BLACK&DECKER®

The Complete Photo Guide to
homeowner basics

100 essential projects every homeowner needs to know

Creative Publishing international

MINNEAPOLIS, MINNESOTA
www.creativepub.com

CONTENTS

Creative Publishing international

Copyright © 2008
Creative Publishing international, Inc.
400 First Avenue North
Suite 300
Minneapolis, Minnesota 55401
1-800-328-3895
www.creativepub.com
All rights reserved

Printed in Singapore

10 9 8 7 6 5 4 3 2

President/CEO: Ken Fund
VP for Sales & Marketing: Kevin Hamric

Home Improvement Group:

Publisher: Bryan Trandem
Managing Editor: Tracy Stanley
Senior Editor: Mark Johanson
Editor: Jennifer Gehlhar

Creative Director: Michele Lanci-Altomare
Senior Design Manager: Brad Springer
Design Managers: Jon Simpson, Sara Holle

Production Managers: Linda Halls,
Laura Hokkanen

Authors: Jodie Carter (Wiring), David Griffin
(Plumbing), Matthew Paymar (Flooring),
Jerri Farris (Painting & Decorating),
Steve Willson (Outdoor)

Page Layout Artist: Lois Stanfield

Library of Congress Cataloging-in-Publication Data

The complete photo guide to homeowner basics :
100 essential projects every homeowner needs
to know.
    p. cm.
    At head of title: Black & Decker.
    By Jodie Carter and others.
    Summary: "Detailed step-by-step guide to the
most common repair and maintenance projects"--
Provided by publisher.
    Includes index.
    ISBN-13: 978-1-58923-376-8 (soft cover)
    ISBN-10: 1-58923-376-X (soft cover)
    1. Dwellings--Maintenance and repair--Amateurs'
manuals. I. Carter, Jodie. II. Creative Publishing
International. III. Black & Decker Corporation
(Towson, Md.)
    TH4817.3.C6565 2008
    643'.7--dc22
                           2007048065

NOTICE TO READERS

For safety, use caution, care, and good judgment when following the procedures described in this book. The Publisher and Black & Decker cannot assume responsibility for any damage to property or injury to persons as a result of misuse of the information provided.

The techniques shown in this book are general techniques for various applications. In some instances, additional techniques not shown in this book may be required. Always follow manufac-

turers' instructions included with products, since deviating from the directions may void warranties. The projects in this book vary widely as to skill levels required: some may not be appropriate for all do-it-yourselfers, and some may require professional help.

Consult your local Building Department for information on building permits, codes and other laws as they apply to your project.

Introduction

OWNING A NEW HOME IS A CHALLENGING YET REWARDING EXPERIENCE. Whether the house itself is new or not, there exists an overwhelming number of remodeling and decorating options you have as a new homeowner. And it doesn't matter if you've bought your first or tenth home, it's still new and brimming with potential to you.

After unpacking all the stuff, where does one start? You'll probably have a list a mile long that looks something like this: install a new toilet, repair the light fixtures, fix the doorbell, replace the exterior siding, hang new window treatments, refinish the kitchen cabinets, install a new livingroom floor or paint the existing floor or refinish the wood that may be under the existing carpet.

With *The Complete Photo Guide to Homeowner Basics* you'll have the information to accomplish all of the most common repairs and installations homeowners face, and you do not need any previous experience because this book explains it all for you in five sections: Wiring, Plumbing, Flooring, Painting & Decorating, and Outdoor Projects. The first few pages of each section give you the background information and technical knowledge that will be helpful. Then the most common projects follow.

Each project has a detailed overview of the parts you'll be working on and the terms you'll need to know as well as photographs that show you all of the tools and materials you'll need. Then step-by-step instructions follow. Virtually every step is photographed so you'll see exactly how to do the work, and along the way you'll find helpful sidebars that show you what to do if something unexpected happens, how to use tools correctly, and which safety precautions to take. Before you know it, you'll be successfully completing one home repair after the next. And because you do it yourself, you'll save hundreds if not thousands of dollars: all the more money to allow you to tackle that next project sooner rather than later.

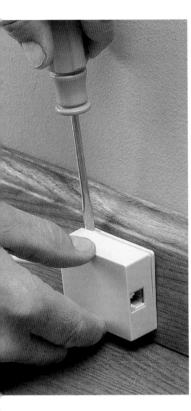

Wiring

THE WIRING SECTION OF THIS BOOK IS UNIQUE IN THAT YOU DON'T NEED TO HAVE ANY PRIOR KNOWLEDGE TO SUCCESSFULLY EXECUTE THE WIRING REPAIRS AND INSTALLATIONS. ALMOST EVERY WIRING BOOK REQUIRES YOU TO HAVE SOME FAMILIARITY WITH THE SUBJECT MATTER BEFORE YOU BEGIN. IF YOU HAPPEN TO BE A TRUE BEGINNER, YOU'RE ALREADY AT A DISADVANTAGE. THIS BOOK DOESN'T ASSUME YOU ALREADY KNOW A LOT ABOUT THE SUBJECT. AND IT'S ALSO A BOOK THAT WON'T LEAVE OUT ANY INFORMATION.

On the following pages you'll find directions for solving the most universal wiring problems and projects in your home. No knowledge is assumed, and no question is left unanswered.

IN THIS CHAPTER:

- ❏ Before You Begin
  - Putting Together a Wiring Kit
  - Understanding Electrical Circuits
- ❏ Replacing Phone Jacks
- ❏ Fixing Lamp Sockets
- ❏ Fixing Doorbells
- ❏ Fixing Pull-Chain Switches
- ❏ Installing Programmable Thermostats
- ❏ Adding Wireless Light Switches
- ❏ Replacing Bad Receptacles
- ❏ Childproofing Receptacles
- ❏ Installing GFCI Receptacles
- ❏ Replacing Bad Light Switches

- ❏ Installing Dimmers
- ❏ Installing Timer Switches
- ❏ Replacing Ceiling-Mounted Fixtures
- ❏ Replacing Hanging Light Fixtures
- ❏ Installing Track Lights
- ❏ Installing Motion-Sensing Floodlights
- ❏ Repairing Fluorescent Light Fixtures
- ❏ Fixing Ceiling Fans
- ❏ Installing Raceway Wiring

Before You Begin:
Putting Together a Wiring Kit

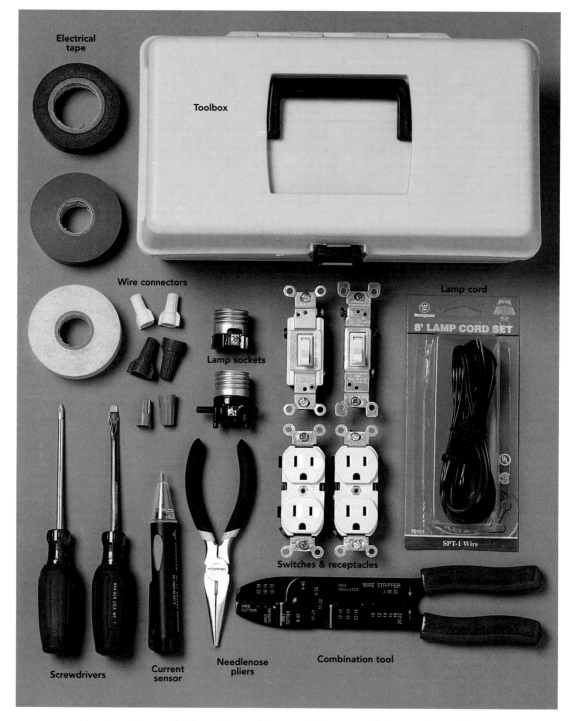

Here's pretty much all you'll need to complete most of the repairs and projects in this book. They are available at any home improvement center or hardware store.

UNLIKE SOME OTHER TYPES OF HOME IMPROVEMENT SKILLS, MAKING BASIC wiring repairs doesn't require very much at all in the way of tools and materials. Investing $30 to $40 puts you in a position to save hundreds of dollars on routine wiring repairs. We recommend that you keep a small toolbox with items dedicated to your wiring tools. That way, you can bring your kit to your work site, and will have the screwdrivers, pliers, and other things you need handy, and won't have to hunt for a screwdriver at the most inconvenient time. Here are the things we recommend for your wiring tool kit:

• **Electrical tape.** These days, tape isn't used to make wire connections, but to help label wires temporarily as you replace fixtures. Some electricians, though, do wrap a loop of electrical tape around plastic wire connectors to reinforce the connections.

• **Toolbox.** A small plastic toolbox is just fine; one with a divided tray for holding wire connectors, screws and other small items is a good choice.

• **Wire connectors.** Sometimes known as "wire nuts," after one manufacturer's product. They're used to join wires together, and you'll be using them a lot. They're color coded for convenience. Green connectors are used for bare copper grounding wires. With most manufacturers, orange connectors are used for two small wires, yellow for two or three wires, red for three or more wires. But you should follow the recommendations on the box, in case you buy a different brand.

• **Lamp sockets.** Repairs to lamps and light fixtures are very common, so you can save yourself time by having a few of these on hand. Besides, they're very inexpensive.

• **Switches & receptacles.** Because these are so frequently needed, and so inexpensive, keep a few on hand. Sooner or later, you'll need them.

• **Cord kit.** Another inexpensive item that's good to have on hand. Lamp cord kits have preattached plugs, to make rewiring a lamp very easy.

• **Screwdrivers.** Have at least two screwdrivers; one with a slot-shaped tip, the other with an X-shaped Phillips tip. It's even better to have several sizes of each type.

• **Needlenose pliers.** This tool is used for almost every wiring project, and is used mostly for bending and connecting wires.

• **Current sensor.** This clever tool tells you if the wires you want to work on are carrying electricity or not. Best of all, this new-style tool doesn't require that you touch any wires.

• **Combination tool.** This workhorse does it all: cuts cables, identifies wire sizes, strips wires. It is the single most important wiring tool you can have.

There are handful of other workshop tools you may use in your wiring projects. They include: a portable drill, a hammer, a level, a utility knife, a tape measure, and a stud finder. If you don't already own them, you may need to buy or borrow them when you get to projects that require them.

Before You Begin: Understanding Electrical Circuits

NO QUESTION ABOUT IT: WIRING AND ELECTRICITY MAKE MOST PEOPLE JUST A LITTLE NERVOUS. Understanding a bit about how electricity behaves in the wires that run through your house will help take away a bit of the scary mystery, and will also give you some confidence to make these repairs. So let's take a short tour of your electrical system. You might even carry the book along with as you walk through your home looking for the things we describe.

Electricity is really nothing more than a form of magnetism running through wires. Electrical energy is obviously invisible, but it's useful to think of it in much the same way as you'd think about water flowing through plumbing pipes. Like water, the electricity is present but not really moving until you "open the faucet" by turning on a light switch, or turning on the motor for an appliance.

Problems occur when the wires (the "pipes") carrying current become broken or blocked, or if they "leak" electricity outside the system. If you're ever been shocked, you know one result of electricity leaking outside its wires. Because flowing electricity generates heat, leaking electricity can also cause fires. These are the reasons electricity makes people a little nervous: it's an invisible energy, it can cause shocks, and it can cause fires.

Fortunately, the system has lots of safety features built in to prevent these problems. And to stay perfectly safe while making repairs to the system, all that's necessary is for you to shut off the flow of electricity in the wires you want a work on. This is very, very easy to do, as you'll soon see. Let's start the tour:

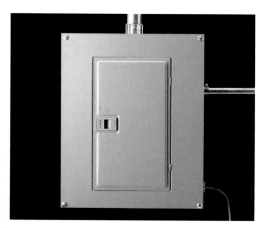

1 For all intents and purposes, your electrical system begins for you with the **main service panel.** Usually this is a gray metal box located in a utility area of your home—the basement, the garage, or a utility room. Sometimes, though, it might be located inside a wooden wall cabinet in a finished basement room.

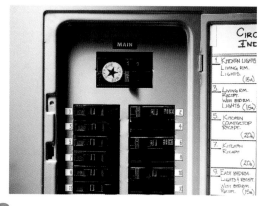

2 Inside the service panel are rows of toggle switches. These are **circuit breakers**. They serve two functions. First, they protect wires from having too much current flowing through them. If you've ever had a circuit breaker trip and lights go out suddenly, you've experienced this safety feature. Secondly, the circuit breakers let you shut off the power to wires when you want to work on them.

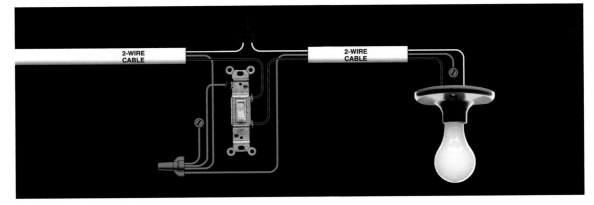

3 Each of the circuit breakers in the service panel sends and controls electricity through a **circuit**—a continuous loop of wire that runs from the service panel, out to one or more receptacles, appliances, or light fixtures, and back again. This diagram shows a simplified circuit. Even the most complicated circuits are just variations of this basic idea. Electricity changes its nature as it flows through the circuit wires. It begins as **"hot" current**. This current is under **"pressure,"** which means that it carries voltage. After the electricity does its work, by creating light or heat or moving mechnical parts in an appliance, it loses its pressure, or charge, and becomes **"neutral"** as it flows back to the service panel. The wires carrying hot current are normally black or red, while neutral wires are usually white. In addition to the hot and neutral wires, a circuit has a loop of bare copper wire (or sometimes an insulated green wire). This **grounding wire** is a safety feature that carries stray electricity back to the service panel if the other wires "leak" their electricity.

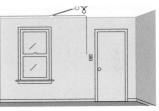

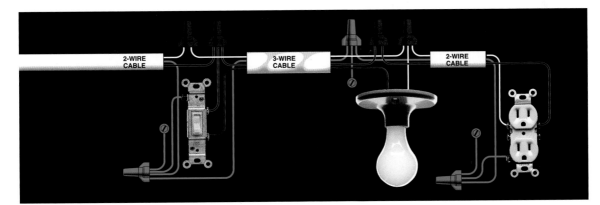

4 Here's another circuit map that shows how a more complicated circuit works. This circuit sends electricity to both a switch/light combination, and a receptacle outlet. If you follow the path of the black wire, you'll see how it works. As the black wire carrying hot current reaches the switch location, it branches, sending one black wire that passes all the way through the light fixture and goes to the receptacle. This allows the receptacle to operate independently from the switch and light. Back at the switch, you'll see that another black wire leads to the switch. The hot current passes through the switch, then is carried to the light fixture through a red wire, which is part of a cable containing three insulated wires. From both the light fixture and the receptacle, white wires carry "depressurized" neutral current back to the service panel.

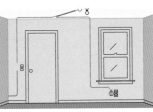

HOW TO TURN OFF THE POWER

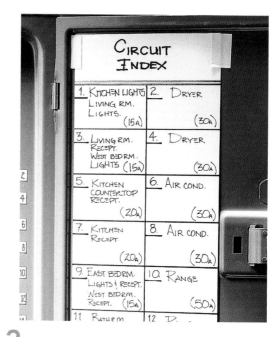

1 Find your main service panel (see page 10). Make sure there is no moisture on the floor below the panel. In very rare instances, people have been shocked when they touch a service panel while standing in water. Open the door of the panel, and look for the index on the inside face of the door. If your electrical service has been properly mapped, the index will tell you exactly which circuit breaker controls the circuit wires you want to work on. This isn't always the case, though. Sometimes you'll need to switch them off one at a time, identifying the correct breaker through trial and error.

2 With your finger, snap the lever on the circuit breaker to the OFF position. You will hear an audible click, and on some breakers a red window will appear on the face of the breaker. Now, close the panel door, and make very sure that everyone in the house knows you'll be working on wires, and that they shouldn't touch the service panel. **DO NOT** actually work on wires until you've tested for current (next page).

WHAT IF...?

If you have an older home with an electrical panel that contains fuses rather than circuit breakers, you will shut off power to the circuits by removing the fuses.

1 Locate the fuse that controls the circuit wires you plan to work on. Like a circuit breaker panel, fuse panels usually have an index that labels the circuits. The circuits that control ordinary wall outlets and light fixtures are usually screw-in fuses. The fuses for large appliances are usually cartridge fuses that fit into a fuse block you pull out of the panel.

2 Unscrew the fuse, being careful to touch only the insulated rim of the fuse.

HOW TO TEST FOR CURRENT

No-touch current testers are very easy to use, but they are accurate only if they are working properly. Before trusting it to test wires to make sure they are safe to work on, test the tool on a fixture that is carrying live current—the power cord on a lamp that is turned on, for example. Turn the tester to ON, then move the probe around the lamp wires until the tester glows or sounds its audible alarm. Now you know the tool works correctly, and can trust it to accurately test wires for live current.

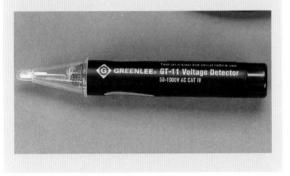

Receptacles: Remove the coverplate on the receptacle. Turn the tester on, and verify it works by testing it on wires you know to be live. Now insert the probe tip on the receptacle into the electrical box on each side of the receptacle. If the tester does not indicate current, you know the wires are now safe to work on.

Light fixtures: Loosen mounting screws and carefully lower the light fixture away from the ceiling box. With the wall switch in the ON position, pass the tip of the current tester within ½" of each wire.

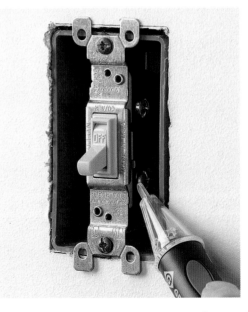

Wall switches: Remove the coverplate on the switch, and insert the tip of the current tester into the box, passing it within ½" of each of the screw terminals on the side of the switch. If the tester does not light up or beep, the wires are safe to work on.

HOW TO MAKE WIRE CONNECTIONS

ONE OF THE FEW SKILLS THAT IS UNIVERSAL TO MOST WIRING PROJECTS IS STRIPPING WIRES OF THEIR OUTER PLASTIC JACKETS, exposing the bare wires, and then connecting those wires to each other or to wire leads or screw connectors on switches, outlet receptacles, light fixtures, or other devices. So before moving on to any actual repairs in this book, practice the following skills:

- Stripping cables and wires
- Connecting wires
- Making screw terminal connections
- Making push-in connections
- Making set-screw connections

HOW TO STRIP WIRES

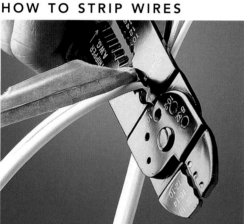

1 If you need to, cut away any plastic sheathing on the cable containing the wires, using the cutting jaws of a combination tool, or a utility knife. (If you use a utility knife, make sure not to nick the plastic jacket on the individual wires. If necessary, you can trim the wires down to size, using the cutting jaws on the combination tool.

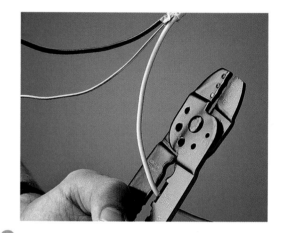

2 Determine how much wire to strip. Many receptacles and other devices come with a gauge that tells you how much wire to strip. Usually, it's about ¾".

3 To strip insulation from the individual wire, select the opening on the combination tool that matches the size of the wires. In most instances, you'll be using the 12-gauge or 14-gauge openings on the tool. Open the jaws and place the wire in the correct slot, then close the jaws of the tool around it. Tug on the wire until it comes free from the insulation.

HOW TO CONNECT WIRES WITH SCREW CONNECTORS

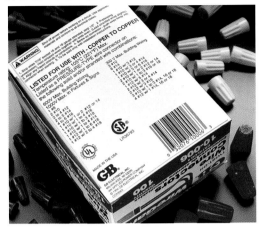

1 Screw connectors are used to join circuit wires together, or to join circuit wires to the wire leads on a light fixture, dimmer switch or other device. Choose a wire connector appropriate for the number of wires you're connecting, and for their size. Wire connector packages come with recommendations for usage. Green wire connectors are reserved for grounding wires.

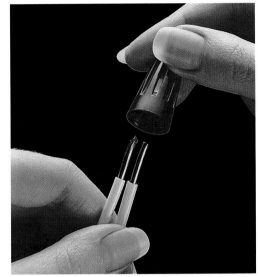

2 Hold the wires together and slide a wire connector onto them. Twist clockwise until the wires are snug. You shouldn't be able to see any bare wire exposed. Tug on the wires gently to make sure they're firmly attached.

HOW TO MAKE SCREW TERMINAL CONNECTIONS

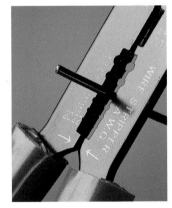

1 Strip about ¾" of insulation from each wire, using your combination tool. Choose the slot in the tool that corresponds to the wire size—this will almost always be 14-gauge or 12-gauge wire for the type of wiring you're doing.

2 Form a C-shaped loop in the end of the wire, using a needlenose pliers. Make sure the wire has no nicks or deep scratches. If it does, clip it off and restrip the ends of the wire.

3 Hook each wire around the appropriate screw terminal on the device, so it forms a clockwise loop. Attach only one wire under each screw terminal. Tighten the screw securely. The plastic insulation on the wire should just touch the screw, and the end of the wire should be under the screw, not extending beyond it.

HOW TO MAKE PUSH-IN CONNECTIONS

1 Although they are not as secure as screw connections, you can also use push-in connections on some switches. Some devices also have push-in connections. To make this connection, use the strip gauge on the back of the device to mark the wire for stripping. Use a combination tool to strip the wire.

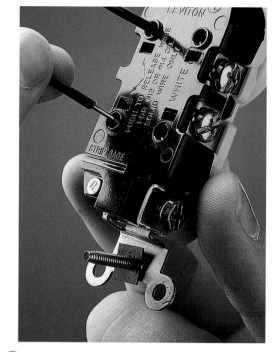

2 Insert the bare copper wires firmly into the push-in fittings on the back of the switch or receptacle. There shouldn't be any bare wire exposed. Tug gently to make sure the wire is firmly gripped. If not, remove the wire and reinsert. If the device won't grip the wire tightly, connect the wire using the screw terminals instead.

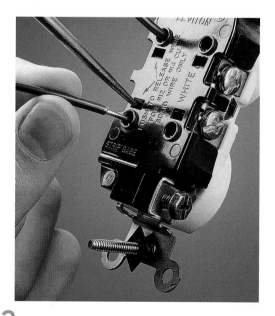

3 If you need to remove a wire from a push-in fitting, insert a small nail or screwdriver into the release opening next to the wire. The wire should pull out easily.

WHAT IF...?

A new type of wire connector looks like a twist connector, but instead uses a simple push-in action. Strip the wires to the length indicated, then simply slide the bare wires into the holes on the connector.

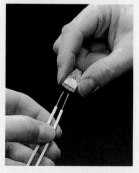

CONTINUITY TESTER

A continuity tester is a specialty tool that can be used to test lamp cords, switches, sockets, switches, and other devices to see if they are working correctly. The continuity tester is a battery-operated tool that sends a very faint electrical current through the metal components on a device, and senses whether or not there is a continuous pathway for household current to follow. If you have doubts about the condition of a device, the continuity tester offers a quick way to tell if the device is faulty or not.

Although there's only one project in this book that calls for a continuity tester, it's useful tool you might want to add to your wiring tool kit.

On lamp cords, use the continuity tester to check the pathway from the prongs on the plug to the ends of the cords.

On pull-chain switches, attach the clip of the tester to one of the switch leads, and hold the tester to the other lead. Pull the chain. If the switch is good, the tester will glow when the switch is in one position, but not in the other.

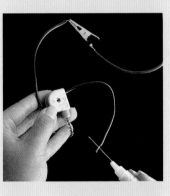

On wall switches, attach the clip of the tester to one of the screw terminals and touch the probe to the other screw. Flip the switch lever from ON to OFF. If the switch is good, the tester will glow when the switch is ON, but not when OFF.

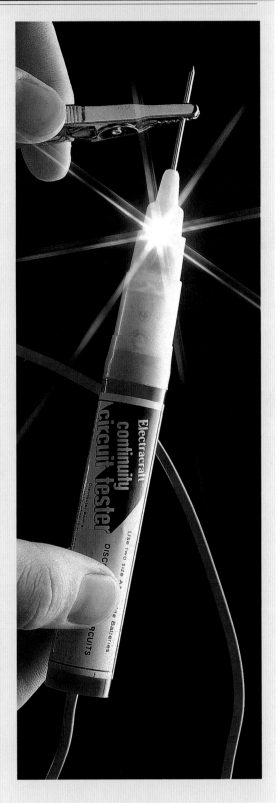

Replacing Phone Jacks

1

Phone jacks are easily damaged. Whether they get smashed by an errant chair leg or their wires get rattled loose, a faulty jack can degrade the quality of the sound on your phone—or disconnect you altogether. The good news is that working on phone wiring is easy and very safe.

REPAIRING OR REPLACING A BROKEN PHONE JACK is a project that offers a lot of bang for the buck. If a phone jack somewhere in your house has stopped working or has very poor sound quality, you can probably fix it by investing $5 and less than an hour of your time.

The phone system is separate from the household wiring, and runs on a very mild current, which means you don't have to worry about shock. You don't have to turn anything off to replace a phone jack.

PHONE JACKS 101

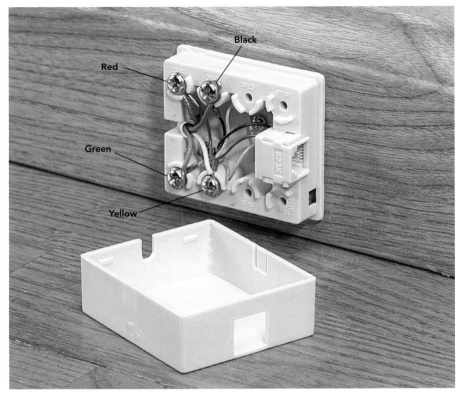

Phone jacks generally have four thin colored wires in them. The wires are connected to screw terminals or to slotted brackets. The four wires are usually colored red, yellow, green and black. Connect the individual system wires to the screw or bracket connected to the matching color leads leading to the modular plug.

CHEAT SHEET

If your wires don't match the color scheme shown here, don't worry. Use this chart as a reference for connecting wires to the screw terminals:

The red terminal will accept:
- a red wire
- a blue wire (or blue with white stripe)

The green terminal will accept:
- a green wire
- a white wire with blue stripe

The yellow terminal will accept:
- a yellow wire
- an orange wire (or orange with white stripe)

The black terminal will accept:
- a black wire
- a white wire with orange stripe

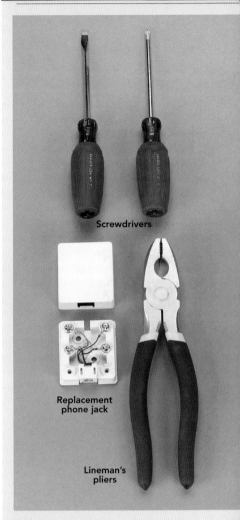

Screwdrivers

Replacement phone jack

Lineman's pliers

SKILLS YOU'LL NEED

- Making wire connections (page 14)

DIFFICULTY LEVEL

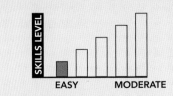

SKILLS LEVEL

EASY   MODERATE

You'll likely finish this in 30 minutes or less.

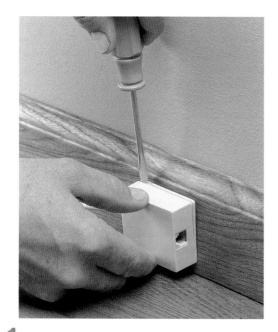

1 If the jack has no visible damage, you may be able to get it working again by reconnecting loose wires inside. Pry the cover off the jack with a small screwdriver.

2 Under the cover, you'll see six or eight wires in four colors. Each of the wires should be firmly seated under a screw terminal or in a forked metal tab. If one of the wires is loose, reattach it to the terminal of matching color. Plug in the phone to test it. If it still doesn't work, continue with replacing the jack.

3 To remove the jack, first disconnect all the wires from their screw terminals or forked tabs. Then, unscrew the screws (there may be one or two) holding the jack to the wall. Tape the phone wires to the wall so they don't get knocked into the wall cavity.

4 Take the old jack to a hardware store or home center and try to find a similar replacement jack so you can use the same mounting holes. Remove the cover from the new jack. Carefully thread the phone wire through the back of the new jack, and connect the wires to the screw terminals of matching color. Attach the jack to the wall, replace the cover, and test the phone.

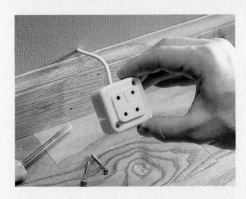

What if I have a *really* old jack? Older style phones used a four-pin system rather than modular plugs. New phones won't work with these jacks, so you'll need to replace them with new modular jacks.

1 Unscrew the old jack from the wall, and carefully pull it away from the wall.

2 On the back of the old jack, you'll find two or four colored wires connected to screws. Unscrew the screws to free the wires and then clip away the stripped portion of the wires. Buy a new modular phone jack.

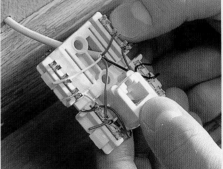

3 If your new jack uses forked tab connectors, thread the phone cable through the opening in the back of the jack, then press each of the four wires into a forked tab that already contains a wire of the same color running to the plug-in opening. If your new jack uses screw terminals, follow the instructions on the opposite page. After all the wires are connected, plug in a phone. You should have a clear dial tone.

4 Set the jack over the old mounting holes and make sure the wire isn't being pinched against the wall. Drive the mounting screws back into the holes. Snap the cover back onto the jack and plug in your phone.

2

Removing Broken Lightbulbs

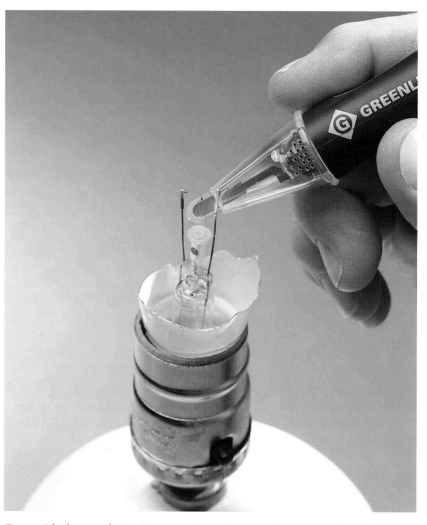

Even with the simplest wiring repairs, using a voltage sensor to check for power is a good idea. We'll then show you how the pros handle this job—using a needlenose pliers to remove the broken lightbulb. This technique works on even the most corroded and rusted light fixture sockets.

IF YOU'VE EVER TRIED TO REMOVE A LIGHTBULB THAT'S CORRODED AND STUCK in a fixture socket, you know that the lightbulb can easily break, leaving the bulb's aluminum base stuck in the fixture. There are several solutions to this common problem; some work better than others. For example, you may have heard of the old potato trick that suggests you push a raw potato into the broken socket and turn. But this introduces moisture and other debris into the fixture, and it doesn't work that well, especially if your broken bulb is really stuck. The bar of soap technique isn't much better. Effective methods include using a pair of needlenose pliers or a bulb extractor device, which can be found at most hardware or home improvement stores.

LIGHT SOCKETS 101

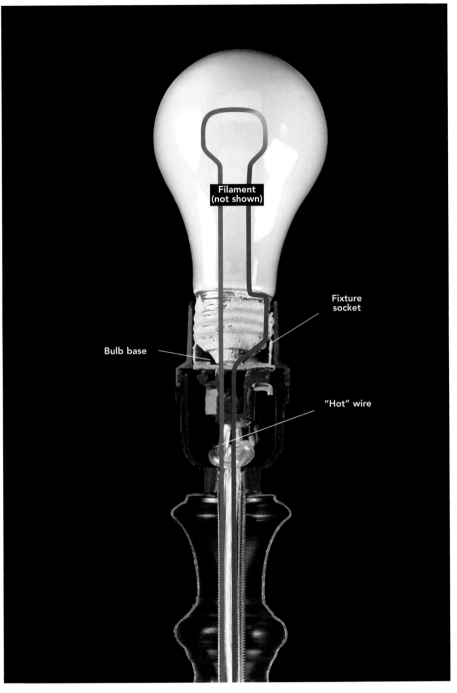

Filament (not shown)

Fixture socket

Bulb base

"Hot" wire

Over time, the aluminum base of a lightbulb may become corroded and difficult to remove from its socket. You can almost always remove the bulb without damaging the socket. In this cutaway lamp, you can see exactly how a light fixture socket works. Current flows up into the lightbulb through the "hot" wire and through the central contact in the base of the bulb. The current flows through the filament inside the light bulb, loses its charge by producing light, then the neutral current flows back to the neutral wire through the threaded metal portion of the bulb and socket.

TOOLS & SUPPLIES YOU'LL NEED

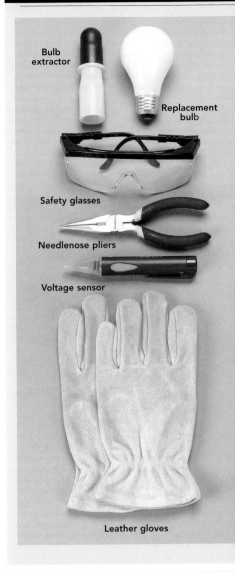

Bulb extractor

Replacement bulb

Safety glasses

Needlenose pliers

Voltage sensor

Leather gloves

SKILLS YOU'LL NEED

• Turning off the power (page 10)
• Testing for current (page 11)

DIFFICULTY LEVEL

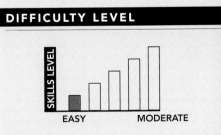

EASY   MODERATE

You'll finish this job in just a few minutes.

HOW TO REMOVE A BROKEN LIGHTBULB

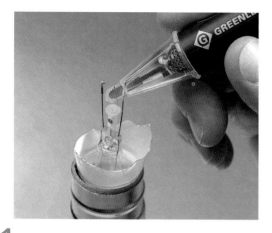

1 Before you start to remove the broken bulb, turn off the power to the light (or unplug the lamp, if that's what you're working on). Then, with the light switch in the ON position, place the tip of your voltage sensor in the broken bulb base. If the sensor beeps or lights up, then the wires are still live and are not safe to work. Check the main circuit panel again and trip the correct breaker to disconnect power to the light. If the sensor does not beep or light up, the circuit is dead and safe to work on.

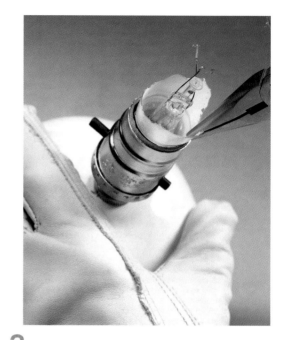

2 Put on safety glasses and a pair of heavy leather work gloves. Use your needlenose pliers to remove any broken shards of glass still attached to the lightbulb base. If you're working on a ladder, have a helper hold the base of the ladder.

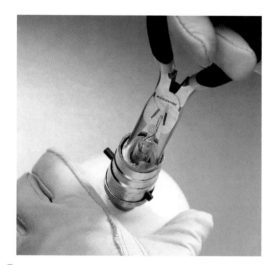

3 Insert the needlenose pliers into the broken bulb base as far as they will go. Spread the handles of the pliers firmly apart (this will cause the jaws to press against the inside of the socket), and turn the pliers slowly counterclockwise, unscrewing the bulb base. If the bulb won't budge, try wrapping the jaws of the pliers in duct tape for extra grip.

TOOL TIP

Needlenose pliers are handy for all sorts of household repairs, not just wiring. They come in many sizes. A good basic pair should have jaws around 3" long and comfortable handles.

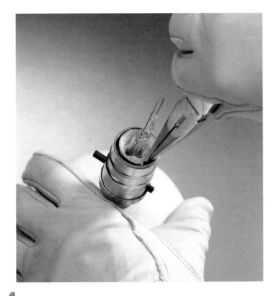

4 If the lamp is still stuck, use the tip of needle-nose pliers to grab the lip of the bulb base and bend it in slightly on one side. Grip the bent portion firmly with the pliers, and pull the base counter clockwise to unscrew the bulb.

WHAT IF...?

What if the bulb still won't turn?

The base of the bulb is soft aluminum, and, if you pull hard enough, it will begin to tear much like a pop can. If you can't twist the bulb out, you may be able to create a little tear in the edge of the base. Try to fold the tear back. You'll probably rip a piece of the bulb off. Eventually, you'll have the whole socket out.

5 If the broken bulb is in a hard-to-reach location or if you're not comfortable working on top of a ladder, you can buy a broken bulb extractor (available at hardware stores for less than $10) and screw it on to the end of a broom handle or extension pole. Simply insert the extractor into the socket. Its rubber sides grip the edge of the bulb base and give enough grip to allow you to turn the base out of the socket.

6 Once the bulb is out, wipe away any corrosion in the socket with a rag. If bulbs often get stuck in a particular fixture, use a bulb socket lubricant (available at hardware stores) to lubricate the lightbulb base and prevent corrosion. And remember, there's no need to twist hard when installing a bulb.

3

Fixing Lamp Sockets

Fixing an old lamp is a satisfying and surprisingly simple process. No matter what a lamp looks like on the outside, they almost always have the same electrical components.

WHEN A LAMP STOPS WORKING, IT'S OFTEN CAUSED BY A BAD LIGHTBULB SOCKET UNIT—that's the piece containing the switch or pull chain that holds the lightbulb. No need to throw the lamp away: for a few dollars, you can replace the socket and restore the lamp to like new. Replacing a socket is easy, and most hardware stores and home centers sell a variety of replacement sockets.

LAMP SOCKETS 101

Lamp sockets and switches are usually interchangeable—choose whatever type you want. Included here from top left: twist knob, remote switch, pull chain, push lever.

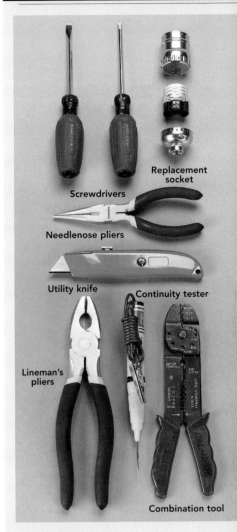

Screwdrivers

Replacement socket

Needlenose pliers

Utility knife

Continuity tester

Lineman's pliers

Combination tool

QUICK FIX

Sometimes, you'll get lucky and you can fix the faulty socket very easily. With the lamp unplugged and its bulb and shade removed, use a small flat screwdriver to pry up the small metal tab on the base of the socket. The tab should be angled slightly upward, not pressed flat in the socket. If the tab doesn't touch the base of the bulb, electricity will not flow though the bulb. Prying it up may restore the current flow. Replace the bulb and test the lamp.

Contact tab

SKILLS YOU'LL NEED

• Stripping and connecting wires (pages 14 and 15)

• Testing for continuity (page 17)

DIFFICULTY LEVEL

SKILLS LEVEL

EASY   MODERATE

This job takes 30 to 60 minutes.

HOW TO FIX A LAMP SOCKET

Outer shell

Insulated sleeve

1 With the lamp unplugged, the shade off, and the bulb out, you can remove the socket. Squeeze the outer shell of the socket just above the base and pull the shell out of the base (the shell is often marked "Press" at some point along its perimeter. Press there and then pull).

3 With the shell and insulation set aside, pull the socket away from the lamp (it will still be connected to the cord). Look at the two screws on the sides of the socket. One half of the cord should be connected securely to each. If the screws are loose or if either of the wires is unattached, you've found the problem. Reconnect the ends of the cord and tighten the screws. But if the connections seem sound, then you'll need to continue by unscrewing the two screws to disconnect the socket.

2 Under the outer shell, you'll find a cardboard insulating sleeve. Pull this off and you'll reveal the socket attached to the end of the cord.

WHAT IF...?

What if my lamp is old and the shell is held in place by screws?

Some older lamps may have an outer shell held together with small screws. Simply undo the screws, remove the outer shell, and proceed as described here.

4 To rule out a bad cord as the cause of the problem, attach the clip of your continuity tester to one prong of the lamp's plug; then touch the probe first to one of the bare wires and then to the other. Do the same test for the other prong. The tester should light up once for each prong. If the tester never lights or lights on both wires for the same prong, you'll need to replace the cord. If it lights up once for each prong, the socket is the problem.

5 Attach the ribbed half of the wire to the silver screw terminal on the new socket. Attach the other wire to the brass-colored screw terminal. If the stripped ends of the cord are frayed or blackened, cut them off with your combination tool and strip away ¾" of insulation to reveal clean wire.

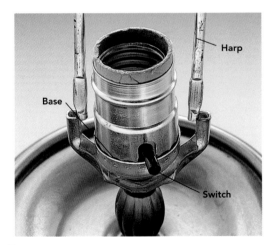

Harp

Base

Switch

6 Set the socket on the base of the lamp. Make sure the switch isn't blocked by the "harp"— the part that holds the shade on some lamps. Slide the cardboard insulating sleeve over the socket, so the sleeve's notch aligns with the switch. Now slide the outer sleeve over the socket, aligning the notch with the switch. It should snap into the base securely. Screw in a lightbulb, plug the lamp in, and test it.

HERE'S HOW

Here's how to buy a replacement socket. First, make sure it accepts the same size bulb (you'll be able to see this by looking). Next, if your old socket has a twist-, push-, or pull-chain-style switch, find a replacement that has the same style. (If the socket doesn't have a switch, you'll need to find a socket without one.) Finally, make sure it has the same watt rating as the old socket. Somewhere on the inside or outside of the socket, you'll find a number (between 20 and 120) followed by a *W*. This is the watt rating.

Fixing Doorbells

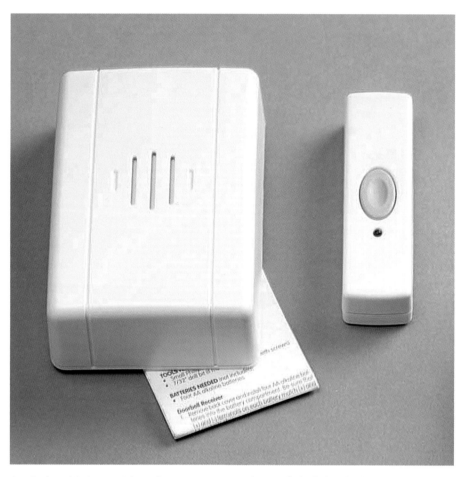

4

A wireless kit is a quick and easy way to replace a failed doorbell system. The kit consists of a battery-powered doorbell button that sends a wireless signal to a plug-in chime unit somewhere in the house. Some models come with two button units, one for the front door and one for the back.

WHAT DO YOU DO IF YOUR DOORBELL DOESN'T CHIME? The repair may be as simple as repairing loose wires or replacing a $2 button. The most common causes of doorball malfunction—loose wiring and worn-out buttons—are the easiest to fix, requiring only a screwdriver.

If the problem is with the wiring itself or the chime unit, it's generally simpler and cheaper to replace the system with a wireless doorbell kit, which take only minutes to install and cost very little.

DOORBELLS 101

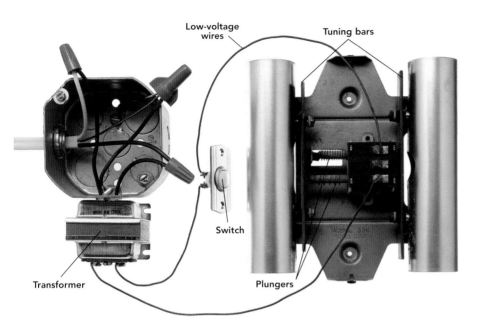

Low-voltage wires • Tuning bars • Switch • Transformer • Plungers

Repairing or replacing a doorbell is a simple project that often doesn't even require you to shut off the power. Doorbells are powered by a transformer that reduces household current to 24 volts or less. This low-voltage current goes from the transformer to the switch by the door and on to a chime unit. When you press the doorbell button, it completes a low-voltage pathway and causes the plunger to strike a musical tuning bar. To distinguish between the front and back door signals, one of the doorbell switch-and-plunger pairs strikes two tuning bars in succession, creating the characteristic "ding-dong" sound. The other switch and plunger strikes only one tuning bar.

HERE'S HOW

Rarely, it may be a loose wire connection on the doorbell chime unit that causes the problem. Remove the cover on the chime unit, look for loose wires, and tighten them with a screwdriver. More often, though, the problem will be with the push-button switch, or with a chime unit that has simply reached the end of its life.

TOOLS & SUPPLIES YOU'LL NEED

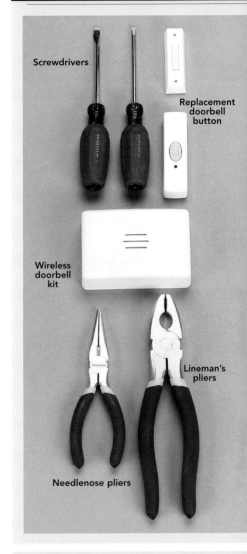

Screwdrivers • Replacement doorbell button • Wireless doorbell kit • Lineman's pliers • Needlenose pliers

SKILLS YOU'LL NEED

- Turning off the power (page 12)
- Testing for power (page 13)
- Making wire connections (page 14)

DIFFICULTY LEVEL

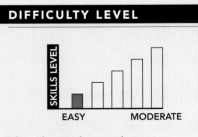

SKILLS LEVEL

EASY — MODERATE

Takes about 1 hour or less.

HOW TO FIX A DOORBELL

1 Begin by testing the button to make sure it works. Doorbell buttons are commonly the culprit. Use a screwdriver to remove the two screws that secure the doorbell cover to the house.

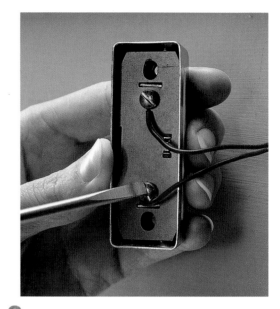

2 Carefully pull the switch away from the wall. Check the two wire connections on the back of the switch. If the wires are loose, reconnect them to the screws on the back of the button. Test the doorbell by pressing the button. Check the two wire connections on the back of the switch. If the wires are loose, reconnect them to the screws on the back of the button. Test the doorbell by pressing the button.

3 If the doorbell still doesn't work, loosen the screws on the back of the doorbell, remove the wires, and touch their bare copper ends together. If the bell sounds, the problem is a faulty button you'll need to replace (go to step 4). If the bell doesn't sound, the problem is elsewhere in the system (go to step 5). If you're replacing the switch, disconnect the wires and tape them to the wall to keep them from falling inside and getting lost.

4 To replace the switch, simply buy a replacement that has the mounting holes in the same location as the old one. Wrap each of the wires around one of the screws on the back of the switch and tighten the screws. Position the button over the mounting holes and attach the new button to the wall with a screwdriver.

5 If the bell didn't ring, check the transformer, which is probably located in the basement or utility room near your main service panel. Check the two wires connected to the surface of the transformer, and reconnect them if they're loose. Test the doorbell by pressing the button. If the doorbell still doesn't sound, go to step 6.

7 Install the battery into the battery compartment of the doorbell button. Go outside your front door and press the button to make sure the chime rings. If not, you may need to move the indoor receiver to a receptacle closer to the door.

6 If nothing else has worked, now it's time to install a new wireless doorbell kit. First, plug in the chime unit to a centrally located receptacle in your house. Disconnect the doorbell switch by your door, and clip off the wires as close to the wall as possible, using lineman's pliers.

8 Mount the button to the door frame where you removed the old doorbell. You may have to drill two new holes before securing the new button to the wall with screws. Some doorbells come with double-sided tape that can be used to secure the button to the wall or to door molding. Push the doorbell button to make sure it works.

Fixing Pull-Chain Switches

5

The pull-chain switch is actually a separate piece of the fixture. It's held in place with a retaining nut and connected to circuit wires with two wire leads.

CHANCES ARE YOU'VE GOT A LIGHT FIXTURE WITH A PULL-CHAIN somewhere in your house—in a closet, attic crawl space, or maybe even your bathrom vanity. And, chances are, if you use it enough, you will eventually pull a little too hard and the switch will fail. Fortunately, you can easily replace a pull-chain switch, generally for only a dollar or two.

This is the first project where you actually touch circuit wires, so make sure you read the information on shutting off power and testing for current, found at the beginning of this book.

PULL CHAINS 101

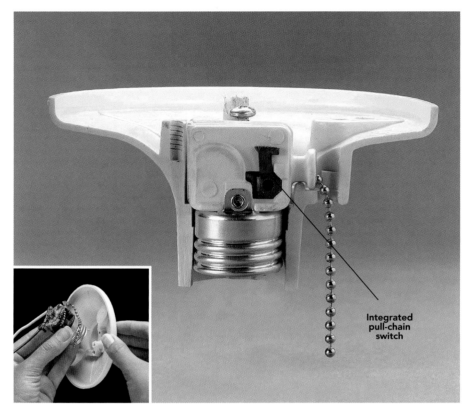

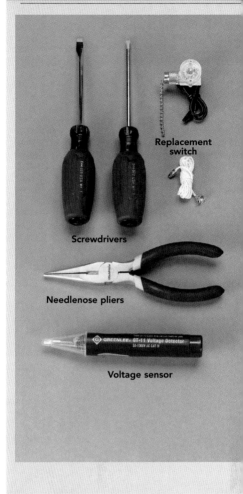

TOOLS & SUPPLIES YOU'LL NEED

Replacement switch

Screwdrivers

Needlenose pliers

Voltage sensor

On some utility light fixtures, the pull-chain switch is part of the lightbulb socket. On these fixtures, you'll need to replace the entire socket/switch unit (inset).

Integrated pull-chain switch

WHAT IF...?

If you have a light fixture or lamp with a push-button switch, replacing the switch is exactly the same as for a pull-chain switch.

Just buy a replacement switch that matches the old switch, and replace it using the same technique described on the following pages.

SKILLS YOU'LL NEED

- Turning off the power (page 12)
- Testing for power (page 13)
- Making wire connections (page 14)

DIFFICULTY LEVEL

EASY   MODERATE

This project takes less than 1 hour.

HOW TO REPLACE A PULL-CHAIN SWITCH

1 First, make sure that the switch is broken, not just the chain. If you find a short bit of chain sticking out of the fixture, pull on it to see if the light turns on and off. If so, you can buy and attach a new length of pull chain. If there's no chain left or if the switch doesn't work when you pull the remaining chain, go ahead and replace the switch.

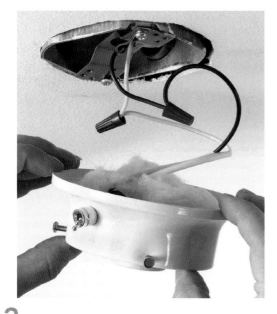

2 First, turn off the power to the fixture. Now, remove the globe and lightbulb, and loosen the mounting screws that hold the fixture to the electrical box. Lower the fixture away from the ceiling.

3 Test for current by holding your voltage sensor within ½" of the circuit wires. The black wires should cause the sensor to beep if power is present. Check all the wires for power in case the light was wired improperly. If the sensor beeps or lights up, then the circuit is still live and is not safe to work. Check the main circuit panel again and trip the correct breaker to disconnect power to the fixture. If the sensor does not beep or light up, the wires are dead and safe to work on.

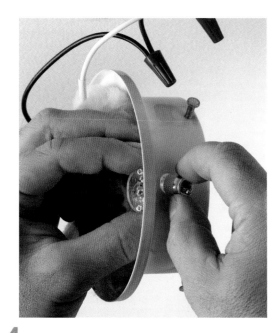

4 Hold the fixture steady with one hand and turn the knurled retaining nut at the base of the pull chain. You should be able to turn it with your fingers. If it sticks, use needlenose pliers to turn it. Once the retaining nut is off, pull the switch out of the fixture.

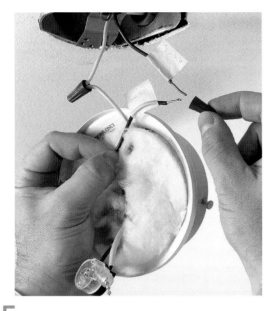

5 Remove the two wire leads coming from the switch from the wires they are attached to by unscrewing the wire connectors. On most fixtures, one of the switch's leads will be connected to a circuit wire, the other lead to the light fixture itself.

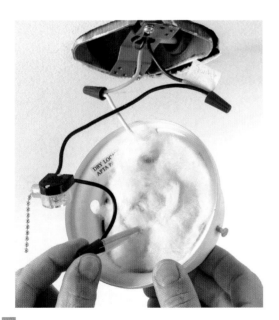

7 Attach the wire leads on the new switch to the disconnected wires, using wire connectors. Then, insert the threaded portion of the switch through the hole. Slip the retaining nut over the pull chain and thread it on to the switch until it is snug.

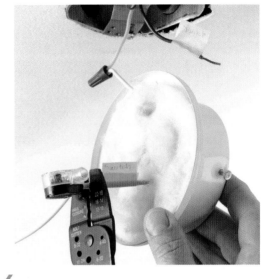

6 If the switch is part of the fixture itself, snip off its connection, using a combination tool. You'll connect the new switch to the wire you've just snipped, so strip about $\frac{3}{4}$" of insulation off that wire.

8 Reattach the fixture to the ceiling by holding it over the electrical box in the ceiling so that the mounting holes in the fixture line up with the screw holes in the box. Make sure all the wires are in the box and not pinched between the ceiling and the fixture. Insert the mounting screws and tighten them down with a screwdriver. Now you can replace the bulbs, restore the power, and test the fixture.

Installing
Programmable Thermostats

6

Programmable thermostats come in many varieties, but all of them will help save on energy costs. Most models have instructions for programming printed on the access plate.

TRADITIONAL FURNACE THERMOSTATS ARE LOW-VOLTAGE MODELS THAT DO A simple, but necessary, job. They sense changes in the house air temperature and when it's too low, the thermostat turns on the heat and when it's too high, the thermostat turns off the heat. For many years this was all we needed to make our homes comfortable and no one gave much thought to improving this performance. Then, fuel shortages and high energy costs made everyone interested in lowering the heating fuel bill.

One innovation that has advanced this effort is the programmable thermostat. This provided more control over furnaces and, as a result, reduced energy consumption. If everyone in the house is gone during the day, there's no reason to keep the heat at 68 or 70 degrees or more. And when everyone goes to sleep at night, these thermostats turn down the heat automatically and turn it back on before anyone gets up. Different models that offer different levels of control are available. Generally, the more capability a unit has, the more it costs. While there is variety in what the units can do, most are easy to install, as shown here.

THERMOSTATS 101

PROGRAMMABLE THERMOSTATS

Programmable thermostats contain sophisticated circuitry that allows you to set the heating and cooling systems in your house to adjust automatically at set times of day. Replacing a manual thermostat with a programmable model is a relatively simple job that can have big payback on heating and cooling energy savings.

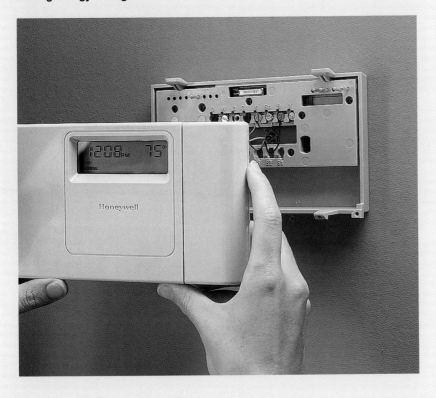

Programmable thermostat

Masking tape

Pencil

Small level

Drill

Screwdrivers

CHECK BEFORE YOU BUY

When buying a new thermostat, make sure the new unit is compatible with your heating/air conditioning system. For reference, bring the brand names and model numbers of the old thermostat, the furnace, and the central air conditioning unit to the store and provide the information to the sales assistant.

SKILLS YOU'LL NEED

- Reading package directions
- Making wire connections (page 14)

TERMS YOU'LL NEED TO KNOW

LOW-VOLTAGE WIRES—Electrical wires that carry lower voltage, usually 12 volts, than the standard household current, which is 120 volts. Often used for thermostats, doorbells, and outdoor lighting.

DIFFICULTY LEVEL

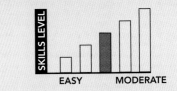

SKILLS LEVEL

EASY   MODERATE

Allow 1 to 2 hours for this project.

1 Turn off the power to the furnace at the main service panel. Then, remove the thermostat cover.

2 The body of the thermostat is held to a wall plate with screws. Remove these screws and pull the body away from the wall plate. Set the body aside.

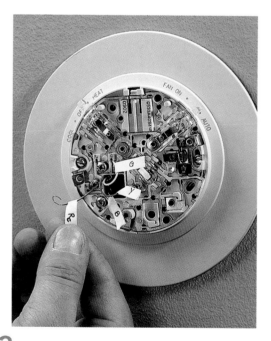

3 The low-voltage wires that power the thermostat are held by screw terminals to the mounting plate. Do not remove the wires until you label them with tape, according to the letter printed on the terminal to which each wire is attached.

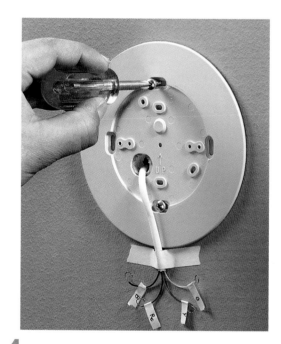

4 Once all the wires are labeled and removed from the mounting plate, tape the cable that holds these wires to the wall to keep it from falling back into the wall. Then unscrew the mounting plate and set it aside (see sidebar, next page).

5 Position the new thermostat base on the wall and guide the wires through the central opening. Screw the base to the wall.

6 Check the manufacturer's instructions to establish the correct terminal for each low-voltage wire. Then connect the wires to these terminals, making sure each screw is secure.

7 These thermostats require batteries to store the programs so they won't disappear if the electric power goes out in a storm. Make sure to install these batteries before you snap the thermostat cover in place. Then program the new unit to fit your needs and turn on the power to the furnace.

MERCURY THERMOSTATS

Older model thermostats (and even a few still being made today) often contained one or more small vials of mercury totaling 3 to 4 grams in weight. Because mercury is a highly toxic metal that can cause nerve damage in humans, along with other environmental problems, DO NOT dispose of an old mercury thermometer with your household waste. Instead, bring it to a hazardous waste disposal site, or a mercury recycling site if your area has one (check with your local solid waste disposal agency). The best way to determine if you old thermostat contains mercury is simply to remove the cover and look for the small glass vials or ampules containing the silver mercury substance. If you are unsure, it is always better to be safe and keep the device in question out of the normal waste stream.

7

Adding Wireless Light Switches

Wireless switch kits are a simple and inexpensive way to add a second switch to an existing fixture.

SOMETIMES A LIGHT SWITCH IS JUST IN THE WRONG PLACE, or it would be more convenient to have two switches controlling a single fixture. Adding a second switch the conventional way generally requires hours of work and big holes in walls. (Electricians call this a "three-way" switch installation.) Fortunately, wireless switch kits are available to perform basically the same function for a fraction of the cost and effort. There is a bit of real wiring involved here, but it's not nearly as complicated as the traditional method of adding a three-way switch installation.

The kits work by replacing a conventional switch with a unit that has a built-in radio-frequency receiver that will "read" a remote device mounted within a 50 ft. radius. The kits come with a remote, battery-powered switch (it looks like a standard light switch) that you can attach to a wall with double-sided tape.

Two other similar types of wireless switch kits are also available. One allows you to control a plugged-in lamp or appliance with a remote light switch. The second type allows you to control a conventional light fixture remotely, but instead of replacing the switch, the receiver screws in below the lightbulb. This is particularly useful if you want to control a pull-chain light from a wall switch.

WIRELESS SWITCHES 101

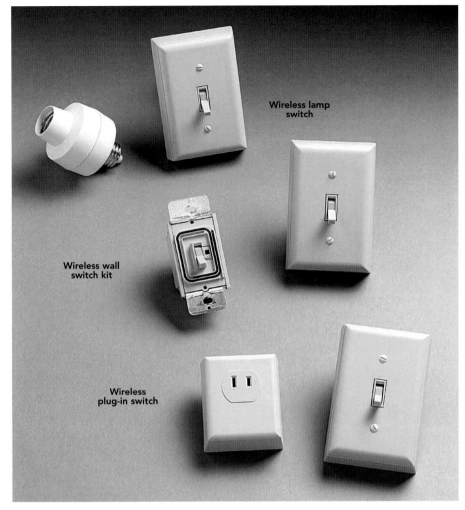

Wireless lamp switch

Wireless wall switch kit

Wireless plug-in switch

Wireless kits are available to let you switch lights on and off remotely in a variety of ways, at the switch, at the plug, or at the bulb socket.

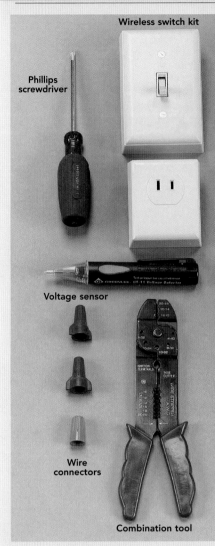

The remote switch is a wireless transmitter that requires a battery. The transmitter switch attaches to the wall with adhesive tape or velcro strips.

HOW TO REMOVE A WALL SWITCH

1 To remove the old switch, first shut off the power to the switch. Remove the decorative cover-plate from the switch by unscrewing the two screws that hold the plate to the switch box. Set the screws and the plate aside. With the cover-plate off, you will be able to see the switch and the electrical box it is attached to.

2 Use a voltage sensor to make sure the wires are dead. Hold your voltage sensor's probe within ½" of the wires on either side of the switch. If the sensor beeps or lights up, then the switch is still live, and you'll need to trip the correct break-er to disconnect power to the switch. If the sensor does not beep or light up, the circuit is dead and you're safe to continue.

3 Remove the switch from the box by unscrew-ing the two long screws that hold the switch to the box at the top and the bottom. Once the screws are out, hold the top and bottom of the switch, and carefully pull the switch away from the box.

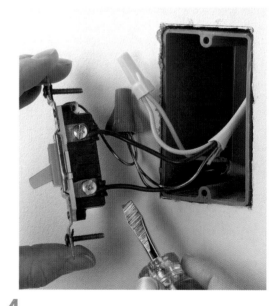

4 Remove the switch completely by disconnect-ing the wires. In many cases, there will also be two white wires connected with a wire connector in the box. You won't have to deal with these in your installation.

HOW TO INSTALL A WIRELESS WALL SWITCH

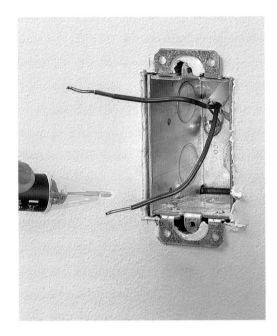

1 To install the receiver switch, you'll need to determine which wire carries current from the service panel. Bend both the wires so they are as far apart as possible. Turn the power back on temporarily. Without touching either wire, pass your voltage sensor over both. One should make your sensor beep and light up and the other won't. The one that trips your sensor carries current. Turn off the power and label that wire with a piece of tape.

3 Once the wires are firmly connected, you can attach the switch to the box. Tuck the new switch and wires neatly back into the box. Then drive the two long screws that are attached to the new switch into the two holes in the electrical box.

2 Identify the wire lead on the receiver switch marked "line" and attach it to the circuit wire you marked with tape, using a wire connector. Connect the other wire lead on the switch to the remaining circuit wire in the same way.

4 Reattach the coverplate. Then, turn the power back on at the main panel and test the switch for operation. You should be able to turn the light on and off as normal.

5 Now you can install the transmitter switch. Install the 9-volt battery in the transmitter switch. Remove the backing from the double-sided tape on the back of the switch and place the switch on a wall within 50 ft. of the receiver switch.

6 Test the operation of both switches. Each switch should successfully turn the light fixture on and off. You've just successfully created a three-way switch installation, without running any new wires.

VARIATION: WIRELESS LAMP SWITCH

1 You can also purchase wireless switch kits that control plug-in fixtures. Plug the receiver unit into any receptacle.

2 The unit has a receptacle on its face. Plug a lamp or any other plug-in device into the unit (this is an especially handy way to control Christmas lights).

VARIATION: WIRELESS SWITCH FOR A CEILING FIXTURE

1 A third type of wireless switch uses a transmitter that screws into the bulb socket of the light fixture. If you need to control a light with a pull-chain switch or if you don't want to replace a wall switch as shown above, this is the best choice. Remove the lightbulb and thread the receiver into the bulb socket.

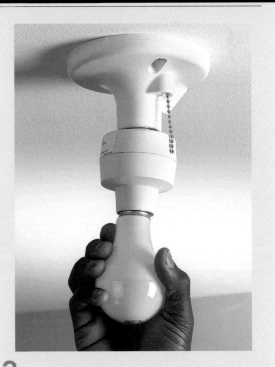

2 Screw the lightbulb into the receiver socket.

Replacing Bad Receptacles

8

Since receptacles don't have moving parts, they don't wear out quickly, but they don't last forever. If a receptacle won't hold a plug or if it's hot to the touch or sparks when you pull a plug, it needs some attention and possibly replacement. If you have a GFCI receptacle (inset) see pages 58 to 63 to replace it.

THE THING YOU'VE PROBABLY CALLED AN "OUTLET" IS MORE PROPERLY KNOWN AS AN ELECTICAL "RECEPTACLE." A receptacle that gets a lot of use will eventually wear out—you'll know this has happened if appliance plugs feel loose in the receptacle, or if a lamp flickers when the plug is jiggled. Another common problem is wires that work loose, causing the receptacle to stop working. This project will show you how to check the wire connections, then replace the receptacle if it's bad.

RECEPTACLES 101

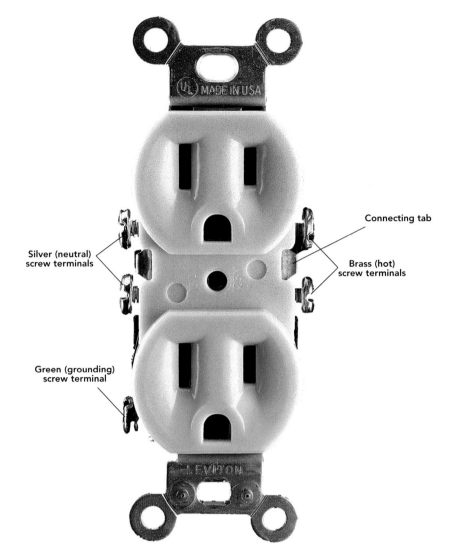

Silver (neutral) screw terminals

Green (grounding) screw terminal

Connecting tab

Brass (hot) screw terminals

Receptacles have five screws for connecting wires: two silver, two brass colored, and one green. Some installations don't use all of these screws. Disconnecting and connecting a switch is only a matter of connecting the right wires to the right screws.

TERMS YOU NEED TO KNOW

MOUNTING STRAP—the metal piece that holds the plastic body of the receptacle to the electrical box.

SCREW TERMINALS—the silver and brass-colored screws used to connect the lamp wire to the socket.

TOOLS & SUPPLIES YOU'LL NEED

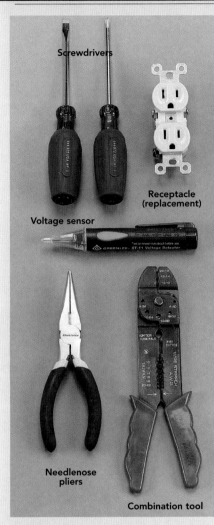

Screwdrivers

Receptacle (replacement)

Voltage sensor

Needlenose pliers

Combination tool

SKILLS YOU'LL NEED

• Turning off the power (page 12)

• Testing for power (page 13)

• Making wire connections (page 14)

DIFFICULTY LEVEL

SKILLS LEVEL

EASY   MODERATE

This project takes about 1 hour.

HOW TO FIX A BAD RECEPTACLE

1 Shut off the power to the switch at the main service panel. Remove the decorative coverplate from the receptacle. Set the screw and the plate aside. With the coverplate off, you will be able to see the receptacle and the electrical box it is attached to.

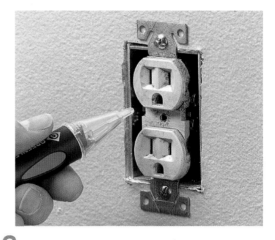

2 Use a voltage sensor to make sure that the circuit is dead. Hold your voltage sensor's probe within ½" of the wires on either side of the receptacle. If the sensor beeps or lights up, then the receptacle is still live, and you'll need to trip the correct breaker to disconnect power to the receptacle. If the sensor does not beep or light up, the receptacle is dead and you're safe to continue.

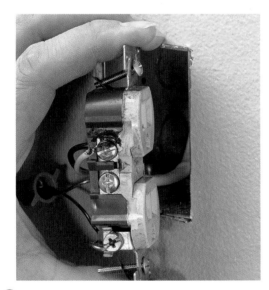

3 Remove the receptacle from the box by unscrewing the two long screws that hold the switch to the box at the top and the bottom. Once the screws are out, carefully pull the receptacle away from the box. Depending on how your receptacle has been wired, it may be connected to two colored wires and a bare grounding wire, or four colored wires and a bare wire.

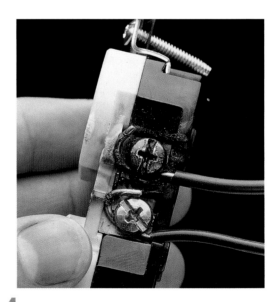

4 Inspect the screws where the wires connect to the switch. They should be tight and the connections should be clean and free of any scorch marks. If the connections were good, the problem is likely with the receptacle itself. If one of the wires is loose or if the connections are scorched, the problem is probably a loose screw causing a short circuit. You can follow the directions below to reattach the old switch or you can install a new one to be on the safe side.

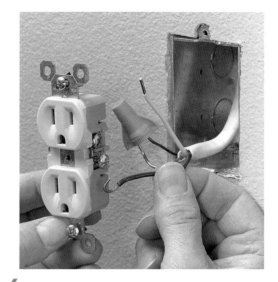

5 Loosen the screw terminals and remove the circuit wires. Inspect the wires, and if they're damaged, clip them off and strip about ¾" of bare wire, using a combination tool. Check the connecting tabs on the sides of the receptacle. If they have been snapped off, you'll need to also do this on the new receptacle, using needlenose pliers.

6 Use needlenose pliers to bend the stripped portions in small, clockwise hooks. Now you can connect the wires to the receptacle. Take one of the black wires and wrap the end of the wire around one of the two brass-colored screws on the side of the switch. Tighten the screw so it's snug. If there is a second black wire, wrap it around the other brass-colored screw in the same way.

7 Now take one of the white wires and wrap the end of the wire around one of the silver screws. Tighten the screw so it's snug. Do the same for the second white wire if there is one. Connect the copper wire to the green-colored screw on the bottom of the receptacle.

8 Once the connections are made, gently tuck the wires and the receptacle in to the box so the holes at top and bottom of the receptacle align with the holes in the box. Use a screwdriver to drive the two long mounting screws that hold the receptacle to the box. Replace the cover plate. Restore the power and test your receptacle.

Childproofing Receptacles

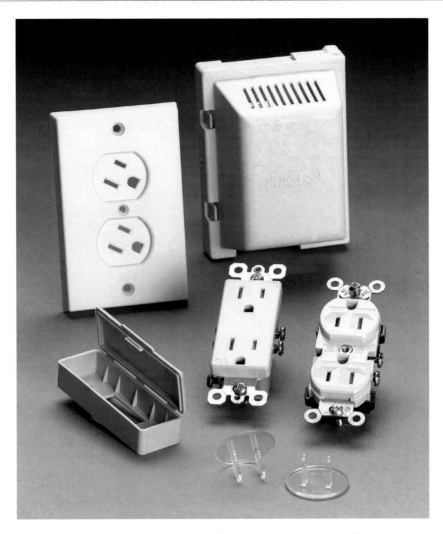

9

Standard receptacles present a real shock hazard to small children. Fortunately, there are many ways you can make receptacles safer without making them less convenient.

THOUSANDS OF CHILDREN ARE SHOCKED EVERY YEAR when they insert foreign objects in receptacles. Plug-in safety caps are an effective solution, but they make receptacles less convenient. Installing a tamper-resistant receptacle is an easy variation of replacing a bad receptacle (pages 54 to 55). And there are some other simple solutions that will allow you to childproof receptacles in just a few minutes.

CHILDPROOFING 101

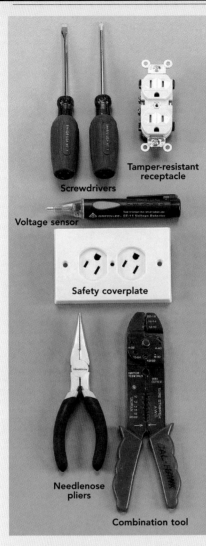

Screwdrivers

Tamper-resistant receptacle

Voltage sensor

Safety coverplate

Needlenose pliers

Combination tool

SKILLS YOU'LL NEED

- Turning off the power (page 12)
- Testing for power (page 13)
- Making wire connections (page 14)

DIFFICULTY LEVEL

EASY · MODERATE

This project will take about 1 hour.

Safety coverplates (A) are designed so plugs need to be twisted before they can be fully inserted. Plug covers (B) replace standard coverplates and allow you to plug in lamps or other devices and then cover the plugs, preventing curious fingers from removing the plugs. Tamper-resistant receptacles (C) feature spring-loaded shutters that remain closed unless the two prongs of a plug enter the slots simultaneously; they won't open for a single pointed object, like a screwdriver or key. A very easy solution is plug-in inserts, which effectively block the receptacle slots completely.

INSTALLING A TAMPER-RESISTANT RECEPTACLE

1 Shut the power to the switch off. Remove the decorative coverplate from the receptacle by unscrewing the screw that holds the plate to the electrical box. Set the screw and the plate aside.

2 Use a voltage sensor to double-check that the circuit is dead. Hold your voltage sensor's probe within ½" of the wires on either side of the receptacle. If the sensor beeps or lights up, then the receptacle is still live, and you'll need to trip the correct breaker to disconnect power to the receptacle. If the sensor does not beep or light up, the receptacle is dead and you can proceed safely.

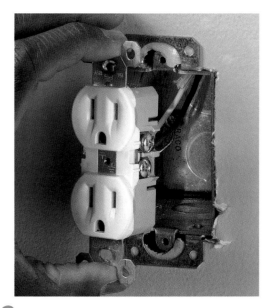

3 Remove the receptacle from the box by unscrewing the two long screws that hold the switch to the box, one at the top and another at the bottom. Once the screws are out, gently pull the receptacle away from the box. Depending on how your receptacle has been wired, there may be two colored wires and a bare wire or four colored wires and a bare wire.

4 Remove the receptacle completely by unscrewing the screws that hold the wires. Disconnect each wire by turning the screws on the sides of the receptacle just enough to free the wires.

5 Clip off the stripped ends of the wires and use your combination tool to strip away about ¾" of insulation. Then use your needlenose pliers to bend the stripped portions in small, clockwise hooks. Take one of the black wires and wrap the end of the wire around one of the two brass-colored screws on the side of the switch. Tighten the screw so it's snug. If there is a second black wire, wrap it around the other brass screw in the same way.

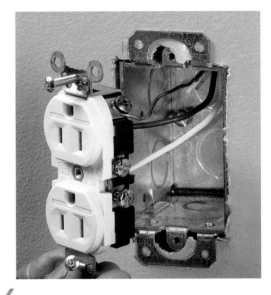

6 Now take one of the white wires and wrap the end of the wire around one of the silver screws. Tighten the screw so it's snug. Do the same for the second white wire, if there is one. Connect the copper wire to the green-colored screw on the receptacle.

WHAT IF...?

What if I want a tamper-resistant GFCI receptacle?

No problem. GFCIs are available with the same shutter mechanism. Follow project #10 on page 58 to install one.

7 Once the connections are made, gently tuck the wires and the receptacle in to the box so the holes at top and bottom of the receptacle align with the holes in the box. Use a screwdriver to drive the two long mounting screws that hold the receptacle to the box. Replace the coverplate. Restore the power and test your receptacle.

INSTALLING SAFETY COVERPLATES

1 You can get much of the protection of a tamperproof outlet with a safety coverplate. Adding one takes only minutes and requires no contact with wiring. Remove the old coverplate from the receptacle by unscrewing the screw that holds the plate to the electrical box.

2 Hold the safety coverplate over the receptacle. Use a small screwdriver to tighten the screws.

SAFETY TIP

Push-in slot covers cost just pennies, and can be very effective at keeping kids from poking objects into electrical receptacles. Buy several packages, and use them to plug any receptacle that your child might be tempted to play with.

3 To plug a device in, push the slider aside and insert the plug. The shutters automatically snap over the slots when nothing is plugged in.

INSTALLING A PLUG COVER

1 Plug covers are designed to replace coverplates on receptacles where devices are plugged in more or less permanently to prevent children from unplugging them. After removing the old cover-plate, hold the plug cover's base plate over the receptacle and screw it in with a small screwdriver.

2 Plug in your lamp or other device and snap the plug cover into the new base plate. Cords should fit through the slots in the plug cover.

SAFETY TIP

Any receptacle is made safer by installing it "upside down" with the rounded grounding slot at the top. Three-prong receptacles are almost always installed with the round third prong facing down, but some experts recommend wiring receptacles with the third prong on top. This is because the third prong is the grounding prong and doesn't carry any current under normal operation. In theory, if something were to fall on a partially inserted plug, it would hit the harmless grounding prong and not the current-carrying slot prongs. Either way, you're wiring it right, but upside down may be slightly safer.

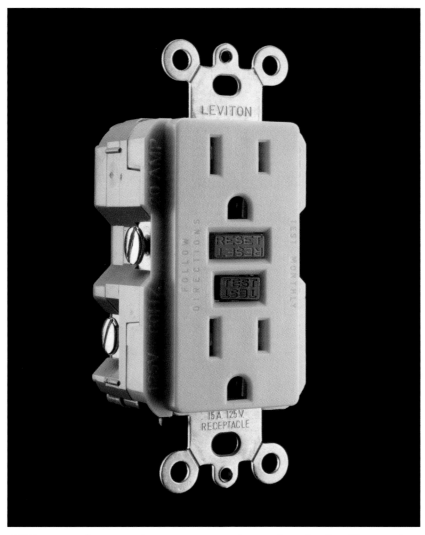

GFCI receptacles are an important protection against shocks. They work just like a normal receptacle, but they have special circuitry that helps prevent shocks. They're required by building code in all wet locations but can help improve safety anywhere.

A GROUND-FAULT CIRCUIT-INTERRUPTER RECEPTACLE (called a GFCI by pros) works just like a standard receptacle with an added feature. In the event of a short, the receptacle shuts off—"trips"—in a tiny fraction of a second. This will protect you from a dangerous shock, and this is why building codes require GFCIs in wet locations like bathrooms, kitchens, and garages.

If you need to replace a faulty receptacle in a kitchen, bathroom, or garage, replace it with a GFCI. Even if your existing receptacles work fine, you can add a measure of safety (and practice your wiring skills) by installing GFCIs. In a child's bedroom, for example, it's a good idea to install a GFCI.

GFCI 101

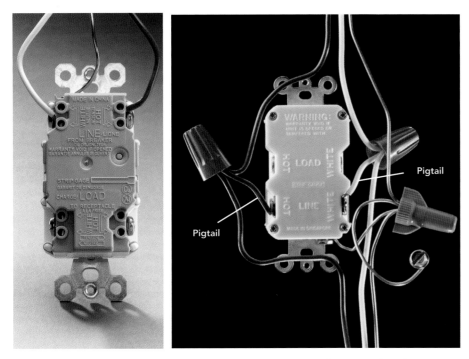

Pigtail

Pigtail

Wiring a GFCI isn't much different from wiring a standard receptacle. The main difference is that, in this installation, you'll only use one pair of the four screws, the ones labeled "line." If there were only two colored wires attached to the old receptacle, the new GFCI is attached in the same way (left photo). But if you have more than one of each color of wire connected to the old receptacle, you'll need to use a technique called pigtailing to connect the GFCI (shown in the image at right). Don't worry; it's easy and you'll see how on the next page.

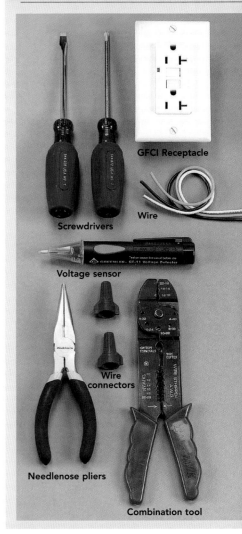
TERMS YOU NEED TO KNOW

LOAD—In this installation, you're ignoring the screws labeled "load" and using only the ones labeled "line." The load screws literally put a load on the GFCI circuitry of the receptacle by making the GFCI protect other devices on the same circuit (so, other receptacles on the same household circuit could also trip the GFCI in the event of a short). This sounds like a good thing and it is in certain situation. But for your purposes, it will cause a lot of "nuisance" trips, where the GFCI will shut down for no apparent reason. This is why you should use the line screws only.

HOW TO REPLACE A GFCI RECEPTACLE

1 Remove the decorative coverplate from the receptacle. With the coverplate off, you will be able to see the receptacle and the electrical box it is attached to.

2 Before you remove the old receptacle, use a voltage sensor to make sure the circuit is dead. Hold your voltage sensor's probe within ½" of the wires on either side of the receptacle. If the sensor beeps or lights up, then the receptacle is still live, and you'll need to trip the correct breaker to disconnect power to the receptacle. If the sensor does not beep or light up, the receptacle is dead and you can proceed safely.

3 Remove the receptacle from the box by unscrewing the long screws at the top and the bottom. Once the screws are out, gently pull the receptacle away from the box. It won't pull away easily, since the wires are still attached, so pull firmly. Depending on how your receptacle has been wired, there may be two colored wires and a bare wire or four colored wires and a bare wire.

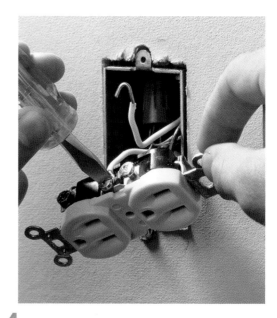

4 Remove the receptacle completely by unscrewing the screws that hold the wires. Disconnect each wire by turning the screws on the sides of the receptacle just enough to free the wires.

5 Now you can start to connect the GFCI. To begin, count the number of wires you just disconnected from the old receptacle. You'll either have three wires—one each of white, black, and bare wires—or you'll have five—a pair of white and black wires and a single bare wire. If you've got five wires, skip to steps 6A and B. If you've got three wires, clip off the stripped ends of the wires and use your combination tool to strip away about ¾" of insulation. Then use your needlenose pliers to bend the stripped portions in small, clockwise hooks and go to step 7.

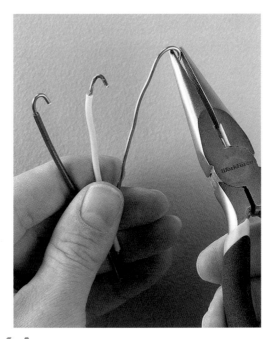

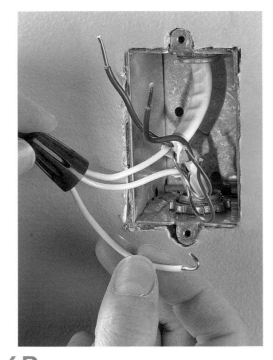

6A If you've got five wires, clip off the stripped ends of the wires and use your combination tool to strip away about ¾" of insulation. Now cut three 3" pieces of 14-gauge wire—one bare, one white, and one black. Strip about ¾" of wire from both ends and then use your needlenose pliers to make a clockwise hook at one end of each. These are your pigtails.

6B Hold the straight end of the white pigtail next to the ends of the two white wires coming from the electrical box. Slide a wire connector over the ends and twist it clockwise until the connector is snug. No bare wire should be visible. Repeat this procedure for the black wires and black pigtail, and then for the two bare wires and the bare pigtail.

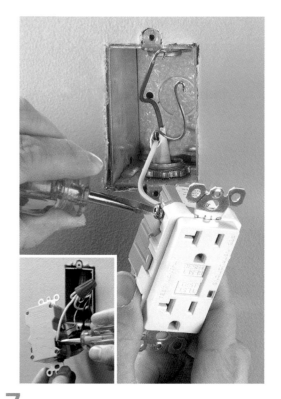

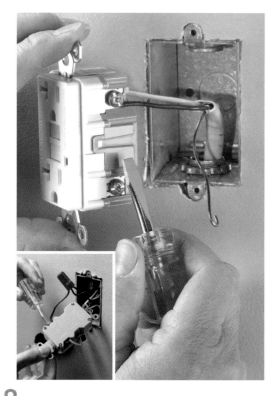

7 Connect the white wire (or the white pigtail; see inset photo) to the silver-colored screw labeled "line."

8 Connect the black wire (or the black pigtail; see inset photo) to the copper-colored screw labeled "line."

BUYING TIP

Not all GFCI receptacles are created alike. Make sure you buy one that's rated the same as the receptacle you're replacing. Many household circuits carry 15 amps of power. Receptacles for 15-amp circuits look like the one on the left. But a 20-amp circuit should have receptacles rated for 20 amps, like the one shown on the right. 20-amp receptacles have one T-shaped slot that accepts special T-shaped plugs on appliances with heavy power loads, such as window air conditioners or hot tubs.

15-amp GFCI   20-amp GFCI

9 Connect the bare wire (or the bare pigtail; see inset photo) to the green grounding screw on the bottom of the receptacle.

10 Once the connections are made, gently tuck the wires and the receptacle into the box so the holes in the top and bottom of the receptacle align with the holes in the box. Use a screwdriver to drive the two long mounting screws that hold the receptacle to the box. Replace the coverplate. If your GFCI didn't come with its own coverplate, you'll need to buy one with a square cutout to fit the GFCI.

11 Restore the power and test your receptacle. In addition to plugging something in to the receptacle, you need to test the two buttons on the face of the receptacle. Press the TEST button. The receptacle should make a clicking noise, the RESET button should pop out, and whatever you've plugged in should stop working. If this happens, the GFCI is wired correctly and working. Push RESET and the receptacle will work again.

Replacing Bad Light Switches

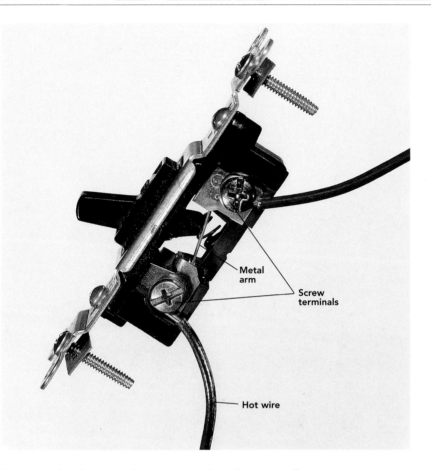

Metal arm

Screw terminals

Hot wire

Light switches have moving parts, so they do eventually wear out or stop working reliably. As shown in this cutaway, most switches have a movable metal arm that opens and closes the electrical circuit, and eventually the metal arm loses its resilience, or snaps off. You might also want to replace a switch just because you want a new look, or to install a dimmer (see page 70 to see how).

THERE ARE SEVERAL REASONS WHY YOU MIGHT NEED TO REPLACE A LIGHT SWITCH. If the switch won't stay in position (won't stay on), if it buzzes, if it gets hot, or if a breaker trips when you flip the switch, it might be time to replace the switch. And, of course, you might want to replace the switch for aesthetic reasons or to gain the added functionality of a dimmer. Dimmers not only provide greater control, but they save energy and make light-bulbs last much longer than they would at full power.

Fortunately, swapping an old switch for a new one is a very simple project. You can easily replace the standard light switch with another standard light switch using basic hand tools.

LIGHT SWITCHES 101

TERMS YOU NEED TO KNOW

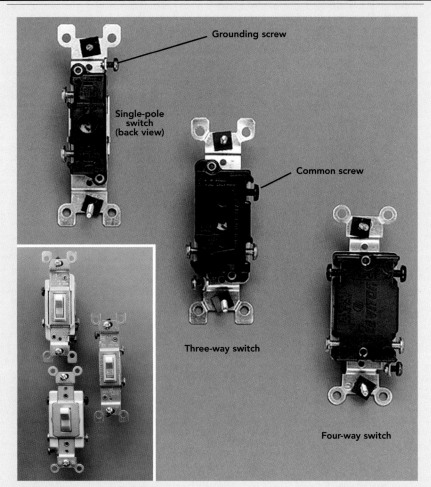

Grounding screw

Single-pole switch (back view)

Common screw

Three-way switch

Four-way switch

Wall switches come in three types, and it's crucial you buy the right replacement. Single-pole switches (left) are used when a light fixture is controlled from one switch location only. Notice that it has two screw terminals on the side of the switch (the screw on the metal strap used to connect the grounding wire isn't counted when you talk about circuit wires). A three-way switch (center) is used when a light fixture is controlled from two different wall locations. It has three screws on the body of the switch. One screw is known as the common terminal, the others are called travelers. A four-way switch (right) is used when a light fixture is controlled from three or more different wall locations. It has four screws on the body of the switch. Four-way switches are a little rare; you may not have any of them in your house.

When replacing a switch, remember to buy a replacement that matches the old switch, and connect the wires in the same way they were connected to the old switch.

TOOLS & SUPPLIES YOU'LL NEED

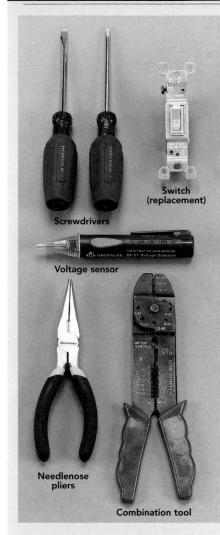

Screwdrivers

Switch (replacement)

Voltage sensor

Needlenose pliers

Combination tool

SKILLS YOU'LL NEED

- Turning off the power (page 12)
- Testing for power (page 13)
- Making wire connections (page 14)

DIFFICULTY LEVEL

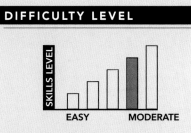

SKILLS LEVEL

EASY   MODERATE

Allow about 1 hour for this project.

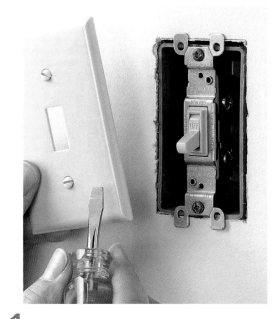

1 First shut off the power to the switch. Remove the decorative coverplate from the switch by unscrewing the two screws that hold the plate to the switch box. Set the screws and the plate aside. With the coverplate off, you will be able to see the switch and the electrical box it is attached to.

2 Use a voltage sensor to make sure the circuit is dead. Hold the sensor's probe within ½" of the wires on either side of the switch. If the sensor beeps or lights up, then the switch is still live, and you'll need to trip the correct breaker to disconnect power to the switch. If the sensor does not beep or light up, the circuit is dead and you're safe to continue.

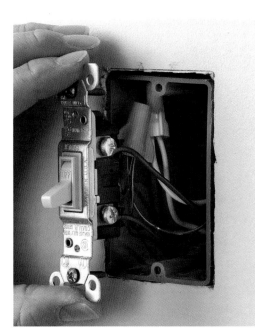

3 Remove the switch from the box by unscrewing the two long screws that hold the switch to the box, one at the top, the other at the bottom. Once the screws are free, gently pull the switch away from the box.

4 Inspect the screw connections. They should be tight and free of any scorch marks. If one of the connections is loose or scorched, the problem is probably a loose screw causing a short circuit. Reattach the wires, reassemble the switch and coverplate, and see if the switch works. If this isn't the problem, continue to the next step.

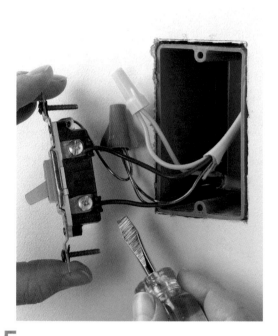

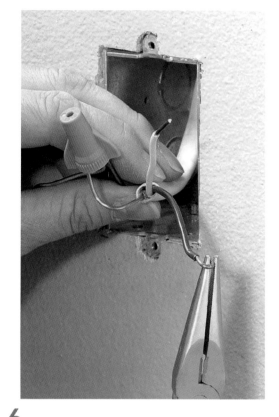

5 Loosen all the screw connections and detach the switch from the wires. (If there are three or four colored wires attached to the switch instead of just two, see the "WHAT IF" variation on the next page.) In many cases, there will also be two white wires connected with a wire connector in the box. You won't have to deal with these in your installation. Take the old switch to a hardware store or home center and purchase an identical replacement.

6 Before you begin to wire your new switch, clip of the ends of the wires and use your combination tool to strip away about ¾"of insulation. Then use your needlenose pliers to bend the stripped portion in a small clockwise hook.

WHAT IF...?

What if there is a white wire connected to the switch?

In certain installations, a switch is connected with one black wire and one white wire. (The pros call this installation a "switch loop.") If the electrician did a good job, the end of the white wire should have black tape, indicating that it carries current. Treat it just like a black wire when you install your new switch. If there is no tape on the end of the white wire, wrap a bit of electrical tape on the end. The next person who works on the circuit will thank you.

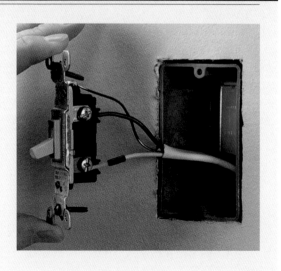

WHAT IF...?

What if there are more than two colored wires connected to the switch? If this is the case, you're dealing with a three-way switch (if there are three colored wires) or a four-way switch (if there are four colored wires). Before removing a three- or four-way switch, use masking tape to label the wires to identify which screw terminals they are attached to.

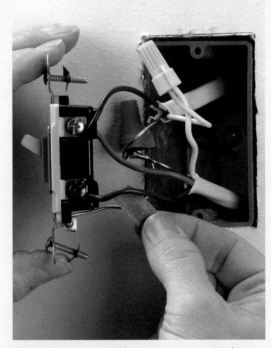

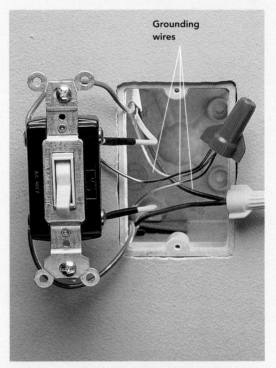

Grounding wires

For a three-way switch, one screw terminal is labeled "common," and is almost always darker in color than the other two. Make sure the wire that was attached to the common screw terminal on the old switch is connected to the common screw terminal on the new switch. The other two wires aren't critical; they can be attached to either of the remaining screw terminals.

Four-way switches are a little trickier. In most cases, you'll be attaching the pair of wires attached to the top two screw terminals on the old switch to the same screws on the new switch. Then you'll attach the other pair of wires to the bottom pair of screws. Some manufacturers, though, use a different pairing system, with one screw terminal pair on the right side of the switch, the other on the left. A good way to avoid problems is by buying a replacement made by the same manufacturer that made the old switch.

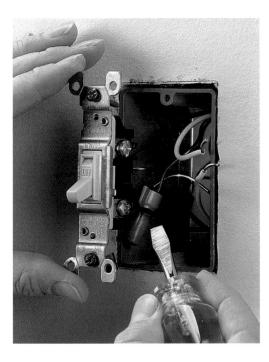

7 Position the switch so the ON/OFF markings read correctly. Take one of the colored circuit wires and wrap the end of the wire clockwise around one of the two screw terminals on the side of the switch. Tighten the screw so it's snug. Wrap the second colored wire around the other screw in the same way. If there was a bare copper wire connected to the old switch, connect it to the green-colored screw on the switch in the same way you connected the two black wires. (If you're installing a three-way or four-way, see the information on the opposite page.) Then connect the rest of the wires as described above. The other two screws are interchangeable, so it doesn't matter which of the remaining colored wires connects to which screw.

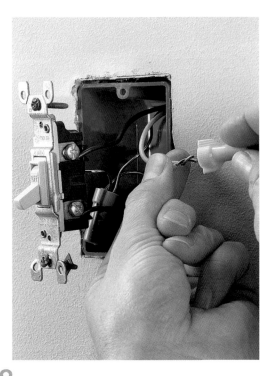

8 Check to make sure the white circuit wires (they're called the neutrals) are snugly connected. If not, then use a wire nut to join them.

9 Once the connections are made, gently tuck the wires and the switch into the box so the holes in the top and bottom of the switch align with the holes in the box. Use a screwdriver to drive the two long mounting screws that hold the switch to the box. Replace the coverplate. Restore the power and test your switch.

12

Installing Dimmers

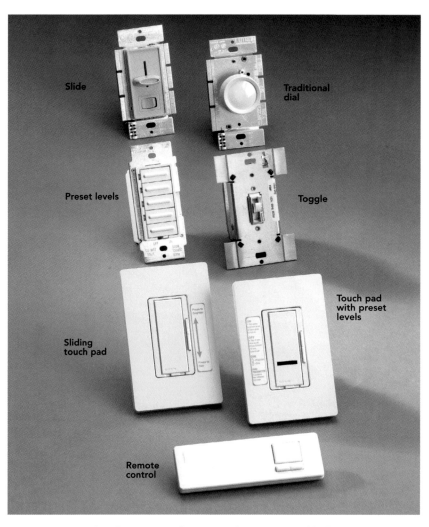

Slide

Traditional dial

Preset levels

Toggle

Touch pad with preset levels

Sliding touch pad

Remote control

Dimmers not only allow you to fine-tune the amount of light in a room, but also they save energy and extend lightbulb life. There is a wide variety of dimmer switches available to replace almost any standard ON/OFF switch. Whether you flip, turn, slide, or touch them, they all work the same. The one exception is an automatic dimmer, which has an electronic sensor that adjusts the light fixture to compensate for the changing levels of natural light. An automatic dimmer also can be operated manually.

DIMMER SWITCHES ARE SIMPLY LIGHT SWITCHES that allow you to control the intensity of light that comes from a fixture. The control may be a dial, a touch pad, a slider, or a faux-toggle switch, but they all function in basically the same way.

Installing a dimmer is no more difficult than installing a light switch. The only possible obstacles are the size of the electrical box and the type of light in the fixture. In some older homes, the metal box that contains the old switch may not be large enough for a dimmer. If the fixture uses fluorescent lightbulbs, you will not be able to use a standard dimmer.

DIMMER SWITCHES 101

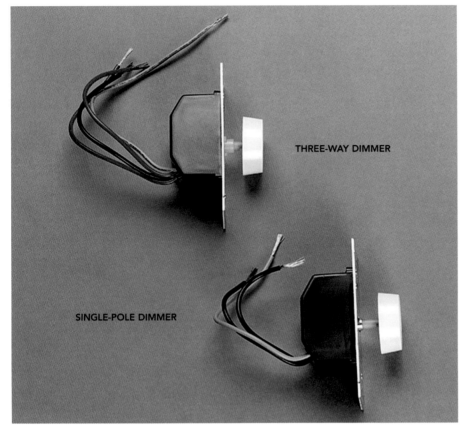

THREE-WAY DIMMER

SINGLE-POLE DIMMER

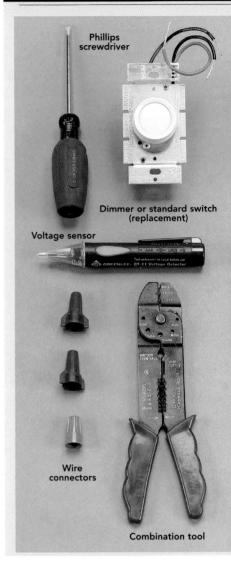

Phillips screwdriver

Dimmer or standard switch (replacement)

Voltage sensor

Wire connectors

Combination tool

Unlike standard light switches, dimmers are connected to the household electrical wires by short lengths of wire called "leads." Leads come pre-attached to the dimmer. You attach them to the household wiring with wire connectors. Single-pole dimmers have two wire leads (plus a green grounding lead). Use this type for switches where the light fixture is controlled from a single wall location. Three-way dimmers have three black and red wire leads, and are used when a light fixture is controlled from two wall locations.

SKILLS YOU'LL NEED

- Turning off the power (page 12)
- Testing for power (page 13)
- Making wire connections (page 14)

DIFFICULTY LEVEL

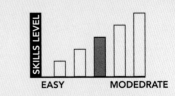

SKILLS LEVEL

EASY   MODEDRATE

Allow 1 to 2 hours for this job.

TERMS YOU NEED TO KNOW

COMMON WIRE—On a three-way wall switch or dimmer, one of the screw terminals or wire leads is designated as "common." Depending on where the switch is in the circuit, the common wire receives electrical current from the power source, or sends current to the light fixture. The common screw terminal or wire lead is the one that is a different color from the other two screws or wire leads.

TRAVELER WIRE—On three way switches and dimmers, the travelers are the two wires other than the common (see above). The traveler wires run between the two switches, providing alternative paths for electrical current.

HOW TO INSTALL A DIMMER SWITCH

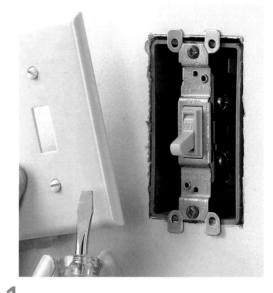

1 First shut off the power to the switch. Remove the decorative coverplate from the switch by unscrewing the two screws that hold the plate to the switch box. Set the screws and the plate aside. With the coverplate off, you will be able to see the switch and the electrical box it is attached to.

2 Use a voltage sensor to make sure that the circuit is dead. Hold your voltage sensor's probe within ½" of the wires on either side of the switch. If the sensor beeps or lights up, then the switch is still live, and you'll need to trip the correct breaker to disconnect power to the switch. If the sensor does not beep or light up, the circuit is dead and you are safe to continue.

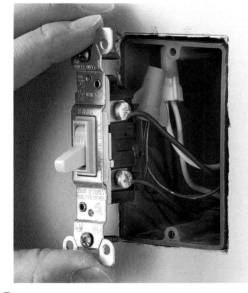

3 Remove the switch from the box by unscrewing the two long screws that hold it. One is at the top and another at the bottom. Once the screws are out, hold the top and bottom of the switch, and gently pull the switch away from the box.

WHAT IF...?

What if my electrical box seems too small to hold the dimmer switch? Dimmer switches have much bigger bodies than standard switches, and they are connected with twist wire connectors rather than screw terminal connections. This means that the electrical box might be too small to hold the switch and the connections. If so, don't try to force the switch into the box. Instead, see the Here's How feature on page 75.

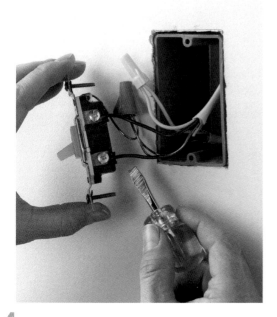

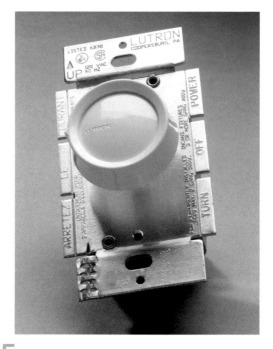

4 Remove the switch completely by unscrewing the screws that hold the wires. There may be as many as four wires connected to the switch: black, white, bare copper, and red. Disconnect each one by turning the screws on the sides of the switch just enough to free the wires. In many cases, there will also be two white wires connected with a wire connector in the box. You won't have to deal with these in your installation.

5 Buy a dimmer suited for your replacement. Choose a single-pole or three-way dimmer, as needed. Second, buy a dimmer rated for the maximum wattage of all light fixtures the switch will serve. For example, if the standard light switch you are replacing controls three recessed 60-watt lights, then the dimmer switch should be rated for 180 watts ($60 \times 3 = 180$).

WHAT IF...?

What if you find four colored wires attached to your switch?

This is a four-way switch, a type of switch used to control light fixtures from three or more different switch locations. A four-way switch can't be replaced with a dimmer, so if you run into this situation, you'll need to reassemble the switch. However, four-way switch installations are always installed in conjunction with three-way switches in the other switch locations. You will be able to replace one of the three-way switches at a different wall location with a three-way dimmer switch.

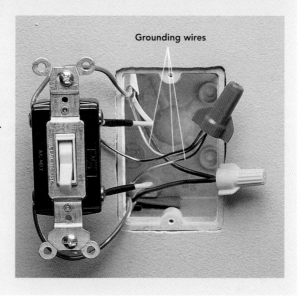

Grounding wires

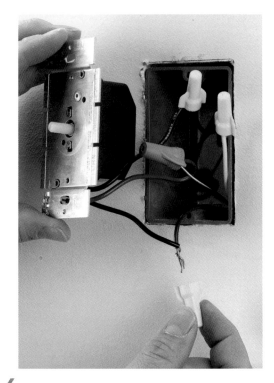

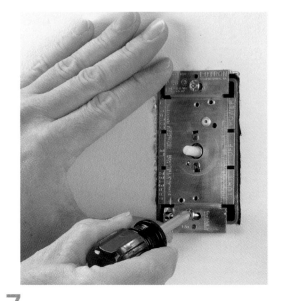

6 The dimmer will have two black wires, called leads, coming out of the dimmer's plastic body. The leads, like the two black wires coming out of the wall, are interchangeable, so you can't mix them up. Place the stripped end of one of the black leads and the end of one of the existing black wires into a wire connector (the dimmer will come with twist-on wire connectors). Twist the wire connector clockwise until it is tight. Hold the wires and tug gently on the connector to ensure that it is tight. Connect the other lead to the other wire from the wall in the same way. (If you are installing a three-way dimmer, see "WHAT IF...?" at right.)

7 Once the wires are firmly connected, you can attach the switch to the box. Tuck the new switch and wires neatly back into the box. Then drive the two long screws that are attached to the new switch into the two holes in the electrical box. These screws are typically long, so an electric screwdriver is handy. Reattach the coverplate. Then, turn the power back on at the main panel and test the switch for operation.

WHAT IF...?

If you're installing a three-way dimmer, attach the wire lead identified as the common to the circuit wire you tagged as the common in step 4. Now attach the other two wire leads to the other two colored circuit wires, using wire connectors. These wires, called the travelers, are interchangeable. It doesn't make any difference which of the two remaining circuit wires they get attached to.

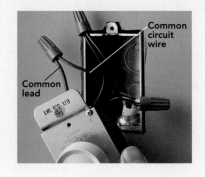

Common circuit wire

Common lead

HERE'S HOW: REPLACE AN ELECTRICAL BOX

Dimmer switches have larger bodies than traditional toggle switches, so you may find that the existing electrical box is too small to comfortably hold the new dimmer switch. Shallow, 2"-deep electrical boxes will not easily accommodate dimmer switches, especially if there are more than one set of wires inside the electrical box. If you purchase a dimmer and can't seem to get it to fit, don't force it. Dimmers produce more heat than standard switches, and it is a potential fire hazard to crowd the electrical box. You may be able to find a dimmer with a smaller body that will fit. Or, you can install a new, larger wall box.

Installing a new wall box is a somewhat advanced project, so you may want to hire a professional to do this work. But if you're up to the task, you can do it yourself by following the directions below. Allow yourself a full afternoon for this graduate school project.

1 Remove the old switch, following steps 1 through 5 on pages 72 and 73. To remove the old box, identify the location of the nails holding the electrical box to the wall studs. Use a reciprocating saw or jigsaw equipped with a metal-cutting blade to cut through the nails holding the box.

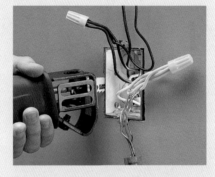

2 Bind the cable ends together and attach them to strings so they don't fall into the wall cavity when the old box is removed. Disconnect the cable clamps and slide the old box out.

3 Feed the cable into the new box, tighten the cable clamps, and secure the box in the opening. The retrofit box shown here uses bracket arms that are inserted into the sides of the box, then bent around the front edges to secure the box in the opening. Other styles of retrofit boxes have other means of attachment. Attach the new dimmer, following steps 6 and 7 on the preceding page.

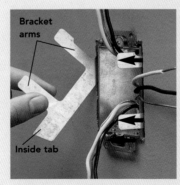

Bracket arms

Inside tab

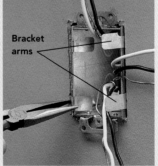

Bracket arms

13

Installing Timer Switches

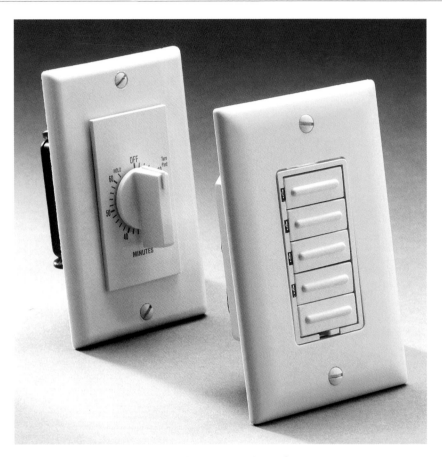

There are two common types of timer switch. Dial-type timers are commonly used to control bathroom vents and outdoor lights. To turn on the light and set the timer, simply twist the dial to the desired setting. When the dial winds down, the light or fan goes off. Push-button timers are commonly used to control lights. They have three or four switches, each with a preset time setting.

TIMER SWITCHES ARE SIMPLY SWITCHES THAT TURN ON OR OFF after a determined amount of time. This is useful for controlling some types of exterior lights and for controlling bathroom vent fans. With outdoor lights, you can use a timer to turn on landscape and security lighting at preset times. In the bathroom, the timer can vastly increase the efficacy of your vent fan by making sure it runs long enough to completely evacuate moist air. You can also use push-button-type timer switches to control room lights, thus assuring that no light is left burning indefinitely.

Installing a timer is no more difficult than installing a light switch. As with dimmers, the size of the box holding the switch in the wall is a consideration. In some older homes, the metal box that contains the old switch may not be large enough for a timer. If so, see page 75 for information on changing the box.

TIMER SWITCHES 101

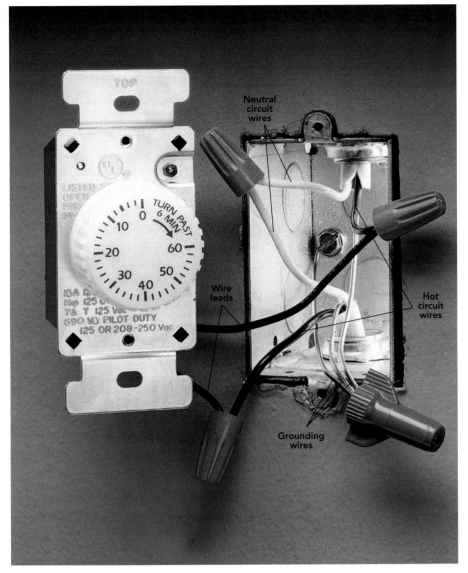

Neutral circuit wires

Wire leads

Hot circuit wires

Grounding wires

Unlike standard light switches and like dimmers, most timers are connected to the household electrical wires by short lengths of wire called leads. Leads come preattached to the timer. You attach them to the household wiring with wire connectors.

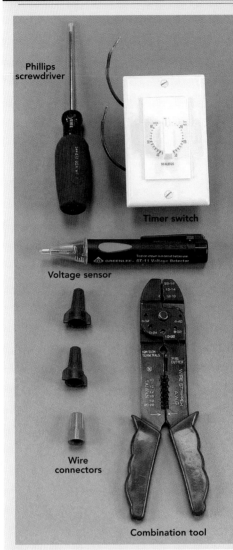

Phillips screwdriver

Timer switch

Voltage sensor

Wire connectors

Combination tool

SKILLS YOU'LL NEED

- Turning off the power (page 12)
- Testing for power (page 13)
- Making wire connections (page 14)

TERMS YOU NEED TO KNOW

LEADS—The preattached black wires attached to a timer switch.

GROUNDING WIRES—The bare copper circuit wires in an electrical box.

DIFFICULTY LEVEL

SKILLS LEVEL

EASY   MODERATE

This project takes about 1 hour.

1 First shut off the power to the switch. Remove the decorative coverplate from the switch by unscrewing the two screws that hold the plate to the switch box. Set the screws and the plate aside.

2 Use a voltage sensor to make sure the circuit is dead. Hold your voltage sensor's probe within ½" of the wires on either side of the switch. If the sensor beeps or lights up, then the switch is still live, and you'll need to trip the correct breaker to disconnect power to the switch. If the sensor does not beep or light up, the circuit is dead and you're safe to continue.

3 Remove the switch from the box by unscrewing the two long screws that hold the switch to the box at the top and at the bottom. Once the screws are out, hold the top and bottom of the switch, and carefully pull the switch away from the box.

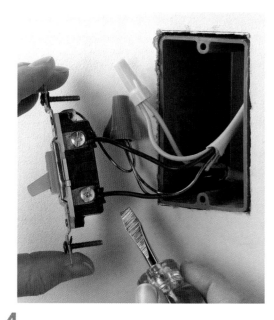

4 Remove the switch completely by unscrewing the screws that hold the two wires to the switch. In most cases, there will also be two white wires connected with a wire connector in the box. You won't have to deal with these in your installation.

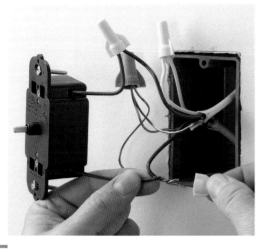

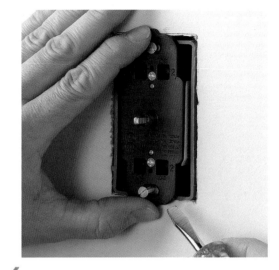

5 The timer will have two black wires, called leads, coming out of the timer's plastic body. The leads, like the two black wires coming out of the wall, are interchangeable, so you can't mix them up. Place the stripped end of one of the black leads and the end of one of the existing black wires into a wire connector (the dimmer will come with twist-on wire connectors). Twist the wire connector clockwise until it is tight. Hold the wires and tug gently on the connector to ensure that it is tight. Connect the other lead to the other wire from the wall in the same way.

6 Once the wires are firmly connected, you can attach the switch to the box. Tuck the new timer switch and wires neatly back into the box. Then drive the two long screws that are attached to the new switch into the two holes in the electrical box. These screws are typically long, so an electric screwdriver is handy. Pull the dial off the timer so the coverplate will fit over it. Reattach the coverplate and push the dial back onto the timer stem. Then, turn the power back on at the main panel and test the switch.

WHAT IF...?

What if there's a light switch right next to the fan switch?

This is a common arrangement. You might even find a group of three switches together. Behind the single coverplate, you'll find one large electrical box, called a "double-gang" box if there are two switches, that contains all the connections. This won't affect your installation except in one way: the coverplate. The coverplate that comes with your timer will be for a single switch. You'll need to buy a double-gang coverplate with a cutout for your timer (a small hole in the center) and one for a standard light switch.

Replacing Ceiling-Mounted Fixtures

14

Installing a new ceiling fixture can provide more light to a space, not to mention an aesthetic lift. It's one of the easiest upgrades you can do.

CEILING FIXTURES DON'T HAVE ANY MOVING PARTS and their wiring is very simple, so, other than changing bulbs, you're likely to get decades of trouble-free service from a fixture. This sounds like a good thing, but it also means that the fixture probably won't fail and give you an excuse to update a room's look with a new one. Fortunately, you can don't need an excuse. Upgrading a fixture is easy and can make a dramatic impact on a room. You can substantially increase the light in a room by replacing a globe-style fixture by one with separate spot lights, or you can simply install a new fixture that matches the room's décor.

CEILING FIXTURES 101

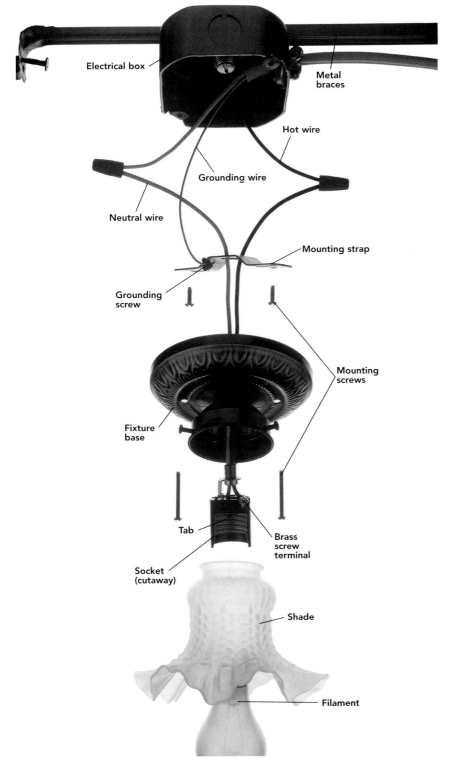

Electrical box

Metal braces

Hot wire

Grounding wire

Neutral wire

Mounting strap

Grounding screw

Mounting screws

Fixture base

Tab

Brass screw terminal

Socket (cutaway)

Shade

Filament

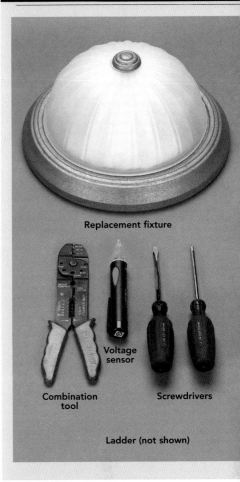
SKILLS YOU'LL NEED

- Turning off the power (page 12)
- Testing for power (page 13)
- Making wire connections (page 14)

DIFFICULTY LEVEL

SKILLS LEVEL

EASY   MODERATE

This project should take you 2 hours or less, and will be easier if you have a helper.

No matter what a ceiling light fixture looks like on the outside, they all attach in basically the same way. An electrical box in the ceiling is fitted with a mounting strap, which holds the fixture in place. The bare wire from the ceiling typically connects to the mounting strap. The two wires coming from the fixture connect to the black and white wires from the ceiling.

HOW TO REPLACE A CEILING-MOUNTED LIGHT FIXTURE

1 Begin by turning off the power to the fixture. Remove the globe by unthreading the globe (turning it counterclockwise) or by loosening the three screws that pinch the globe in place (the screws usually go through a collar around the base of the globe). Next, remove the lightbulbs from the fixture.

2 Detach the old light from the ceiling electrical box. Most traditional fixtures use two long screws to secure the fixture base to the metal electrical box in the ceiling. Have a helper hold the fixture with one hand so it doesn't fall, while you use a screwdriver to remove the two screws. Gently pull the light straight down, exposing the wiring that powers the fixture.

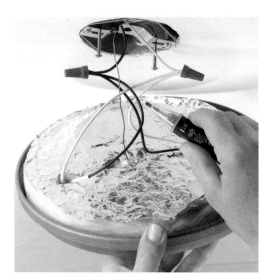

3 Before you touch the wires that feed the existing light, use a voltage sensor to verify that the circuit is now dead. With the fixture's switch in the ON position, insert the sensor's probe into the electrical box and hold the probe within ½" of the black wires inside. If the sensor beeps or lights up, then the circuit is still live, and you'll need to trip the correct breaker to disconnect power to the fixture. If the sensor does not beep or light up, the circuit is dead and you can proceed safely.

HERE'S HOW

Here's how to remove the shade. Most are secure in the center by a decorative nut. You can probably unscrew it by hand (hold on to the shade or have a helper support it). If it's stuck, try a pliers.

4 Once you have verified that the power to the light is off at the main panel, remove the fixture by disconnecting the wires. Use your hands to unscrew the wire connectors by turning them counterclockwise. After removing the wire connectors, pull the fixture completely away from the box (you can recycle it or save it). If you need to stop working and restore the power, first separate the wires coming from the ceiling box and cap them each with a wire connector.

5 Before you install the new fixture, check the ends of the wires coming from the ceiling electrical box. They should be clean and free of nicks or scorch marks. If they're dirty or worn, clip off the stripped portion with your combination tool. Then, strip away about ¾" of insulation from the end of each wire.

WHAT IF...?

What if there are no wire connectors?

If the fixture is small, the wires from the box may be connected directly to the fixture. To disconnect them, simply loosen the screws enough to free the wires.

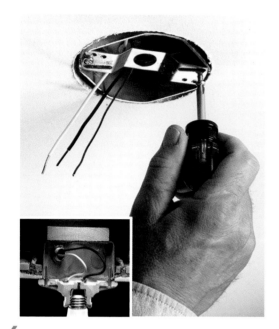

6 Now, take a look at the electrical box. Most fixtures installed in the last few decades are attached to a mounting strap, a strip of metal reaching from one side of the electrical box to another and attached with two screws. Older light fixtures were often mounted directly to the holes in the box (inset), a less safe installation that doesn't meet current electrical codes.

8 You will probably find a bare copper wire in the box. Connect this wire to the screw near the center of the mounting strap. Wrap the wire clockwise around the screw and turn the screw until it is snug.

7 If the box doesn't have a mounting strap, attach one. One might be included with your new fixture; otherwise, you can buy one at any hardware store or home center.

9 Set the new fixture on top of a ladder or have a helper support it. You'll find two short wires—called leads—coming from the fixture, one white and one black. If the ends of the leads are not already stripped, remove about ¾" of insulation from each wire end. Hold the white lead from the fixture next to the white wire from the ceiling. Push the ends into a wire connector, and twist the connector clockwise until it is snug.

11 Tuck the wire connections into the ceiling box on either side of the mounting strap. Hold the fixture over the electrical box so its two mounting holes line up with the holes on the mounting strap. Secure the light to the ceiling box by driving the fixture's mounting screws through the holes in the fixture base and into the strap. These screws are typically quite long, so an electric screwdriver is helpful.

10 Now connect the black wire to the black lead with a wire connector in the same way. Give both connections a gentle tug to make sure the connectors are tight.

SAFETY TIP

When picking a new ceiling fixture, select one with a bulb wattage rating appropriate to the bulb size you'll be using. For example, if you're installing a fixture that uses two bulbs, and you want to use 100-watt bulbs for maximum light, your fixture must be rated for 200 watts or more. A 120-watt fixture, on the other hand, can accept two 60-watt bulbs.

12 With the fixture secured to the box, you can install the lightbulbs and shades. Each fixture is a little different; follow the manufacturer's instructions. Once the bulbs are in, restore power to the fixture and test it.

15 Replacing Hanging Light Fixtures

Replacing an old chandelier is a quick and easy way to make a big change to a room's character, not to mention the quality of its light.

CHANDELIERS AND OTHER HANGING FIXTURES EXIST IN A HUGE VARIETY OF STYLES, so chances are good that you might acquire a house with a chandelier you find less than attractive. Of course, you might also have a chandelier stop working for some reason. Either way, they're easy enough to replace.

A properly installed chandelier has more bracing behind it than a standard ceiling fixture, so don't try to replace a simple ceiling globe with a 50-pound chandelier. You'll likely find a broken chandelier on your dining room table if you do.

CHANDELIERS 101

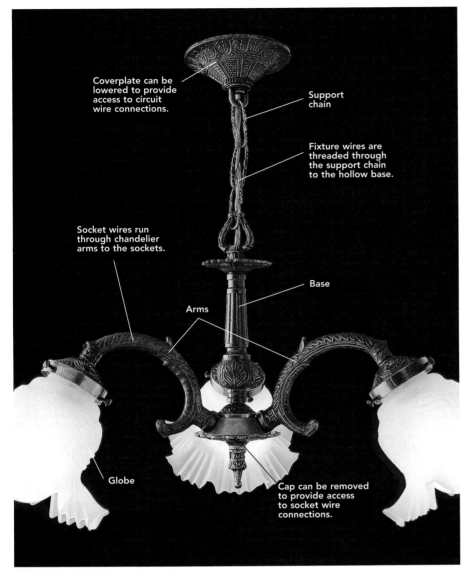

Coverplate can be lowered to provide access to circuit wire connections.

Support chain

Fixture wires are threaded through the support chain to the hollow base.

Socket wires run through chandelier arms to the sockets.

Base

Arms

Globe

Cap can be removed to provide access to socket wire connections.

Chandeliers can be a maze of wires, but fortunately, to install one, you only need to deal with the two fixture wires that snake up the chain.

HERE'S HOW

Heavy chandeliers and ceiling fans are suspended from electrical boxes that are secured between ceiling joists with heavy-duty braces.

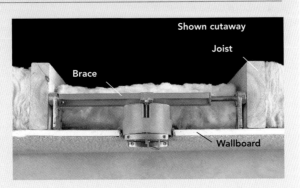

Shown cutaway

Joist

Brace

Wallboard

TOOLS & SUPPLIES YOU'LL NEED

Combination tool

Screwdriver

Voltage sensor

Replacement chandelier

SKILLS YOU'LL NEED

• Making wire connections (page 14)

Note: This job is easier with two people.

DIFFICULTY LEVEL

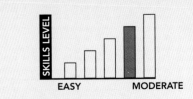

SKILLS LEVEL

EASY   MODERATE

Allow about 2 hours for this project.

HOW TO INSTALL A NEW CHANDELIER

Chandeliers are heavy, as you will learn very quickly when you're removing or installing one. It's better to rig up some means of temporary support for the fixture than to rely on a helper to hold it or—worse still—try to hold it yourself (you will need both hands to make the connections). One solution is to position a tall stepladder directly below the work area so you can rest the fixture on the top platform. And just in case the fixture falls, remove all the bulbs and globes before you do any of the work.

Retainer nut with integral chain loop

1 Remove the old light fixture. To gain access to the wiring connections, unfasten the retainer nut that secures the coverplate for the electrical box. On some chandeliers (such as the one above), the ring that holds the support chain for the chandelier is integral to the retainer nut, so unfastening it will mean the fixture is being supported only by the electrical wires.

2 Turn off the power to the old fixture at the main service panel. Use a voltage sensor to verify that the circuit is dead. With the light switch turned on, insert the sensor's probe into the electrical box within ½" of the wires inside. If the sensor beeps or lights up, then the circuit is live and you've shut off the wrong circuit. Shut off additional circuits until the probe confirms that you've shut off the correct one.

3 Remove the wire connectors from all the wires in the box and separate the wires. If the support chain is still attached, unscrew the mounting nut from the end of the threaded nipple inside the box. Disconnect the bare copper wire from the screw near the center of the mounting strap. Pull the old wires down through the threaded nipple.

Lamp shroud
(not the coverplate)

4 Adjust the length of the support chain on the new chandelier (if necessary) so it will hang at the desired height when mounted. This is normally done by disconnecting the chain from the support ring on the fixture, removing the required number of links and then reattaching the chain.

5 There will be two insulated wires and a bare copper ground woven in with the chain on your new fixture. There should be 6" to 12" of extra wire at the top of the chain. If the ends of these wires aren't stripped, use your combination tool to strip away ¾" of insulation.

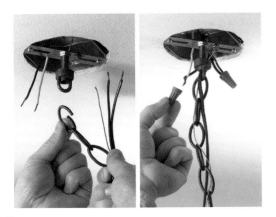

6 Hang the new fixture from the threaded nipple (unless the chain support nut is integral to the coverplate retainer, as in step 1). You may need to screw the threaded nipple farther into the mounting plate so it does not extend past the coverplate. Or, you may need to replace the mounting strap and nipple with correctly sized hardware (usually provided with the new fixture). Make the wire connections, including attaching the bare copper wire to the grounding screw on the mounting strap.

7 Carefully tuck the wires into the electrical box and then tighten the retainer for the coverplate so it is snug against the ceiling. Restore power and test the fixture.

16

Installing Track Lights

If you currently have a ceiling-mounted light fixture that is not meeting your lighting needs, it's simple to replace it with a track-lighting fixture. With track lighting you can easily change the type and number of lights, their position on the track, and the direction they aim. These fixtures come in many different styles, including short three-foot track systems with just one or two lights up to 12-foot systems with five or more lights.

TRACK LIGHTING OFFERS A BEAUTIFUL AND FUNCTIONAL WAY TO INCREASE THE AMOUNT OF LIGHT in a room or simply to update its look. A variety of fixture and lamp options lets you control the shape, color, and intensity of the light. Installing track lighting in place of an existing ceiling-mounted light fixture involves basic wiring and hand-tool skills, but the connections are even easier to make than with traditional light fixtures. Once installed, the system is very easy to upgrade or expand in the future.

TRACK LIGHTING 101

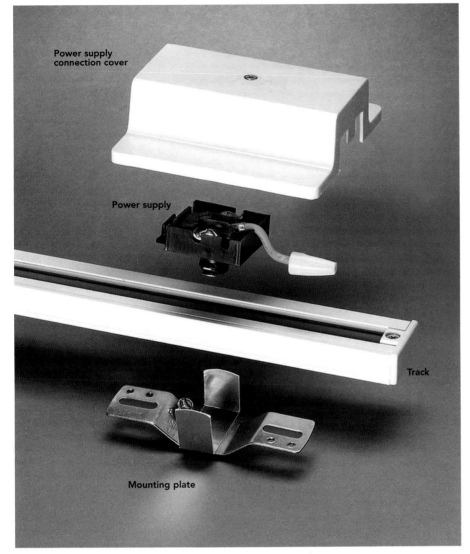

Power supply connection cover

Power supply

Track

Mounting plate

Track systems include a lot of components, but fortunately you can buy all-inclusive starter kits containing everything you need for a basic installation, as well as a foundation for later upgrades if you wish.

TERMS YOU NEED TO KNOW

POWER SUPPLY—This little piece of hardware varies in appearance from kit to kit, but in all cases, it feeds power from the household wiring to the electrified pathways inside the track (and this powers the lights).

TOOLS & SUPPLIES YOU'LL NEED

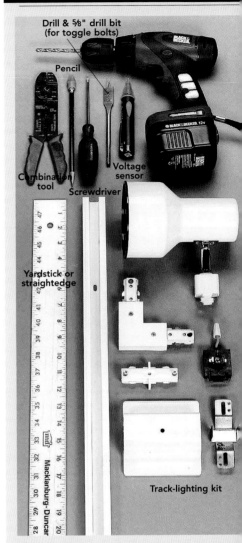

Drill & ⅝" drill bit (for toggle bolts)

Pencil

Combination tool

Screwdriver

Voltage sensor

Yardstick or straightedge

Track-lighting kit

SKILLS YOU'LL NEED

- Turning off power (page 12)
- Testing for power (page 13)
- Making wire connections (page 14)
- Light carpentry skills

DIFFICULTY LEVEL

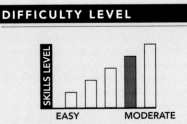

EASY   MODERATE

This project will take about half a day.

1 Locate the breaker for the light circuit you're working on and switch that breaker into the OFF position. If you have an older electrical service panel, you may have glass fuses instead of breakers. If so, pull the fuse for that circuit. Close the cover of the breaker or fuse cabinet.

2 Remove the globe and the lightbulbs from the fixture. Detach the old light from the ceiling electrical box. Most fixtures use two long screws to secure the fixture base to the electrical box in the ceiling. Hold the fixture with one hand while you use a screwdriver to remove the two screws. Gently pull the light straight down, exposing the wiring.

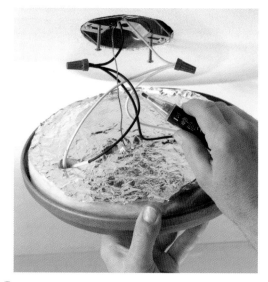

3 Use a voltage sensor to verify that the circuit is dead. Insert the sensor's probe into the electrical box within ½" of the black wires inside. If the sensor beeps or lights up, then the circuit is still live, and you'll need to trip the correct breaker to disconnect power to the fixture. If the sensor does not beep or light up, the circuit is dead and you can proceed safely.

4 Remove the fixture by disconnecting the wires. Use your hands to unscrew the wire connectors by turning them counterclockwise. After removing the wire connectors, pull the fixture completely away from the box (you can recycle it or save it). If you need to stop working and restore the power, first separate the wires coming from the ceiling box and cap them each with a wire connector.

HOW TO INSTALL TRACK LIGHTING

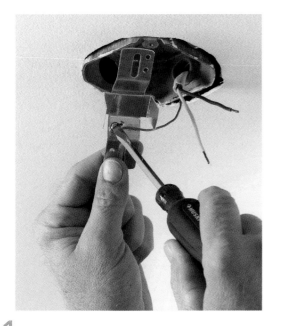

1 Turn off power (step 1, opposite page). Thread the three wires from the power supply hardware through the hole in the center of the mounting plate. Connect the power supply wires using wire connectors (the kit will come with them). The green wire on the power supply is connected to the bare copper wire coming out of the electrical box. Connect the white and black wires from the power supply to the white wire and black wires coming from the electrical box in the same way.

2 Carefully tuck the wires back up into the ceiling box and attach the mounting plate using the screws provided with the kit. The power supply can simply hang by its wires for the time being.

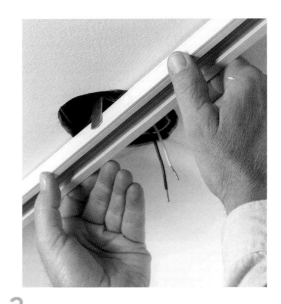

WHAT IF...?

What if the track is too long? Most types of track can be cut to length easily with a hacksaw. Use a saw fitted with a sharp blade and make a straight cut.

3 Draw a reference line on the ceiling to mark the track's path from the mounting plate to the end of the track. If possible, position the track directly underneath a ceiling joist so you can screw it to the joists. Otherwise, you will need to use toggle bolts to hold the tracks in the ceiling. Snap the track temporarily onto the mounting plate so it follows the reference line.

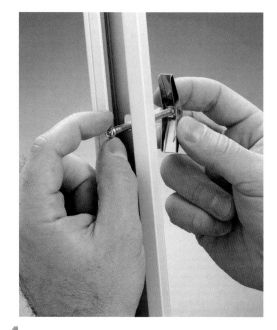

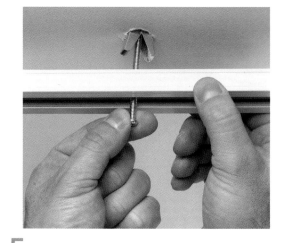

4 Mark the screw hole locations on the ceiling by making a dot through each hole in the track. After you mark the screw locations, remove the track and drill holes in the ceiling for the mounting screws. Begin by threading the bolts onto the track. First, unscrew the toggle bolt from the spring-loaded wings. Insert the toggle bolts through the holes in the track. Hold the wing on the ceiling-side of the track, then screw the bolt back into the toggle wings with two or three turns of the bolt.

5 Drill holes slightly larger then the thickness of the closed toggle wings. Pinch the wings of one toggle together and push it into the hole in the ceiling. The wings will snap open once they enter the cavity and hold the bolt in place. Push the other toggle bolts into their holes in the same way. Once all the bolts for a track section are in their holes, fit the track end to the mounting plate, and then tighten all the toggle bolts. Tighten the two screws on the mounting plate.

HERE'S HOW

Here's how to add another section of track. You can link sections of track together with connectors (your kit may include some or you can buy them separately, along with additional track sections). Connector pieces will also allow you to make 90-degree turns or T's on your track path. The connectors snap into the end of the track and are secured with screws.

6 Now you can connect the power supply to the track. Insert the power supply into the track and twist the connector until it snaps securely into place (connector installation may vary by manufacturer). The connector is made so that it cannot be snapped in the wrong way, so you'll know when it's in correctly. Attach the white and black wires to the screw terminals on the power supply.

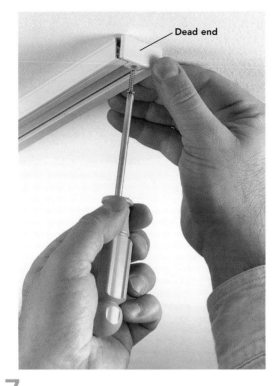

Dead end

7 Most kits will require you to cap the open ends of track dead ends. Snap them onto the ends of track pieces and secure them with screws.

8 Now you can fit the decorative cover over the mounting plate. It may snap in place or be secured with screws. This will cover up the mounting plate completely.

9 You can begin inserting the light heads into the track at this point. These should simply twist-lock into place. Turn on power and test the light head.

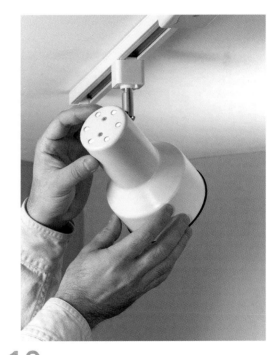

10 If the light works, locate a position you like and push down the locking tab on the side of the fixture to secure the light in this location. Install appropriate bulbs in the light sockets, according to the manufacturer's instructions. Install the remaining heads.

Installing
Motion-Sensing Floodlights

17

An exterior floodlight with a motion sensor is an effective security measure.
Make sure you keep the motion sensor adjusted so it doesn't give false alarms.

MOST HOUSES AND GARAGES HAVE FLOODLIGHTS ON THEIR EXTERIORS. You can easily upgrade these fixtures so that they provide additional security by replacing them with motion-sensing floodlights. Motion-sensing floods can be set up to detect motion in a specific area—like a walkway or driveway—and then cast light into that area. And there are few things intruders like less than the spotlight. These lights typically have timers that allow you to control how long the light stays on and photosensors that prevent the light from coming on during the day.

FLOODLIGHTS 101

A motion-sensing light fixture provides inexpensive and effective protection against intruders. It has an infrared eye that triggers the light fixture when a moving object crosses its path. Choose a light fixture with: a photo cell (A) to prevent the light from turning on in daylight; an adjustable timer (B) to control how long the light stays on; and range control (C) to adjust the reach of the motion-sensor eye.

TOOLS & SUPPLIES YOU'LL NEED

Combination tool

Screwdriver

Voltage sensor

Floodlight with motion sensor

SKILLS YOU'LL NEED

- Turning off the power (page 12)
- Testing for power (page 13)
- Making wire connections (page 14)

HERE'S HOW

Here's how to make sure no one accidentally turns off your security lights—or any other light you don't want turned off. Switch locks are inexpensive plastic covers that lock a switch in the ON or OFF position. You can find them at any hardware store or home center.

DIFFICULTY LEVEL

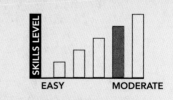

SKILLS LEVEL

EASY   MODERATE

This project will take about 1 hour.

HOW TO INSTALL A MOTION-SENSING FLOODLIGHT

1 Turn off power to the old fixture. To remove it, unscrew the mounting screws on the part of the fixture attached to the wall. There will probably be four of them. Carefully pull the fixture away from the wall, exposing the wires. Don't touch the wires yet.

2 Before you touch any wires, use a voltage sensor to verify that the circuit is dead. With the light switch turned ON, insert the sensor's probe into the electrical box and hold the probe within ½" of the wires inside to confirm that there is no voltage flow. Disconnect the wire connectors and remove the old fixture.

3 Examine the ends of the three wires coming from the box (one white, one black, and one bare copper). They should be clean and free of corrosion. If the ends are in poor condition, clip them off and then strip ¾" of wire insulation with a combination tool.

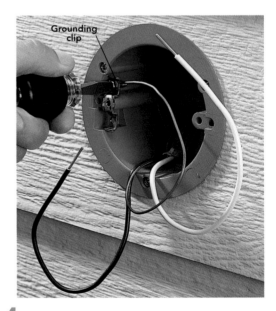

Grounding clip

4 If the electrical box is nonmetallic and does not have a metal grounding clip, install a grounding clip or replace the box with one that does have a clip and make sure the ground wire is attached to it securely. Some light fixtures have a grounding terminal on the base. If yours has one, attach the grounding wire from the house directly to the terminal.

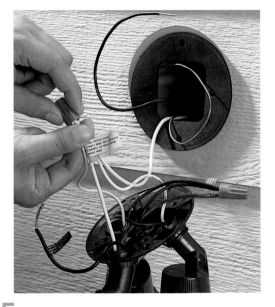

5 Now you can attach the new fixture. Begin by sliding a rubber or foam gasket (usually provided with the fixture) over the wires and onto the flange of the electrical box. Set the new fixture on top of a ladder or have a helper hold it while you make the wiring connections. There may be as many as three white wires coming from the fixture. Join all white wires, including the feed wire from the house, using a wire connector.

6 Next, join the black wire from the box and the single black wire from the fixture with a wire connector. You may see a couple of black wires and a red wire already joined on the fixture. You can ignore these in your installation.

7 Neatly tuck all the wires into the box so they are behind the gasket. Align the holes in the gasket with the holes in the box, and then position the fixture over the gasket so its mounting holes are also aligned with the gasket. Press the fixture against the gasket and drive the four mounting screws into the box. Install floodlight bulbs (exterior rated) and restore power.

8 Test the fixture. You will still be able to turn it on and off with the light switch inside. Flip the switch to ON and pass your hand in front of the motion sensor. The light should come on. Adjust the motion sensor to cover the traffic areas and pivot the light head to illuminate the intended area.

Repairing Fluorescent Light Fixtures

18

Troubleshooting a fluorescent light that's flickering or won't work is a process of testing and checking that begins with inspecting the fluorescent tubes to make sure they're making good contact with the fixture sockets and are in good condition.

FLUORESCENT FIXTURES ARE GREAT LIGHTING CHOICES because they save energy and offer many different quality-of-light options, from the hue and color of the light to its brightness. And fluorescent lamps have a much longer life than regular incandescent lamps. But as fluorescent fixtures age, small parts begin to fail. Replacing the tubes is easy, and replacing the ballast (a transformer-type part that distributes power to the sockets) is only slightly more difficult. But if the fixture is old it may make more sense to replace the entire fixture with a newer (and probably quieter) model.

FLUORESCENT LIGHTS 101

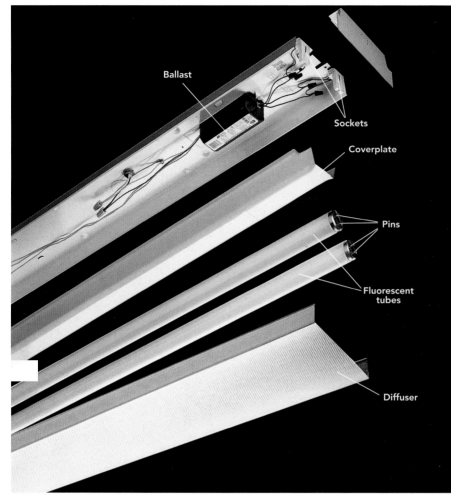

Ballast

Sockets

Coverplate

Pins

Fluorescent
tubes

Diffuser

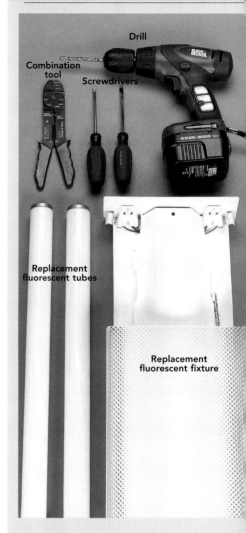

Drill

Combination
tool

Screwdrivers

Replacement
fluorescent tubes

Replacement
fluorescent fixture

Fluorescent fixtures come in lots of different lengths, from 6 inches to 6 feet. They all work basically the same. The fixture consists of a diffuser and a coverplate and housing that contain a ballast that connects to the sockets that hold the tubes.

BUYER'S TIP

Here's how to buy a fluorescent tube: You'll need three pieces of information: the length of the tube, the end type, and the wattage. There are a couple different styles of pin configuration for the ends of tubes. The two-pin style shown here is most common, but there are others. If yours looks different, take it with you to the hardware store to find an exact match. The wattage of the fluorescent tube will be printed somewhere along its length. Buy a new tube with the same watt rating. For best value, buy fluorescent tubes in multiple tube packs, as you would with other types of lightbulbs.

SKILLS YOU'LL NEED

- Turning off power (page 12)
- Testing for power (page 13)
- Making wire connections (page 14)

Note: This may be easier with two people.

DIFFICULTY LEVEL

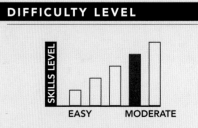

SKILLS LEVEL

EASY   MODERATE

Allow about 2 hours for this project.

HOW TO REPLACE A FLUORESCENT TUBE

1 If your fluorescent light is flickering or not working, check the tubes first. Start by removing the plastic diffuser that covers the light so you can access the florescent tubes. The diffuser normally snaps into place. Squeeze it slightly at its sides to remove it.

2 Twist the tubes to confirm that they are seated correctly in the sockets. If they are securely in the sockets but the light won't light, remove the tubes by rotating them a quarter turn in each direction and pulling down.

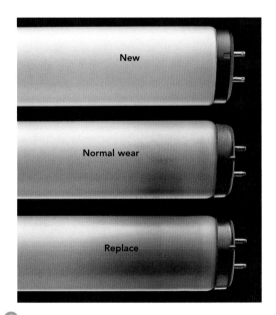

New

Normal wear

Replace

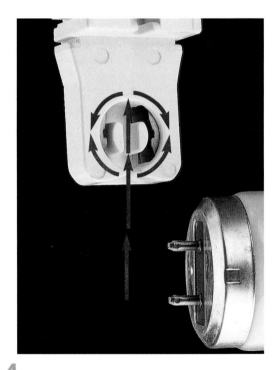

3 Take a look at the ends of the bulb. A little light gray coloring at the ends of a used fluorescent bulb is normal. But if one or more of the tube ends is blackened, the tube should be replaced.

4 Purchase a replacement tube (see page 101) and install the new tubes by holding the tube so the pins are vertical. Slide the pins into the grooves in the sockets and push up. Then, turn the tube a quarter turn in each direction. Replace the diffuser and test the fixture.

HOW TO REPLACE A BALLAST

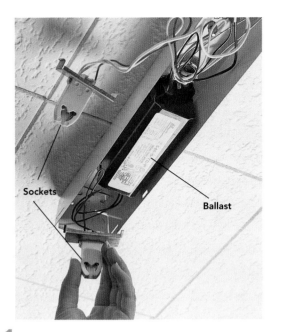

Sockets

Ballast

1 Turn off the power at the main service panel, then remove the diffuser, fluorescent tube, and coverplate. Test for power. Remove the sockets from the fixture housing by sliding them out, or by removing the mounting screws and lifting the sockets out.

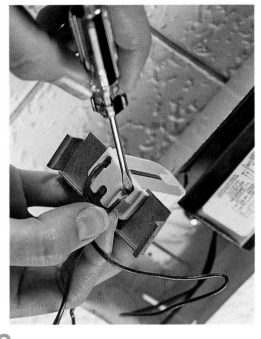

2 Disconnect the wires that lead from the ballast to the sockets by pushing a small screwdriver into the release openings (as seen above) or loosening the screw terminals. On some socket styles you'll need to cut the wires to within 2" of the socket to remove the ballast.

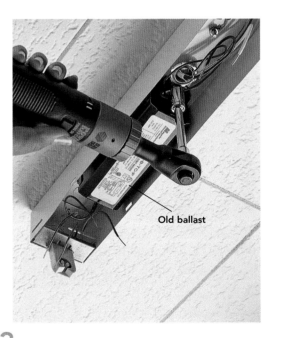

Old ballast

3 Remove the old ballast, using a ratchet wrench or screwdriver. Make sure to support the ballast so it does not fall (a little duct tape will do the job).

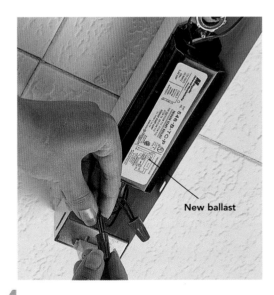

New ballast

4 Install a new ballast that has the same ratings as the old ballast. Attach the ballast wires to the socket wires and reinstall the coverplate, fluorescent tube, and diffuser. Turn on power to the light fixture at the main service panel.

HOW TO REPLACE A FLUORESCENT FIXTURE

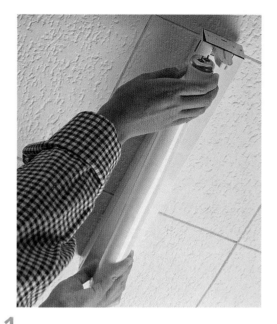

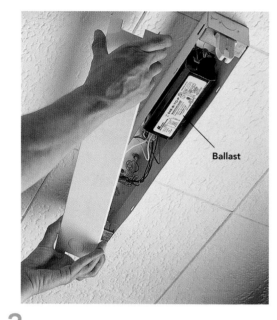

Ballast

1 If replacing the tube or ballast doesn't fix the problem, it's best to replace the whole light fixture. Start by removing the diffuser and the tubes. Then, turn off the power to the fixture at the service panel and test with a voltage tester.

2 Loosen the screws at each end of the metal coverplate on the fixture. If there are no screws, you may be able to remove the cover by pinching its ends and pulling down. Pull the coverplate free and set it aside.

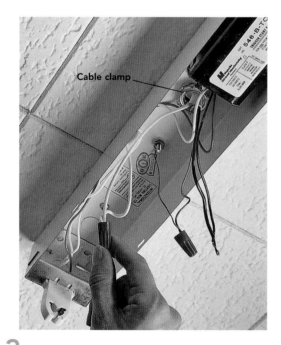

Cable clamp

3 Disconnect the fixture by unscrewing the wire connectors inside the fixture housing. Straighten out the three wires feeding into the fixture through the cable clamp and then unscrew the cable clamp.

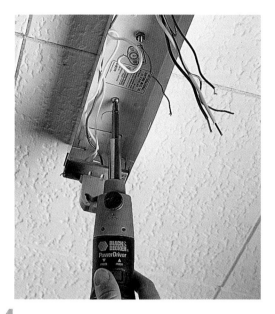

4 You can now completely remove the fixture by unscrewing the mounting screws. It's a good idea to have a helper support the fixture as you undo the screws. Move the fixture away from the ceiling, pulling the three wires through the hole.

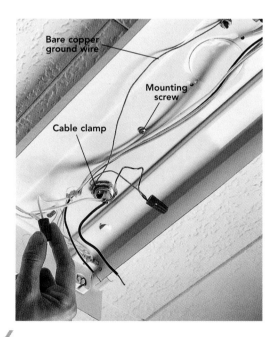

Bare copper ground wire

Mounting screw

Cable clamp

6 Attach the fixture to the ceiling with screws or toggle bolts driven up through mounting screw holes in the top of the fixture, and then tighten a retaining nut around the cable clamp. Make the wire connections (white to white, black to black, bare copper ground to grounding screw on fixture).

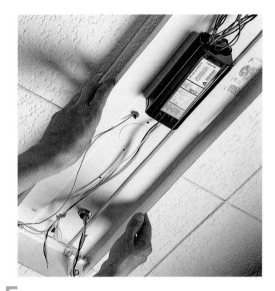

5 Remove the coverplate from the new fixture. On the bottom of the new fixture, you'll find several knockout holes. Remove a knockout that will fall under the electrical box in the ceiling when the fixture is installed (drive a screwdriver through the knockout to remove it). Attach a cable clamp in the knockout hole and feed the three wires from the ceiling box through the cable clamp as you raise the fixture up against the ceiling.

7 Reattach the coverplate on the new fixture, install the fluorescent tubes and snap in the diffuser. Restore power and test the fixture.

Fixing Ceiling Fans

19

Even ceiling fans that are operated only occasionally are prone to failure or problems like excess wobble. Following the steps in this chapter will help you diagnose and solve common ceiling fan maladies.

CEILING FANS THAT WORK PROPERLY WILL SAVE MONEY on heating and cooling costs and add to the comfort of your home. But over time ceiling fans can fail to work, become noisy, the blades may wobble, or the pull-chain switch may become unreliable or just plain faulty. Before putting many hours of time and hard labor—not to mention the expense—into a new fan installation, diagnose the old fan to see if it can be easily repaired using these steps. Keep in mind that most consumer-level ceiling fans will never be completely silent when the fan is operating—moving air does make some noise, after all.

CEILING FANS 101

Mounting bracket

Canopy

Motor

Fan blades

Switch housing

Pull chain

Bottom cap

A ceiling fan is suspended from a sturdy mounting bracket and the connection is concealed by a decorative canopy.

FAN NOT WORKING? TRY THIS FIRST:

1 Make sure that the wall switch that controls the ceiling fan is in the ON position. Reach up to the fan and move the fan direction switch back and forth to confirm that it is fully engaged in one of the two positions (clockwise blade movement for summer, counterclockwise for winter). If the fan blades do not start rotating, even though the switch feels secure in one of the two positions, go to step 2.

Fan direction switch

2 Put your hand on the switch housing to feel for vibration. If a vibration or humming is present, the fan motor is malfunctioning and you should consider replacing the entire unit. No hum or vibration? Proceed to the further diagnostics beginning on page 108.

TOOLS & SUPPLIES YOU'LL NEED

Masking tape

Phillips screwdriver

Fan switch

Voltage sensor

Needlenose pliers

Combination tool

SKILLS YOU'LL NEED

- Turning off power (page 12)
- Testing for power (page 13)
- Making wire connections (page 14)

DIFFICULTY LEVEL

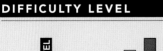

SKILLS LEVEL

EASY   MODERATE

Allow 2 to 4 hours, and work with a helper.

HOW TO FIX A CEILING FAN

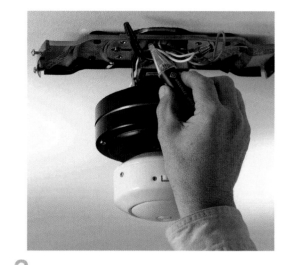

1 A leading cause of fan failure is loose wire connections. To inspect these connections, first shut off the power to the fan. Remove the fan blades to gain access, then remove the canopy that covers the ceiling box and fan mounting bracket. Most canopies are secured with screws on the outside shell. Have a helper hold the fan while you remove the screws so it won't fall.

2 Once the canopy is lowered, you'll see black, white, green, copper, and possibly blue wires. Hold a voltage sensor within ½" of these wires with the wall switch that controls the fan in the ON position. The black and blue wires should cause the sensor to beep if power is present.

HERE'S HOW

One common problem with older ceiling fans is that over time or due to incorrect initial installation, the blades begin to wobble as they spin. If you're within earshot, the vibration from wobbling is irritating, but it can also damage the fan and shorten its life. Wobbling has three main causes: (1) the fan blades may not be balanced properly, (2) the fan may not be tightly secured to the ceiling fan box, or (3) one or more of the fan blades may have become warped. Fixing any of these situations requires minimal effort and time.

1 Start by checking and tightening all hardware used to attach the blades to the mounting arms and the mounting arms to the motor. Hardware tends to loosen over time and this is frequently the cause of wobble.

2 If wobble persists, try switching around two of the blades. Often, this is all it takes to get the fan back into balance. If a blade is damaged or warped, try to locate a replacement blade.

3 If you still have wobble, turn the power off at the panel, remove the fan canopy, and inspect the mounting brace and the connection between the mounting pole and the fan motor. Tighten any loose connections and replace the canopy.

3 When you have confirmed that there is no power, check all the wire connections to make certain each is tight and making good contact. You may be able to see that a connection has come apart and needs to be remade. But even if you see one bad connection, check them all by gently tugging on the wire connectors. If the wires pull out of the wire connector or the connection feels loose, unscrew the wire connector from the wires.

4 Twist the wires back together the same way you found them, making sure the bare wires are making good contact with each other. Secure them with a new wire twist connector.

HERE'S HOW

Bad wiring connections often are caused by failed wire connectors. Inspect connections for signs of burning, corrosion, or rust. If the inside of any wire connector does not look clean and shiny, replace it with a new connector of the same size.

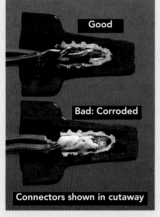

Good

Bad: Corroded

Connectors shown in cutaway

5 If everything works, reinstall the canopy by replacing the screws that were holding it in place. Reattach the fan blades and then restore power. If all connections are secure but the fan still doesn't work, try replacing the pull chain to resolve the problem (see next page).

1 Turn off the power at the main service panel. Use a screwdriver to remove the three to four screws that secure the bottom cap on the fan switch housing. Lower the cap to expose the wires that supply power to the pull-chain switch.

2 Test the wires by placing a voltage sensor within ½" of the wires. If the sensor beeps or lights up, then the circuit is still live, and is not safe to work. When the sensor does not beep or light up, the circuit is dead and may be worked upon.

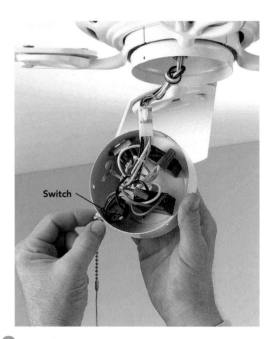

Switch

3 Locate the switch unit (the part that the pull chain used to be attached to if it broke off); it's probably made of plastic. You'll need to replace the whole switch. Fan switches are connected with from three to eight wires, depending on the number of speed settings.

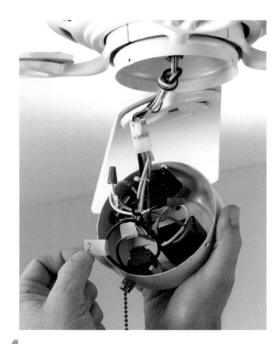

4 Attach a small piece of tape to each wire that enters the switch and write an identifying number on the tape. Start at one side of the switch and label the wires in the order they're attached.

BUYER'S TIP

Here's how to buy a new switch. Bring the old switch to the hardware store or home center, and find an identical new switch—one with the same number and color of wires. It should also attach to the fan motor wires in the same way (slots or screw terminals or with integral wires and wire connectors) and that attaches to the fan in the same way. If you are unable to locate an identical switch, find the owners manual for your ceiling fan and contact the manufacturer. Or, find the brand and model number of the fan and order a switch from a ceiling fan dealer or electronics supply store.

5 Disconnect the old switch wires, in most cases by cutting the wires off as close to the old switch as possible. Unscrew the retaining nut that secures the switch to the switch housing.

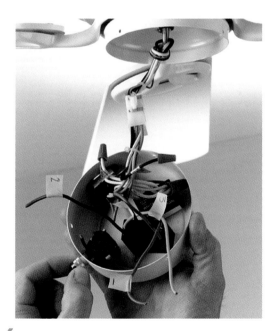

6 Remove the switch. There may be one or two screws that hold it in place or it may be secured to the outside of the fan with a small, knurled nut, which you can loosen with needlenose pliers. Purchase an identical new switch.

7 Connect the new switch using the same wiring configuration as on the old model. To make connections, first use a wire stripper to strip ¾" of insulation from the ends of each of the wires coming from the fan motor (the ones you cut in step 5). Attach the wires to the new switch in the same order and configuraion as they were attached to the old switch. Secure the new switch in the housing and make sure all wires are tucked neatly inside. Reattach the bottom cap. Test all the fan's speeds to make sure all the connections are good.

20

Installing Raceway Wiring

Raceway wiring systems are surface-mounted networks of electrical boxes and hollow metal tracks that allow you to expand an existing wiring circuit without cutting into your walls.

SURFACE WIRING CAN BE USED TO EXTEND POWER FROM ANY EXISTING RECEPTACLE to another location without cutting into walls, floors, or ceilings. If you're relying on an ugly (not to mention dangerous) tangle of extension cords to compensate for a shortage of proper receptacles, a raceway system of surface wiring may be your solution. Surface wiring uses inconspicuous metal channels that are mounted to the walls. The channels are easily removed and can be extended again or rerouted as your needs change.

RACEWAYS 101

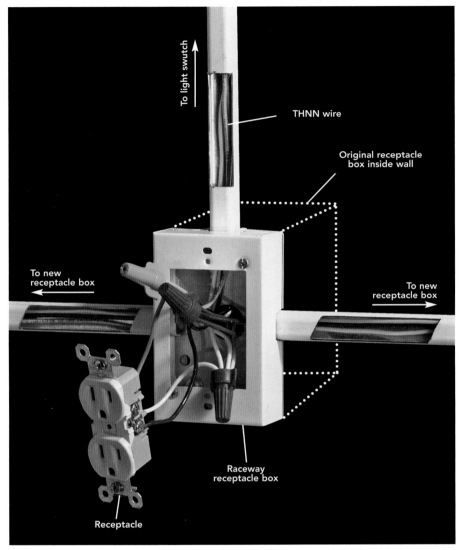

To light swutch

THNN wire

Original receptacle box inside wall

To new receptacle box

To new receptacle box

Raceway receptacle box

Receptacle

The raceway receptacle box is mounted directly to the original electrical box (usually for a receptacle) and raceway tracks are attached to it. The tracks house THNN wires that run from the raceway box to new receptacles and light switches.

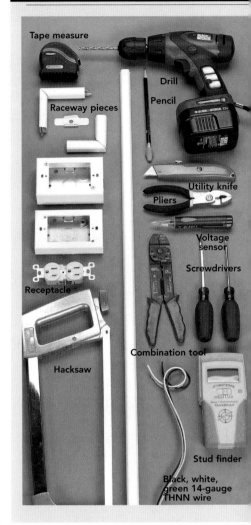

Tape measure

Raceway pieces

Drill

Pencil

Utility knife

Pliers

Voltage sensor

Screwdrivers

Receptacle

Combination tool

Hacksaw

Stud finder

Black, white, green 14-gauge THNN wire

SKILLS YOU'LL NEED

- Turning off power (page 12)
- Testing for power (page 13)
- Making wire connections (page 14)
- Light carpentry skills

HERE'S HOW

Here's how to determine if an electrical circuit has enough capacity for you to add a new receptacle or light. Count the number of receptacles and lights that are already part of the circuit. Multiply this number by 1.5 amps. The result should not exceed the amperage of the circuit (usually 15 or 20 amps). The 1.5 amps estimate is for everyday small appliances, lamps, and lighting. Do not add onto a circuit if it supplies or is intended to supply power to high-draw appliances such as a refrigerator, microwave oven, or electric heater. Overloading a circuit is unsafe and will cause the circuit breaker to trip. It's always a good idea to consult your local electrical inspector before you start.

DIFFICULTY LEVEL

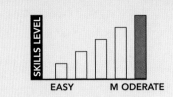

SKILLS LEVEL

EASY   M ODERATE

Allow half a day for this project.

HOW TO INSTALL RACEWAY WIRING

1 Confirm that the circuit you want to expand will support a new receptacle or light (see page 113). Mark the planned location of the new receptacle or switch on the wall and mea-sure to the nearest existing receptacle. Purchase enough raceway to cover this distance plus about 10 percent extra. Buy a surface-mounted starter box, new receptacle box, and fittings for your project (the raceway product packaging usually provides guidance for shopping).

2 First shut off the power to the switch. Remove the coverplate from the receptacle by unscrewing the screw that holds the plate to the electrical box. Set the screws and the plate aside. With the coverplate off, you will be able to see the receptacle and the electrical box it is attached to.

3 Before you remove the old receptacle, use a voltage sensor to double-check that the circuit is dead. Hold your voltage sensor's probe within ½" of the wires on each side of the receptacle. If the sensor beeps or lights up, then the receptacle is still live, and you'll need to trip the correct breaker to disconnect power to the receptacle. If the sensor does not beep or light up, the receptacle is dead and you can proceed safely.

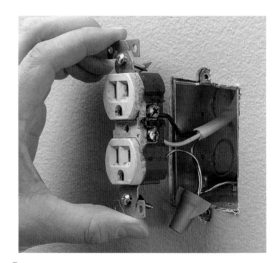

4 Remove the receptacle from the box by unscrewing the two long screws that hold the switch to the box. Once the screws are out, gently pull the receptacle away from the box. It won't pull away easily, since the wires are still attached, so pull firmly. Depending on how your receptacle has been wired, you may find two insulated wires and a bare copper wire or four insulated wires and a bare wire. Detach these wires and set the receptacle aside.

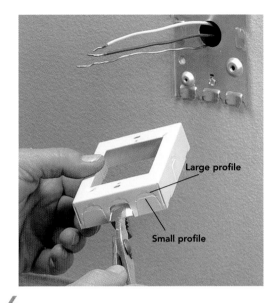

5 Your starter box includes a box and a mounting plate with a hole in its center. Pull all the wires you just disconnected through the hole, taking care not to scrape them on the edges of the hole. Screw the mounting plate to the existing receptacle box with the included mounting screws.

6 Remove a knockout from the starter box to create an opening for the raceway track, using pliers. Often, the prepunched knockouts have two profile options—make sure the knockout you remove matches the profile of your track.

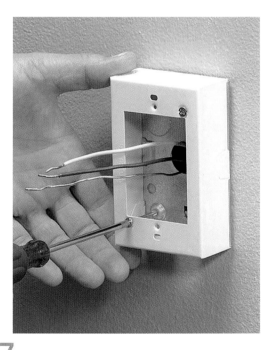

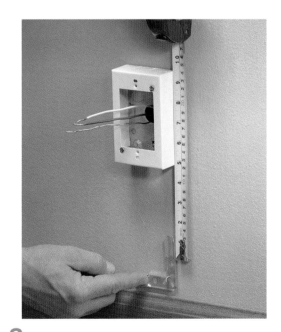

7 Hold the box portion of the starter box over the mounting plate on the existing receptacle. Drive the mounting screws through the holes in the box and into the threaded openings in the mounting plate.

8 Set the mounting bracket for an elbow connector ¼" above the baseboard (having the track run along the baseboard edge looks better than running it in a straight line out of the starter box). Measure from the knockout in the starter box to the top of the bracket and cut a piece of raceway ½" longer than this measurement.

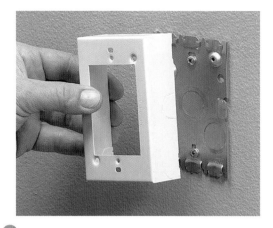

9 At the new receptacle location, use a laser level to transfer the height of the top of the starter box and mark a reference line. If possible, locate the box so at least one screw hole in the mounting plate falls over a wall stud. Position the mounting plate for the receptacle box up against the laser line and secure it with screws driven through the mounting plate holes. If the plate is not located over a wall stud, use wall anchors (see below left).

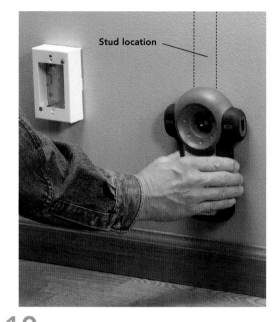

Stud location

10 Use a stud finder to locate and mark all of the wall framing members between the old receptacle and the new one. There should be a stud every 16" along the wall, and the studs should be about 1½" wide.

TOOL TIP

Here's how to cut metal raceway. Secure the track in a vise or clamping work support and cut with a hacksaw. Make sure the mounting bracket and the track cover are aligned at the end and cut through both at the same time. For best results, use long, slow strokes and don't bear down too hard on the saw.

11 At stud locations, use a laser level as a reference for marking a line ¼" above the top of the baseboard. Attach mounting clips for the raceway track at these marks.

Here's how to install wall anchors. Mark screw locations on the wall, then drill ¼" holes through the wall at the marks. Tap a plastic wall anchor into the hole with a hammer so the underside of the top flange is flush against the surface of the wall. When a screw is driven into the wall anchor sleeve, the sleeve will expand in the hole and hold the screw securely.

13 At the starter box slide one end of the short piece of raceway into the knockout so that about ⅛" extends into the box. Snap the raceway into the clip below the knockout. Repeat this same procedure at the new receptacle box. Slip a bushing (included with installation kit) over the ends of the tracks where they enter the box.

12 Install mounting clips ½" or so below the knockouts on both the starter box and the new receptacle box. The clips should line up with the knockouts.

14 The elbow piece will have two parts, a mounting plate and a cap. Install the mounting plates directly below the pieces of track entering the receptacle boxes.

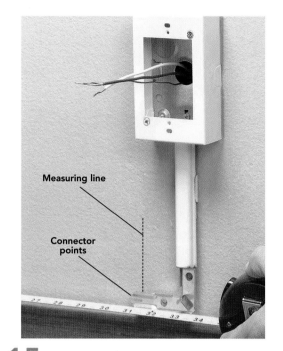

Measuring line

Connector points

15 Now you can measure and cut the long piece of raceway that fits between the two receptacles. Measure the distance between the ends of the horizontal parts of the elbows, and cut a length of raceway to that length. Be sure to measure all the way to the base of the clip, not just to the tips of the connector points.

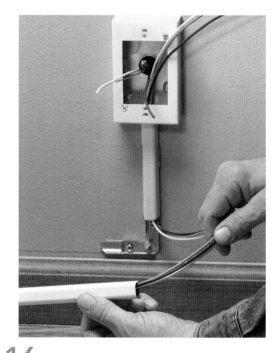

16 Cut black, white, and green THNN wire about 2-ft. longer than the length of each wiring run. Snake the end of each wire into the starter box, through the knockout, and into the vertical raceway. Then snake the wire all the way through the long piece of raceway so about 12" to 16" come out on each side.

WHAT IF...?

What if I need to go around a corner? Use corner pieces to guide raceway around corners. Corners are available for inside or outside corners and consist of a mounting plate and a cap piece. Inside corners may be used at wall/ceiling junctures.

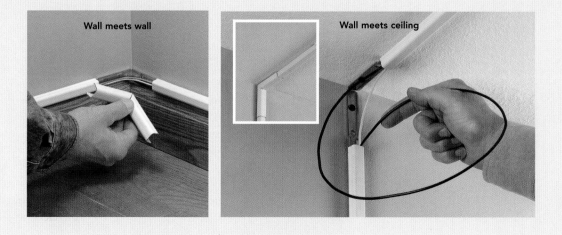

Wall meets wall

Wall meets ceiling

WHAT IF...?

What if I need a piece of raceway track that's longer than the longest piece available at the hardware store (usually 5 ft.)?

You can use straight connector pieces to join two lengths of raceway. Much like an elbow piece, they have a mounting plate and a cover that snaps over the wiring.

17 Now you can snap the long piece of raceway into the mounting clips. Line one end of the raceway up with the end of an elbow and begin pressing the raceway into the clips until it is snapped into all of the clips. At the new receptacle location, snake the ends of the wires up through the vertical piece of raceway and into the new receptacle box. There should be about 6" of wire coming out at each box.

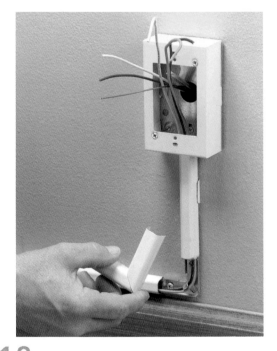

18 Finish the raceway by snapping the elbow cover pieces into place over the mounting plates, one at the starter box and another at the new receptacle location. You may need to rap the plate with a rubber mallet to get enough force to snap it on. Make sure all of the wire fits completely within the cover pieces.

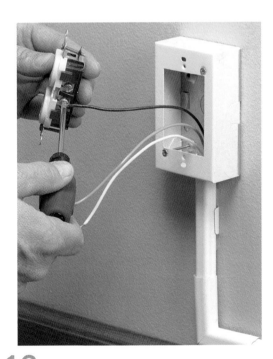

19 Now you can wire the receptacles. Begin at the new receptacle location. Take the black wire and wrap the end of the wire around the bottom gold screw on the side of the receptacle. Tighten the screw so it's snug.

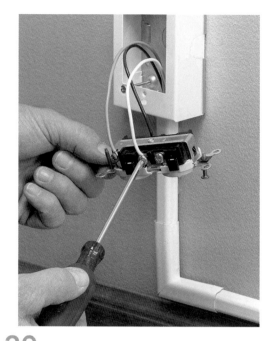

20 Now take the white wire and wrap the end of the wire around the silver screw opposite the copper one you just used. Tighten the screw so it's snug. Connect the green wire to the green-colored screw on the bottom of the receptacle.

21 Once the connections are made, gently tuck the wires and the receptacle into the box so the holes in the top and bottom of the receptacle align with the holes in the box. Use a screwdriver to drive the two long mounting screws that hold the receptacle to the box. Attach the cover plate.

22 Now you can reinstall the old receptacle (or a replacement) at the starter box. First, make sure the power is still off with your voltage tester. Take the old black wire and wrap the end of the wire around the top gold screw on the side of the receptacle. Tighten the screw so it's snug.

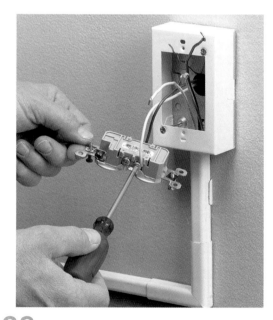

23 Take the old white wire and wrap the end of the wire around the silver screw opposite the copper one you just used. Tighten the screw so it's snug.

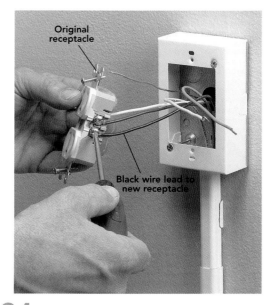

Original receptacle

Black wire lead to new receptacle

24 The next step connects the old receptacle to the new one. Take the black wire that goes into the raceway and wrap the end of the wire around the bottom gold screw on the side of the receptacle. Tighten the screw so it's snug.

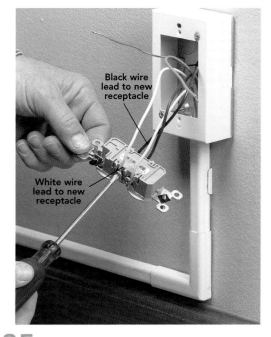

Black wire lead to new receptacle

White wire lead to new receptacle

25 Take the old white wire and wrap the end of the wire around the silver screw opposite the copper one you just used. Tighten the screw so it's snug.

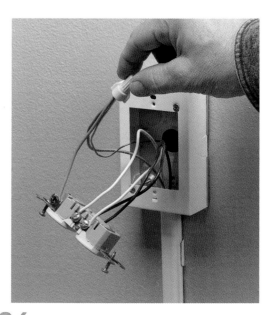

26 Finally, cut a piece of green wire about 6" long and strip ¾" from both ends (this is called a pigtail wire). Join one end of the pigtail with the ends of the bare and green wires in the box, using a wire connector. Wrap the other end of the pigtail around the green screw on the receptacle. Tighten the screw until it's snug.

27 Once the connections are made, gently tuck the wires and the receptacle into the box so the holes in the top and bottom of the receptacle align with the holes in the box. Use a screwdriver to drive the two long mounting screws that hold the receptacle to the box. Install the coverplate. You can now restore the power and test your new receptacle.

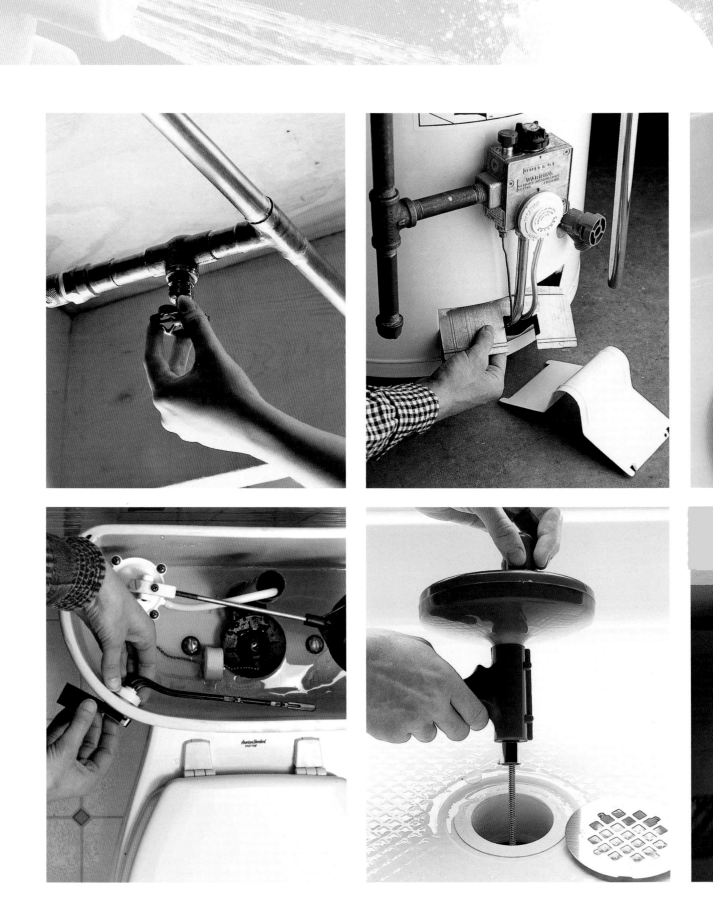

Plumbing

LET'S FACE IT, PLUMBERS SPEND A LOT OF TIME FISHING SOCKS OUT OF TOILETS AND REPLACING FIVE-CENT WASHERS ON DRIPPY FAUCETS. NOTHING WRONG WITH THAT, EXCEPT THEY CHARGE $100 AN HOUR AND PROMISE TO MEET YOU AT THE DOOR "OH, SOMETIME BETWEEN TEN AND THREE O'CLOCK." WE THINK YOU HAVE BETTER WAYS TO SPEND YOUR TIME AND MONEY.

In this section you'll find down-to-earth repairs and replacements—the kinds of projects that will keep the plumbing in your house running smoothly and looking good. Most important, they're doable.

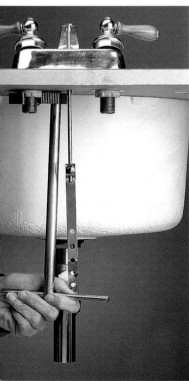

Before You Begin:
The Home Plumbing System

A TYPICAL HOME PLUMBING SYSTEM INCLUDES THREE BASIC PARTS: a water supply system, a fixture and appliance set, and a drain system. These three parts can be seen clearly in the photograph of the cut-away house on the opposite page.

Fresh water enters a home through a main supply line (1). This fresh water source is provided by either a municipal water company or a private underground well. If the source is a municipal supplier, the water passes through a meter (2) that registers the amount of water used. A family of four uses about 400 gallons of water each day.

Immediately after the main supply enters the house, a branch line splits off (3) and is joined to a water heater (4). From the water heater, a hot water line runs parallel to the cold water line to bring the water supply to fixtures and appliances throughout the house. Fixtures include sinks, bathtubs, showers, and laundry tubs. Appliances include water heaters, dishwashers, clothes washers, and water softeners. Toilets and exterior sillcocks are examples of fixtures that require only a cold water line.

The water supply to fixtures and appliances is controlled with faucets and valves. Faucets and valves have moving parts and seals that eventually may wear out or break, but they are easily repaired or replaced.

Waste water then enters the drain system. It first must flow past a trap (5), a U-shaped piece of pipe that holds standing water and prevents sewer gases from entering the home. Every fixture must have a drain trap.

The drain system works entirely by gravity, allowing waste water to flow downhill through a series of large-diameter pipes. These drain pipes are attached to a system of vent pipes. Vent pipes (6) bring fresh air to the drain system, preventing suction that would slow or stop drain water from flowing freely. Vent pipes usually exit the house at a roof vent (7).

All waste water eventually reaches a main waste and vent stack (8). The main stack curves to become a sewer line (9) that exits the house near the foundation. In a municipal system, this sewer line joins a main sewer line located near the street. Where sewer service is not available, waste water empties into a septic system.

Water meter and main shutoff valves are located where the main water supply pipe enters the house. The water meter is the property of your local municipal water company. If the water meter leaks, or if you suspect it is not functioning properly, call your water company for repairs.

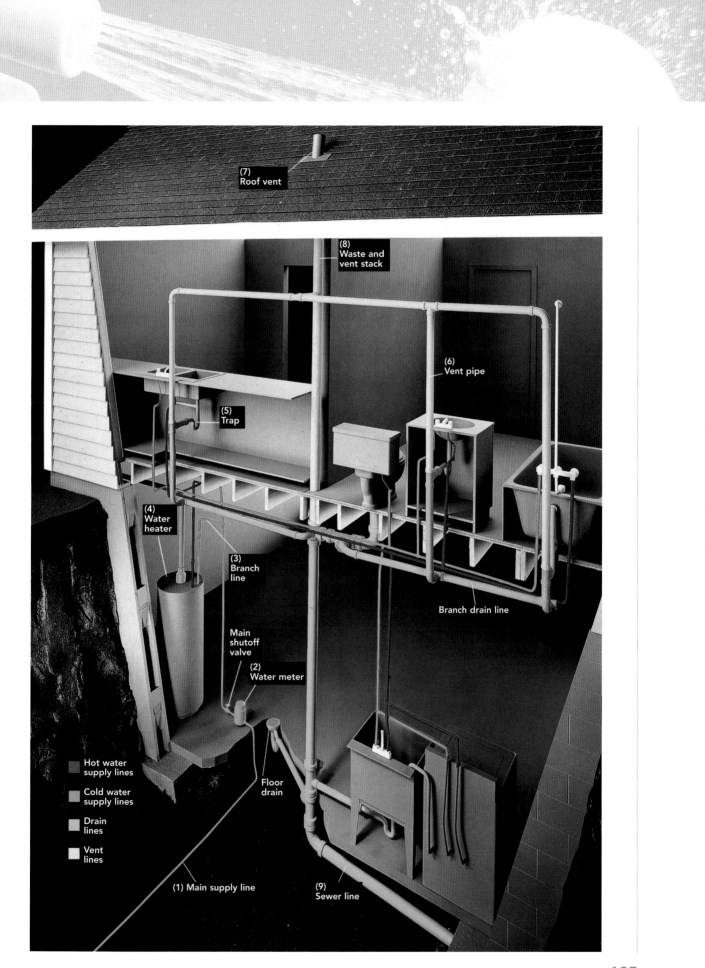

(7) Roof vent

(8) Waste and vent stack

(6) Vent pipe

(5) Trap

(4) Water heater

(3) Branch line

Main shutoff valve

(2) Water meter

Branch drain line

Hot water supply lines

Cold water supply lines

Drain lines

Vent lines

Floor drain

(1) Main supply line

(9) Sewer line

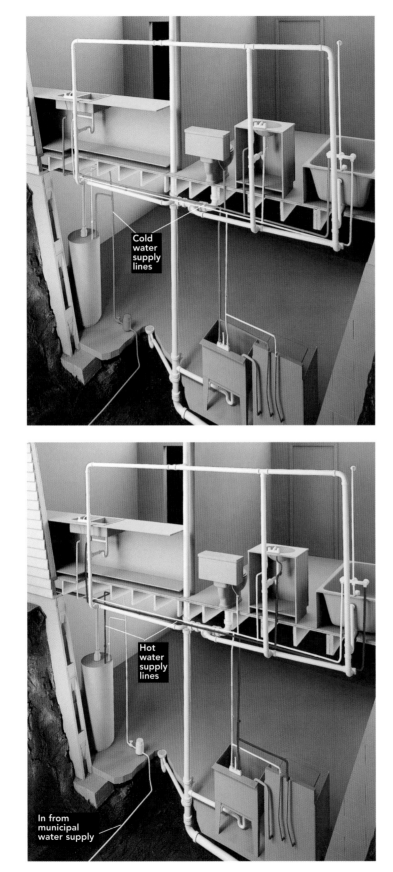

Cold water supply lines

Hot water supply lines

In from municipal water supply

WATER SUPPLY SYSTEM

Water supply pipes carry hot and cold water throughout a house. In homes built before 1960, the original supply pipes are usually made of galvanized iron. Newer homes have supply pipes made of copper. In most areas of the country, supply pipes made of rigid plastic or PEX are accepted by local plumbing codes. Water supply pipes are made to withstand the high pressures of the water supply system. They have small diameters, usually ½" to ¾", and are joined with strong, watertight fittings. The hot and cold lines run in tandem to all parts of the house. Usually, the supply pipes run inside wall cavities or are strapped to the undersides of floor joists.

Hot and cold water supply pipes are connected to fixtures or appliances. Fixtures include sinks, tubs, and showers. Some fixtures, such as toilets or hose bibs, are supplied only by cold water. Appliances include dishwashers and clothes washers. Tradition says that hot water supply pipes and faucet handles are found on the left-hand side of a fixture, with cold water on the right.

Because it is pressurized, the water supply system is prone to leaks. This is especially true of galvanized iron pipe, which has limited resistance to corrosion.

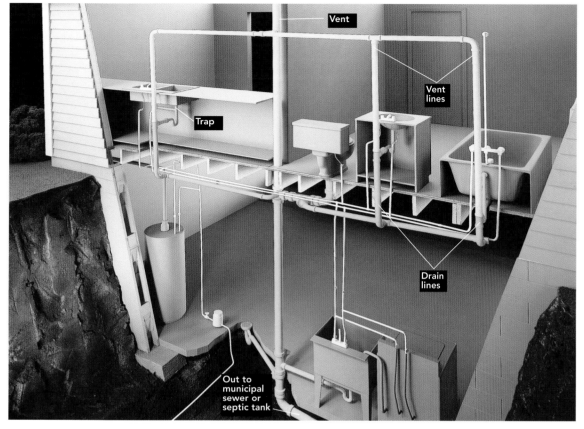

Vent

Vent lines

Trap

Drain lines

Out to municipal sewer or septic tank

DRAIN-WASTE-VENT SYSTEM

Drain pipes use gravity to carry waste water away from fixtures, appliances, and other drains. This waste water is carried out of the house to a municipal sewer system or septic tank.

Drain pipes are usually plastic or cast iron. In some older homes, drain pipes may be made of copper or lead. Because they are not part of the supply system, lead drain pipes pose no health hazard. However, lead pipes are no longer manufactured for home plumbing systems.

Drain pipes have diameters ranging from 1½" to 4". These large diameters allow waste water to pass through easily.

Traps are an important part of the drain system. These curved sections of drain pipe hold standing water, and they are usually found near any drain opening. The standing water of a trap prevents sewer gases from backing up into the home. Each time a drain is used, the standing trap water is flushed away and is replaced by new water.

In order to work properly, the drain system requires air. Air allows waste water to flow freely down drain pipes.

To allow air into the drain system, drain pipes are connected to vent pipes. All drain systems must include vents, and the entire system is called the drain-waste-vent (DWV) system. One or more vent stacks, located on the roof, provide the air needed for the DWV system to work.

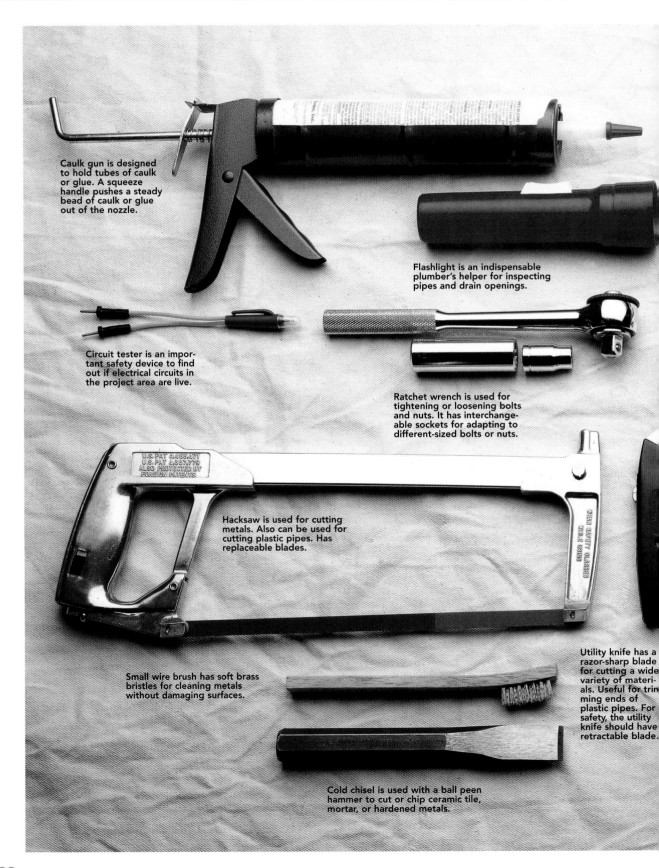

Caulk gun is designed to hold tubes of caulk or glue. A squeeze handle pushes a steady bead of caulk or glue out of the nozzle.

Flashlight is an indispensable plumber's helper for inspecting pipes and drain openings.

Circuit tester is an important safety device to find out if electrical circuits in the project area are live.

Ratchet wrench is used for tightening or loosening bolts and nuts. It has interchangeable sockets for adapting to different-sized bolts or nuts.

Hacksaw is used for cutting metals. Also can be used for cutting plastic pipes. Has replaceable blades.

Utility knife has a razor-sharp blade for cutting a wide variety of materials. Useful for trimming ends of plastic pipes. For safety, the utility knife should have retractable blade.

Small wire brush has soft brass bristles for cleaning metals without damaging surfaces.

Cold chisel is used with a ball peen hammer to cut or chip ceramic tile, mortar, or hardened metals.

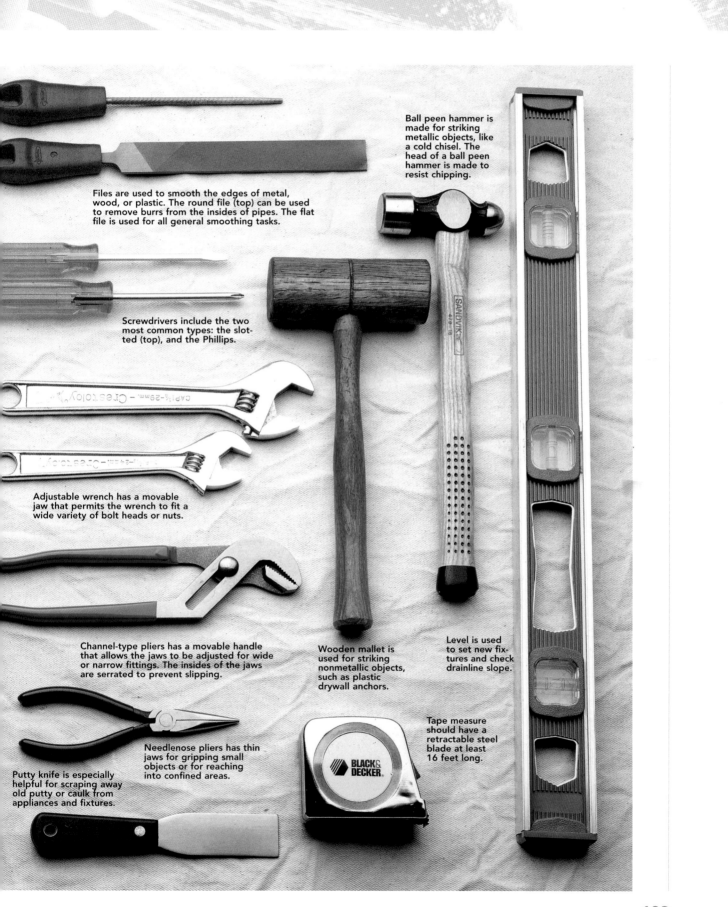

Files are used to smooth the edges of metal, wood, or plastic. The round file (top) can be used to remove burrs from the insides of pipes. The flat file is used for all general smoothing tasks.

Ball peen hammer is made for striking metallic objects, like a cold chisel. The head of a ball peen hammer is made to resist chipping.

Screwdrivers include the two most common types: the slotted (top), and the Phillips.

Adjustable wrench has a movable jaw that permits the wrench to fit a wide variety of bolt heads or nuts.

Channel-type pliers has a movable handle that allows the jaws to be adjusted for wide or narrow fittings. The insides of the jaws are serrated to prevent slipping.

Wooden mallet is used for striking nonmetallic objects, such as plastic drywall anchors.

Level is used to set new fixtures and check drainline slope.

Needlenose pliers has thin jaws for gripping small objects or for reaching into confined areas.

Tape measure should have a retractable steel blade at least 16 feet long.

Putty knife is especially helpful for scraping away old putty or caulk from appliances and fixtures.

BLACK & DECKER

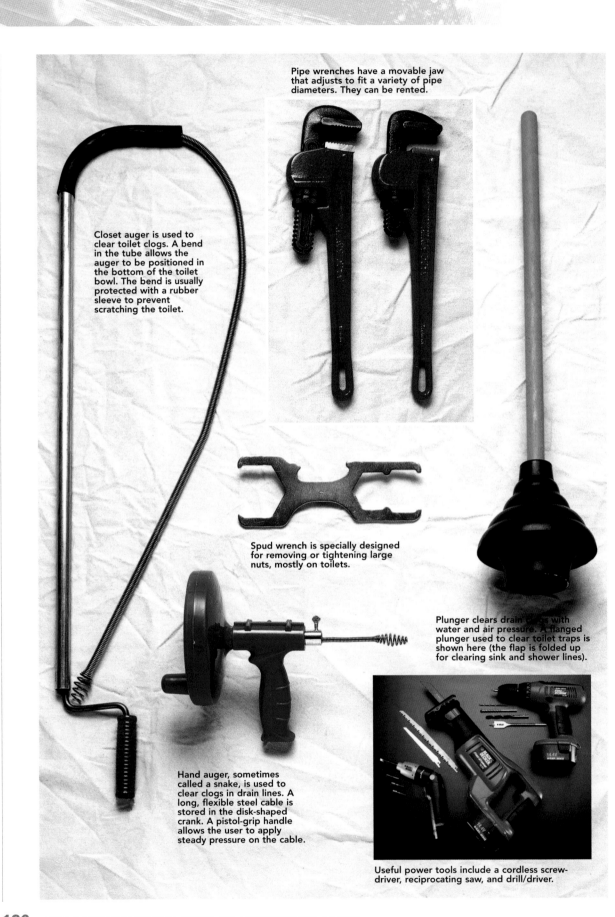

Pipe wrenches have a movable jaw that adjusts to fit a variety of pipe diameters. They can be rented.

Closet auger is used to clear toilet clogs. A bend in the tube allows the auger to be positioned in the bottom of the toilet bowl. The bend is usually protected with a rubber sleeve to prevent scratching the toilet.

Spud wrench is specially designed for removing or tightening large nuts, mostly on toilets.

Plunger clears drain clogs with water and air pressure. A flanged plunger used to clear toilet traps is shown here (the flap is folded up for clearing sink and shower lines).

Hand auger, sometimes called a snake, is used to clear clogs in drain lines. A long, flexible steel cable is stored in the disk-shaped crank. A pistol-grip handle allows the user to apply steady pressure on the cable.

Useful power tools include a cordless screw-driver, reciprocating saw, and drill/driver.

PLUMBING MATERIALS

Check local plumbing code for materials allowed in your area. Common pipe types include:

A) Cast iron for main drain stack

B) ABS drain pipe (no longer allowed)

C) PVC drain pipe

D) Chromed brass fixture drain pipe

E) CPVC supply pipe

F) Galvanized supply pipe (seldom used)

G) Rigid copper supply tube

H) Chromed copper fixture supply pipe

I) PE plastic supply tube (mostly used in irrigation)

J) Flexible copper supply tube

K) PEX (cross-linked polyethylene) flexible supply line

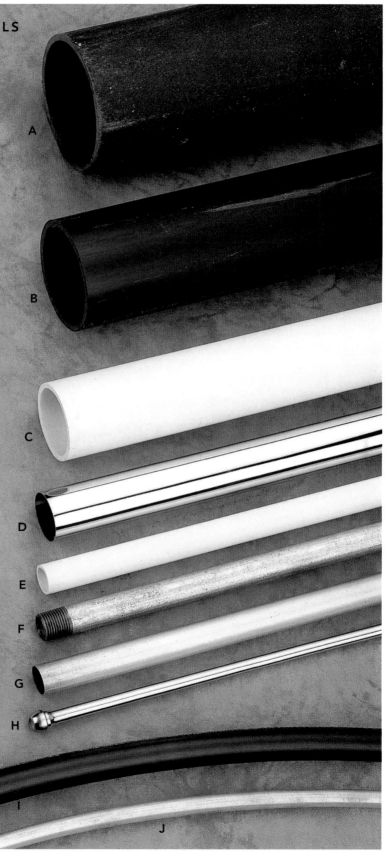

Before You Begin:
Evaluating Your Plumbing

You don't have to possess the knowledge and experience of a journeyman plumber to do some basic evaluations of your plumbing system. Taking a few moments to examine the system helps you learn which parts are which and identify any parts of your system that may be in disrepair or hold the potential for future problems.

Fixture Units	Minimum Gallons per Minute (GPM)
10	8
15	11
20	14
25	17
30	20

The tips on the next page offer a bit of guidance on how to be a home plumbing sleuth. By following them you can quickly and accurately identify cold and hot supply lines, drain lines, the water main, and shutoff valve locations. And the tips below will help you test your water supply capacity to find out if the pressure and volume are adequate to meet your water needs.

Minimum recommended water capacity is based on total demand on the system, as measured by fixture units, a standard of measurement assigned by the plumbing code. First, add up the total units of all the fixtures in your plumbing system (see chart above). Then, perform the water supply capacity test described below. Finally, compare your water capacity with the recommended minimums listed above. If it falls below that recommended GPM, then the main water supply pipe running from the city water main to your home is inadequate and should be replaced with a larger pipe by a licensed contractor.

HOW TO DETERMINE YOUR WATER SUPPLY CAPACITY

1 Shut off the water at the valve on your main water meter, run a faucet on every floor to empty the supply lines, and then disconnect the pipe on the house side of the meter. You can do this by counter-rotating the large nuts on the line with two pipe wrenches (you can rent these if you don't want to invest in a pair).

2 Make a downspout like the one seen above from 2" PVC pipe sections and position it over the water line to direct water down into a garbage can. Open the main supply valve and let the water run for 30 seconds. Shut off the water, then measure the water in the container by bailing with a 1-gallon container. Multiply this figure by two to find your water capacity in gallons per minute (GPM).

HOW TO INSPECT YOUR PLUMBING

There are two basic kinds of pipes in a plumbing system: supply pipes and drain pipes. Supply pipes are always full of water under pressure and drain pipes (which include vent pipes that only move air) are empty when not in use. Supply pipes usually are ½" or ¾" in diameter and drain pipes are anywhere from 1½" to 4" or more. The largest drain pipes are the main drain stack (multi-level houses) and horizontal house drains fed by branch lines.

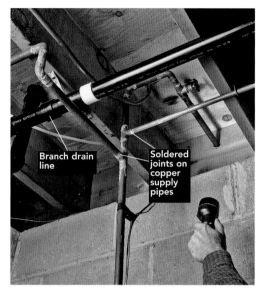

In your basement, branch drain lines run horizontally at a very low slope and ultimately feed into the main drain stack or house drain. They enter the basement through the floor, usually directly under walls. Look for moisture or discoloration around joints. On copper supply lines, visually inspect the soldered joints for pinholes or other signs of deterioration.

Trace hot water pipes from the water heater (the outlet side will be labeled "Hot" on the appliance). Hot supply lines will be hot to the touch when the fixture they connect to is in use.

To identify which supply pipes feed which fixture, you can sometimes measure from the fixture to a heating register. Then, locate the ductwork directly below the register and measure out from it and look for supply lines.

Shutting Off the Water

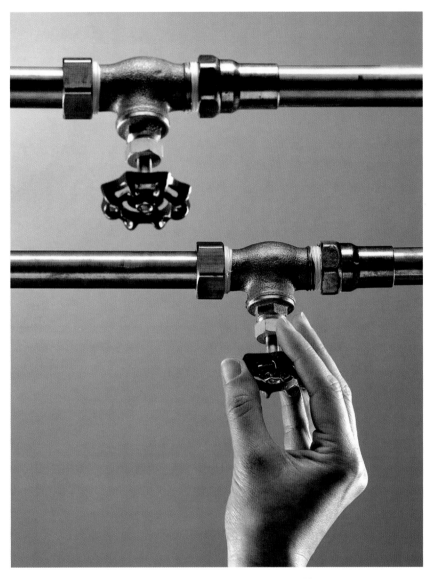

1

Just as the first step in any wiring project is to shut off the power at the main service panel, most plumbing projects begin with shutting off the water supply at one of the shutoff valves in the plumbing system.

USUALLY THERE ARE TWO OR THREE WAYS TO TURN OFF THE WATER. First, try to close the stop valves at the fixture or appliance that's broken. If these are damaged or absent, turn off the water at intermediate shutoff valves that control the hot and cold water to the part of the house with the problem. The whole hot water system usually can be turned off near the hot water heater. Finally, you can stop the water to the entire house at a main shut-off located near the water meter. As a last resort, your municipal water works can shut off your water before it gets to your house. If you have a well, find the shutoff on the pipe between the pressure tank and the rest of your plumbing.

WATER STOP VALVES 101

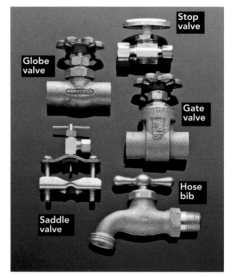

Globe valve

Stop valve

Gate valve

Hose bib

Saddle valve

Main shutoff

Water meter

Access panel with door opens to shut-offs for tub/shower

Water stop valves and shutoff valves function much like faucets, except most of them are left open all the time. Unfortunately, valves used on potable water (water for drinking and cooking) lines may be similar to valves used on natural gas lines, heating oil pipes, and hot water heating pipes. Finding the valves you need may require some careful tracing of pipes from a fixture back to the water meter. The photos here show common water shutoff valves.

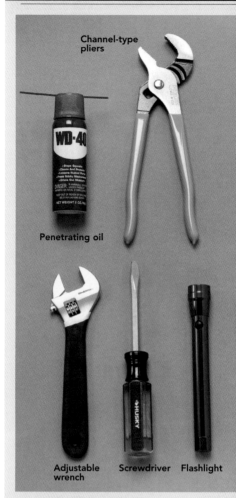
SKILLS YOU'LL NEED

- Using locking pliers
- Loosening stuck valve handles

TERMS YOU NEED TO KNOW

VALVE— any device that regulates the flow of fluids or gases through a pipe.

STOP VALVE—a valve used to stop hot or cold water to a single faucet, toilet, or appliance.

INTERMEDIATE SHUTOFF VALVE—a valve on a pipe used to stop hot or cold water to part of a house or building; often a gate valve or globe valve.

HOT WATER SHUTOFF VALVE—a valve that shuts off cold water supply to the hot water tank.

MAIN SHUTOFF VALVE—a valve that shuts off all the water to a house or building.

DIFFICULTY LEVEL

SKILLS LEVEL

EASY   MODERATE

Time: A few minutes to ½ hour

HOW TO SHUT OFF HOT AND COLD WATER

1 Try to shut off the water locally first. Toilets and sinks usually have stop valves under them. Tubs and showers may have hot and cold shutoffs on the faucet itself or through a wall access panel in a room adjoining the bathroom. Washing machines are connected to shutoff valves with hot and cold supply hoses. Dishwashers sometimes share a two-outlet shutoff with the hot water supply tube for the kitchen faucet.

2 If you can't locate or operate the stop valve, look for intermediate shutoffs that control multiple fixtures in a supply line. Finding the right intermediate shutoff(s) can require trial and error and detective work. Hot water pipes will always lead back to a hot water heater and cold water pipes will lead back to a water meter (below) or a well pressure tank.

3 The hot water shutoff is located at or near the water heater and lets you turn off all the hot water in the house. There will usually be a valve on the pipe supplying cold water to the heater, and there may also be a valve on the outgoing pipe from the heater. If your water is heated by gas, do not be confused by the gas pipe and gas shutoff. The gas pipe leads to the thermostat at the bottom of the water heater.

4 The main water shutoff will be located near the water meter, generally found in your basement. Do not confuse it with the gas meter shutoff, which has a disc shaped device associated with it and generally turns off with a wrench or lever, rather than by hand-spinning. In an emergency, your municipal water works may be contacted to shut off the water with a key (a special wrench) between the public water main on the street and your house. NOTE: Some municipal water works do not meter water use.

What if the valve is stuck?

1 Stop valves and shutoff valves may become fused by corrosion if they are not used regularly. If your valve won't operate, rap lightly on the valve body with a wrench handle or hammer and try again to turn the handle clockwise.

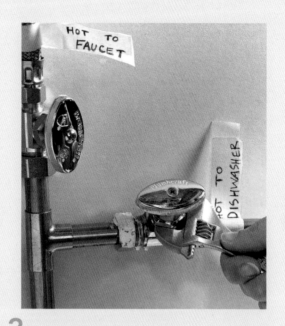

2 If rapping the valve doesn't work, try loosening the packing nut with your adjustable wrench until it leaks just a little bit of water. Then, retighten the nut and try the handle again.

3 If the valve handle won't turn the stem, remove it so you can grip the valve stem directly. Start by unscrewing the screw that secures the handle to the valve. Remove the screw and the handle.

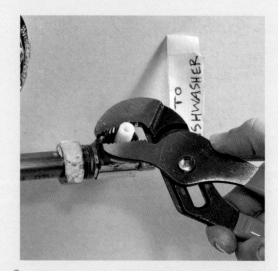

4 Grip the end of the handle stem with channel-type pliers or locking pliers and twist clockwise. Don't overdo it; you can break the valve and create a flood.

Recovering Items from Drains

2

Your wedding ring fell down the drain? Don't panic yet. Chances are good that the P-trap caught it.

EVERY PLUMBING FIXTURE IN YOUR HOUSE HAS A TRAP—a downward facing drainage loop that can collect small, heavy items (like wedding rings) that accidentally fall into the drain. The main function of a trap is not to catch rings, but to hold water. The water in a trap acts as a plug to keep sewer gases from rising into the house. Sink traps are located beneath the sink basin. Bathtub and shower traps are located near the drain and are sometimes accessible through a panel in an adjoining room. A toilet trap is an integral part of the fixture—the front part of the trap is the bowl itself. You can fish out an object from a toilet trap with coat-hanger wire since the bend only goes back a little way from the visible side before bending up again. But if an object is swept out of a trap, it has embarked on a journey through the sewer system, and you may be out of luck.

TRAPS 101

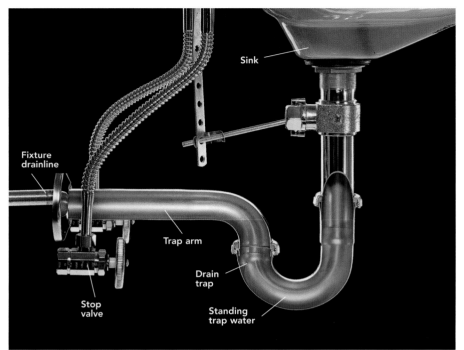

A *drain trap* is a section of pipe attached near the top of a *fixture drain* that loops downward and then upward again. This creates a "trap" for water that blocks sewer gases from rising up though your drainlines and out the drain opening of a *fixture*. It also creates a blockage point for debris and a catch basin for small objects that find their way into the drain opening. Traps are designed to be easy to take apart for cleaning or retrieval.

TERMS YOU NEED TO KNOW

TRAP—downward bend in a drain in or near a fixture that can catch small objects. The standing water in a trap keeps sewer gases from rising into the house.

S-TRAP—The S-shaped trap is an older design used when the waste pipe comes out of the floor.

P-TRAP—Modern sink, tub, and shower traps are shaped like a P tipped on its face.

J-BEND—also called a "drain bend" or simply a "trap", this is the part that forms the low bend on a P-Trap or S-Trap.

TRAP ARM—also called a "wall tube," this extends from the J-bend to the trap adapter at the wall on a P-trap.

TRAP ADAPTER—also called a "drain pipe connector," this is a common transition fitting that lets you attach a light gauge chromed-brass or plastic trap arm to the larger heavy-gauge waste pipe coming out of the wall. It uses a washer and slip nut.

TOOLS & SUPPLIES YOU'LL NEED

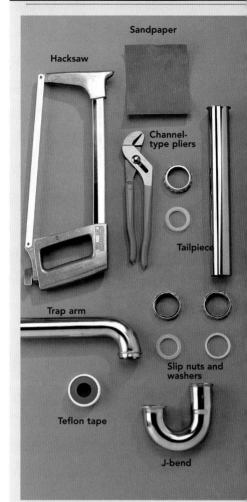

SKILLS YOU'LL NEED

- Unscrewing and retightening compression-style slip joints

DIFFICULTY LEVEL

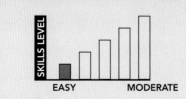

Time: ½ hour to 1 hour

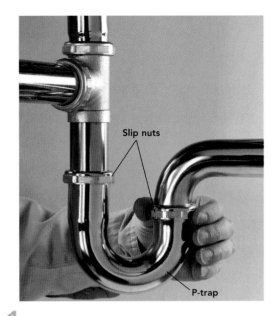

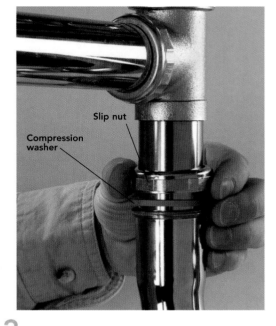

1 Before removing a sink trap, place a bucket under the trap to catch water that spills out. Loosen the slip nut at one end of the trap (a P-trap is seen here). Use channel-type pliers if the nut won't unscrew by hand.

2 Loosen the slip nut on the other end of the trap and pull both nuts away from the union. You will find a compression washer at each union. Slide these back as well and remove the trap by pulling down on it.

3 Keep track of slip nuts and washers and note their up/down orientation. Clean out debris within the trap and examine it. If the trap or the slip nuts and washers are in poor repair (very common), purchase replacement parts, making sure they are made from the same material and are the same size as the rest of the trap.

4 Reassemble the trap pieces just as they came off, or follow instructions on replacement parts. If the trap is made of plastic, hand tighten only. Wrap Teflon tape onto the male threads of metal tubes and then tighten a quarter turn beyond hand tight with channel-type pliers. Tighten joints that leak.

What if your trap looks like this?

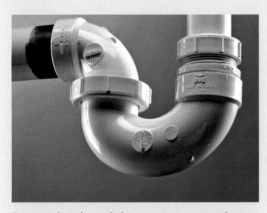

Some sink, tub, and shower traps are made out of the same heavy plastic (Schedule 40 PVC) or metal as the rest of your DWV plumbing and do not fit together like light plastic or chromed drain traps. But even if some parts are permanently fused together by a process called solvent-welding (these typically have a tell-tale purple band of color around the joint) you may still be able to access the trap by untwisting a union. Threaded joints are a sign that you've got a removable trap.

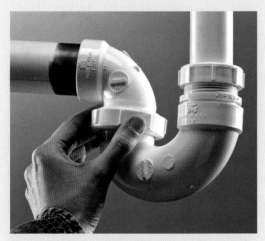

To access the trap, simply unscrew the joint fittings as on the previous page. Unlike a tubular trap, the nut at the DWV trap arm union unscrews counterclockwise from below. That's because the nut faces up instead of down. The slip nut on the fixture side of the trap is loosened like that of a tubular trap.

What if my trap is permanently solvent-welded to the drain and trap arm?

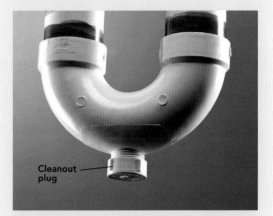

Cleanout plug

Often, bathtubs or showers have a drain trap system that is completely solvent-welded together, making it impossible to disassemble without cutting the pipes. But if you're lucky, the trap will have a cleanout plug at the bottom, like the one above.

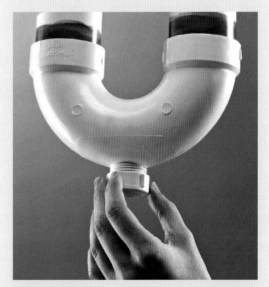

The cleanout plug can be removed to clear the trap and retrieve lost items. Try hand-loosening the plug first, although unless your plumbing is virtually brand new you'll probably need an adjustable wrench to remove the plug. Fair warning—your hand is very likely to be drenched with fairly disgusting drain water, but hopefully, it will be worth it.

Preventing Frozen Pipes

3

Spending a little time and money on protecting your water pipes from freezing is one of the best investments a homeowner can make.

BURST FREEZING PIPES lead to about a quarter million families suffering catastrophic water damage to their houses each year. That's the big picture. The small picture works like this: A section of one of your hot or cold water pipes is exposed to below freezing temperatures. You don't use the water in that pipe during the time it takes for an ice plug to develop. As the ice plug grows, it compresses the water between the plug and the faucet(s) at the end of that line. The pressure becomes extreme and bursts the pipe, sometimes in an area away from the ice plug. The plug thaws. Water spews out of the crack, irreparably damaging walls, floors and your possessions. Another scenario goes like this: You take immediate action to thaw and relieve pressure on frozen pipes and then take short- and long-term steps to prevent refreezing. We'll give you pointers here.

FREEZE-PROOFING 101

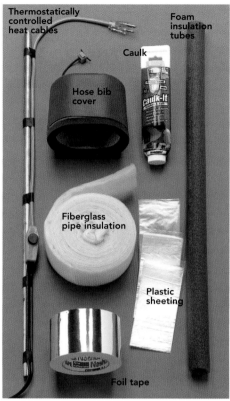

Thermostatically controlled heat cables

Foam insulation tubes

Caulk

Hose bib cover

Fiberglass pipe insulation

Plastic sheeting

Foil tape

Paintable acrylic caulk is good for sealing small gaps, especially in areas where appearance is important. Pipe insulation products include narrow strips of *fiberglass*, *foam insulation tubes* sized to fit common pipe sizes, and *preformed valve covers* for protecting outdoor faucets (hose bibs). *Foil tape* may be used to secure and seal pipe insulation products. *Thermostatically controlled heat cables* prevent pipes that are exposed to long periods of below freezing temperatures from freezing. Expanding foam (not shown here) is effective for stopping large cold air leaks, although it can be unsightly.

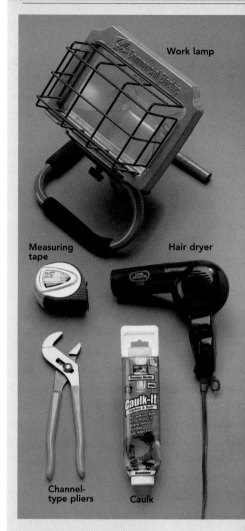

Work lamp

Measuring tape

Hair dryer

Channel-type pliers

Caulk

HOW TO THAW PIPES

Open the faucet affected by the frozen pipes. Beginning at the faucet, use a hair dryer to warm the pipe, working back toward the likely area of the freeze. Leave water on until full flow is restored, then take steps to prevent refreezing. If the pipe has burst, see pages 218 to 221. WARNING: Never use an open flame to thaw pipes.

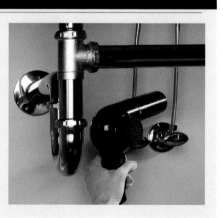

SKILLS YOU'LL NEED

• Investigative skills
• Cutting and fitting

TERMS YOU NEED TO KNOW

CPVC—This is a kind of plastic water pipe that's incompatible with some kinds of foam insulation (which cause it to soften) and needs to be protected with foil if heat tape is used.

THERMAL ENVELOPE—is the sometimes-murky boundary that divides heated from unheated space. Inside spaces that may be outside the thermal envelope include crawl spaces, attics, garages, basements, and three-season rooms. Pipes that may need your attention are those near or outside the thermal envelope.

DIFFICULTY LEVEL

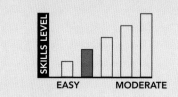

SKILLS LEVEL

EASY   MODERATE

Time: variable

HOW TO FROST-PROOF YOUR PLUMBING

OUTDOOR FAUCETS. Remove hoses from all outside faucets when freezing weather approaches. Shut off the water to the faucet at the shutoff valve inside. Drain the pipe from the shut off to the spout by opening a waste nut on the shutoff and the outside faucet itself.

PIPES NEAR EXTERIOR WALLS. Permit air to circulate from the heated interior of the house to plumbing near outside walls. This could mean opening the dishwasher door and service panel, sink cabinet doors, and plumbed rooms that aren't heated directly. WARNING: Inappropriate warming of pipes is a major cause of house fires.

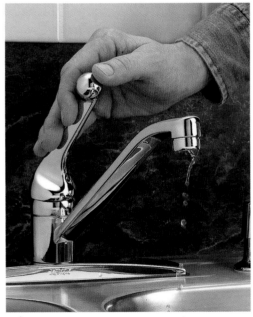

IMMINENT DANGER OF FREEZING. Leave vulnerable lines open to a fast drip if you suspect any of your supply pipes may be in imminent danger of freezing. Even slowly moving water will not freeze. This may not be water and energy efficient (although if you're around, you can collect water in a bucket), but it gives you time to come up with a permanent solution.

AIR LEAKS NEAR PIPES. Seal gaps that can jet cold air onto pipes. Use caulk for small gaps and expanding foam or fiberglass for large gaps. WARNING: Expanding foam expands more than you think it will and cures to an unsightly rust color when exposed to sun.

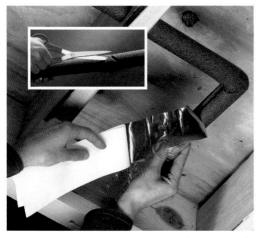

INSULATE SUPPLY PIPES. Insulate pipes that pass through unavoidably cold spaces like crawl spaces and attics. Measure a pipe's diameter by closing an adjustable wrench on it and then measuring the span of the wrench jaws. Measure the length of pipes to be insulated so you know how many linear feet of insulation to buy. Buy self-sealing side-slit foam tubes for pipes of your diameter(s). Cut double 45-degree notches with a scissors to turn corners (inset photo). Seal all slits and joints that are not self-adhering with foil tape.

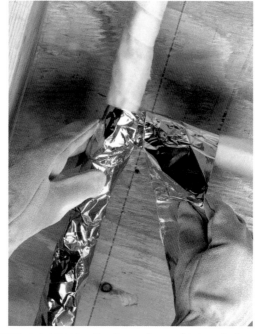

PIPE UNIONS. For irregular and jointed pipes, use fiberglass strip insulation secured with foil tape. Wind the insulation in an overlapping spiral. The tape should not compress the fiberglass too tightly and should form a continuous vapor seal to prevent condensation on the pipes in the summer.

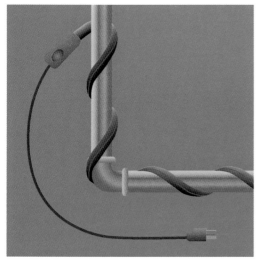

PIPES EXPOSED TO BELOW FREEZING TEMPERATURES for long periods will freeze, insulated or not. Wrap your most vulnerable pipes with U.L. approved thermostatically controlled heat cables according to manufacturer instructions. In the long run, these pipes should be moved to a more protected location or the thermal envelope should be extended to include the pipes.

WHILE YOU'RE AWAY. Don't set the thermostat below 55 degrees F, and have somebody who knows how to shut off the water check on the house daily.

Fixing Dripping Sink Faucets

4

Eventually, just about every faucet develops leaks and drips. Repairs can usually be accomplished simply by replacing the mechanical parts inside the faucet body (the main trick is figuring our which kind of parts your faucet has).

IT'S NOT SURPRISING THAT SINK FAUCETS LEAK AND DRIP. Any fitting that contains moving mechanical parts is susceptible to failure. But add to the equation the persistent force of water pressure working against the parts, and the real surprise is that faucets don't fail more quickly or often. It would be a bit unfair to say that the inner workings of a faucet are regarded as disposable by manufacturers, but it is safe to say that these parts have become more easy to remove and replace.

The most important aspect of sink faucet repair is identifying which type of faucet you own. In this chapter we show all of the common types and provide instructions on repairing them. In every case, the easiest and most reliable repair method is to purchase a replacement kit with brand new internal working parts for the model and brand of faucet you own.

SINK FAUCETS 101

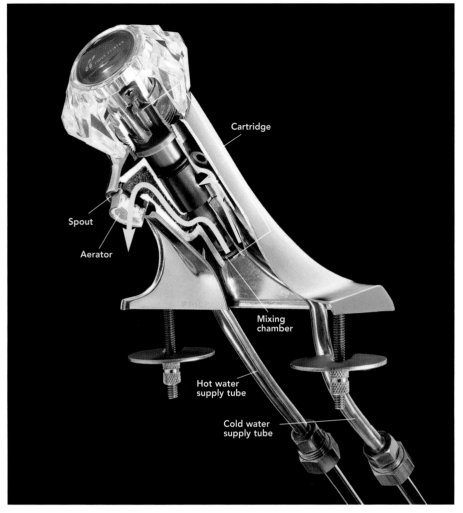

Cartridge

Spout

Aerator

Mixing chamber

Hot water supply tube

Cold water supply tube

Almost all leaks are caused by malfunctioning faucet valve mechanisms. Whether your sink faucet is a one-handle cartridge type (above) or a two-handle compression type or anything in between, the solution to fixing the leak is to clean or replace the parts that seal off the hot and cold water inlets from the spout.

TERMS YOU NEED TO KNOW

COMPRESSION VALVE—a valve type in which a spindle moves a washer up and down to stop or allow water flow through a valve seat.

CARTRIDGE VALVE—a valve type containing a cartridge, usually made of plastic or plastic and metal, in which a channel is slid open and closed by rotating a handle (see the example above).

NEOPRENE—a rubber-like, usually black material from which washers, rings, gaskets, and other seal-forming valve parts are made.

TELEPHONE—an invaluable tool used to contact your faucet's manufacturer, a font of information specific to the repair of your particular faucet.

TOOLS & SUPPLIES YOU'LL NEED

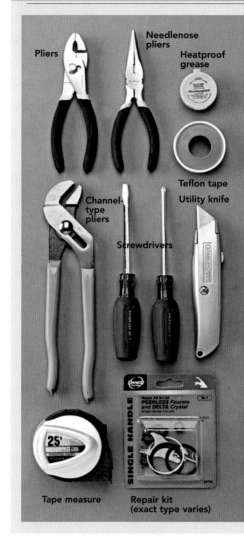

Pliers

Needlenose pliers

Heatproof grease

Teflon tape

Channel-type pliers

Utility knife

Screwdrivers

SINGLE HANDLE

Tape measure

Repair kit (exact type varies)

SKILLS YOU'LL NEED

- Using channel-type pliers
- Tracking the order and arrangement of parts
- Phone or computer research

DIFFICULTY LEVEL

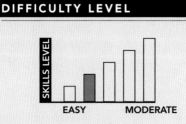

SKILLS LEVEL

EASY

MODERATE

Time: 30 minutes to 1 hour plus research and shopping

HOW TO FIX A COMPRESSION FAUCET

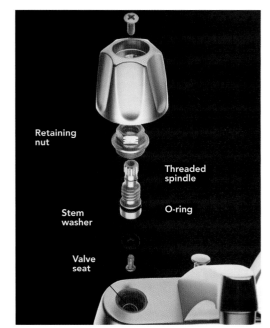

Most compression valves have a threaded metal spindle with a disc-shaped stem washer on the end. When the spindle is screwed all the way in, the stem washer covers a hole, and water flow to the spout is stopped. Drips from the spout happen when the seal between the stem washer and the rim of the hole (called the "valve seat") is imperfect. Usually, replacing the stem washer is enough to stop the drip.

1 Turn off the water at the stop valves for the faucet you are fixing then open the faucet and let the water drain out. Remove the handles by prying an index cap off the top with a dull knife or screwdriver and removing the screw hidden underneath.

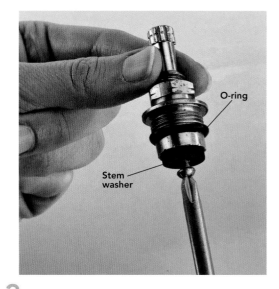

3 Unscrew the stem screw and remove the stem washer. You must find an exact replacement. A flat washer should always be replaced with a flat washer, for example, even if a profiled washer fits. Your washer may have a size code printed on the back, but it's usually easiest to bring the whole stem into the hardware store or home center and try on new neoprene parts there.

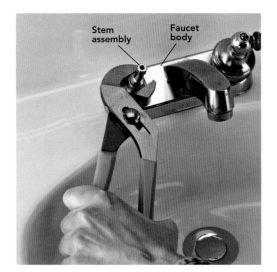

2 Use channel-type pliers to unscrew a retaining nut or the entire stem assembly from the faucet body. If what you find looks similar to the stem assembly shown in step 3, you're in the right place.

4 Pry or cut off the O-ring on the stem with a utility knife. This keeps water from leaking under the handle when the faucet is on.

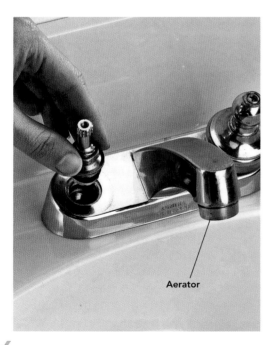

Aerator

6 Wrap Teflon tape onto the retaining nut threads and screw it onto the faucet body. Tighten lightly with channel-type pliers. Replace the handle, the handle screw, and the index cap. **TIP:** Unscrew the aerator at the tip of the spout and open the faucet before turning the water back on. This will flush debris from the system.

5 Coat the new O-ring and washer with heat-proof grease and install them. Tighten the stem screw enough to hold the washer in place, but do not distort the washer by overtightening. Coat the large threaded spindle threads with heatproof grease to lubricate the action of the faucet valve.

HERE'S HOW

There are many ways to classify sink faucets, but perhaps the most useful distinction is compression style versus washerless. These names refer to the type of mechanism inside the faucet. Many older faucets are compression type, but most newer ones are washerless, which can be one of three principal types: cartridge, ball, or disc. All one-handle faucets are washerless. The best way to tell if your faucet is a compression type or washerless is to turn the handle. With compression faucets you can feel the compression building as you crank the handle, even after the water flow has stopped. On washerless models, the handle comes to an abrupt stop.

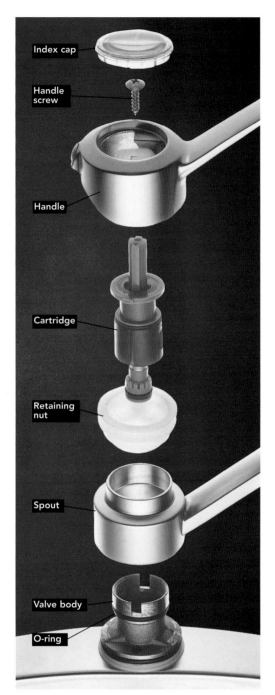

1 Turn off the water at the stop valves. To avoid losing small parts, put a rag in the drain if it has no stopper. Some cartridge faucets have an index cap covering a handle screw. Other handles, especially on one-handle faucets, are secured with a recessed set screw that can be loosened with a ³⁄₃₂" or ⁷⁄₆₄" hex wrench. A lever type handle with no set screw may be removed with channel-type pliers.

SHOPPING TIP

Replacement cartridges are not interchangeable among brands or sometimes even among models from the same manufacturer. It's always a good idea to bring the old cartridge with you to the hardware store to help you select the correct replacement.

Both one- and two-handle faucets are available with replaceable plastic cartridges inside the faucet body. These cartridges (used by Price-Pfister, Sterling, Kohler, Moen, and others) regulate the flow of water through the spout, and in single-handle faucets they also mix the hot and cold water to alter the temperature out of the spout. To locate the correct replacement cartridge for your faucet, knowing the manufacturer and model number is a great help.

Retaining nut

2 Remove the retaining nut, if there is one, with channel-type pliers. A recessed nut with notches can be removed with open needlenose pliers or a tool provided by the faucet manufacturer. With other kinds, you'll remove a sleeve and three screws before extracting the cartridge.

3 Record the direction the cartridge is facing by noting the orientation of some distinctive part of the cartridge (some are cast with an orientation tab that generally should point straight forward). Pull the cartridge straight up and out with pliers. You may need to twist the cartridge back and forth to break the seal.

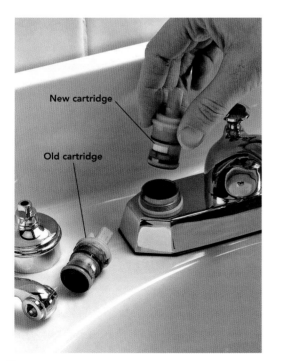

New cartridge

Old cartridge

4 Purchase a replacement cartridge. Apply heat-proof grease to the valve seat and O-rings, then install the cartridge in the correct orientation and with its tabs seated in the slotted body of the faucet.

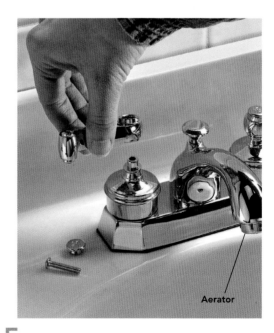

Aerator

5 Reattach the handle, remove the aerator, turn on the water, and test. If the faucet doesn't work, the cartridge may be facing the wrong direction. Remove it and reinsert it facing the other way, still making sure the tabs fit into the slots on the valve body.

HOW TO FIX A BALL FAUCET

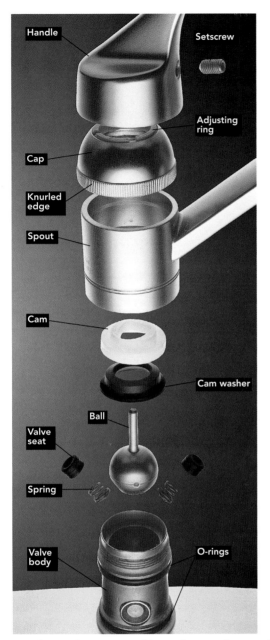

Handle
Setscrew
Adjusting ring
Cap
Knurled edge
Spout
Cam
Cam washer
Ball
Valve seat
Spring
Valve body
O-rings

The ball-type faucet is used by Delta, Peerless, and a few others. The ball fits into the faucet body and is constructed with three holes (not visible here)—a hot inlet, a cold inlet, and the outlet, which fills the valve body with water that then flows to the spout or sprayer. Depending on the position of the ball, each inlet hole is open, closed, or somewhere in-between. The inlet holes are sealed to the ball with valve seats, which are pressed tight against the ball with springs. If water drips from the spout, replace the seats and springs. Or go ahead and purchase an entire replacement kit and replace all or most of the working parts.

Ball faucet tool

1 Turn off the hot and cold water at the stop valves and open the faucet to let any water drain from the pipes. Plug the sink drain with a towel to avoid losing small parts. Pry off a red and blue hot/cold button or a knob-handle button, if present, with a small screwdriver or dull knife. Loosen the setscrew hidden underneath with the hex wrench on the ball faucet tool. Now remove the handle.

Faceted edge

2 Wrap the jaws of your channel-type pliers with masking tape to protect the faucet finish. Grasp the faceted or knurled edges of the round ball cap with the pliers and twist to remove.

3 Pull out the ball, noticing for later how a pin in the faucet body fits in a slit in the ball. Clean the ball with white vinegar and a toothbrush or replace it if it is scratched.

4 If your faucet drips from the spout, it's because the seal between the ball and the hot- or cold-water intake has failed. Pull the neoprene valve seats and springs from the intakes with a screwdriver. Note how the cupped sides of the valve seats fit over the narrow sides of the springs and how the wide base of the springs fit into holes in the intakes.

5 Replace parts in the reverse order they came off. Each spring/seat washer combo can be lined up on a screwdriver, set in place, and pushed in with a finger. The pin in the faucet body fits in a slit on the ball. The pointy side of the cam faces forward, and lugs on the sides of the cam fit in notches in the valve body.

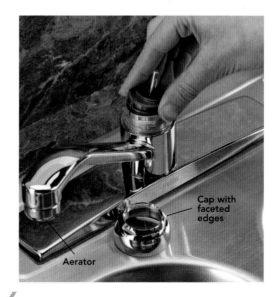

6 Make sure the adjusting ring is partly backed off before screwing the cap on. After the cap is on, gently tighten down the adjusting ring with the ball faucet tool. Remove the aerator, turn on the water supply and test. If water leaks from under the handle or if the handle action is stiff, tighten or loosen the adjusting ring. Replace the aerator.

HOW TO FIX A DISC FAUCET

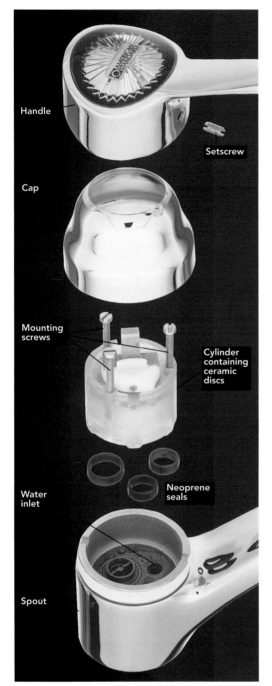

The disc-type faucet used by American Standard, among others, has a wide disc cartridge hidden beneath the handle and the cap. Mounting screws hold the cartridge in the valve body. Two tight-fitting ceramic discs with holes in them are concealed inside the cartridge. The handle slides the top disc back and forth and from side to side over the stationary bottom disc. This brings the holes in the disks into and out of alignment, adjusting the flow and mix of hot and cold water.

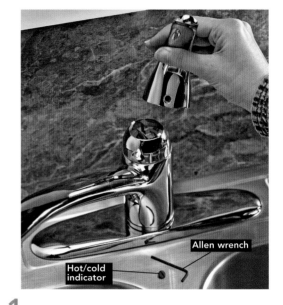

1 Turn off the hot and cold water at the stop valves, open the faucet to let any water drain out, and plug the sink drain. Pry the index cap (and possibly a hot/cold indicator) off the handle with a small screwdriver or a dull knife. Loosen the handle setscrew with a Phillips or slotted screwdriver or an Allen wrench and remove the handle.

2 Remove the chrome cap and/or a plastic or metal retaining ring with channel-type pliers (cover the jaws with masking tape). Remove the cylinder containing the discs, generally by first removing three long retaining screws. Take time to line up parts in the orientation and order in which they were installed.

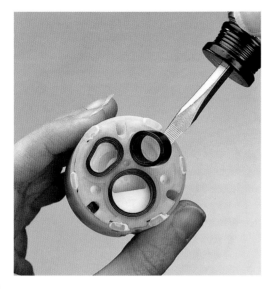

3 If your faucet leaks under the handle, remove the three neoprene seals from the underside of the disc cylinder. Bring them to the hardware store and find matching replacements. For a leak out of the spout, you need to replace the entire cylinder.

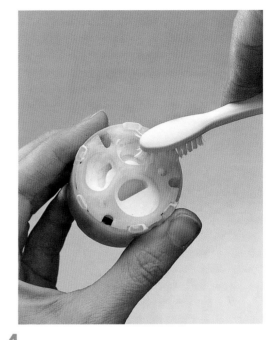

4 If you are reusing the cylinder, clean the water inlets, scouring with a toothbrush and white vinegar if they are crusty.

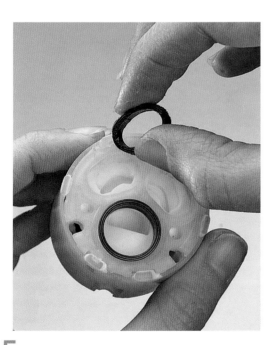

5 Lightly coat the new neoprene seals with heatproof grease and insert them in the appropriate openings in the cylinder. The seals will be slippery and you'll need to contort them a bit to fit the shapes of the openings, so be sure to do this over a clean, light colored surface so you don't lose the seals.

6 Insert the cylinder and secure it to the faucet body with the cylinder screws. Reattach the retaining nut. Reattach the handle, then turn on the hot and cold supplies and test the faucet. Remove the aerator from the spout to allow debris to escape.

Adjusting Water Pressure

5

Restoring vigorous water pressure to your water outlets can be as simple as cleaning a filter in a faucet or showerhead.

CORRECTING LOW WATER PRESSURE AT A SINK OR SHOWER MAY BE EASIER THAN YOU'D EXPECT. Minerals and rust can collect in the finely perforated screens and sprayers in sink spouts and showerheads. Clean these out and, voilà, the water flows with vigor; no plumber needed. Before water reaches any fixture or appliance, it passes through a shutoff valve or two. Make sure these are fully open. Washing machines also draw water through filters. Clean these screens and your washer may fill faster. Old iron water pipes are subject to mineral buildup. A professional can replace these with modern copper or plastic pipes that resist buildup and corrosion.

WATER FLOW 101

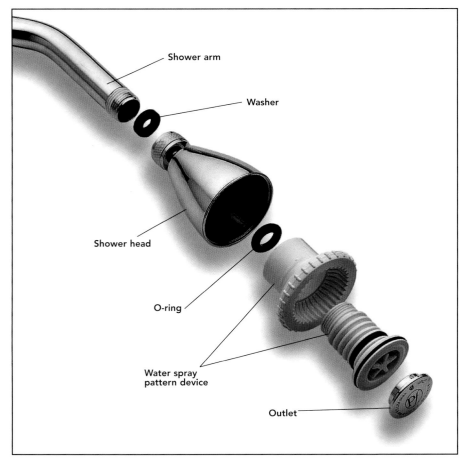

- Shower arm
- Washer
- Shower head
- O-ring
- Water spray pattern device
- Outlet

A showerhead is easy to remove for cleaning or repair. Once you remove it from the shower arm, you take it apart, clean the parts (you may need to check the flow restrictor), and then reassemble it and reattach it to the arm.

TERMS YOU NEED TO KNOW

AERATOR—a small cylinder on the end of a bathroom or kitchen sink spout that breaks up the water stream so it doesn't splash.

FLOW RESTRICTOR—a disc-shaped part on the inlet side of a showerhead with a small hole or holes designed to restrict water flow and conserve water.

TOOLS & SUPPLIES YOU'LL NEED

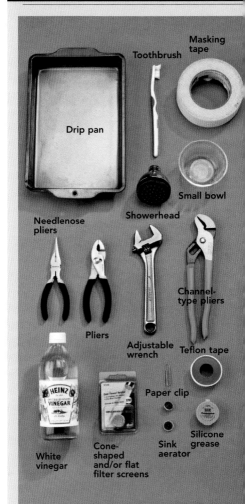

- Masking tape
- Toothbrush
- Drip pan
- Small bowl
- Showerhead
- Needlenose pliers
- Channel-type pliers
- Pliers
- Adjustable wrench
- Teflon tape
- White vinegar
- Cone-shaped and/or flat filter screens
- Paper clip
- Sink aerator
- Silicone grease

SKILLS YOU'LL NEED

- Using channel-type pliers
- Using a wrench

DIFFICULTY LEVEL

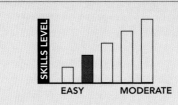

SKILLS LEVEL

EASY   MODERATE

Time: less than ½ hour per fixture

HOW TO CLEAN A SHOWERHEAD

1 Remove the showerhead from the shower arm by unscrewing the collar nut that houses the swivel ball and is threaded onto the shower arm. You may need to grip the shower arm with channel-type pliers to keep it from twisting. Wrap the jaws of the pliers with masking tape to protect shower parts.

2 Once the showerhead is fully removed, run water through the shower arm for a couple of minutes to clear it.

THE FIRST SPOT TO CHECK

Water may flow through two or three shut-off valves between the city water line or the well and your shower or sink. Make sure all the shutoff valves are functioning properly and are opened fully. If the valves are all open, the problem could be in the internal working of your outlet valves. Check the filters and aerators first, as we show you in this project. If the water flow is still subpar, refer to the project that show you how to repair and replace faucets.

3 Disassemble the showerhead. On newer showerheads, the swivel ball or the inlet side of the showerhead will have flow restriction parts. These contain one or more small holes and exist mainly to conserve water. Remove these parts, if you can, with a small knife or screwdriver.

4 Keep all parts in order and oriented in the correct up/down position. If the house water pressure is very poor, you may leave the flow restriction parts (inset photo) out when you put the showerhead back together. WARNING: Removing flow restrictor parts can dramatically increase your water and energy bills.

6 Coat the rubber O-ring that contacts the swivel ball with silicone grease before reassembling the head. Hand-tighten the collar nut that holds the swivel fitting to the showerhead.

5 Use a paper clip or pin to clean the outlet holes on the showerhead then flush all parts clean with water. Soak encrusted parts overnight in white vinegar to soften mineral deposits.

7 Wrap the shower arm threads with two or three layers of Teflon tape in a clockwise direction before replacing the head. Tighten the head to the shower arm a little more than hand tight using your adjustable wrench. Tighten a little more if the joint drips with the shower on. If the showerhead does not work to your satisfaction, replace it.

HOW TO CLEAN A FAUCET AERATOR

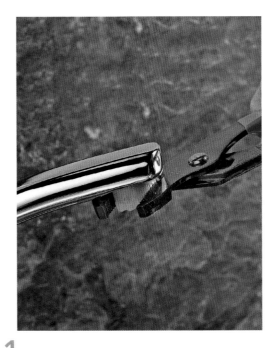

1 Dry and wrap the aerator with masking tape to protect the finish. Adjust channel-type pliers to fit comfortably over the aerator and twist the aerator counterclockwise to loosen.

2 Finish unscrewing the aerator by hand then gently prod apart its components with your finger or a needle or other pointed tool. Be careful to lay out pieces in the order they fit together and in the correct up/down orientation. TIP: Turn on the water while the aerator is removed to flush any built-up materials out the spout.

3 Clean parts with white vinegar and a toothbrush. Soften mineral deposits by soaking overnight in the vinegar. Replace the aerator at a hardware store or home center if parts are damaged or difficult to clean. A standard replacement aerator has both male and female threads and fits most faucets, but take in your old aerator in case yours is a non-standard size.

4 Reassemble the aerator exactly as it came apart and hand-tighten it onto the spout. Remove the tape. Replace the aerator if it still doesn't work right.

WASHING MACHINE FILLS SLOWLY?

1 Turn off hot and cold water to the machine and unscrew supply hoses where they join the machine or at the first accessible coupling.

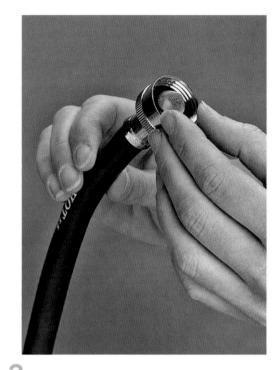

2 Some water supply hoses for washing machines contain filter screens in the hose couplings that connect to the water supply and to the water inlets in the washing machine. If you find these filters, carefully remove and clean them.

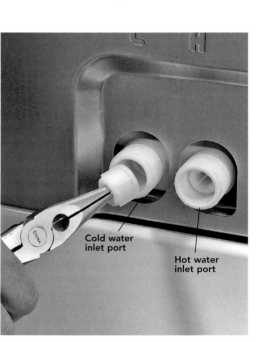

Cold water
inlet port

Hot water
inlet port

3 Most washing machines contain filter screens at the water inlet port. Remove the cone filter with needlenose pliers and clear debris from the filter screen. If the filter is in poor condition, replace it.

4 Apply Teflon tape to the male pipe threads at the water inlet connection and retighten all hoses.

Fixing Running Toilets

6

Jiggling the handle can make a running toilet stop, but it's only a temporary solution. Making real repairs is a lot easier than you might think.

SNORING, TICKING CLOCKS, DRIPPING FAUCETS, AND RUNNING TOILETS are perhaps the four greatest nighttime annoyances. Together they conspire to keep you from the blissful slumber you deserve. For help on fixing leaky faucets, see pages 146 to 155. If your toilet runs and runs and you just can't seem to catch up with it, you're in the right place. This project will show you how to diagnose and remedy the most common causes for the perpetually running toilet.

TOILET TROUBLE SHOOTING 101

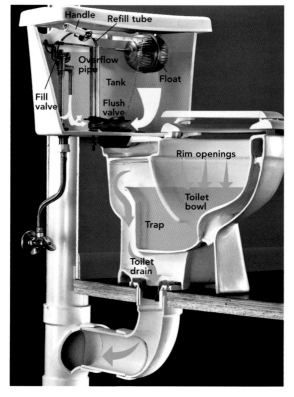

Five steps of a perfect flush: 1.The *handle* opens the *flush valve,* emptying the *tank* into the *toilet bowl.* 2. Water races through *rim openings* and the *siphon jet* at the base of the bowl. 3. The sudden surge causes the water to exit the *trap* and bowl as a unit, siphoning itself down the *toilet drain.* 4. The *ballcock* (fill valve) opens when the *float* drops to refill the tank. The *refill tube* directs some of the water down the *overflow pipe* to refill the bowl. 5. The *float* turns off the *fill valve* when enough water has entered the *tank.*

Most toilets can be fixed with generic replacement parts. However, some brands require special parts, especially newer models, which may have larger flush valves. Contact your manufacturer or go to a well-equipped plumbing-supply house. Identify your toilet brand, which is often written behind (not on) the seat, and its model number (usually stamped inside the tank or tank lid). Always bring old parts with you to the store for reference.

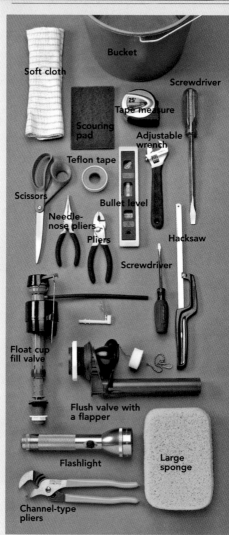
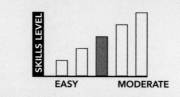
TERMS YOU NEED TO KNOW

BALLCOCK/FILL VALVE—These terms both refer to the valve that fills the tank after you flush the toilet. Traditionally, the ballcock is turned on and off by a float ball on a rod. Modern cup-float fill valves can be used to replace most old ballcocks.

FLUSH VALVE—the assembly that releases water from the tank into the bowl when the toilet is flushed. It includes the overflow pipe, the valve seat (hole), and the flapper or tank ball that covers the hole. Universal flapper-style flush valves can replace old tank ball or flapper flush valves on most toilets.

STOP VALVE—the valve that turns off water to the toilet.

SUPPLY—the hose or tube that takes water from the stop valve to the tank.

HOW TO RESET THE TANK WATER LEVEL

1 Perhaps the most common cause of running toilets is a minor misadjustment that fails to tell the water to shut off when the toilet tank is full. The culprit is usually a float ball or cup that is adjusted to set a water level in the tank that's higher than the top of the overflow pipe, which serves as a drain for excess tank water.

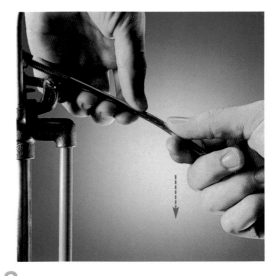

2 A ball float is connected to a float arm that's attached to a plunger on the other end. As the tank fills, the float rises and lifts one end of the float arm. At a certain point, the float arm depresses the plunger and stops the flow of water. By simply bending the float arm downward a bit you can cause it to depress the plunger at a lower tank water level, solving the problem.

3 A diaphragm fill valve usually is made of plastic and has a wide bonnet that contains a rubber diaphragm. Turn the adjustment screw clockwise to lower the water level and counter-clockwise to raise it.

Spring clip

4 A float cup fill valve is made of plastic and is easy to adjust. Lower the water level by pinching the spring clip with fingers or pliers and moving the clip and cup down the pull rod and shank. Raise the water level by moving the clip and cup upward.

WHAT IF THE FLUSH STOPS TOO SOON?

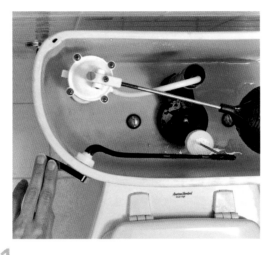

1 Sometimes there is plenty of water in the tank, but not enough of it makes it to the bowl before the flush valve shuts off the water from the tank. Modern toilets are designed to leave some water in the tank, since the first water that leaves the tank does so with the most force. (It's pressed out by the weight of the water on top). To increase the duration of the flush, shorten the length of the chain between the flapper and the float (yellow in the model shown).

2 The handle lever should pull straight up on the flapper. If it doesn't, reposition the chain hook on the handle lever. When the flapper is covering the opening, there should be just a little slack in the chain. If there is too much slack, shorten the chain and cut off excess with the cutters on your pliers. Turn the water back on at the stop valve and test the flush.

3 If the toilet is not completing flushes and the lever and chain for the flapper or tank ball are correctly adjusted, the problem could be that the handle mechanism needs cleaning or replacement. Remove the chain/linkage from the handle lever. Remove the nut on the backside of the handle with an adjustable wrench. It unthreads clockwise (the reverse of standard nuts). Remove the old handle from the tank.

4 Unless the handle parts are visibly broken, try cleaning them with an old toothbrush dipped in white vinegar. Replace the handle and test the action. If it sticks or is hard to operate, replace it. Most replacement handles come with detailed instructions that tell you how to install and adjust them.

HOW TO REPLACE A FILL VALVE

1 Toilet fill valves degrade eventually and need to be replaced. Before removing the old fill valve, shut off the water supply at the fixture stop valve located on the tube that supplies water to the tank. Flush the toilet and sponge out the remaining water. Then, remove the old fill valve assembly by loosening and removing the mounting nut on the outside of the tank wall that secures the fill valve.

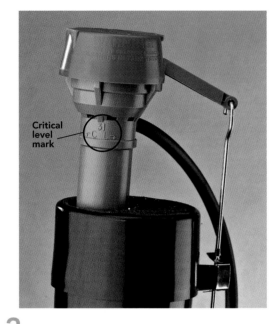

Critical level mark

2 Fill valves need to be coordinated with the flush valve so the tank water level is not higher than the overflow pipe and so the fill valve is not low enough in the tank that it creates a siphoning hazard. New fill valves have a "critical level" mark ("CL") near the top of the valve.

3 The new fill valve must be installed so the Critical Level ("CL") mark is at least 1" above the overflow pipe. Slip the shank washer on the threaded shank of the new fill valve and place the valve in the hole so the washer is flat on the tank bottom. Compare the locations of the CL mark and the overflow pipe.

4 Adjust the height of the fill valve shank so the "CL" line and overflow pipe will be correctly related. Different products are adjusted in different ways—the fill valve shown here telescopes when it's twisted.

Threaded valve stem

5 Position the valve in the tank. Push down on the valve shank (not the top) while hand tightening the locknut onto the threaded valve stem (thread the mounting nut on the exterior side of tank). Hand-tighten only.

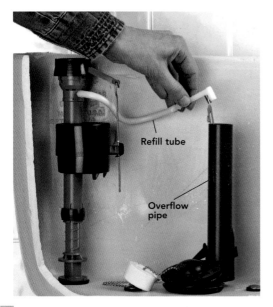

Refill tube

Overflow pipe

7 If the overflow pipe has a cap, remove it. Attach one end of the refill tube from the new valve to the plastic angle adapter and the other end to the refill nipple near the top of the valve. Attach the angle adapter to the overflow pipe. Cut off excess tubing with scissors to prevent kinking. WARNING: Don't insert the refill tube into the overflow pipe. The outlet of the refill tube needs to be above the top of pipe for it to work properly.

6 Hook up the water by attaching the coupling nut from the supply riser to the threaded shank at the bottom end of the new fill valve. Hand-tighten only.

8 Turn the water on fully. Slightly tighten any fitting that drips water. Adjust the water level in the tank by squeezing the spring clip on the float cup with needlenose pliers and moving the cup up or down on the link bar. Test the flush.

HOW TO REPLACE A FLUSH VALVE

1 If the fixes on the previous pages still do not stop your toilet from running, the next step it to try replacing the flush valve. Before removing the old flush valve, shut off the water supply at the fixture stop valve located on the tube that supplies water to the tank. Flush the toilet and sponge out the remaining water. To make this repair you'll need to remove the tank from the bowl. Start by unscrewing the water supply coupling nut from the bottom of the tank.

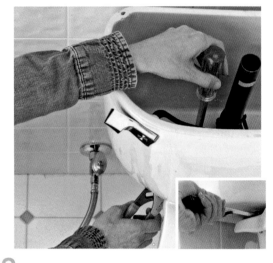

2 Unscrew the bolts holding the toilet tank to the bowl by loosening the nuts from below. If you are having difficulty unscrewing the tank bolts and nuts because they are fused together by rust or corrosion, apply penetrating oil or spray lubricant to the threads, give it a few minutes to penetrate and then try again. If that fails, slip an open-ended hacksaw (or plain hacksaw blade) between the tank and bowl and saw through the bolt (inset photo).

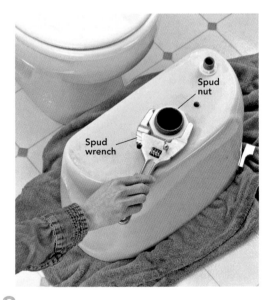

3 Unhook the chain from the handle lever arm. Remove the tank and carefully place it upside-down on an old towel. Remove the spud washer and spud nut from the base of the flush valve using a spud wrench or large channel-type pliers. Remove the old flush valve.

4 Place the new flush valve in the valve hole and check to see if the top of the overflow pipe is at least 1" below the Critical Level line (see page 166) and the tank opening where the handle is installed. If the pipe is too tall, cut it to length with a hacksaw.

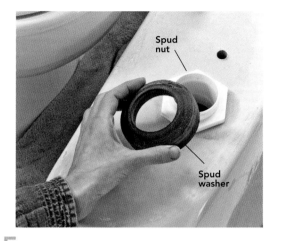

Spud
nut

Spud
washer

5 Position the flush valve flapper below the handle lever arm and secure it to the tank from beneath with the spud nut. Tighten the nut one-half turn past hand tight with a spud wrench or large channel-type pliers. Over tightening may cause the tank to break. Put the new spud washer over the spud nut, small side down.

Intermediate nut goes
between tank and bowl

6 With the tank lying on its back, thread a rubber washer onto each tank bolt and insert it into the bolt holes from inside the tank. Then, thread a brass washer and hex nut onto the tank bolts from below and tighten them to a quarter turn past hand tight. Do not overtighten.

Intermediate
nut

7 With the hex nuts tightened against the tank bottom, carefully lower the tank over the bowl and set it down so the spud washer seats neatly over the water inlet in the bowl and the tank bolts fit through the holes in the bowl flange. Secure the tank to the bowl with a rubber washer, brass washer, and nut or wing nut at each bolt end. Press the tank to level as you hand-tighten the nuts. Hook up the water supply at the fill valve inlet.

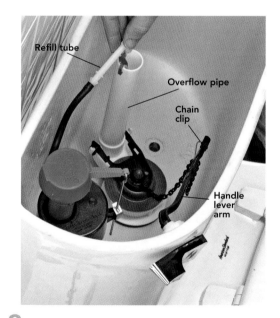

Refill tube

Overflow pipe

Chain
clip

Handle
lever
arm

8 Connect the chain clip to the handle lever arm and adjust the number of links to allow for a little slack in the chain when the flapper is closed. Leave a little tail on the chain for adjusting, cutting off remaining excess. Attach the refill tube to the top of the overflow pipe the same way it had been attached to the previous refill pipe. Turn on the water supply at the stop valve and test the flush. (Some flush valve flappers are adjustable.)

Clearing Clogged Toilets

7

A blockage in the toilet bowl leaves flush water from the tank nowhere to go but on the floor.

THE TOILET IS CLOGGED AND HAS OVERFLOWED, or perhaps its gorge has simply risen, lapped the canyon walls but not yet topped the rim. Have patience. Now is the time for considered action. A second flush is a tempting but unnecessary gamble. First, do damage control. Mop up the water if there's been a spill. Next, consider the nature of the clog. Is it entirely "natural" or might a foreign object be contributing to the congestion? Push a natural blockage down the drain with a plunger. A foreign object should be removed, if possible, with a closet auger. Pushing anything more durable than toilet paper into the sewer may create a more serious blockage in your drain and waste system. If the tub, sink, and toilet all become clogged at once, the branch drainline that serves all the bathroom fixtures is probably blocked and your best recourse is to call a drain clearing service.

CLOGGED TOILETS 101

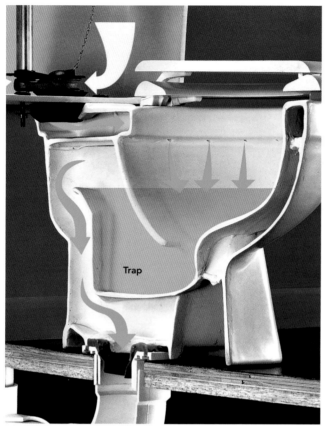

Trap

The *trap* is the most common catching spot for toilet clogs, Once the clog forms, flushing the toilet cannot generate enough water power to clear the trap, so flush water backs up. Traps on modern 1.6-gallon toilets have been redesigned to larger diameters and are less prone to clogs than the first generation of 1.6 gallon toilets.

Not all plungers were created equal. The *standard plunger* (left) is simply an inverted rubber cup and is used to plunge sinks, tubs, and showers. The *flanged plunger,* also called a *force cup,* is designed to get down into the trap of a toilet drain. But in a pinch you can fold the flange up into the flanged plunger cup and use it as a standard plunger.

TERMS YOU NEED TO KNOW

WATER SEAL—Because of the loop-like shape of a toilet's plumbing, there is always water in the bowl and in the passage directly behind the bowl. This water seal keeps sewer gases from rising into the house.

TOILET TRAP—A "trap" in plumbing refers to a bend that holds a water seal, so technically, the toilet bowl is part of the trap. But usually people are talking about the back, hidden portion of that bend when they speak of the toilet trap.

FLUSH VALVE—is the flapper covering the hole in the bottom of the tank that sits behind the bowl. The toilet flushes when this is opened.

CONTROLLED FLUSH—the letting of water from the tank to bowl by manually lifting and closing the flush valve. This prevents bowl overflow when you're not sure the clog is gone.

TOOLS & SUPPLIES YOU'LL NEED

Towels

Plunger with foldout skirt (force cup)

Closet auger

SKILLS YOU'LL NEED

- Vigorous plunging
- Using a closet auger

DIFFICULTY LEVEL

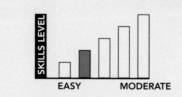

SKILLS LEVEL

EASY   MODERATE

Time: 15 to 30 minutes

HOW TO PLUNGE A CLOGGED TOILET

A flanged plunger fits into the mouth of the toilet trap and creates a tight seal so you can build up enough pressure in front of the plunger to dislodge the blockage and send it on its way.

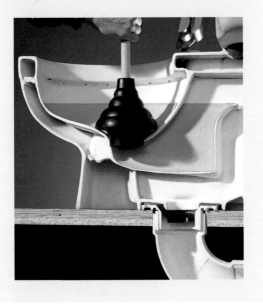

1 Plunging is the easiest way to remove "natural" blockages. Take time to lay towels around the base of the toilet and remove other objects to a safe, dry location, since plunging may result in splashing. Sometimes, allowing a very full toilet to sit for twenty or thirty minutes will permit some of the water to drain to a less precarious level, or you can bail it out. WARNING: Don't use a plunger if the toilet is plugged with a diaper, washcloth, or other object that could get pushed into the drainpipe. It may create a worse clog in a pipe that's beyond your reach. Try to remove the object with a closet auger.

2 There should be enough water in the bowl to completely cover the plunger. Fold out the skirt from inside the plunger to form a better seal with the opening at the base of the bowl. Pump the plunger vigorously half-a-dozen times, take a rest, and then repeat. Try this for 10 to 15 cycles.

3 If you force enough water out of the bowl that you are unable to create suction with the plunger, put a controlled amount of water in the bowl by lifting up on the flush valve in the tank. Resume plunging. When you think the drain is clear, you can try a controlled flush, with your hand ready to close the flush valve should the water threaten to spill out of the bowl. Once the blockage has cleared, dump a five-gallon pail of water into the toilet to blast away any residual debris.

HOW TO CLEAR CLOGS WITH A CLOSET AUGER

A closet auger is a semirigid cable housed in a tube. The tube has a bend at the end so it can be snaked through a toilet trap (without scratching it) to snag blockages.

Protective rubber boot

1 Place the business end of the auger firmly in the bottom of the toilet bowl with the auger tip fully withdrawn. A rubber sleeve will protect the porcelain at the bottom bend of the auger. The tip will be facing back and up, which is the direction the toilet trap takes.

2 Rotate the handle on the auger housing clockwise as you push down on the rod, advancing the rotating auger tip up into the back part of the trap. You may work the cable backward and forward as needed, but keep the rubber boot of the auger firmly in place in the bowl. When you feel resistance, indicating you've snagged the object, continue rotating the auger counterclockwise as you withdraw the cable and the object.

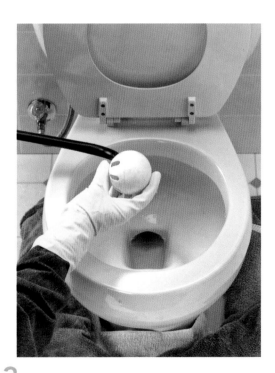

3 Fully retract the auger until you have recovered the object. This can be frustrating at times, but it is still a much easier task than the alternative—to remove the toilet and go fishing.

Fixing Leaky Tubs & Showers

8

Tub/shower plumbing is notorious for developing drips from the tub spout and the showerhead. In most cases, the leak can be traced to the valves controlled by the faucet handles.

DOES YOUR TUB/SHOWER DRIP, DRIP, DRIP from the spout or the showerhead even when the water is turned off? Chances are, a washer or cartridge in the faucet valve needs attention or replacement. But these parts vary widely by type and by brand name. The most critical part of a good repair job does not involve wrenches and screwdrivers, but the telephone and possibly a computer. That's because finding the brand name, model number, and ultimately part numbers will let you get the exact materials you'll need to do the job right. From there, it's a pretty easy repair.

TUB & SHOWER FAUCETS 101

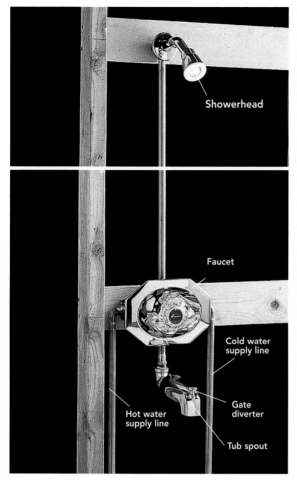

Showerhead

Faucet

Cold water
supply line

Hot water
supply line

Gate
diverter

Tub spout

If you could make your tub/shower and the tub surround above it disappear, you'd see pipes and plumbing parts similar to this. The *faucet* seen here only has one handle that controls the water volume and temperature. The water is directed to either the *tub spout* or the *showerhead* with a *diverter* located in the tub spout. Some two-handle models are joined by a third handle that serves as a diverter instead of the gate on the spout.

As the stem assemblies (right) demonstrate, sink and tub compression valves share the same genetics but vary in size and the particulars.

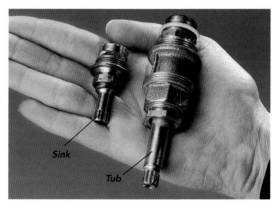

Sink

Tub

TOOLS & SUPPLIES YOU'LL NEED

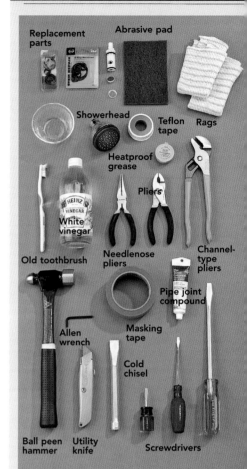

Replacement parts

Abrasive pad

Showerhead

Teflon tape

Rags

Heatproof grease

Pliers

Old toothbrush

Needlenose pliers

Channel-type pliers

Pipe joint compound

Allen wrench

Masking tape

Cold chisel

Ball peen hammer

Utility knife

Screwdrivers

White vinegar

SKILLS YOU'LL NEED

- Using channel-type pliers
- Tracking the order and arrangement of parts
- Phone or computer research

DIFFICULTY LEVEL

SKILLS LEVEL

EASY   MODERATE

Time: 1 hour plus research and shopping

HOW TO FIX A LEAKY ONE-HANDLE FAUCET

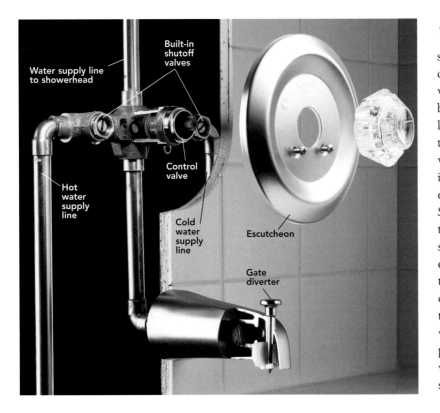

1 Single-handle tub and shower faucets have one valve controlling both hot and cold water. This valve sits directly behind the one large knob or lever. If your tub spout drips all the time, you need to fix this valve. The first step involves information and materials gathering (see "Steps to Successful Shopping" on page 179). Next, turn off the hot and cold water supplies. Make sure the diverter is in the tub-filling position, then drain residual water out of the plumbing by opening the faucet to hot and cold water. Lay towels in the tub to prevent damaging the finish with tools and losing small parts.

2 Remove the handle of the damaged valve by first prying an index cap off the front with a dull knife or screwdriver and removing the screw hidden underneath. Pull off the handle. Remove any other parts obstructing the escutcheon, then remove the escutcheon. Keep parts in a safe place. Line them up and orient them as they sit in the faucet. If it's helpful, take digital pictures to remember how the parts went together.

3 Many one-handle tub and shower faucets have hot and cold shutoffs built in to the faucet body. Turn these off clockwise with a large slotted screwdriver. Integral stops are useful if you need to leave the water off for some time during a repair, and the only other turnoff to the tub and shower takes other fixtures out of commission. If you'd rather, you may turn off water at the nearest shutoff valves instead.

A balancing cartridge is included in many newer single-handle faucets. This unit prevents sudden swings in water temperature due to relative pressure changes in the hot and cold supplies (such as those that result from flushing a toilet or turning on a sink tap). The relative pressure of the hot and cold water exiting the cartridge remains the same. If your faucet has a balancing cartridge, note that the faucet will not work at all if only one of the supply pipes is open. If the O-rings on the back of the balancing cartridge are worn, replace them.

4 Remove the threaded retaining ring that secures the cartridge or stem and bonnet assembly (some models may use retaining screws to hold the stem). This unit is what turns the water on and controls the mix of hot and cold water.

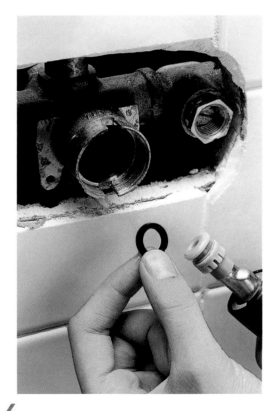

5 Remove the cartridge, pulling gently on the stem with a pair of pliers if necessary. With the cartridge out, now is a good time to flush out the system by opening the shutoffs in the valve or in the supply line. Watch out, though, the water will come out of the valve opening, not the spout.

6 Clean the cartridge by flushing with warm water and replace the O-ring at the end (coat the new O-ring with heatproof grease). If the cartridge is old or visibly damaged, replace it. Reinstall the faucet parts in reverse order.

HOW TO FIX A LEAKY TWO- OR THREE-HANDLE FAUCET

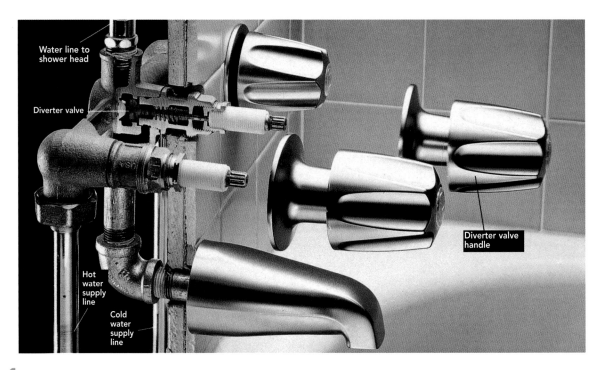

Water line to shower head

Diverter valve

Hot water supply line

Cold water supply line

Diverter valve handle

1 Both three-handle and two-handle faucets have a hot-water valve and a cold-water valve behind their hot and cold faucet handles. If water drips from the spout when the faucet is off, you need to determine which valve isn't working by shutting off the water supply on each line in turn at the shutoff valve. Two- and three-handle faucets are repaired in the same manner, except that the middle handle on the three-handle models is a diverter valve (the diverter on two-handle models is in the spout). If the showerhead on your three-handle system drips, or if you continue to get a high volume of water through the spout when it should be coming out the showerhead, it's the diverter handle that needs attention.

2 Determine which valve is causing the leak (see previous step) and remove the handle cover for that valve (in this case, the diverter valve is being worked upon). Also remove the escutcheon that covers the wall opening for that valve.

3 Remove the bonnet nut from the stem assembly using an adjustable wrench. If your faucet has cartridges, not compression valves as shown here, simply remove the cartridge (see p. 177).

4 Unscrew the stem assembly using a deep-set socket and a ratchet wrench. You may need to enlarge the opening in the wall slightly with a cold chisel and ball-peen hammer to gain clearance for the socket. TIP: You can purchase a shower valve socket wrench at most hardware stores. The most common sizes are $^{29}\!/_{32}$" and $^{31}\!/_{32}$".

5 Remove the brass stem screw from the compression valve. Find an exact match for the stem washer that's held in place by the stem screw. Disassemble the spindle and the valve retaining nut.

6 Clean the valve parts with white vinegar and a toothbrush or small wire brush. Coat all washers with heatproof grease and reassemble then reinstall the valve.

SHOPPING TIP

STEPS TO SUCCESSFUL SHOPPING

Identify the brand. This may be written on the faucet handle, on a plate behind the handle or handles, or elsewhere on the hardware of the tub or shower. Be aware that a name on a pop-up stopper, overflow cap, or showerhead may or may not be the manufacturer of your faucet.

Identify the model. The major brands have web sites and toll-free numbers. Use these to identify your model.

Identify replacement parts. It may be that all you will need for replacement parts are washers, screws, and a few common valve parts available at a well-equipped home center or hardware store. But if you need to replace a cartridge or other intricate faucet component, your manufacturer can provide parts numbers and tell you how to order these.

Adjusting Bathtub or Shower Drainage

9

As with bathroom sinks, tub and shower drain pipes may become clogged with soap and hair. The drain stopping mechanisms can also require cleaning and adjustment.

TUB OR SHOWER NOT DRAINING? First, make sure it's only the tub or shower. If your sink is plugged, too, it may be a coincidence or it may be that a common branch line is plugged. A sure sign of this is when water drains from the sink into the tub. This could require the help of a drain cleaning service, or a drum trap that services both the sink and tub needs cleaning. If the toilet also can't flush (or worse, water comes into the tub when you flush the toilet), then the common drain to all your bathroom fixtures is plugged. Call a drain cleaning service. If you suspect the problem is only with your tub or shower, then read on. We'll show you how to clear drainlines and clean and adjust two types of tub stopper mechanisms. Adjusting the mechanism can also help with the opposite problem: a tub that drains when you're trying to take a bath.

BATH DRAINS 101

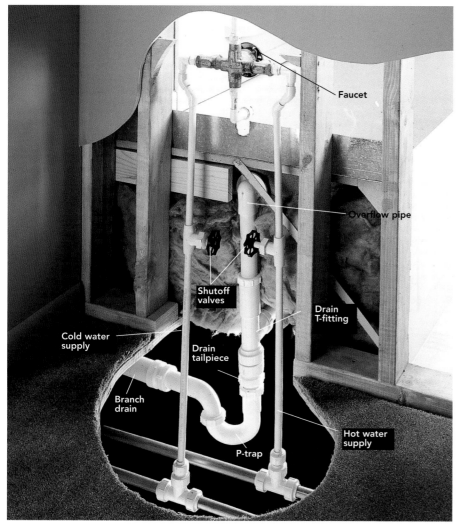

Faucet

Overflow pipe

Shutoff valves

Drain T-fitting

Cold water supply

Drain tailpiece

Branch drain

P-trap

Hot water supply

If you removed the wall behind your tub/shower along with part of the floor, this is pretty much what you would see. From the photo you can tell that having to access your drain for outside the tub is not easy, and that maintaining the drain system to avoid major problems and blockages is well worth the effort. Fortunately, maintenance is not difficult, and minor clogs are relatively easy to track down and eliminate.

TERMS YOU NEED TO KNOW

POP-UP DRAIN—a mechanical drain stopper where a metal drain cover is raised and lowered with a lever mounted on the cover of the overflow opening.

PLUNGER-TYPE DRAIN—another mechanical drain stopper where a plunger is lowered through the overflow pipe to block the drain.

HAND AUGER—a long bendable cable with a crank at one end that is snaked into a drain line to retrieve or break up a blockage.

TOOLS & SUPPLIES YOU'LL NEED

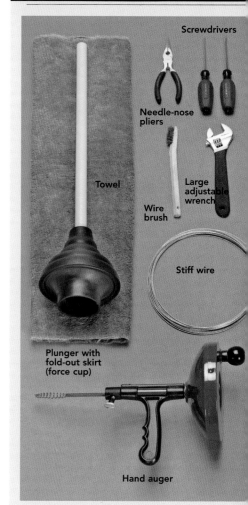

Screwdrivers

Needle-nose pliers

Towel

Wire brush

Large adjustable wrench

Stiff wire

Plunger with fold-out skirt (force cup)

Hand auger

SKILLS YOU'LL NEED

- Vigorous plunging
- Using an auger

DIFFICULTY LEVEL

SKILLS LEVEL

EASY   MODERATE

Time: ½ to 1½ hours

HOW TO FIX A PLUNGER-TYPE DRAIN

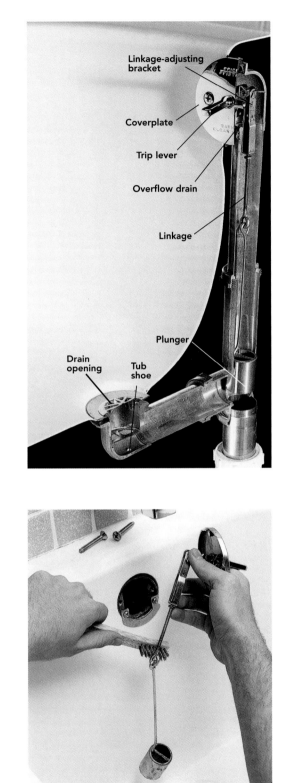

Linkage-adjusting bracket

Coverplate

Trip lever

Overflow drain

Linkage

Plunger

Drain opening

Tub shoe

1 A plunger-type tub drain has a simple grate over the drain opening and a behind-the-scenes plunger stopper. Remove the screws on the overflow coverplate with a slotted or Phillips head screwdriver. Pull the coverplate, linkage, and plunger from the overflow opening.

2 Clean hair and soap off the plunger with a scrub brush. Mineral buildup is best tackled with white vinegar and a toothbrush or a small wire brush.

3 Adjust the plunger. If your tub isn't holding water with the plunger down, it's possible the plunger is hanging too high to fully block water from the tub shoe. Loosen the locknut with needlenose pliers then screw the rod down about ⅛". Tighten the locknut down. If your tub drains poorly, the plunger may be set too low. Loosen the locknut and screw the rod in an ⅛" before retightening the locknut.

HOW TO FIX A POP-UP DRAIN

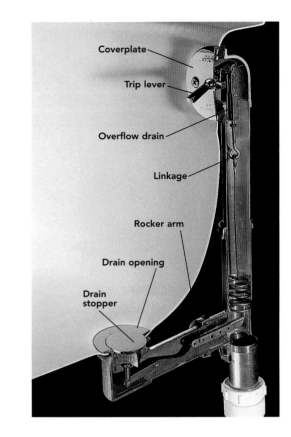

- Coverplate
- Trip lever
- Overflow drain
- Linkage
- Rocker arm
- Drain opening
- Drain stopper

1 Raise the trip lever to the open position. Pull the stopper and rocker arm assembly from the drain. Clean off soap and hair with a dishwashing brush in a basin of hot water. Clean off mineral deposits with a toothbrush or small wire brush and white vinegar.

2 Remove the screws from the cover plate. Pull the trip lever and the linkage from the overflow opening. Clean off soap and hair with a dish scrubbing brush in a basin of hot water. Remove mineral buildup with white vinegar and a wire brush. Lubricate moving parts of the linkage and rocker arm mechanism with heatproof grease.

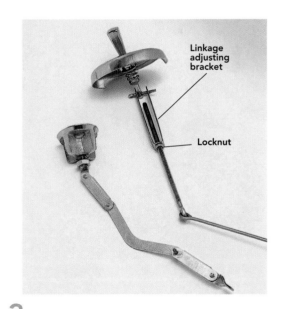

- Linkage adjusting bracket
- Locknut

3 Adjust the pop-up stopper mechanism by first loosening the locknut on the lift rod. If the stopper doesn't close all the way, shorten the linkage by screwing the rod ⅛" farther into the linkage-adjusting bracket. If the stopper doesn't open wide enough, extend the linkage by unscrewing the rod ⅛". Tighten the locknut before replacing the mechanism and testing your adjustment.

1 To plunge a shower drain, first remove the drain stopper equipment, including the strainer cover (if there is one) from the drain of a tub or shower. Pop the strainer out with a screwdriver, or remove a screw in the middle. Clear any hair from the pipe below the drain with a stiff bent wire.

TIP: If you can't clear a stubborn clog with a plunger, insert the tip of a hand auger into the drain opening (see next page).

2 If you can't see and remove an obstruction in the drain, try plunging. Position the plunger over the drain opening. If using a force-cup type of plunger, as seen above, fold the skirt up inside the plunger head. Completely cover the plunger with water. Plunge rhythmically through half-a-dozen ups and downs with increasing vigor, then yank up hard on the plunger. Repeat this cycle for up to 15 minutes. Promising signs: crud from the clog may rise into the tub before the weight of the water pushes the clog down the drain.

MAINTENANCE TIP

Like bathroom sinks, tubs and showers face an ongoing onslaught from soap and hair. When paired, this pesky combination is a sure-fire source of clogs. The soap scum coagulates as it is washed down the drain and binds the hair together in a mass that grows larger with every shower or bath. To nip these clogs in the bud, simply pour boiling hot clean water down the drain from time to time to melt the soapy mass and wash the binder away.

USING A HAND AUGER ON A SHOWER DRAIN

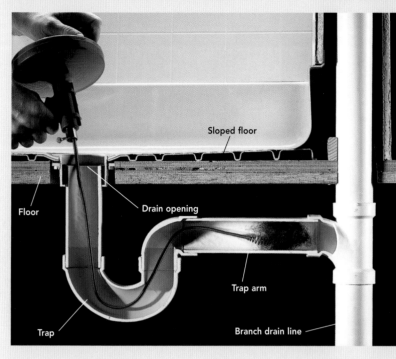

Floor

Drain opening

Sloped floor

Trap arm

Trap

Branch drain line

On shower drains, feed the head of the auger in through the *drain opening* after removing the strainer. Crank the handle of the auger to extend the cable and the auger head down into the trap and, if the clog is further downline, toward the branch drain. When clearing any drain, it is always better to retrieve the clog than to push it further downline.

USING A HAND AUGER ON A TUB DRAIN

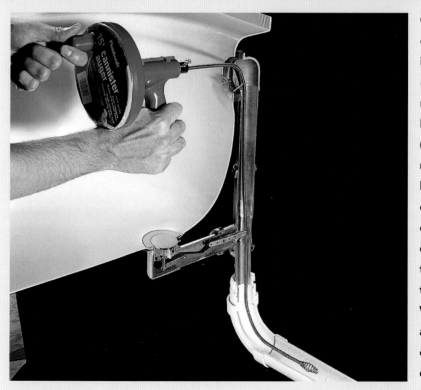

On combination tub/showers, it's generally easiest to insert the auger through the *overflow opening* after removing the coverplate and lifting out the drain linkage (see pages 182 to 183 for more information on drain linkages). Crank the handle of the auger to extend the cable and the auger head down into the trap and, if the clog is further downline, toward the branch drain. When clearing any drain, it is always better to retrieve the clog than to push it further downline.

10

Clearing Kitchen Sink Drains

Drain clearing isn't all drudgery and filth. Some people find the plunger to be as much a tool of personal transformation as an implement for removing clogs.

IT'S A WEEK TO PAYDAY, and that austerity plan you've arranged with your creditors gives you 67 dollars and change to last until then. Alas, the kitchen sink is clogged; you can't afford a plumber! Don't despair—your enemy is merely a wad of coffee grounds and some bacon fat. If plunging doesn't work, you'll go after it where it lives, remove the trap, look in the disposer, explore the fixture drain with a hand auger. With the right tool, you are like Thor and his thunderbolt, Zeus and his trident. You, we are confident, will locate the clog and break it up or drag it into the light, slap it into a basin, and sluice its slimy spawn into the sewer with a triumphant blast of tap water. You. Will. Win.

TIP: Avoid chemical clog removers. They can damage your pipes, your fixtures, and you, and they don't work very well. They're so dangerous to people, in fact, that drain cleaning services often charge extra if you've used them prior to their visit.

KITCHEN SINKS 101

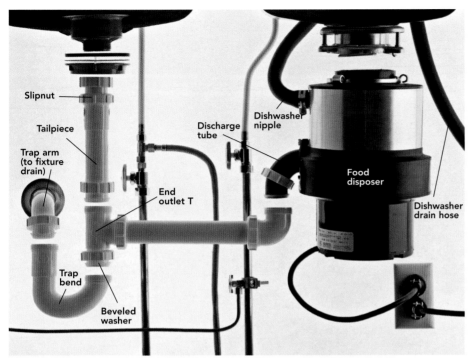

Slipnut
Tailpiece
Trap arm (to fixture drain)
End outlet T
Trap bend
Beveled washer
Discharge tube
Dishwasher nipple
Food disposer
Dishwasher drain hose

Kitchen sink drain components are usually connected with *slipnuts,* which means everything from the *tailpiece* beneath a basket strainer to the *trap arm* can be removed for cleaning. Clogs commonly occur in the *trap bend* and the *end outlet T.* With the trap arm off, the *fixture drain* can be augered. Make sure your *beveled washers* are facing the right direction when you put things back together. Clogs can happen in the *discharge tube* and *drain chamber* of a disposer. The *impellers* in the grinding chamber of a disposer can get stuck to the *grinding ring* with tough or fibrous waste materials. The *dishwasher drain hose* should be clamped where it joins the disposer if you wish to plunge the sink drain.

TERMS YOU NEED TO KNOW

BASKET STRAINER—This is the typical strainer, plug, and drain found on a kitchen sink that doesn't have a disposer.

TAILPIECE—takes the waste from the basket strainer to the trap.

GRINDING CHAMBER—the chamber visible through the drain of a disposer where wastes are ground.

IMPELLER—one of two or four steel lugs on the metal plate at the bottom of a disposer grinding chamber. Its function is to push food waste against the grinding ring as the plate rotates.

GRINDING RING—a stationary, toothed ring at the bottom perimeter of the disposer grinding chamber. Food wastes are ground against it until they are small enough to be washed into the drain chamber below.

TOOLS & SUPPLIES YOU'LL NEED

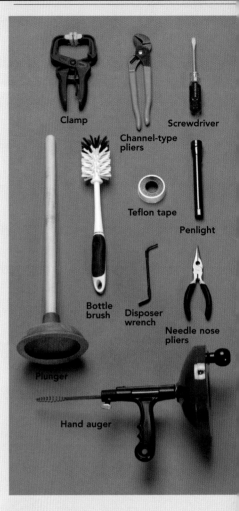

Clamp
Channel-type pliers
Screwdriver
Teflon tape
Penlight
Bottle brush
Disposer wrench
Needle nose pliers
Plunger
Hand auger

SKILLS YOU'LL NEED

- Working with slip joints
- Plunging
- Flexibility

DIFFICULTY LEVEL

SKILLS LEVEL

EASY   HARD

Time: ½ to 1½ hours.

KITCHEN SINK STOPPED? PLUNGE IN

CLEARING THE TRAP AND BEYOND

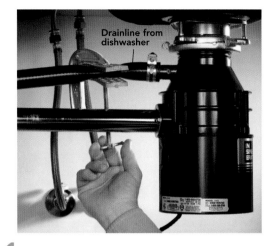

Drainline from dishwasher

1 Plunging a kitchen sink is not difficult, but you need to create an uninterrupted pressure lock between the plunger and the clog. If you have a dishwasher, the drain tube needs to be clamped shut and sealed off at the disposer or drainline. The pads on the clamp should be large enough to flatten the tube across its full diameter (or you can clamp the tube ends between small boards).

2 If there is a second basin, have a helper hold a basket strainer plug in its drain or put a large pot or bucket full of water on top of it. If you just set the strainer plug in place, the pressure of your plunging will pop the plug instead of the clog. Unfold the skirt within the plunger and place this in the drain of the sink you are plunging. There should be enough water in the sink to cover the plunger head. Plunge rhythmically for six repetitions with increasing vigor, pulling up hard on the last rep. Repeat this sequence until the clog or you are vanquished. Flush out a cleared clog with plenty of hot water.

1 If plunging doesn't work, remove the trap and clean it out. With the trap off, see if water flows freely from both sinks (if you have two). Sometimes clogs will lodge in the T-fitting or one of the waste pipes feeding it. These may be pulled out manually or cleared with a bottlebrush or wire. When reassembling the trap, apply Teflon tape clockwise to the male threads of metal waste pieces. Tighten with your channel-type pliers. Plastic pieces need no tape and should be hand-tightened only.

2 If you suspect the clog is downstream of the trap, remove the trap arm from the fitting at the wall. Look in the fixture drain with a penlight. If you see water, that means the fixture drain is plugged. Clear it with a hand auger (page 185).

DISPOSER NOT GRINDING?

1 Press the reset button located on the base of the disposer and switch the appliance on. If the motor hums but cannot move, the grinders are clogged and need to be cleared.

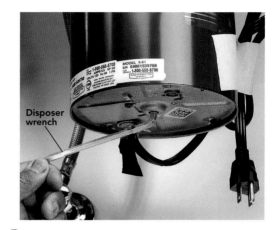

Disposer wrench

2 Unplug the disposer. Look for a wrench with a hex shaped head that came with the disposer. Stick this in a fitting in the base of the disposer. This manipulates the metal plate that holds the impellers. Typically, some hard or fibrous object is binding an impeller to the grinding ring. Rock the plate back and forth with the wrench to unbind the impeller. You can also attempt to rotate the plate from above by pushing against an impeller with a broom handle.

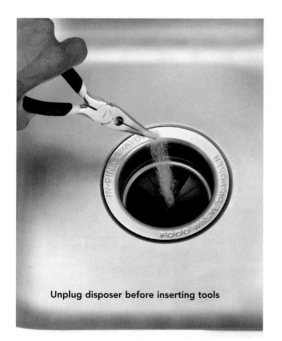

Unplug disposer before inserting tools

3 Look for and remove any material that's keeping the metal plate from rotating. Make sure the disposer is unplugged and then shine a light into the disposer and look for hard or fibrous debris between the impellers and the grinding ring. Use needlenose pliers to pull debris free.

DRAINING SLOWLY?

Discharge elbow

Waste buildup in the drain chamber beneath the impeller disc can lead to a slow-draining disposer. Remove the discharge elbow from the disposer body by withdrawing one or two screws or bolts. These may require a screwdriver or an adjustable wrench. Clear debris from the discharge elbow then shine a light into the drain chamber. Reach into the drain chamber with needlenose pliers to remove any fibrous buildup.

Fixing Leaky Sink Strainers

11

If your waste water takes a wrong turn on the way to the sewer, it may be time to reseat, or replace, your sink strainer.

THE SINK STRAINER IS THE PERFORATED BASKET IN THE BOTTOM OF YOUR KITCHEN SINK THAT CATCHES SPAGHETTI AND BROCCOLI SPEARS BEFORE THEY DIVE DOWN THE DRAIN. If your sink is simply not holding water, you may need to replace only the basket. These are available at any hardware store. If water is leaking onto the floor in the cabinet, you may need to reseat or replace the sink strainer body. A replacement includes the basket and the metal well that cradles the basket and forms a seal with your sink and the drain pipe.

FIXING A LEAKY SINK STRAINER

1 Clear out the cabinet under the sink. Unscrew slipnuts from both ends of the drain tailpiece with channel-type pliers. Lower the tailpiece into the trap bend or remove the tailpiece. NOTE: If you have a double sink and your tailpiece is very short, you may need to loosen slipnuts elsewhere and remove a larger piece of the drain assembly to access the strainer body.

3 Remove old putty from the drain opening with a putty knife. If reusing the old strainer body, clean off the old putty from under the flange. Knead plumber's putty into a snake shape and apply to the lip of the drain opening. Press the strainer body into the drain opening. Any writing on the strainer should be read from the front.

2 Loosen the locknut with a spud wrench or channel-type pliers. Unthread the locknut completely, then push the strainer body up out of the sink.

4 From under the sink, place the rubber gasket and the friction washer over the strainer body and secure the body to the sink deck with the locknut. Tap the nubs on the locknut with a screwdriver to tighten it. Reattach the drain by tightening the slipnut over the threaded end of the tailpiece.

TOOLS & SUPPLIES YOU'LL NEED

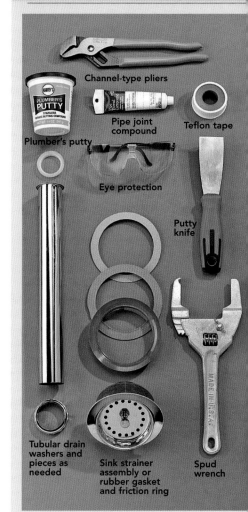

Channel-type pliers

Pipe joint compound

Teflon tape

Plumber's putty

Eye protection

Putty knife

Tubular drain washers and pieces as needed

Sink strainer assembly or rubber gasket and friction ring

Spud wrench

SKILLS YOU'LL NEED

- Using wrenches
- Putty rolling
- Making slip-joint connections

DIFFICULTY LEVEL

SKILLS LEVEL

EASY   MODERATE

Time: ½ to 1 hour plus shopping

TERMS YOU NEED TO KNOW

PLUMBER'S PUTTY—a clay-like material used to seal metal hardware to the sink.

TEFLON TAPE—a thin white tape used to lubricate and seal threaded fittings and keep them from sticking together.

PIPE JOINT COMPOUND—a paste that may be used instead of Teflon tape.

BASKET STRAINER—another name for a sink strainer.

Clearing Clogged Floor Drains

12

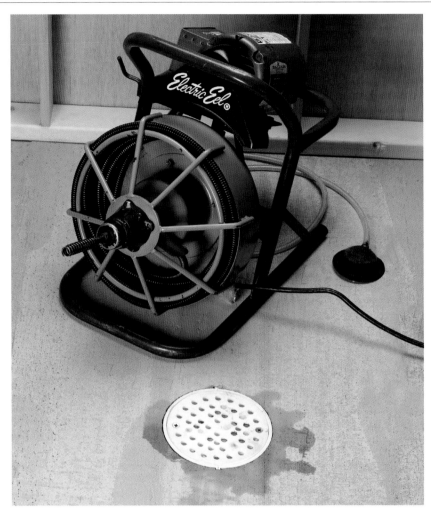

When the going gets tough, the tough rent power tools. The medium duty auger shown here is perfect for augering the 2-inch-diameter floor drain-lines and branch drainlines.

WHEN PLUNGERS AND HAND AUGERS MEET A CLOG THEY CAN'T DISLODGE, you have one more DIY option before you call a professional drain cleaning service. Most rental centers stock power augers in several sizes. These electric tools work in much the same manner as a hand auger, but with much more tenacity. With spear tools, cutting tools, and spring tools, they can push or cut through a clog, or snag an object and drag it out from your floor or branch drainline.

Always read the instructions carefully and be sure to get through operating instructions at the rental center. If used improperly, power augers can cause major damage to your plumbing system. They are designed to be inserted beyond the trap or through cleanouts in the drainline, so they do not need to be forced through the drain trap. Never run a power auger through a toilet—it could scratch the porcelain or even break the fixture.

POWER AUGERING 101

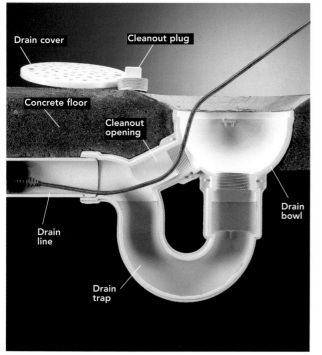

Drain cover

Cleanout plug

Concrete floor

Cleanout opening

Drain bowl

Drain line

Drain trap

Floor drains can develop extremely robust clogs, especially if the drain cover is absent. A *power auger* that's inserted through the cleanout opening can travel 50 feet or more to hunt down and remove stubborn clogs. These rental tools come in several sizes and may also be used to clear tub/shower drainlines, branch drainlines and even a 3- to 4-inch diameter soil stack or house drain.

TOOL TIP

Power augers can be fitted with three different head styles. The spring tool is affixed to the cable end to snag and retrieve an obstruction. The spear tool is used to penetrate a clog and puncture it to create a starter hole for the cutting tool, which can cut apart very resistant clogs (often tree roots).

Spring tool

Spear tool

Cutter tool

TERMS YOU NEED TO KNOW

TRAP—a U-shaped bend of drain pipe behind or under every fixture. It's always full of water to keep sewer gases from rising into the house. If possible, remove the trap before augering the drainline to a fixture. With the floor drain, you bypass the trap by opening a cleanout plug.

CLEANOUTS—are access ports in drain pipes kept covered with threaded caps.

CLEANING TOOL—the spring, spear, or cutter attached to the tip of a cable auger. These are interchangeable.

BRANCH OR FIXTURE DRAIN—the run of pipe in the wall or floor that drains a fixture (except a toilet). It's usually 1½ to 2-inches in diameter. It may join with a toilet drain, a stack, or the house drain.

TOOLS & SUPPLIES YOU'LL NEED

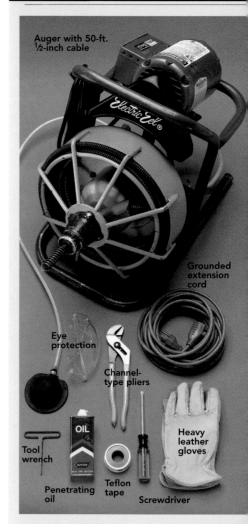

Auger with 50-ft. ½-inch cable

Grounded extension cord

Eye protection

Channel-type pliers

Heavy leather gloves

Tool wrench

OIL

Penetrating oil

Teflon tape

Screwdriver

SKILLS YOU'LL NEED

- Driving to rental center
- Exercising caution

DIFFICULTY LEVEL

SKILLS LEVEL

EASY   MODERATE

Time: ½ to 1 hour plus renting equipment

HOW TO POWER-AUGER A FLOOR DRAIN

1 Remove the cover from the floor drain using a slotted or Phillips screwdriver. On one wall of the drain bowl you'll see a cleanout plug. Remove the cleanout plug from the drain bowl with your largest channel-type pliers. This cleanout allows you to bypass the trap. If it's stuck, apply penetrating oil to the threads and let it sit a half an hour before trying to free it again. If the wrench won't free it, rent a large pipe wrench from your home center or hardware store. You can also auger through the trap if you have to.

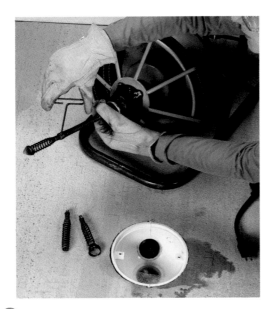

2 Rent an electric drum auger with at least 50 feet of ½-inch cable. The rental company should provide a properly sized, grounded extension cord, heavy leather gloves, and eye protection. The auger should come with a spear tool, cutter tool, and possibly a spring-tool suitable for a 2-inch drainline. Attach the spearhead first (with the machine unplugged).

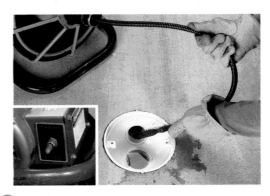

3 Wear close-fitting clothing and contain long hair. Place the power auger machine in a dry location within three feet of the drain opening. Plug the tool into a grounded, Ground Fault Interrupted (GFI) protected circuit. Put on eye protection and gloves; you will be holding a rotating metal cable and may be exposed to dangerous bacteria and caustic drain cleaning chemicals. Position the footswitch where it is easy to actuate; visualize using the machine without having to overreach the rotating drum or exposed belts. Make sure the FOR/REV switch is in the Forward position (inset photo). Hand feed the cleaning tool and some cable into the drain or cleanout before turning the machine on.

4 Stationary power augers (as opposed to pistol-grip types) are controlled by a foot pedal called an actuator so you can turn the power on and off hands-free.

6 Gradually work through the clog by pulling back on the cable whenever the machine starts to bog down and pushing it forward again when it gains new momentum. Again, never let the cable stop turning when the motor is running. When you have broken through the clog (or if you are using the spring head and believe you have snagged an object) withdraw the cable from the line. Manually pull the cable from the drain line while continuing to run the drum Forward. If it's practical, have a helper hose off the cable as its withdrawn and recoiled. When the cleaning tool is close to the drain opening, release the foot actuator and let the cable come to a stop before feeding the remaining two or three feet of cable into the drum by hand.

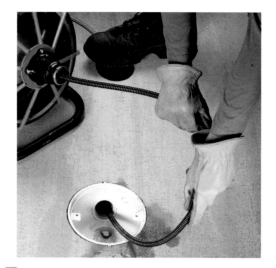

5 With both gloved hands on the cable, depress the foot actuator to start the machine. Gradually push the rotating cable into the drain opening. If the rotation slows or you cannot feed more cable into the drain, pull back on the cable before pushing it forward again. Don't force it. The cable needs to be rotating whenever the motor is running or it can kink and buckle, destroying the cable (although a clutch on the drum should prevent this). If the cleaning tool becomes stuck, turn the FOR/REV switch to Reverse and back the tool off the obstruction before switching back to Forward again.

7 After clearing the drain pipe, run the auger through the trap. Finish cleaning the auger. Wrap Teflon tape clockwise onto the plug threads and replace the plug. Run hot water through a hose from the laundry sink or use a bucket to flush remaining debris through the trap and down the line.

13

Adding a Shower to a Tub

Converting a plain bathtub into a tub/shower is a relatively easy task when you use a flexible shower adapter that fits onto a special replacement tub spout.

FORGET THE LAZY 8 TRUCK STOP. Forget the locker room at the health club. You may be able to enjoy the luxury of a real shower right in your own home or apartment. If you have an old built-in tub but no shower, we'll show you how you can remove the spout and replace it with one equipped with an adapter hose outlet. A flexible shower hose can be screwed to this. We'll also show you how to install a mounting bracket so you can hang the showerhead and free up your hands. Add a telescoping shower curtain rod and a shower curtain and your new shower stall is ready for duty.

SHOWER ADAPTERS 101

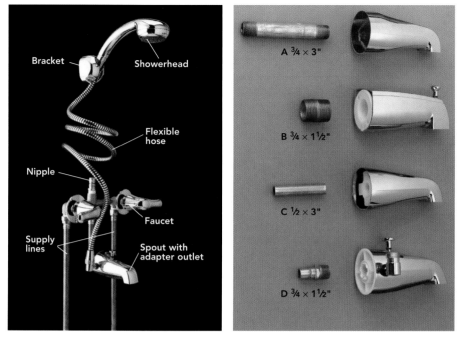

Bracket · Showerhead
Flexible hose
Nipple
Faucet
Supply lines
Spout with adapter outlet

A ¾ × 3"
B ¾ × 1½"
C ½ × 3"
D ¾ × 1½"

The appearance of the spout gives good clues as to which kind of nipple it is connected to. A) Spout with no diverter is probably connected to a 3" long threaded nipple. To install a diverter spout you'll need to replace the 3" threaded nipple with a shorter threaded nipple that sticks out no more than ½" from the wall—not too big of a job. B) If the spout already has a diverter knob, it already has a showerhead, and you're doing the wrong project (although there is no reason you couldn't hook up a shower adapter if you want a handheld shower). C) If the spout has a small setscrew in a slot on the underside, it is probably attached with a slip fitting to a ½" copper supply nipple. Unless you are able to solder a new transition fitting onto the old pipe after cutting it, call a plumber to install the new spout here. D) Spouts with outlets for shower adapters require a short threaded nipple (or comparable union) that sticks out from the wall no more than ¾".

TERMS YOU NEED TO KNOW

NIPPLE—a short piece of iron or brass pipe that's threaded on both ends. It may be unscrewed from the wall.

COPPER STUB—a short piece of copper pipe with or without a threaded adapter on the end. It cannot be unscrewed from the wall.

REDUCING BUSHING—a little piece of pipe with interior and exterior threads. In this case, to allow a ¾-inch tub spout to screw onto a ½-inch nipple.

TEFLON TAPE—a white or thin tape wound on pipe threads to seal and lubricate the joint.

TOOLS & SUPPLIES YOU'LL NEED

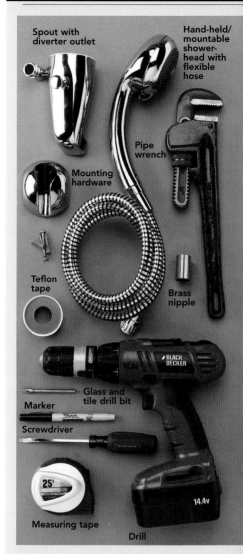

Spout with diverter outlet
Hand-held/mountable showerhead with flexible hose
Pipe wrench
Mounting hardware
Teflon tape
Brass nipple
Marker
Glass and tile drill bit
Screwdriver
Measuring tape
Drill
BLACK & DECKER
14.4v

SKILLS YOU'LL NEED

- Making pipe connections
- Cutting tile or tileboard
- Working with wall anchors

DIFFICULTY LEVEL

SKILLS LEVEL

EASY   MODERATE

Time: 1 to 2 hours

HOW TO ADD A SHOWER WITH AN ADAPTER SPOUT

1 Make sure the old spout is not held in place with a setscrew (see previous page) and then remove it by wrapping it with a cloth and turning the spout with channel-type pliers or a pipe wrench.

2 If you have a long iron or brass nipple like this, you need to replace it with a short one. Threaded nipples have threads at each end, so you can usually unscrew the old ones. Mark the nipple at the face of the wall and write "front" on your side. Unscrew it counterclockwise with a pipe wrench. Get a threaded brass nipple of the same diameter that is about half an inch longer than the distance from the back of your old nipple to your line.

TOOL TIP

A long-bladed screwdriver or a dowel inserted into the mouth of the spout can be used to spin the spout free from the nipple.

3 Wrap six layers of Teflon tape clockwise on the nipple and thread into the wall. Thread the reducing bushing onto the nipple if it will fit. Thread the adapter spout on. Tighten further with a screwdriver or dowel to orient the spout correctly.

4 Attach flexible shower hose to the adapter hose outlet. Tighten with an adjustable wrench.

5 Determine the location of showerhead bracket. Use hose length as a guide, and make sure showerhead can be easily lifted off the bracket.

6 Mark hole locations. Obtain a glass-and-tile drill bit for your electric drill in the size recommended by the shower bracket manufacturer. Put on eye protection and drill holes in ceramic tile on your marks.

7 Insert anchors into holes, and tap in place with a wooden or rubber mallet. Fasten showerhead holder to the wall using a Phillips screwdriver and the mounting screws.

Replacing Bathtub Spouts

14

The bathtub spout may need replacing for many reasons, including a failed diverter like the one above. You also may want to add a flexible shower adapter (see pages 196 to 199), or the old spout could just be disgusting beyond repair.

IN MANY SITUATIONS, REPLACING A BATHTUB SPOUT can be almost as easy as hooking up a garden hose to an outdoor spigot. There are some situations where it is a bit more difficult, but still pretty simple. The only time it's a real problem is when the spout is attached to a plain copper supply nipple, rather than a threaded nipple. You'll know this is the case if the spout has a setscrew on the underside where it meets the wall. Many bathtub spouts are sold in kits with a matching showerhead and handle or handles. But for a simple one-for-one replacement, spouts are sold separately. You just need to make sure the new spout is compatible with the existing nipple (see pages 202 and 203).

TUB SPOUTS 101

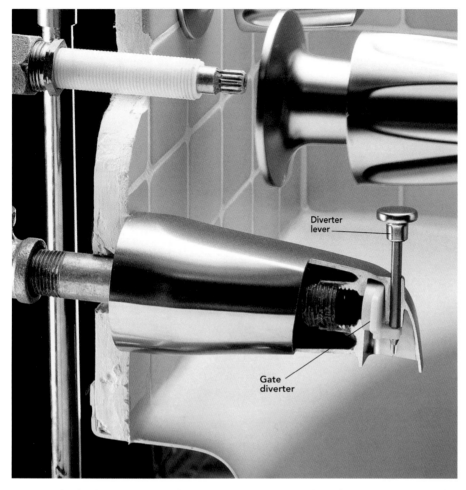

Diverter lever

Gate diverter

In many bathtub/shower plumbing systems, the *spout* has the important job of housing the diverter switch—a *gate* inside the spout that is operated by a lever with a knob for pulling. When the gate is open, water comes out of the spout when the faucet is turned on. When the *diverter* is pulled shut, the water is redirected up a *riser pipe* and to the *showerhead*. Failure of the diverter is one of the most common reasons for replacing a spout.

TERMS YOU NEED TO KNOW

TUB SPOUT GATE DIVERTER—a knob-operated gate valve on the tip of a tub spout. When it's pulled up, water cannot pass through the spout and is forced to rise to the showerhead.

HANDLE-OPERATED DIVERTER VALVE—the diverter valve behind the central handle on a three-handle faucet. It uses a compression stem and washer or a cartridge to divert water from the spout so the shower can be used.

TOOLS & SUPPLIES YOU'LL NEED

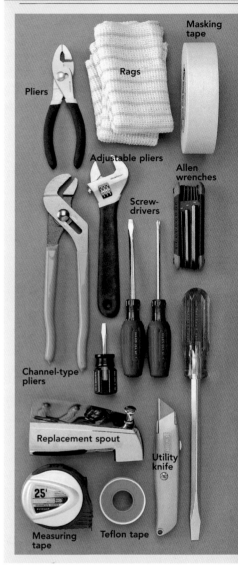

Masking tape

Rags

Pliers

Adjustable pliers

Allen wrenches

Screw-drivers

Channel-type pliers

Replacement spout

Utility knife

Measuring tape

Teflon tape

SKILLS YOU'LL NEED

• Using channel-type pliers

• Tracking the order and arrangement of parts

DIFFICULTY LEVEL

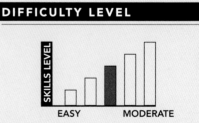

SKILLS LEVEL

EASY   MODERATE

Time: 1 hour plus research and shopping

HOW TO REPLACE A SLIP-FIT SPOUT

1 Check underneath the tub spout to look for an access slot or cutout, which indicates the spout is a slip-fit style that is held in place with a setscrew and mounted on a copper supply nipple. Loosen the screw with a hex (Allen) wrench. Pull off the spout.

2 Clean the copper nipple with steel wool. If you find any sharp edges where the nipple was cut, smooth them out with emery paper. Then, insert the O-ring that comes with spout onto the nipple (see the manufacturer's instructions) and slide the spout body over the nipple in an upside-down position.

3 With the spout upside down for ease of access, tighten the setscrews on the clamp, working through the access slot or cutout, until you feel resistance.

4 Spin the spout so it's right-side up and then tighten the setscrew from below, making sure the wall end of the spout is flush against the wall. Do not overtighten the setscrew.

HOW TO REPLACE A THREADED SPOUT

1 If you see no setscrew or slot on the underside of the spout, it is attached to a threaded nipple. Unscrew the tub spout by inserting a heavy-duty flat screwdriver into the spout opening and spinning it counterclockwise.

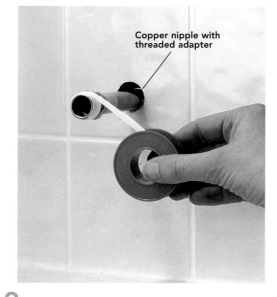

Copper nipple with threaded adapter

2 Wrap several courses of Teflon tape clockwise onto the pipe threads of the nipple. Using extra Teflon tape on the threads creates resistance if the spout tip points past six o'clock when tight.

3 Twist the new spout onto the nipple until it is flush against the wall and the spout is oriented properly. If the spout falls short of six o'clock, you may protect the finish of the spout with tape and twist it a little beyond hand tight with your channel-type pliers—but don't over do it; the fitting can crack.

Replacing Widespread Bathroom Faucets

15

Three-piece (widespread) faucets are as classy as a good three-piece suit, and the styles are virtually unlimited.

WIDESPREAD FAUCETS COME IN THREE PIECES INSTEAD OF ONE: a hot tap, a cold tap, and the spout. Each piece is mounted separately in its own hole in the sink. The hot and cold taps (valves) are connected to hot and cold water supplies respectively. The spout is connected to the valves with reinforced flexible hoses. The great advantage to this configuration is that you gain flexibility when locating your spout and handles. If your faucet set has a long enough hose, you can even create arrangements such as locating the handles near one end of the tub and the spout near the other so you can turn the water on and off or adjust the temperature without getting up. Even models made for bathroom lavatories, like the one you see here, offer many creative configuration options.

TIP: Save your paperwork. Should you ever need to service your faucet, the product literature will be useful for troubleshooting and identifying and replacing parts.

WIDESPREAD FAUCETS 101

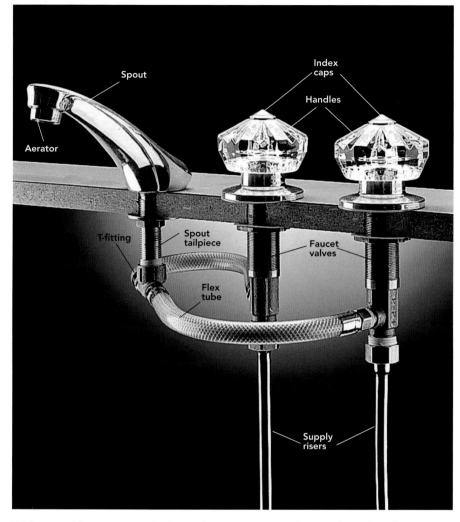

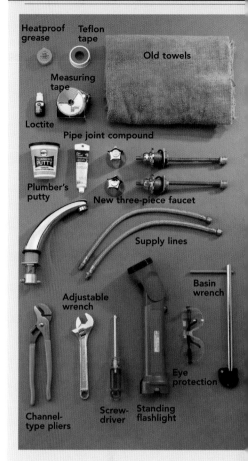

Heatproof grease · Teflon tape · Old towels · Measuring tape · Loctite · Pipe joint compound · Plumber's putty · New three-piece faucet · Supply lines · Adjustable wrench · Basin wrench · Eye protection · Channel-type pliers · Screwdriver · Standing flashlight

Widespread faucets come in three pieces, a *spout* and two *valves. Supply risers* carry hot and cold water to the valves, which are turned to regulate the amount of water going to the spout, where the water is mixed. Water travels from the valves to the spout through *flex tubes,* which attach to the *spout tailpiece* via a *T-fitting.* Three-piece faucets designed to work with a pop-up stopper have a *clevis* and a *lift rod* (see pages 228 to 229). The *handles* attach with *handle screws* that are covered with *index caps.* An *aerator* is screwed on the faucet spout after debris is flushed from the faucet.

SKILLS YOU'LL NEED

- Using a basin wrench
- Working in confined spaces
- Making compression unions

TERMS YOU NEED TO KNOW

PLUMBER'S PUTTY—a soft clay-like material used to seal faucet parts to sink parts.

TEFLON TAPE—a thin, white tape used to lubricate and seal threaded fittings.

PIPE JOINT COMPOUND—a paste that may be used instead of Teflon tape.

LAVATORY—another name for a bathroom sink.

DIFFICULTY LEVEL

SKILLS LEVEL

EASY · MODERATE

Time: 1 to 3 hours

HOW TO REMOVE A WIDESPREAD FAUCET

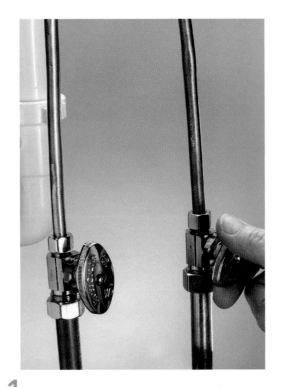

1 Clear out the cabinet under the sink and lay down towels. Turn off the hot and cold stop valves, and open the hot and cold taps. If you have difficulty turning the water off, turn to page 134.

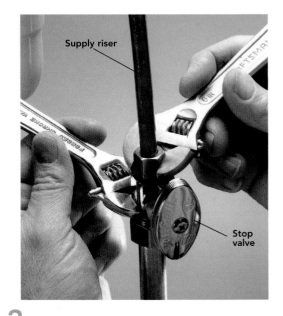

Supply riser

Stop valve

2 Unthread the compression nuts that connect the hot and cold supply risers to the stop valves. If a compression nut is frozen, stabilize the valve body with another wrench before applying more force.

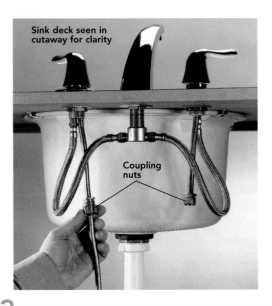

Sink deck seen in cutaway for clarity

Coupling nuts

3 Remove the coupling nuts holding the risers to the supply tubes from the faucet, stabilizing the tubes with a second wrench. Don't reuse old metal supply risers; the soft metal ends have been press-formed to the supply tubes of the old faucet.

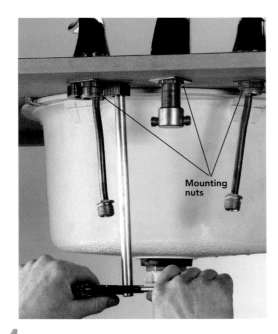

Mounting nuts

4 Using a basin wrench, disconnect all three mounting nuts holding the two faucet handles and the spout. You may need to have somebody hold the spout or valve steady from above. Remove the old faucet parts and clean the installation area in preparation for the new faucet.

HOW TO INSTALL A WIDESPREAD FAUCET

1 Insert the shank of the faucet spout through one of the holes in the sink deck (usually the center hole but you can offset it in one of the end holes if you prefer). If the faucet is not equipped with seals or O-rings for the spout and handles, pack plumber's putty on the undersides before inserting the valves into the deck. N O T E : If you are installing the widespread faucet in a new sink deck, drill three holes of the size suggested by the faucet manufacturer (see page 204 for tips on locating the holes).

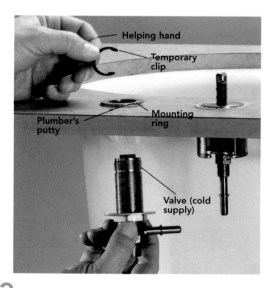

3 Mount the valves to the deck using whichever method the manufacturer specifies (it varies quite a bit). In the model seen here, a mounting ring is positioned over the deck hole (with plumber's putty seal) and the valve is inserted from below. A clip snaps onto the valve from above to hold it in place temporarily (you'll want a helper for this).

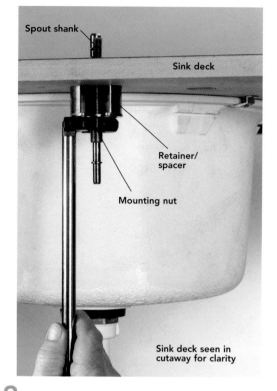

2 In addition to mounting nuts, many spout valves for widespread faucets have an open retainer fitting that goes between the underside of the deck and the mounting nut. Others have only a mounting nut. In either case, tighten the mounting nut with pliers or a basin wrench to secure the spout valve. You may need a helper to keep the spout centered and facing forward.

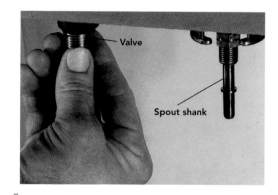

4 From below, thread the mounting nuts that secure the valves to the sink deck. Make sure the cold water valve (usually has a blue cartridge inside) is in the right-side hole (from the front) and the hot water valve (red cartridge) is in the left hole. Install both valves.

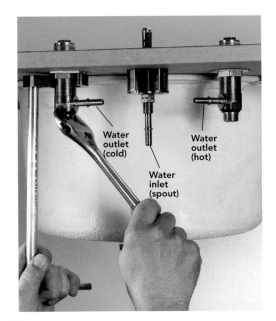

5 Once you've started the nut on the threaded valve shank, secure the valve with a basin wrench squeezing the lugs where the valve fits against the deck. Use an adjustable wrench to finish tightening the lock nut onto the valve. The valves should be oriented so the water outlets are aimed at the inlet on the spout shank.

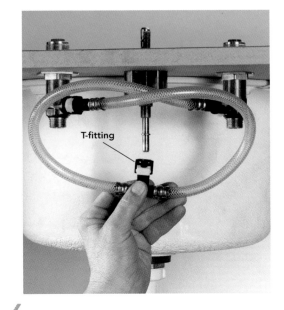

6 Attach the flexible supply tubes (supplied with the faucet) to the water outlets on the valves. Some twist onto the outlets, but others (like the ones above) click into place. The supply hoses meet in a T-fitting that is attached to the water inlet on the spout.

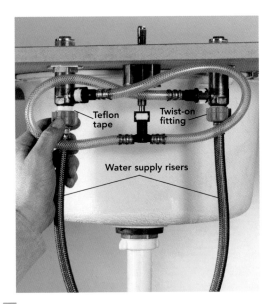

7 Attach flexible braided metal supply risers to the water stop valves and then attach the tubes to the inlet port on each valve (usually with Teflon tape and a twist-on fitting at the valve end of the supply riser).

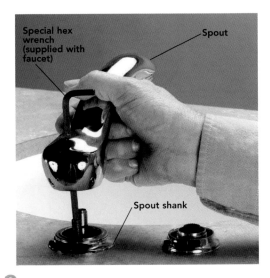

8 Attach the spout. The model shown here comes with a special hex wrench that is threaded through the hole in the spout where the lift rod for the pop-up drain will be located. Once the spout is seated cleanly on the spout shank you tighten the hex wrench to secure the spout. Different faucets will use other methods to secure the spout to the shank.

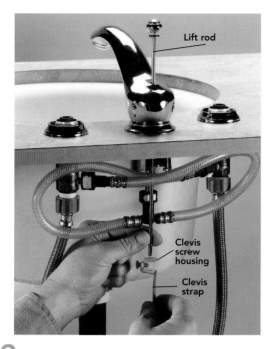

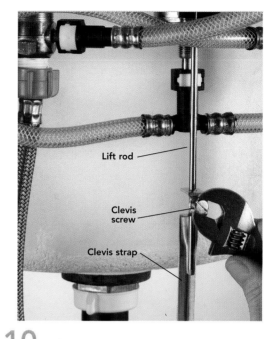

9 If your sink did not have a pop-up stopper, you'll need to replace the sink drain tailpiece with a pop-up stopper body (often supplied with the faucet). See pages 228 to 231. Insert the lift rod through the hole in the back of the spout and, from below, thread the pivot rod through the housing for the clevis screw.

10 Attach the clevis strap to the pivot rod that enters the pop-up drain body and adjust the position of the strap so it raises and lowers properly when the lift rod is pulled up. Tighten the clevis screw at this point. It's hard to fit a screwdriver in here, so you may need to use a wrench or pliers.

11 Attach the faucet handles to the valves using whichever method is required by the faucet manufacturer. Most faucets are designed with registration methods to ensure that the handles are symmetrical and oriented in an ergonomic way once you secure them to the valves.

12 Turn on the water supply and test the faucet. Remove the faucet aerator so any debris in the lines can clear the spout.

Installing New Bathroom Faucets

16

Standard one-handle, deck-mounted bathroom faucets are interchangeable with two-handle models, fitting in the same two or three holes in the bathroom sink.

ONE-PIECE BATHROOM FAUCETS ARE EASY TO REPLACE. They're attached to the sink with a couple of mounting nuts and to the water supply with coupling nuts. With the faucet gone, you'll be looking at two or three holes in the faucet deck. The outside holes take tailpieces or mounting posts for the faucet, and the middle hole is for the pop-up stopper lift rod. The outside holes are spaced four inches apart and will accept any standard deck-mounted, one-piece bathroom faucet, except if you don't have a middle hole, you can't have one with a pop-up stopper. We'd advise you to buy a heavy, quality faucet made of brass (chrome or another metal on the outside). Cheap chromed-plastic faucets tend to wear out at the handle attachments, and chrome-plated steel tends to rust. Faucets usually come with a pop-up stopper mechanism. We show you how to replace these on pages 228 to 231.

ONE-PIECE FAUCETS 101

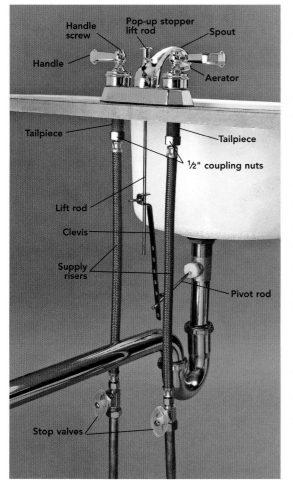

Handle screw
Handle
Pop-up stopper lift rod
Spout
Aerator
Tailpiece
Tailpiece
½" coupling nuts
Lift rod
Clevis
Supply risers
Pivot rod
Stop valves

The tailpieces of a standard deck-mounted, one-piece bathroom sink faucet are 4" apart on center. As long as the two outside holes in the back of your sink measure 4" from center to center, and you have a middle hole for a pop-up stopper, you can put in any standard one-piece bathroom faucet with *pop-up stopper.*

The faucet is secured to the sink with *mounting nuts* that screw onto the tailpieces from below. Also get two *flexible stainless steel supply risers* for sinks, long enough to replace the old tubes. These typically attach to the stop valves with ⅜-inch *compression-sized coupling nuts* and to the faucet with standard *faucet coupling nuts.* But take your old tubes and the old compression nuts from the stop valves to the store to ensure a match. The *clevis, lift rod,* and *pivot rod* are parts of the pop-up stopper assembly. (Replaced on pages 126 to 129.) The handles attach with *handle screws* that are covered with *index caps.* An *aerator* is screwed on the faucet spout after debris is flushed from the faucet.

(Replaced on pages 126 to 129.)

TERMS YOU NEED TO KNOW

PLUMBER'S PUTTY—a soft clay-like material used to seal faucet parts to sink parts.

TEFLON TAPE—a thin white tape used to lubricate and seal threaded fittings.

PIPE JOINT COMPOUND—a paste that may be used instead of Teflon tape.

DECK-MOUNTED FAUCET—another name for a one-piece faucet.

LAVATORY—another name for a bathroom sink.

TOOLS & SUPPLIES YOU'LL NEED

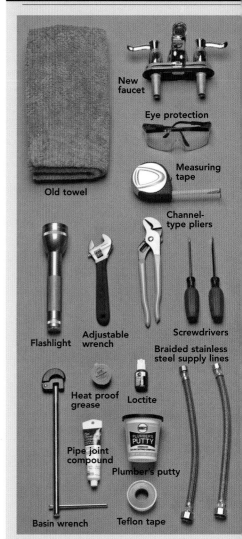

New faucet
Eye protection
Old towel
Measuring tape
Channel-type pliers
Flashlight
Adjustable wrench
Screwdrivers
Braided stainless steel supply lines
Heat proof grease
Loctite
Pipe joint compound
Plumber's putty
Basin wrench
Teflon tape

SKILLS YOU'LL NEED

- Making plumbing connections
- Ability to work in confined space

DIFFICULTY LEVEL

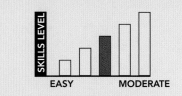

SKILLS LEVEL

EASY   MODERATE

TIME: 1 to 2 hours plus shopping

HOW TO REPLACE A ONE-PIECE FAUCET

1 Clear out the cabinet under the sink and lay down towels. Turn off the hot and cold stop valves and open the faucet. Unscrew the compression nuts that are holding the hot and cold supply tubes in the stop valves. Remove the coupling nuts holding the supply tubes to the tailpieces of the faucet and remove the tubes.

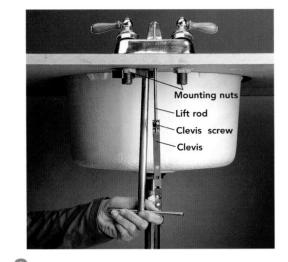

Mounting nuts
Lift rod
Clevis screw
Clevis

2 Put on protective eyewear! Debris will be falling in your face. Loosen the clevis screw (counterclockwise) holding the clevis strap to the lift rod. Remove the mounting nuts on the tailpieces of the faucet with a basin wrench or channel-type pliers. If the mounting nuts are rusted in place, apply penetrating oil, let stand ten minutes, and try again. **TIP:** Attach locking pliers to the basin wrench handle for greater leverage.

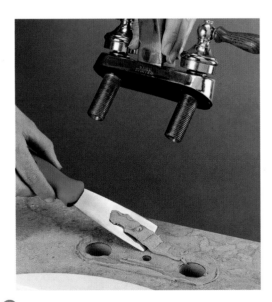

3 Pull the faucet body from the sink. Scrape off old putty or caulk with a putty knife and clean off the sink with a scouring pad and an acidic scouring cleaner like Barkeeper's Friend. Take your old supply tubes and the stop valve compression nuts to the home center so you'll know what size flexible supply risers to get.

4 Most faucets come with a plastic or foam gasket to seal the bottom of the faucet to the sink deck. These gaskets will not always form a watertight seal. If you want to ensure no splash water gets below the sink, discard the seal and press a ring of plumber's putty into the sealant groove built into the underside of the faucet body.

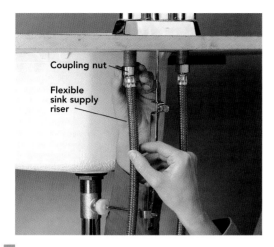

Coupling nut

Flexible sink supply riser

5 Insert the faucet tailpieces through the holes in the sink. From below, thread washers and mounting nuts over the tailpieces, then tighten the mounting nuts with a basin wrench until snug. Put a dab of pipe joint compound on the threads of the stop valves and thread the metal nuts of the flexible supply risers to these. Wrench tighten about a half turn past hand tight. Overtightening these nuts will strip the threads. Now tighten the coupling nuts to the faucet tailpieces with a basin wrench.

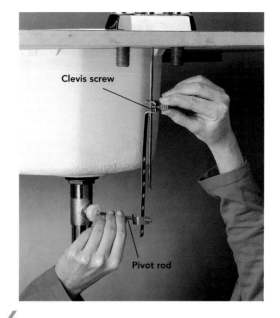

Clevis screw

Pivot rod

6 Slide the lift rod of the new faucet into its hole behind the spout. Thread it into the clevis past the clevis screw. Push the pivot rod all the way down so the stopper is open. With the lift rod also all the way down, tighten the clevis to the lift rod.

7 Grease the fluted valve stems with heatproof grease, then put the handles in place. Put a drop of Loctite on each handle screw before tightening it on. (This will keep your handles from coming loose). Cover each handle screw with the appropriate index cap—Hot or Cold.

8 Unscrew the aerator from the end of the spout. Turn the hot and cold water taps on full. Turn the water back on at the stop valves and flush out the faucet for a couple of minutes before turning off the water at the faucet. Check the riser connections for drips. Tighten a compression nut only until the drip stops.

Replacing Kitchen Sprayers

17

When most of us think of kitchen sprayers, the image that comes to mind doesn't closely resemble the powerful stream of accurately directed water that's cleansing the fresh apples in the photo above. For a variety of reasons, sink sprayers seldom seem to function as designed. But improving the performance of your kitchen sprayer is a simple job with a high likelihood of success.

IF THE FLOW TO YOUR SPRAYER IS WEAK, first make sure the hose under the sink isn't kinked. If the hose is damaged, you will need to replace the hose and sprayer. If the screen at the base of the sprayer is clogged with debris, remove it and flush it clean. If you dislodged other parts from the base of the sprayer, clean these and put them back in the order in which they were removed. If the sprayer leaks from the base, replace the neoprene washer. If the sprayer doesn't turn off fully, replace the sprayer. If water isn't fully diverted from spout to sprayer, you may need to replace the diverter.

KITCHEN SPRAYERS 101

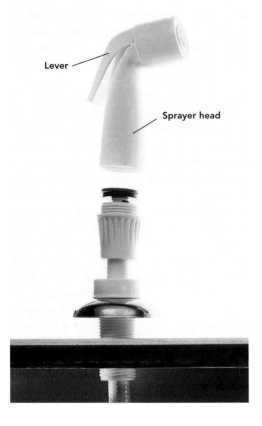

Lever

Sprayer head

When you squeeze the *lever* on your properly functioning kitchen sprayer, water flows out through the *sprayer head*, which causes a diverter valve in the faucet to close off water to the spout.

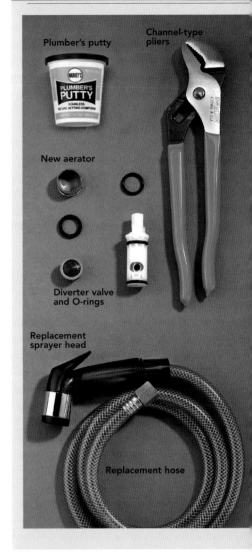
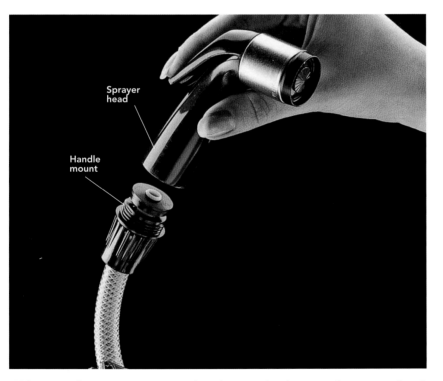

Sprayer head

Handle mount

Older spray hoses are easy to work with—you simply grasp the *sprayer head* and twist counterclockwise. The screen inside can then be removed and cleaned or replaced. Twist the sprayer head back on in a clockwise direction.

SKILLS YOU'LL NEED

- Making pipe connections
- Working with putty

DIFFICULTY LEVEL

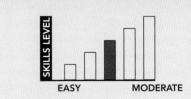

SKILLS LEVEL

EASY   MODERATE

Time: About an hour

HOW TO REPLACE A SPRAYER DIVERTER VALVE

1 Shut off the water at the stop valves and remove the faucet handle to gain access to the faucet parts. Disassemble the faucet handle and body to expose the diverter valve. Ball-type faucets like the one shown here require that you also remove the spout to get at the diverter.

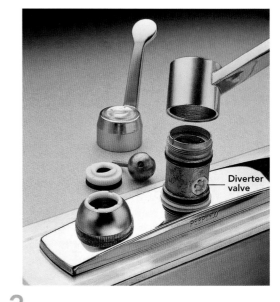

2 Locate the diverter valve, seen here at the base of the valve body. Because different types and brands of faucets have differently configured diverters, do a little investigating beforehand to try and locate information about your faucet. The above faucet is a ball type (see page 152).

3 Pull the diverter valve from the faucet body with needlenose pliers. Use a toothbrush dipped in white vinegar to clean any lime buildup from the valve. If the valve is in poor condition, bring it to the hardware store and purchase a replacement.

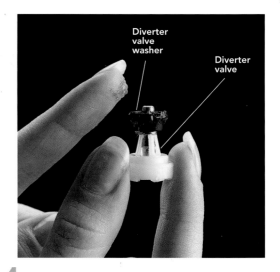

4 Coat the washer or O-ring on the new or cleaned diverter valve with heatproof grease. Insert the diverter valve back into the faucet body. Reassemble the faucet. Turn on the water and test the sprayer. If it still isn't functioning to your satisfaction, remove the sprayer tip and run the sprayer without the filter and aerator in case any debris has made its way into the sprayer line during repairs.

HOW TO REPLACE A KITCHEN SPRAYER

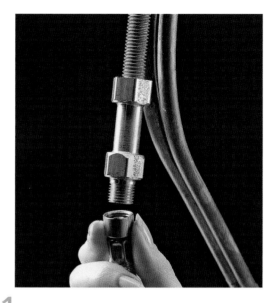

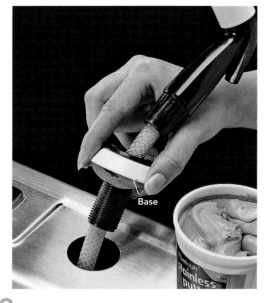

1 To replace a sprayer hose, start by shutting off the water at the shutoff valves. Clear out the cabinet under your sink and put on eye protection. Unthread the coupling nut that attaches the old hose to a nipple or tube below the faucet spout. Use a basin wrench if you can't get your channel-type pliers on the nut.

2 Unscrew the mounting nut of the old sprayer from below and remove the old sprayer body. Clean the sink deck and then apply plumber's putty to the base of the new sprayer. Insert the new sprayer tailpiece into the opening in the sink deck.

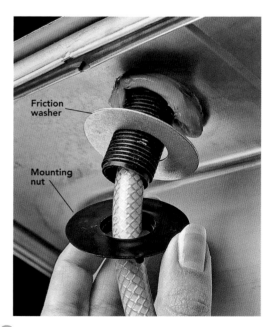

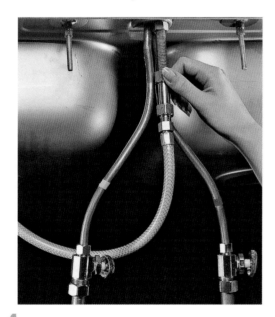

3 From below, slip the friction washer up over the sprayer tailpiece. Screw the mounting nut onto the tailpiece and tighten with a basin wrench or channel-type pliers. Do not over-tighten. Wipe away any excess plumber's putty.

4 Screw the coupling for the sprayer hose onto the hose nipple underneath the faucet body. For a good seal, apply pipe joint compound to the nipple threads first. Tighten the coupling with a basin wrench, turn on the water supply at the shutoff valves, and test the new sprayer.

Repairing Burst Pipes

18

Water supply pipes can burst for many reasons, but the most common cause is water freezing and expanding inside the pipe. First turn off the water, then apply a fix.

IF A WATER PIPE FREEZES AND BREAKS, your first priority may be getting it working again—whatever it takes. There are a number of temporary fix products out there, some involving clamps and sleeves, others, epoxy putties and fiberglass tape. These repairs usually can get you through a weekend okay. We also show you how to apply full slip repair couplings, a more permanent fix. Whatever repair approach you take, please, please, please, don't leave for the store without first determining a) the diameter of your pipe and b) the material of your pipe.

WATER PIPE REPAIR PRODUCTS 101

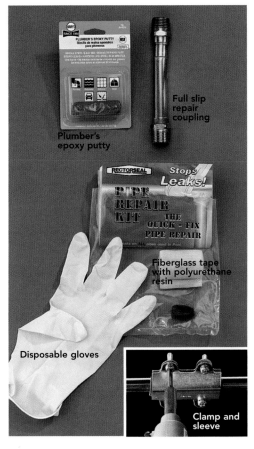

Plumber's epoxy putty

Full slip repair coupling

Fiberglass tape with polyurethane resin

Disposable gloves

Clamp and sleeve

Plumber's epoxy putty may stem a leak at a fitting, at least partially or temporarily. *Fiberglass tape with polyurethane resin* can produce a durable patch; it's sometimes used in conjunction with epoxy putty. A *clamp and sleeve* is quick and cheap. A *full slip repair coupling* is the closest to a permanent fix, but it requires straight and unblemished pipes of the right diameter and material. All of these products require that you carefully follow manufacturer's directions, or they simply will not work.

WARNING: A damaged pipe section with a patch should be replaced as soon as possible. Because of the natural movement of pipes, patches may leak again in time.

TOOLS & SUPPLIES YOU'LL NEED

Metal file

Channel-type pliers

Adjustable wrench

Screwdriver

Tubing cutter

Tape measure

If a water supply pipe bursts, your first stop should be a shutoff. If there is a shutoff near the burst pipe, go ahead and turn off the water there or shut off the water to the whole house (right). Open faucets on every floor of the house to drain the supply system if your repair product requires dry pipe.

SKILLS YOU'LL NEED

- Using a tubing cutter
- Making a compression joint

DIFFICULTY LEVEL

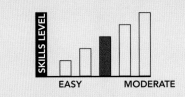

SKILLS LEVEL

EASY   MODERATE

Time: a few minutes plus shopping

TERMS YOU NEED TO KNOW

OUTSIDE DIAMETER—clamps and slip couplings require that you know the outside diameter of the pipe. Close an adjustable wrench on the pipe then measure the distance between the jaws.

PIPE MATERIAL—Certain repair products work on certain pipe types. Make sure you know yours before heading out to the home center.

HOW TO APPLY A SLEEVE AND CLAMP REPAIR KIT

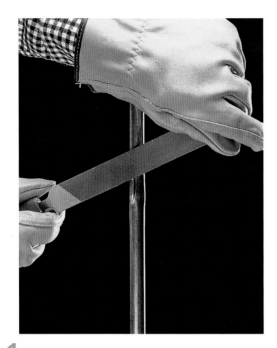

1 Make temporary repairs to a burst copper supply pipe with a sleeve clamp repair kit, available at most hardware stores. With the water supply shut off at the main, smooth out any rough edges around the damage with a metal file.

2 Center rubber sleeve of repair clamp over the rupture. If the sleeve enfolds the pipe, the seam should be opposite the rupture.

3 Place the two metal repair clamps around the sleeve.

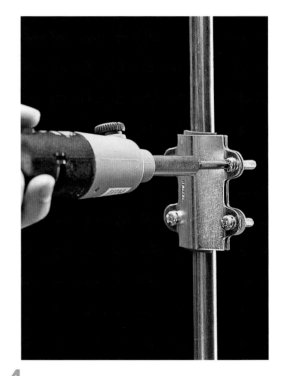

4 Tighten the screws with a Phillips screwdriver. Open water supply and watch for leaks. If it does leak, start from the beginning with the sleeve in a slightly different place. Have the section of ruptured pipe replaced as soon as possible.

HOW TO APPLY A REPAIR COUPLING TO A COPPER PIPE

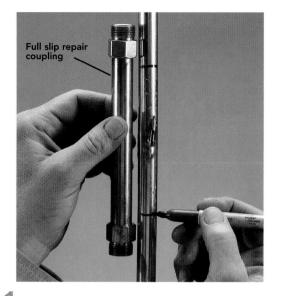

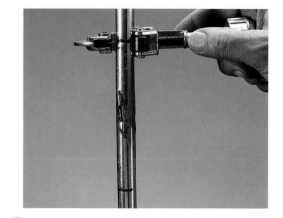

1 For a longer-lasting (not permanent) repair, use a compression-fit, full slip repair coupling (these come with parts to make a compression union—you can also buy a slip coupling that's just a piece of copper tubing with an inside diameter equal to the outside diameter of the tubing being repaired, but these require soldering). Turn off water at the meter. Mark the boundaries of the pipe to be replaced. This should include pipe beyond the damaged area. The cutout section must fall within the bare copper section of the repair coupling.

2 Lightly tighten the tubing cutter onto the pipe on a cutting line. Both wheels of the cutter should rest evenly on the pipe. Rotate the cutter around the pipe. The line it cuts should make a perfect ring, not a spiral. Tighten the cutter a little with each rotation until the pipe snaps. Repeat at your other mark.

3 Deburr the inside of the pipes with the triangular blade on the tubing cutter.

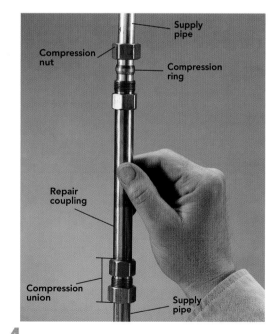

4 Slip the compression nuts and rings supplied with the repair coupling onto the cut ends of the pipe being repaired and then slip the repair coupling over one end. Slide the coupling further onto the pipe and then slide it back the other way so it fits over the other pipe section and the repair area is centered inside the coupling. Tighten each compression nut with pliers while stabilizing the coupling with an adjustable wrench.

Replacing Kitchen Faucets

19

Kitchen faucets don't last forever: in styling or in function. When it's time for you to say goodbye to yours, take comfort in knowing that if you choose one that's the same configuration, the project is quite simple.

MOST MODERN KITCHEN SINK FAUCETS ARE DECK MOUNTED, which means the bulk of the faucet sits on top of the back rim of the sink or counter. Typically, these faucets attach to the sink or counter and to their hot and cold water supplies through three holes. A fourth hole may hold a kitchen sprayer. Standard kitchen sinks (or pre-drilled counters) have three or four holes spaced 4" apart. It's best to look for a new faucet that uses the same number of holes as your current model, although any old holes that aren't used may be covered with a cap or a stand-alone accessory, like a liquid soap dispenser, that doesn't require additional plumbing work (there are several plumbed options, too, such as a water filter spout and a dishwasher air gap).

KITCHEN SINK FAUCETS 101

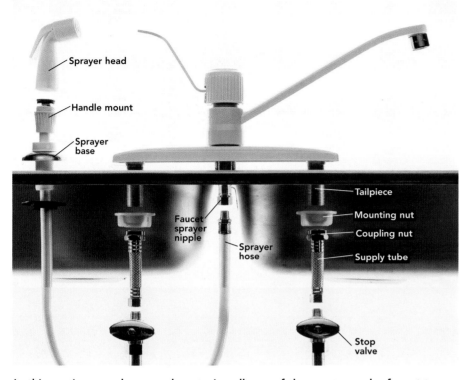

Sprayer head
Handle mount
Sprayer base
Faucet sprayer nipple
Sprayer hose
Tailpiece
Mounting nut
Coupling nut
Supply tube
Stop valve

In this section, we show you how to install one of the most popular faucet types for home use: a *single-lever kitchen sink faucet* with *hose sprayer*, configured for a four-hole sink with standard 4-inch spacing between the holes. If the faucet you want to install isn't quite the same type as this, keep reading anyway. The basic installation requirements are the same: the *faucet body* must be secured firmly to the sink or counter, and the *hot and cold supply tubes* must be connected to the *hot and cold water supplies.*

TOOLS & SUPPLIES YOU'LL NEED

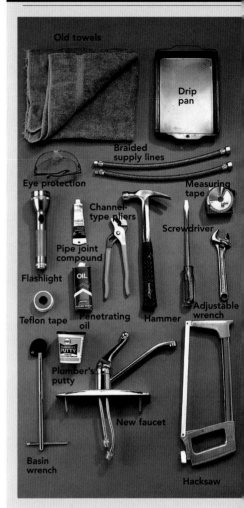

Old towels
Drip pan
Braided supply lines
Eye protection
Measuring tape
Channel-type pliers
Pipe joint compound
Screwdriver
Flashlight
Teflon tape
Penetrating oil
Hammer
Adjustable wrench
Plumber's putty
New faucet
Basin wrench
Hacksaw

SKILLS YOU'LL NEED

• Working with tools in tight spots
• Making compression joints

DIFFICULTY LEVEL

SKILLS LEVEL

EASY   MODERATE

Time: 2 to 3 hours for removal and installation plus shopping

TERMS YOU NEED TO KNOW

COMPRESSION FITTING—a way of attaching copper tubes to stop valves.

FLEXIBLE SUPPLY LINES—flexible hoses that are used to attached to the hot and cold stop valves.

PLUMBER'S PUTTY—a soft clay-like material used to seal faucet parts to sink parts.

TEFLON TAPE—a thin, white tape used to lubricate and seal threaded fittings.

PIPE JOINT COMPOUND—a paste that may be used instead of Teflon tape.

DECK-MOUNTED FAUCET—a faucet that mounts on top of a sink or counter, usually in two to four holes spaced 4 inches on center.

HOW TO REMOVE THE OLD FAUCET

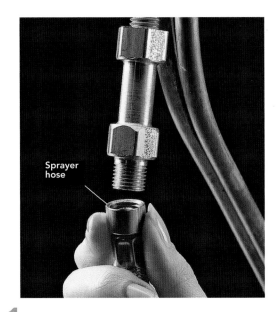

1 To remove the old faucet, start by clearing out the cabinet under the sink and laying down towels. Turn off the hot and cold stop valves and open the faucet to make sure the water is off. Detach the sprayer hose from the faucet sprayer nipple and unscrew the retaining nut that secures the sprayer base to the sink deck. Pull the sprayer hose out through the sink deck opening.

2 Spray the mounting nuts that hold the faucet or faucet handles (on the underside of the sink deck) with penetrating oil for easier removal. Let the oil soak in for a few minutes.

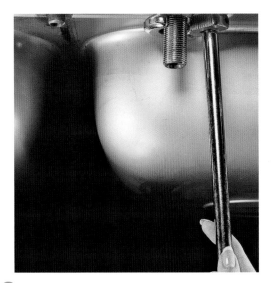

3 Unhook the supply tubes at the stop valves. Don't reuse old chrome supply tubes. If the stops are missing or unworkable, replace them. Then, remove the coupling nuts and the mounting nuts on the tailpieces of the faucet with a basin wrench or channel-type pliers.

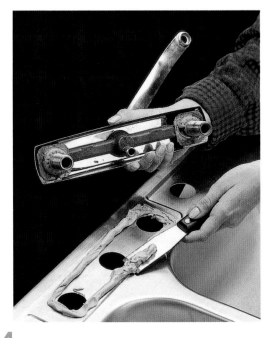

4 Pull the faucet body from the sink. Remove the sprayer base, if you wish to replace this. Scrape off old putty or caulk with a putty knife and clean off the sink with a scouring pad and an acidic scouring cleaner like Barkeeper's Friend.

TIP: Scour stainless steel with a back and forth motion to avoid leaving unsightly circular markings.

HOW TO INSTALL A KITCHEN FAUCET

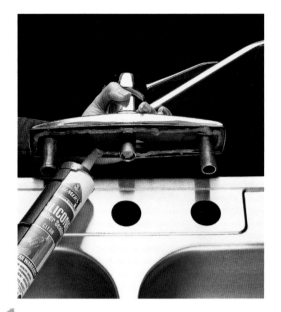

1   Apply a thick bead of silicone caulk to the underside of the faucet base then insert the tail-pieces of the faucet through the appropriate holes in the sink deck. Press down lightly on the faucet to set it in the caulk.

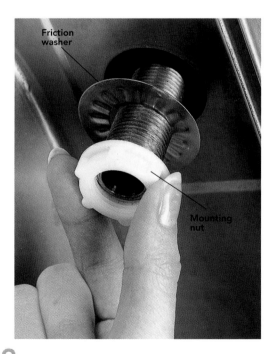

Friction washer

Mounting nut

2   Slip a friction washer onto each tailpiece and then hand-tighten a mounting nut. Tighten the mounting nut with channel-type pliers or a basin wrench. Wipe up any silicone squeeze-out on the sink deck with a wet rag before it sets up.

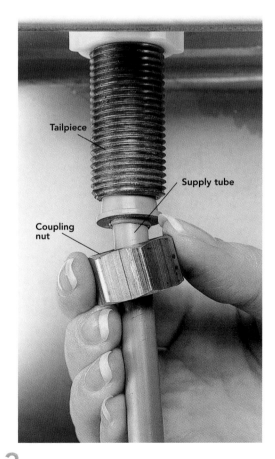

Tailpiece

Supply tube

Coupling nut

3   Connect supply tubes to the faucet tail-pieces—make sure the tubes you buy are long enough to reach the stop valves and that the coupling nuts will fit the tubes and tailpieces.

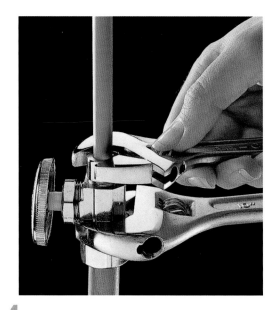

4 Attach the supply tubes to the shutoff valves, using compression fittings. Make sure you connect the hot supply to the hot stop valve. Hand-tighten the nuts, then use an adjustable wrench to tighten them an additional quarter turn. It's a good idea to hold the shutoff valve with another wrench to stabilize it while you tighten the nut. It's also a good idea to wrap some Teflon tape around the threads of the shutoff body.

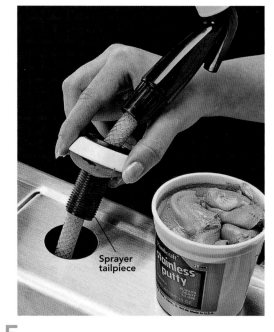

Sprayer tailpiece

5 Apply a ¼" bead of plumber's putty or silicone caulk to the underside of the sprayer base. With the base threaded onto the sprayer hose, insert the tailpiece of the sprayer through the opening in the sink deck.

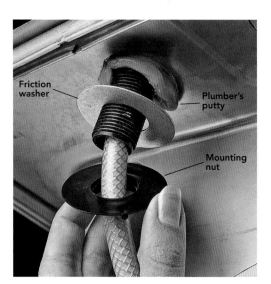

Friction washer

Plumber's putty

Mounting nut

6 From beneath, slip the friction washer over the sprayer tailpiece and then screw the mounting nut onto the tailpiece. Tighten with channel-type pliers or a basin wrench. Wipe any excess putty or caulk on the sink deck from around the base.

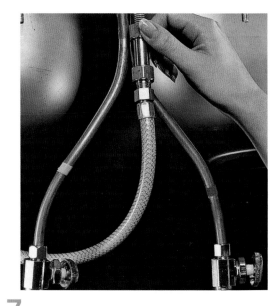

7 Screw the sprayer hose onto the hose nipple on the bottom of the faucet. Hand-tighten and then give the nut one quarter turn with pliers or a basin wrench. Turn on the water supply at the shutoff, remove the aerator and flush debris from the faucet.

VARIATION: INSTALLING A KITCHEN FAUCET WITH PREATTACHED COPPER SUPPLY TUBES

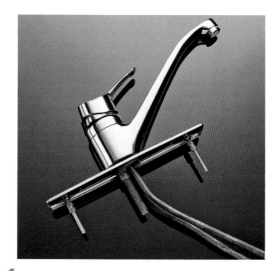

1 Some faucets come with the copper supply tubes preattached to the faucet body. This minimizes the number of connections so you can hook the new faucet directly to the shutoff valves. To install a single-handle lever-type faucet with preattached supply tubes, start by caulking the faucet base and setting it on the deck, as in step 1, on page 123. The copper supply tubes and the sprayer nipple should go through the center hole and then mounting bolts on each side should go through the two outside holes.

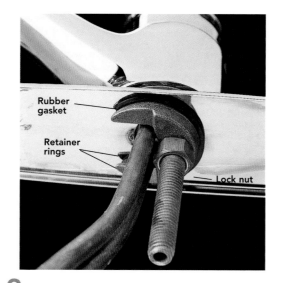

2 Secure the faucet to the sink deck by placing a rubber gasket between the retainer rings and the underside of the countertop. Orient the cutout in the retainer to fit around the supply tubes. Thread a lock nut onto the threaded sprayer nipple and hand-tighten up to the retainer.

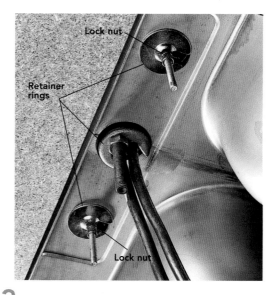

3 Attach retainer rings and washers to the two mounting bolts as well and hand-tighten the mounting nuts. Tighten all nuts with pliers or a basin wrench.

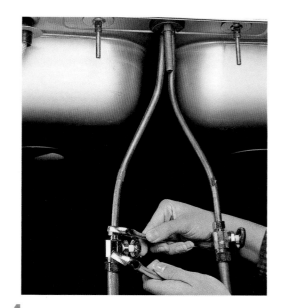

4 Bend the copper faucet tubes so they are in straight up-and-down positions as they meet the stop valves. You may need to trim them with a tubing cutter. Connect the tubes to the stop valves with compression nuts and rings (attach the hot supply tube to the hot supply pipe). Install the sprayer as shown on the previous page. Turn on the water at the shutoffs and test the faucet.

Replacing Pop-up Stoppers

20

A bum pop-up stopper may require complete regime change. Not just the stopper, but the tube and lever apparatus under it may need to be replaced.

POP-UP STOPPERS ARE THOSE CHROME-PLATED, LONG-LEGGED PLUGS IN BATH-ROOM SINKS that are opened and closed with a knob behind the spout. The stopper itself is just the glory guy for a behind-the-scenes assembly that makes sure the stopper sits and stands on cue. New faucets come with their own pop-up stopper assemblies, assuming they use one, but you may also purchase one by itself. This will include everything from the stopper to the pipe that drops into the trap (the trap is that drooping piece of drainpipe under your sink). If you choose to buy a pop-up stopper assembly, we recommend one that's heavy brass under the chrome finish. This will hold up better to time and abuse than a plastic or light-gauge metal model.

POP-UP STOPPERS 101

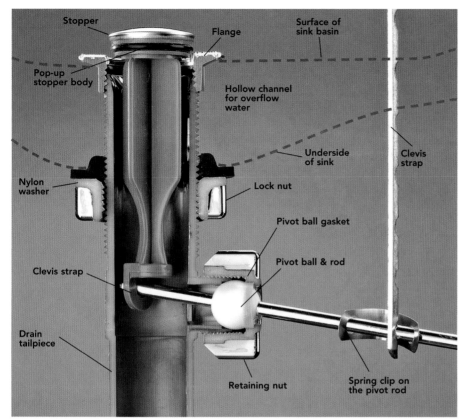

Stopper
Flange
Surface of sink basin
Pop-up stopper body
Hollow channel for overflow water
Nylon washer
Underside of sink
Clevis strap
Lock nut
Pivot ball gasket
Clevis strap
Pivot ball & rod
Drain tailpiece
Retaining nut
Spring clip on the pivot rod

Pop up stoppers keep objects from falling down the drain, and they make filling and draining the sink easy. When you pull up on the *lift rod*, the *clevis strap* is raised, which raises the *pivot rod*, which seesaws on the *pivot ball* and pulls the *pop-up stopper* down against the *flange.* This blocks water through the sink drain, but water may still overflow into the *overflow channel*, and get into the stopper body and down the drain through *overflow ports* in the pop-up body, which is a nice feature if you leave the water running in a plugged basin by mistake.

TERMS YOU NEED TO KNOW

PLUMBER'S PUTTY—a soft clay-like material used to seal metal parts to the sink.

TEFLON TAPE—a thin, white tape used to lubricate and seal threaded fittings.

PIPE JOINT COMPOUND—a paste that may be used instead of Teflon tape.

POP-UP WASTE—another term for a pop-up assembly.

TAILPIECE—takes the waste from the pop-up stopper body to the J-bend.

J-BEND—a J-shaped bend of drainpipe below the sink. It's the part of the trap that's always full of water to keep sewer gases from rising into the house.

TOOLS & SUPPLIES YOU'LL NEED

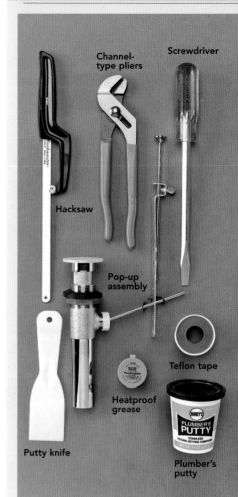

Channel-type pliers
Screwdriver
Hacksaw
Pop-up assembly
Teflon tape
Heatproof grease
Putty knife
Plumber's putty

SKILLS YOU'LL NEED

- Making slip joints
- Handling small parts
- Cutting metal with a hacksaw

DIFFICULTY LEVEL

SKILLS LEVEL

EASY   MODERATE

Time: 1 to 2 hours plus shopping

HOW TO REPLACE A POP-UP STOPPER

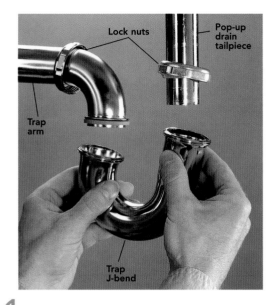

1 Put a basin under the trap to catch water. Loosen the nuts at the outlet and inlet to the trap J-bend by hand or with channel-type pliers and remove the bend. The trap will slide off the pop-up body tailpiece when the nuts are loose. Keep track of washers and nuts and their up/down orientation by leaving them on the tubes.

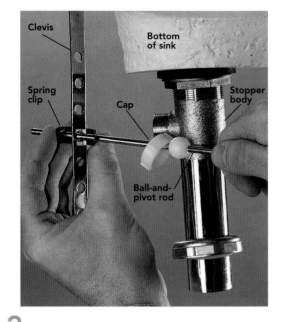

2 Unscrew the cap holding the ball-and-pivot rod in the pop-up body and withdraw the ball. Compress the spring clip on the clevis and withdraw the pivot rod from the clevis.

3 Remove the pop-up stopper. Then, from below, remove the lock nut on the stopper body. If needed, keep the flange from turning by inserting a large screwdriver in the drain from the top. Thrust the stopper body up through the hole to free the flange from the basin, and then remove the flange and the stopper body.

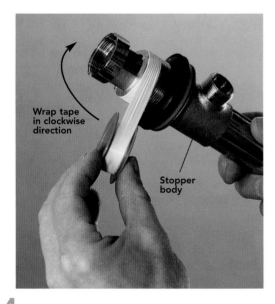

4 Clean the drain opening above and below, and then thread the locknut all the way down the new pop-up body followed by the flat washer and the rubber gasket (beveled side up). Wrap three layers of Teflon tape clockwise onto the top of the threaded body. Make a ½"-dia. snake from plumber's putty, form it into a ring and stick the ring underneath the drain flange.

Plumber's putty

5 From below, face the pivot rod opening directly back toward the middle of the faucet and pull the body straight down to seat the flange. Thread the locknut/washer assembly up under the sink, then fully tighten the locknut with channel-type pliers. Do not twist the flange in the process, as this can break the putty seal. Clean off the squeezeout of plumber's putty from around the flange.

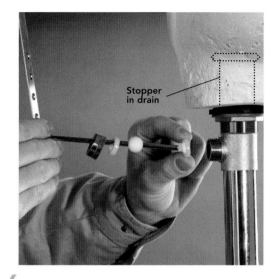

Stopper in drain

6 Drop the pop-up stopper into the drain hole so the hole at the bottom of its post is closest to the back of the sink. Put the beveled nylon washer into the opening in the back of the pop-up body with the bevel facing back.

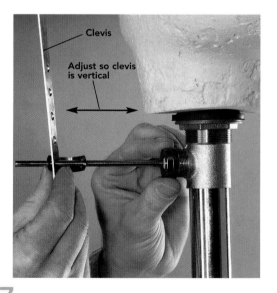

Clevis

Adjust so clevis is vertical

7 Put the cap behind the ball on the pivot rod as shown. Sandwich a hole in the clevis with the spring clip and thread the long end of the pivot rod through the clip and clevis. Put the ball end of the pivot rod into the pop-up body opening and into the hole in the the stopper stem. Screw the cap on to the pop-up body over the ball.

Clevis screw

8 Loosen the clevis screw holding the clevis to the lift rod. Push the pivot rod all the way down (which fully opens the pop-up stopper). With the lift rod also all the way down, tighten the clevis screw to the rod. If the clevis runs into the top of the trap, cut it short with your hacksaw or tin snips. Reassemble the J-bend trap.

21

Replacing Toilets

Replacing a toilet is simple, and the latest generation of 1.6-gallon water-saving toilets has overcome the performance problems of earlier models.

YOU CAN REPLACE A POORLY FUNCTIONING TOILET WITH A HIGH-EFFICIENCY, HIGH-QUALITY NEW TOILET FOR UNDER TWO HUNDRED AND FIFTY DOLLARS, but don't, as Ben Franklin would say, be penny wise and pound foolish. All toilets made since 1996 have been required to use 1.6 gallons or less per flush, which has been a huge challenge for the industry. Today, the most evolved 1.6-gallon toilets have wide passages behind the bowl and wide (three-inch) flush valve openings—features that facilitate short, powerful flushes. This means fewer second flushes and fewer clogged toilets. These problems were common complaints of the first generation of 1.6-gallon toilets and continue to beleaguer inferior models today. See what toilets are available at your local home center in your price range, then go online and see what other consumers' experiences with those models have been. New toilets often go through a "de-bugging" stage when problems with leaks and malfunctioning parts are more common. Your criteria should include ease of installation, good flush performance, and reliability. With a little research, you should be able to purchase and install a high-functioning economical gravity-flush toilet that will serve you well for years to come.

TOILETS 101

Round front

Floor bolt (cap on)

Rough-in distance 10", 12" or 14" (12" most common)

Buy a toilet that will fit the space. Measure the distance from the floor bolts back to the wall (if your old toilet has two pairs of bolts, go by the rear pair). This is your *rough-in distance* and will be either 10" or approximately 12". Make note of the *bowl shape,* round or oval (long). Oval bowls (also called elongated bowls) are a few inches longer for greater comfort, but may be too big for your space. The safest bet is to buy a replacement with the same bowl shape.

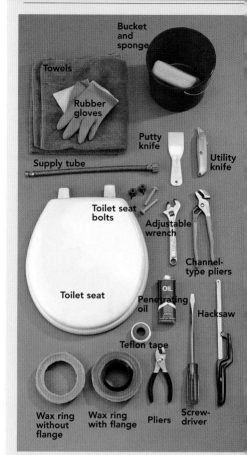
SKILLS YOU'LL NEED

• Making compression joints

• Lifting 50 pounds

• Hand tool usage

TERMS YOU NEED TO KNOW

CLOSET FLANGE—the metal or plastic slotted ring on the floor around the drain opening to which the toilet is bolted.

CLOSET ELBOW—the drain elbow the closet flange attaches to.

WAX RING—a compressible ring that forms a seal between the toilet and the closet flange; it fits either a 3-inch or 4-inch closet elbow.

CLOSET BOLTS—the pair of bolts that attach the toilet to the flange.

DIFFICULTY LEVEL

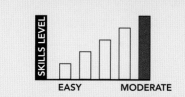

SKILLS LEVEL

EASY   MODERATE

Time: Allow about 1 hour for this project

HOW TO REPLACE A TOILET

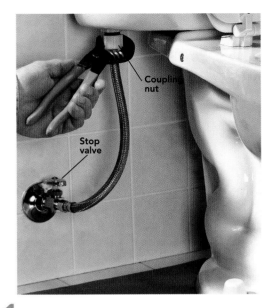

1 Remove the old toilet. First, turn off the water at the stop valve (see page 136 if you have trouble). Flush the toilet holding the handle down for a long flush, and sponge out the tank. Unthread the coupling nut for the water supply below the tank using channel-type pliers if needed. **TIP:** If you have a wet vac, use this here and in step three to clear any remaining water out of the tank and bowl.

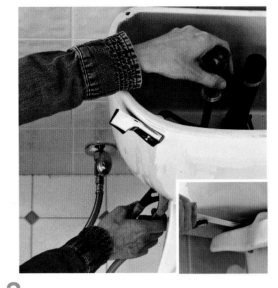

2 Grip each tank bolt nut with a box wrench or pliers and loosen it as you stabilize each tank bolt from inside the tank with a large slotted screwdriver. If the nuts are stuck, apply penetrating oil to the nut and let it sit before trying to remove them again. You may also cut the tank bolts between the tank and the bowl with an open-ended hacksaw (inset). Remove and discard the tank.

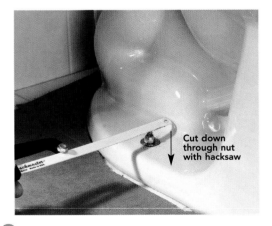

Cut down through nut with hacksaw

3 Remove the nuts that hold the bowl to the floor. First, pry off the bolt covers with a screwdriver. Use a socket wrench, locking pliers, or your channel-type pliers to loosen the nuts on the tank bolts. Apply penetrating oil and let it sit if the nuts are stuck, then take them off. As a last resort, cut the bolts off with a hacksaw by first cutting down through one side of the nut. Tilt the toilet bowl over and remove it.

TECHNIQUE TIP

Removing an old wax ring is one of the more disgusting jobs you'll encounter in the plumbing universe (the one you see here is actually in relatively good condition). Work a stiff putty knife underneath the plastic flange of the ring (if you can) and start scraping. In many cases the wax ring will come off in chunks. Discard each chunk right away—they stick to everything. If you're left with a lot of residue, scrub with mineral spirits. Once clean, stuff a rag in a bag in the drain opening to block sewer gas.

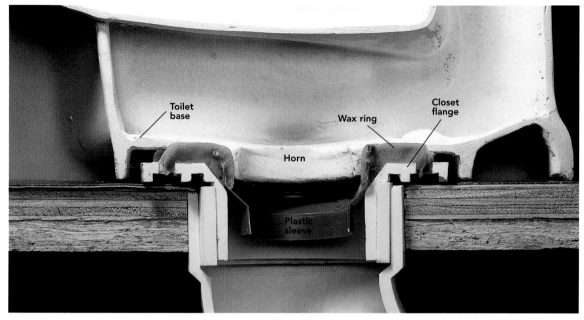

A cross-section of the connection between the toilet stool and the drain reveals that it really is only a ring of wax that makes the difference between a pleasant water closet and something that smells like an open sewer.

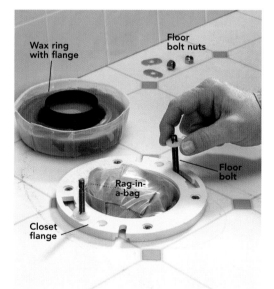

4 Remove the rag-in-a-bag from the drain opening and put new all-brass toilet bolts into the slots on the closet flange at 3 and 9 o-clock and rotate each ¼ turn so the elongated heads cannot be withdrawn. Put the plastic keepers or extra washers and nuts on the bolts to secure them to the flange. Unwrap the wax ring and position it over the flange so it looks like the one in the cross section photo at the top of this page.

5 Lower the new toilet down over the wax ring so the bolts go through the holes on the bottom of the stool (this can be tricky—be patient and get help). Press down on the toilet to seat it in the wax ring and check for level. If the bowl is not quite level, you can shim the low side with a few pennies. Thread washers and nuts onto the floor bolts and tighten them a little at a time, alternating. Do not overtighten. Cut the bolts off above the nuts with a hacksaw and add the caps. Lay a bead of tub and tile caulk around the base of the toilet, but leave the back open to let water escape so you'll know if there's ever a leak.

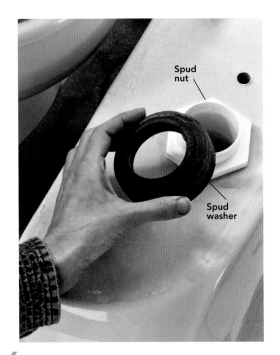

6 Attach the toilet tank. Some tanks come with a flush valve and a fill valve preinstalled, but if yours does not, insert the flush valve through the tank opening and tighten a spud nut over the threaded end of the valve. Place a foam spud washer on top of the spud nut.

7 If necessary, adjust the fill valve as noted in the directions (also see pages 166 to 169).

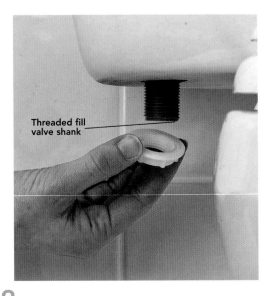

8 Position the valve in the tank. Push down on the valve shank (not the top) while hand-tightening the locknut onto the threaded valve shank (thread the nut on the exterior side of tank). Hand-tighten only.

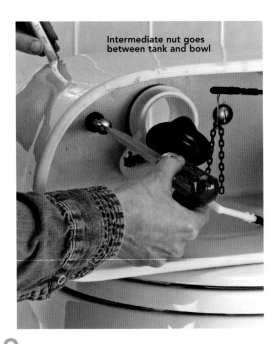

9 With the tank lying on its back, thread a rubber washer onto each tank bolt and insert it into the bolt holes from inside the tank. Then, thread a brass washer and hex nut onto the tank bolts from below and tighten them to a quarter turn past hand tight. Do not overtighten.

10 Position the tank on the bowl, spud washer on opening, bolts through bolt holes. Put a rubber washer followed by a brass washer and a wing nut on each bolt and tighten these up evenly.

11 You may stabilize the bolts with a large slotted screwdriver from inside the tank, but tighten the nuts, not the bolts. You may press down a little on a side, the front, or the rear of the tank to level it as you tighten the nuts by hand. Do not overtighten and crack the tank. The tank should be level and stable when you're done.

12 Hook up the water supply by connecting the supply tube to the threaded fill valve with the coupling nut provided. Turn on the water and test for leaks.

13 Attach the toilet seat by threading the plastic or brass bolts provided with the seat through the openings on the back of the rim and attaching nuts.

Flooring

FLOORING PLAYS A VITAL ROLE IN THE LOOK AND FEEL OF YOUR HOME. BECAUSE IT IS ONE OF THE LARGEST ELEMENTS IN A ROOM, A FLOOR CREATES INSTANT IMPACT. IT'S IMPORTANT TO ADDRESS BOTH THE FUNCTION AND BEAUTY OF THE FLOORING IN YOUR HOME. AND, OF COURSE, IT'S IMPORTANT TO MAINTAIN THE FLOORS IN YOUR HOME TO GET THE MOST OUT OF THEM.

This section of the book will help you better understand the basic types of flooring so you can approach repairs and installations with confidence. It will walk you, step by step, through 16 very common flooring projects. Even if you have no previous experience with flooring, you'll find everything you need right here to make your project a success.

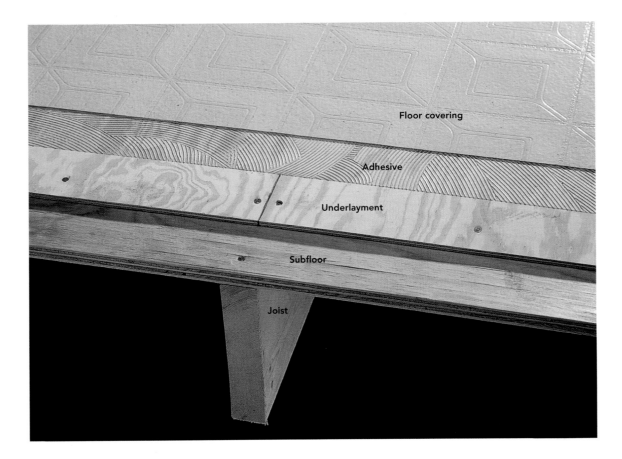

Floor covering

Adhesive

Underlayment

Subfloor

Joist

ANATOMY OF A FLOOR

When most of us think of a floor we envision the top layer: in effect, the decorative covering—hardwood, ceramic tile, laminate, or carpet. The "real" floor is hidden underneath.

Your floor is made of a sturdy plywood or composite panel subfloor that spans supportive floor joists. The subfloor may be large sheets or planks (and the planks may be arranged in a staggered or diagonal fashion). The joists sit on sills along the foundation and are often supported at a midpoint by a steel girder or wood beam.

An elevated framed floor, like the one shown above, is supported by beams that run perpendicular to the joists. In most cases, the joists are tied together with bridging for extra stability (see photo next page, lower right).

Depending on the type of flooring used, the subfloor may be covered with an additional layer of underlayment, such as a cement board. The top layer of flooring is installed on the underlayment or subfloor and may rest on some type of cushioning layer. Of course, there are always custom options, such as soundproofing or heating, that may be layered into your floor plan. It's important to know what is under your floor covering and how your floor is supported before starting any repairs on that floor.

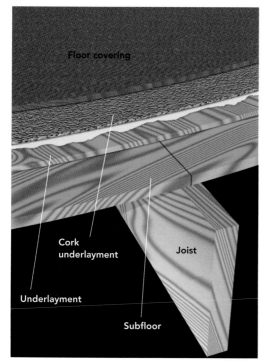

Soundproofed floors have an extra layer to dampen noise. When patching a damaged area of your floor, replace the floor covering on top of the sound barrier material. The sound barrier is not altered.

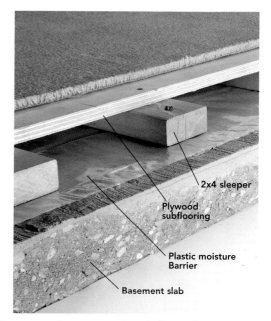

Basement floors are uniquely layered to compensate for the hard concrete base. When patching your damaged floor, only remove the floor covering on top of the plywood subfloor.

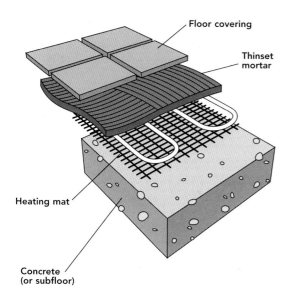

Radiant floor heating systems use hot water coils or electricty. Even concrete floors without floor covering may be heated.

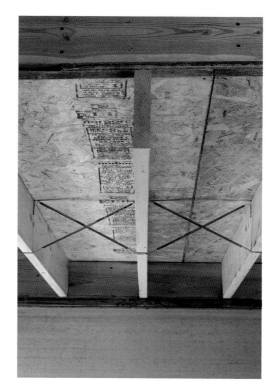

The bridging between joists for extra stability could be wood or metal.

Before You Begin: Choosing Flooring

Today's homeowner is faced with an extensive range of flooring choices. Selecting the right floor can almost be harder than installing it.

If installing new floors, it is fun to choose the colors, patterns, and other design qualities of the floor you desire. But there are some other qualities to consider, including: cost, comfort, ease of maintenance, and durability.

The varying characteristics of the floors discussed here will help you decide which floor is best for your space. For example, hard flooring—such as ceramic tiles or concrete—is tough, attractive, and great for high-traffic areas. Soft floors, like carpet, are still popular in both bedrooms and living areas because they offer comfort, warmth, and a feeling of luxury.

If your floors are already installed—often homes have four or more types of flooring—the following discussion will help you recognize their strong points. Knowing what your floor can handle helps with maintenance, decorating, and cleaning.

Parquet tile floors offer the beauty and feel of wood in the block shape of tiles. Decorative patterns make these floors appear to be high end when they are actually quite affordable. All parquet tiles feature tongue-and-groove edges that snap together. You can find parquet tiles with self-adhesive backs, but dry-back tiles to which you apply standard flooring adhesive stay put longer.

Concrete floors are typically found in basements and garages for obvious reasons. They are tough and can withstand high traffic, heavy equipment, messy spills (including sitting water), scratches, and scuffs. But concrete is increasingly popular for interior spaces, especially when finished with paint or decorative acid stains.

Laminate floors are available in planks or squares. They snap together with tongue-and-groove joints and then "float" on top of the floor, meaning they are not fastened directly to the subfloor or underlayment. A laminate floor consists of a very durable surface-wear layer; a photographic print layer, which allows it to replicate the appearance of other surfaces; and a solid core.

Ceramic tile floors look spectacular, and they are durable. At the same time, they tend to be cold, they conduct sound, and they are expensive. Upon installation, they are evenly spaced and then the joints are filled with grout. These joints are then sealed.

Manufactured wood flooring materials include: fiberboard surfaced with a synthetic laminate layer (right), plywood topped with a thin hardwood veneer (center), and parquet tile made of wood strips (left). Wood floors come in planks or strips. The planks fit together with tongue-and-groove joints or square edges and, depending on manufacturer recommendations, they float on top of the subfloor or are secured in place with nails, staples, and/or glue.

Resilient floors include vinyl, linoleum, cork, and rubber. They are comfortable underfoot and easy to clean. They are impervious to water—except at the seams or where torn. Depending upon the material, resilient flooring comes in either large sheets, which need to be cut to size, or easy-to-install tiles. Resilient floors are often cost effective and are available in a staggering number of patterns and colors. They are usually thin, which means the subfloor must be level.

Carpet is the most popular choice for living rooms and bedrooms because it produces a warm, comfortable environment. It is available in conventional, cushion-back, or tile forms. Wall-to-wall carpet is laid with fittings, such as tackless strips and padding. Cushion-backed carpet is glued directly to the subfloor.

Before You Begin:
Evaluating Floors

Floor coverings wear out faster than other interior surfaces because they get more wear and tear. Surface damage can affect more than just appearance. Scratches in resilient flooring and cracks in grouted tile joints allow moisture to wear away at adhesive, eventually pushing up the floor covering or tile. Hardwood floors lose their finish and become discolored. And loose floorboards squeak. If that problem appears to be minor now, the question is: Clean, repair, or replace?

Before answering that question, you must thoroughly inspect your entire floor. Look for stains, tears, rips, cracks, buckles, bubbles, or damp spots. Specific concerns for each type of flooring material are listed in this section. Once the problem is classified, you may move on to the repair project specific to the problem.

Concrete floors are hard and durable, but still require care. If unsealed, concrete is vulnerable to all kinds of stains. Oil and grease are particularly troublesome. Cracks are also common.

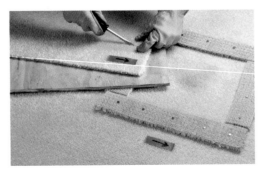

Look for tears, stains, or excessive wear in carpet. Cleaning the spots should always be the first step, and there are carpet-cleaning products for almost every possible stain. If this doesn't do the trick, these damaged areas may be fixed with a patch (as shown in photo).

A severely damaged section of tile or plank may be completely removed (as is being done in photo) and replaced. Normal wear and tear is probably the result of years of accumulated dirt from foot traffic. Unfortunately, this is unavoidable. Often touch-up sticks to repair scratches are available from manufacturers.

Moisture can cause wood floors to swell. Swollen planks should be removed so you can inspect the subfloor. Allowing the subfloor to dry out allows you to then replace the damaged boards with new, tight-fitting planks.

Though quite durable, parquet tiles are still vulnerable to stains, especially from heavy spills or water that sits on the floor for some time. It is important to clean up spills immediately. Soak a cloth in mineral spirits for troublesome stains.

Even durable ceramic tiles develop signs of wear. To evaluate ceramic tiles, check for loose, cracked, or dirty grout joints. Remove failed grout and regrout tile joints.

A common problem for resilient sheet floors is air bubbles. For resilient tiles (inset), the most common problem is loose seams. Tiles with small curls may be reattached, but tiles with dirt under them must be completely removed and replaced.

Before You Begin: Cleaning Floors

Immediately clean spills with a dry cloth. Avoid rubbing the spill into the floor. Once the spill is soaked up, use a damp cloth to blot the remaining residue on the floor. Rinse your cloth often and thoroughly wring it out before using it again. Use a dry, clean cloth to dry the area when you are done. If it is still sticky, allow the area to dry and then use a damp mop.

As a last resort, stubborn sticky wood floors need to be wet mopped. Only wet mop the floor if the finish is in good condition. A sponge mop moistened with a mixture of water and a mild wood floor cleaner or a neutral pH soap or detergent (1 gal.: ½ cup cleaner) is all that is required. The mop should just barely be damp at any given time. Excess water can seriously damage wood floors. After cleaning, use a towel to thoroughly dry the floor.

If a liquid spill fades your hardwood floor, lightly sand the damaged area and apply new finish. Do not use a wax finish over a surface finish.

WHAT IF . . . ?

If you have laminate flooring, follow the cleaning recommendations provided by the manufacturer. Many manufacturers caution against cleaning with water or any cleaner that's mixed with water.

Use nonmarking floor protectors on your furniture's "feet." Sets often include nails or screws to attach the feet. There are also special protectors for wheels. Be sure to buy the correct size and style for your furniture.

HERE'S HOW

Make sure you know what sort of finish (wax or urethane) is on your wood floor, and use products specifically for your floor surface. Look for products labeled "for wood floor cleaning," for example. Avoid ammonia products or soaps with oil; use pH-balanced cleaners for routine cleaning.

CLEANING CARPET

Carpet cleaning machines can be rented by the hour or by the day. To deep clean your carpet push the machine forward over a 3-ft. square area, releasing the detergent and rotating the brush. At this time hot water is often used, causing steam. When you pull back, cold water is used as a rinse. Some machines allow you to manually adjust the water temperature. Always be sure to rinse thoroughly. Slowly go over the same area a couple of times to work the cleaner into the carpet. Repeat this process until the entire carpet is cleaned. Allow the carpet to dry. Vacuum.

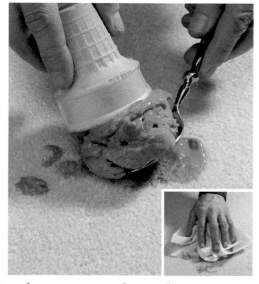

Use a large spoon to pick up spills. Spoons capture liquids well without damaging fibers. Scoop toward the center of the stain to avoid spreading. Do not rub stains—blot them (see inset). Apply cleaning solution to a cloth or paper towel, then blot the stain, working from the outside toward the center to avoid spreading the stain.

Raise crushed fibers by first dampening the area with water (or allow a small ice cube to melt on each dent overnight). Work up the crushed fibers with your hand (or a spoon, if they are stubborn). A hair dryer on medium temperature not only helps dry the spots while you raise the fibers, but the heat helps raise the fibers. Sometimes simply holding a steam iron above the dent will pop up the crushed carpet.

CLEANING CERAMIC TILE

Dry mop daily to gently remove particles that could scratch your tile.

Use pH-balanced cleaners or soapless detergents for bi-weekly mopping. Having a bucket with a wringer helps to ensure you do not oversaturate the mop. Alternatively, use a sponge mop with an attachment to wring out sponge. Always dry mop or vacuum first. If you prefer not to use commercial cleaning products, use a steam cleaner (be sure not to buy a deep cleaner, which often incorporates shampoo).

If water doesn't bead on tiles or on grout joints during regular cleaning, it's time to apply another coat of sealer. For instructions on grouting and sealing ceramic tile joints, see pages 274 to 277.

For heavy stains on natural stone tile, try a manufacturer poultice specifically for porous stone materials. Cover the stain with the poultice, then tape plastic over it. Let the poulitice set, according to the manufacturer's instructions, then remove it.

HERE'S HOW

Add glass cleaner to the water in your cleaning bucket to prevent streaks from showing up once the floor is dry. If the floor has a dull finish, it may be time to reseal the floor. If water absorbs into the grout lines, the grout joints need to be resealed. It is still necessary to clean the floor before sealing.

Vacuum grout joints with a bare-floor attachment once a week. Use a soft-bristle broom or handheld broom and dustpan to pick up debris that the vacuum missed. If dirt or sand is a regular problem, try to find out how it is tracked in. Place rugs or mats at those entryways. Be sure to regularly shake out the rugs.

Remove tough stains with mineral spirits or household bleach. Wet a rag with the solution, and place it over the stain. Lay a plastic bag over the rag to slow evaporation. Wait 1 to 2 hours, then wipe up the stain. Always test solvents in an inconspicuous area before using them elsewhere on the floor. Bleach may strip the protective finish off the floor, leaving it dull.

Occasionally wet mop. Regular dry mopping and vacuuming is necessary, but it doesn't remove sticky spots. Sometimes all that is necessary is a little warm water. Also be sure to inspect seams in tile and the perimeter of full-spread sheet flooring. Use a slightly damp cloth to pick up dirt or dust stuck in seams or corners—especially around thresholds, where material tends to settle after sweeping.

If your floor is dull even after you clean it, you should polish. Put manufacturer polish into a clean bucket, dip a cloth into it, and wring about half the polish out of the cloth. Working in a 3- to 4-ft. square, wipe the cloth over the floor in straight lines. Apply 2 to 3 coats; let the polish dry for at least 30 minutes between coats and about an hour (minimum) when you're done.

On vinyl and laminate, you can remove tough spots like shoe polish or tar with nail polish remover containing acetone. When the spot is gone, wipe the area with a clean, damp cloth.

Repairing Splinters & Gouges

1

Ouch! If a floorboard begins to splinter, it's a good idea to repair it before the splinter completely dislodges and disappears—or worse, completely dislodges into someone's bare foot.

IT IS COMMON FOR SPLINTERS TO APPEAR IN FLOORS THAT ARE DRIED OUT and brittle. When hardwood floors are damaged by high heels or pushed chair legs, a portion of the grain may dislodge; because the grain of wood runs only in one direction, it splinters rather than simply creating a hole. Floorboards that have splinters or gouges don't necessarily have to be replaced; a splinter can be reattached with some glue and a hole can be filled with some wood putty.

SPLINTERS & GOUGES 101

Fiberboard

Plywood

Parquet

Wood flooring is susceptible to splintering and gouges. How you repair the damage depends on whether the planks are laminated or solid wood.

TERMS YOU NEED TO KNOW

RECONDITIONING FLOORS—Lightly sanding only the finish of the floor (to dull the surface) and then reapplying a new coat of finish.

FEATHER SAND—Sanding with lighter and lighter strokes as you move away from a more heavily sanded area. This creates a smooth transition between sanded and non-sanded areas.

TOOLS & SUPPLIES YOU NEED

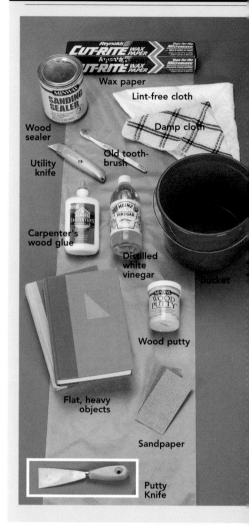

Wax paper

Lint-free cloth

Wood sealer

Damp cloth

Utility knife

Old tooth-brush

Carpenter's wood glue

Distilled white vinegar

Bucket

Wood putty

Flat, heavy objects

Sandpaper

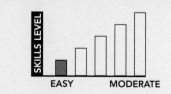

Putty Knife

SKILLS YOU NEED

- Gluing
- Using a putty knife
- Sanding
- Applying a top coat (polyurethane and wax)

DIFFICULTY LEVEL

SKILLS LEVEL

EASY   MODERATE

This project can be completed in less than an hour (not including drying time).

HOW TO GLUE DOWN A SPLINTER

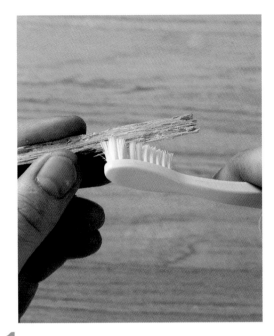

1 If you still have the splintered piece of wood, but it has been entirely dislodged from the floor, it's a good bet that the hollowed space left by the splinter has collected a lot of dirt and grime. Combine a 1:3 mixture of distilled white vinegar and water in a bucket. Dip an old toothbrush into the solution and use it to clean out the hole left in the floor. While you're at it, wipe down the splinter with the solution, too. Allow the floor and splinter to thoroughly dry.

2 If the splinter is large, apply wood glue to the hole and splinter. Use a cotton swab or toothpick to apply small amounts of wood glue under smaller splinters. Soak the cotton swab in glue; you don't want cotton swab fuzz sticking out of your floor once the glue dries.

3 Press the splinter back into place. To clean up the excess glue, use a slightly damp, lint-free cloth. Do not oversoak the cloth with water.

4 Allow the adhesive to dry. Cover the patch with wax paper and a couple of books. Let the adhesive dry overnight.

1 Repair small holes with wood putty. Use putty that matches the floor color. Force the compound into the hole with a putty knife. Continue to press the putty in this fashion until the depression in the floor is filled. Scrape excess compound from the area. Use a damp, lint-free cloth while the putty is still wet to smooth the top level with the surrounding floor. Allow to dry.

2 Sand the area with fine (100- to 120-grit) sandpaper. Sand with the wood grain so the splintered area is flush with the surrounding surface. To better hide the repair, feather sand the area. Wipe up dust with a slightly damp cloth.

3 With a clean, lint-free cloth, apply a matching stain (wood sealer or "restorer") to the sanded area. Read the label on the product to make sure it is appropriate for sealing wood floors. Work in the stain until the patched area blends with the rest of the floor. Allow area to completely dry. Apply two coats of finish. Be sure the finish is the same as that which was used on the surrounding floor.

HERE'S HOW

Surface finish (poly or wax)

Penetrant finish

Wax finish

To determine what kind of surface you have, use a coin to lightly scrape the floor in a hidden corner. If flakes appear, you have either a surface finish or a wax coat. If no flakes appear, it's a penetrant. To check for wax, sprinkle water on the floor. If the beads turn white after 10 minutes, it's waxed.

Fixing Squeaky Floors from Below

2

Squeak-elimination tools, such as the Squeak-Ender (shown), tighten the joist to the subfloor and eliminate squeaks. See page 256 for instructions.

LOTS OF HOUSES SQUEAK, SO MOST OF US JUST ACCEPT IT AS A FACT OF LIFE. It doesn't have to be, though. With a little work, you can get rid of those pesky squeaks. The cause of a floor talking back to you is no mystery; it's just the sound of wood rubbing against a nail or another piece of wood. More often than not the squeaking is just caused by the wood expanding due to humidity, contracting due to dryness. Wood is a very porous material. It just does that.

So how do we make it stop? If you have access to the area below the squeaky floor (as is the case if the immediate level below has an unfinished ceiling), please read on. . . .

FLOOR SQUEAKS 101

To pinpoint the source of a squeak, have someone walk around upstairs while you're below the floor (on the lower level). Make a pencil mark on the unfinished ceiling where you hear the offending chirp or squawk. The subfloor may even visually move away from the joists when you hear the squeak. If you don't see any movement, the finished flooring has buckled up away from the subfloor. If this is the case, have the person upstairs place a heavy weight, such as a couch leg or cinder block, on the spot that squeaks. If the squeak is immediately over a joist, use a hammer to tap a wood shim in between the joist and subfloor. Directions to do so are given in this project (starting on the next page).

(starting on the next page)

TERMS YOU NEED TO KNOW

SUBFLOOR—The base layer of wood or plywood that supports the underlayment and surface flooring.

UNDERLAYMENT—The intermediate layer between the surface flooring material and the subfloor. The underlayment for laminate flooring combines a poly-water barrier and a foam cushion sound barrier in a rollout or rigid-plank form.

JOISTS—Supporting beams set parallel from wall to wall to support the subfloor.

SQUEAK-ENDER FLOOR SQUEAK ELIMINATOR—A commercial squeak-elimination tool. It consists of a threaded rod attached to a flat mounting plate and a steel bracket fitted with a squared-off hook on one end.

TOOLS & SUPPLIES YOU NEED

Hammer
Electric drill
Flashlight
Masking tape
Squeak-elimination tool, such as the Squeak-Ender
Folding ruler
Wood glue
#8 drill bit
¾" spade bit
#10 flat-head wood screws
Wrench
Wood shims
Washers
#10 drill bit
Phillips screwdriver

SKILLS YOU NEED

- Drilling
- Hammering
- Wrench and screwdriver work

DIFFICULTY LEVEL

SKILLS LEVEL

EASY   MODERATE

This project can be completed in as little as 10 minutes or as much as 2 hours.

HOW TO FILL GAPS BETWEEN JOISTS & FLOORBOARDS

1 If there is a gap or movement between the subfloor and joist at the squeak location, tap a tapered wood shim into the gap. First smear it with construction adhesive or wood glue. Squirt some glue into the gap, too. Don't overtap; it makes the gap bigger. Wait for the glue to dry. If this doesn't stop the squeak, go to Step 2.

2 To use a Squeak-Ender, or another comparable squeak-elimination tool, insert the head of the hanger bolt into the concave part of the anchor plate. Use a Phillips screwdriver to screw the mounting plate to the underside of the subfloor (four screws are often provided). You want the plate to be touching the nearest joist in the general area of the squeak.

3 Slide the top part of the joist bracket through the threaded hanger rod and the bottom part under the joist.

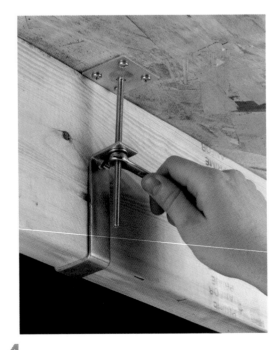

4 Slip the washer and hex nut onto the rod. With a wrench, tighten the nut until the subfloor is pulled snug against the joist. Avoid overtightening.

HOW TO CINCH FLOORING TO JOISTS

1 If you've made it this far, the squeak is not caused by a gap between the subfloor and the joist. It's likely the floorboards have buckled up, creating a gap between the floor and the subfloor. We're going to drill up through the subfloor and pull the flooring down tight against the subfloor with some wood screws. To figure out how long the screws should be, first determine the combined thickness of the floor and subfloor by measuring at existing cutouts in the floor.

2 Drill pilot holes. The length of screw we need is ¼" less than the total depth of the top floor and subfloor combined. Mark that depth with masking tape on a #8 wood drill bit. On a #10 drill bit, mark the depth of the subfloor only. Now, drill some pilot holes around the squeak: 1. Drill through the subfloor with the thicker #10 bit. 2. Drill into the same holes a little deeper with the #8 bit. Make sure you don't drill deeper than the masking tape marks.

WHAT IF . . . ?

If there are no cutouts, determine the thickness by carefully boring a hole up into the subfloor. The hole should be large enough to fit a tape measure into it. Just to be safe, work in an inconspicuous corner of the basement. Use a ¾" spade drill bit to drill up into the subfloor. Stop drilling every so often to see how close to the finish floor you are—you may need a flashlight to see clearly. Stop once you get to the finish floor. Measure. Do not drill all the way through your wood floor above.

To find out the thickness of the top floor, measure the depth of the floor on the first stair down to the basement, if you have one.

HERE'S HOW

The length of screw we need for Step 2 is the same length we marked on the #8 drill bit. The thread thickness, though, is going to be a #10. This way, as the screw is tightened, the hole left in the subfloor by the #10 drill bit will not offer any resistance, but the hole left in the top flooring with the #8 drill bit will be snug and pull the loose board down against the subfloor. To distribute the pressure around the screw, slip each screw through a large fender washer before driving the screws into each pilot hole. This will secure the subfloor to the wood floor and stop the squeak.

Fixing Squeaky Floors from Above

3

It's a little more work to fix squeaks from above the floorboards than from below, but it's a lot easier than you might think.

THE SOUND OF WOOD RUBBING ON WOOD OR AGAINST A NAIL CAN BE infuriating, but fortunately this problem is not too complicated to fix. If the ceiling below the squeaky floor is unfinished, you can go downstairs and actually watch for movement in the subfloor while someone else walks on the floor upstairs. If you can't get to the floor from below, you have to fix the squeak from above. This is done by setting loose boards or surface nailing them down. Alternatively, a squeak-ender designed specifically for above floors may be used.

There are a few key topics discussed in this section. Learn how to:

- Apply lubricants to the floorboards to eliminate subtle squeaks caused by dryness.

- Safely use a hammer to tap loose floorboards into place.

- Carefully drill a small hole through the surface of the floor to surface-nail gaps, and then hide the evidence.

SQUEAK ELIMINATION 101

There are squeak-elimination tools for working above and below the floor. Even if your floor is carpeted, a squeak-elimination tool can drive screws through the subfloor and into the joists for you. The device controls the depth.

Keep in mind, that annoying squeak in your floor is caused by any of four things: 1. two floorboards rubbing together; 2. the subfloor rubbing against the joist below it; 3. the subfloor rubbing against the floorboards above it; 4. a loose nail in any of these places.

TERMS YOU NEED TO KNOW

SUBFLOOR—The base layer of wood or plywood that supports the underlayment and surface flooring.

JOISTS—Supporting beams set parallel from wall to wall to support the subfloor.

TOOLS & SUPPLIES YOU NEED

SKILLS YOU NEED

- Hammering
- Drilling
- Using a putty knife
- Using a nail set

DIFFICULTY LEVEL

This project can be completed in as little as 10 minutes or as much as 2 hours.

HERE'S HOW

Because small squeaks can be caused by dirt between floorboards or by dryness, clean the floor at least once a week and apply lubricants to areas that tend to be extra dry or squeaky.

Oils: graphite, mineral oil, or floor oil. Use powdered or liquid graphite sparingly; it can make a mess. Similarly, a few drops of mineral oil will do the trick, but using too much can stain the surface. Floor oil, applied generously into the joints, soaks into the wood, making it expand. This results in a snug tongue-and-groove fitting. That pesky squeak may just disappear at this stage, at least temporarily.

Powders: graphite and talcum powder. To use talcum powder, dust a generous amount of the powder wherever the floor makes noise. Use a dry, clean cloth to work it into the tongue-and-groove joints, especially near any visible nails. Slightly dampen the cloth with water to wipe away excess powder.

1 Make a "beater" block. If loose nails are the problem, you can tap the floorboards down where you hear the squeak. Wrap a 2 × 4 scrap (length of 1 ft. should do) in a heavy towel or scrap of carpet so that you don't scratch the floor surface. Tack the carpet to the top of the 2 × 4 with nails.

3 Squeaks in hardwood floors caused by floorboards rubbing against each other or against a nail can sometimes be eliminated for a few weeks or months just by adding a hardwood floor lubricant at the point of friction. First remove dirt and debris from between the floorboards, using an old toothbrush. With a clean toothbrush or a clean cloth, apply the lubricant to the floor joints.

2 Place the 2 × 4 at right angles to the squeaky floorboards. Tap the 2 × 4 with a hammer to reseat any loose boards or nails. Start at the perimeter of the squeaky section, moving the 2 × 4 in a rectangular pattern until you get to the center.

HOW TO FASTEN LOOSE BOARDS

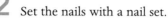

1 As a last resort, reattach buckled floorboards to the subfloor by nailing them down (from above the floorboards) with flooring nails. To reduce the risk of the boards splitting, drill pilot holes slightly smaller than the diameter of the nails. For maximum holding power, drill at opposing angles in a staggered pattern every 4" to 6" along the squeaky boards. The goal is to drill through the surface flooring of the buckled board and into the subfloor; better yet, drill into the subfloor and a joist.

HERE'S HOW

LOCATE JOISTS Not all of the nails can hit a joist, but you get a stronger connection wherever they do. Use a stud finder to find the joists.

COUNTERSINK NAILS Hide the head of the nails beneath the surface of the wood by gently tapping the nails down with a nail set. This is called "countersinking" the nails. Fill nail holes with tinted putty. Use a slightly damp sponge to smooth excess putty.

PROTECT YOUR FLOOR FROM DENTS Before tapping nails into your pre-drilled holes, cut out small squares of cardboard to set around the nailing area. It's a good idea to use a smooth-faced hammer as well.

REMOVE DENTS Some hammer dents can be removed by placing a damp cloth on the spot and applying pressure with a hot iron. This raises the damaged surface back to the common surface.

2 Set the nails with a nail set.

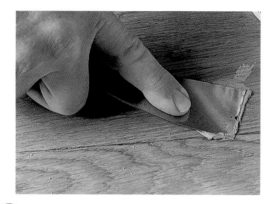

3 Fill nail holes with wood putty, using a putty knife. Force the compound into the hole by pressing the knife blade downward until it lies flat on the floor. Allow the patch to dry completely.

4 Sand the patch flush with the surrounding surface. Use fine-grit sandpaper and sand in the direction of the wood grain. Apply wood restorer to the area (inset) until it blends with the surrounding floor.

Repairing Resilient Flooring

4

Air pockets and curls are unsightly and they only get worse over time. Curls invite debris and moisture to settle under the tile, thus weakening the surrounding tiles; and bubbles continue to swell, destroying the adhesive holding the sheet of flooring in place. These problems must be addressed immediately.

RESILIENT FLOORING IS DURABLE, BUT FROM TIME TO TIME MINOR REPAIRS must be addressed. Air pockets are caused by the adhesive no longer working. This is common as floors age, and the resulting bubble is fairly easy to deflate and rebond to the subfloor. If not attended to, the area will eventually harden, split, and crack—making the problem more noticeable and difficult to fix. Even a curled edge on an otherwise healthy vinyl tile can be easily glued back into place. If the repair doesn't hold, the entire tile must be replaced.

HOW TO FIX A BUBBLE

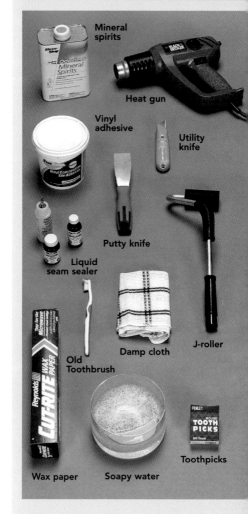

1 Deflate air pocket. Use a utility knife to lightly score and then slice through the bulge. This allows air to escape. Extend the cut a little (½") beyond the blister at both ends. If possible, cut along a line in the pattern to hide the cut.

2 Choose an appropriately sized tool to force fresh vinyl adhesive through the slit and under the bubble. Press the edges together. Wipe up any excess adhesive with a damp cloth. Cover the patch with wax paper and some books while the adhesive dries.

HOW TO FIX A CURL

1 If the corner or edge of vinyl tile is curling, but the rest of the tile is in good shape, you can refasten it. Use an electric heat gun to warm the area. This makes the vinyl easier to work with and it softens the underlying adhesive.

2 Use a flexible tool (such as a small putty knife) to lift the tile just enough to spread the underside with fresh adhesive. Wipe up excess glue with a damp cloth or sponge.

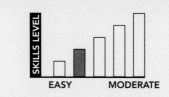

Patching Resilient Sheet Flooring

5

Resilient flooring is vulnerable when it comes to extreme heat and heavy objects falling on it. Burn marks and dents can be fixed by cutting out the damaged section and replacing it with a new patch of matching flooring.

RESILIENT SHEET FLOORING IS A DURABLE, PRACTICAL MATERIAL. There are no seams, so it is impervious to spills. However, it is not impervious to tears, dents, gouges, punctures, or burns. To repair a damaged section of sheet flooring, cut out the damaged area and glue in a replacement patch from a leftover remnant. If you don't have any leftover pieces available, you could settle for a close match or choose a piece that offers an interesting contrast.

SHEET VINYL PATCHES 101

TOOLS & SUPPLIES YOU NEED

Warm water

Lacquer thinner

Vinyl Adhesive

Goo Gone or mineral spirits

Large carpenter's square

Clean cloth

Asbestos-rated respirator

Heat gun or iron and aluminum foil

Duct tape

Liquid seam sealer

Utility knife

Painter's tape

Small carpenter's square

J-roller

Vacuum

Chisel

Floor scraper

Tape measure

Putty knife

⅛" notched trowel

Remember to thoroughly sweep and vacuum underlayment before installing a vinyl patch. Sometimes the tiniest bits and pieces of debris create noticeable bumps. And if old adhesive is not completely removed, a yellow discoloration will form on your new patch.

SKILLS YOU NEED

- Measuring
- Cutting
- Scraping
- Vacuuming
- Simple trowel work

TERMS YOU NEED TO KNOW

UNDERLAYMENT—The intermediate layer between the surface flooring material and the subfloor.

PERIMETER-INSTALL—Vinyl sheet flooring that is glued only around the edges.

TROWEL—A flat-blade hand tool with a raised handle used for scooping, spreading, leveling, smoothing, or shaping substances such as cement, mortar, or adhesive. Usually, a tile trowel has notches on one edge for combing mortar or adhesive into even rows.

DIFFICULTY LEVEL

SKILLS LEVEL

EASY   MODERATE

This project can be completed in 1 hour, not including drying time.

1 Measure the width and length of the damaged area. Place the new flooring remnant on a surface you don't mind making some cuts on—like a scrap of plywood. Use a carpenter's square for cutting guidance. Make sure your cutting size is a bit larger than the damaged area.

2 Lay the patch over the damaged area, matching pattern lines. Secure the patch with duct tape. Using a carpenter's square as a cutting guide, cut through the new vinyl (on top) and the old vinyl (on bottom). Press firmly with the knife to cut both layers.

3 Use tape to mark one edge of the new patch with the corresponding edge of the old flooring as placement marks. Remove the tape around the perimeter of the patch and lift up.

4 Soften the underlying adhesive with an electric heat gun and remove the damaged section of floor. Work from edges in. When the tile is loosened, insert a putty knife and pry up the damaged area.

5 Scrape off the remaining adhesive with a putty knife or chisel. Work from the edges to the center. Dab mineral spirits (or Goo Gone) or spritz warm water on the floor to dissolve leftover goop, taking care not to use too much; you don't want to loosen the surrounding flooring. Use a razor-edged scraper (flooring scraper) to scrape to the bare wood underlayment.

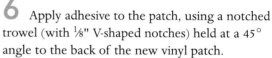

6 Apply adhesive to the patch, using a notched trowel (with ⅛" V-shaped notches) held at a 45° angle to the back of the new vinyl patch.

7 Set one edge of the patch in place. Lower the patch onto the underlayment. Press into place. Apply pressure with a J-roller or rolling pin to create a solid bond. Start at the center and work toward the edges, working out air bubbles. Wipe up adhesive that oozes out the sides with a clean, damp cloth or sponge.

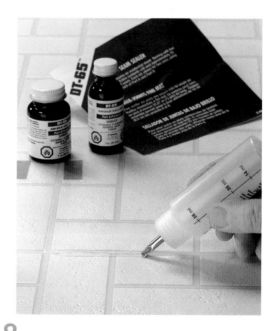

8 Let the adhesive dry overnight. The next day, hide the seams with liquid seam sealer. Use a soft cloth dipped in lacquer thinner to clean the area. Mix the seam sealer according to the manufacturer's directions. Use an applicator bottle to apply a thin bead of sealer onto the cutlines.

Repairing Loose Carpet Seams

6

Sliding furniture across the floor can catch loose carpet seams and further pull them away from the seam tape, leaving a big gap to invite dust and other debris under your carpet. To avoid further problems down the road, fix loose carpet seams immediately—and always lift furniture, instead of sliding it.

SEAM PROBLEMS CAN BE CAUSED BY A SNAG, HEAVY FOOT TRAFFIC, POOR quality, longterm wear, or improper installation. Whatever the cause, if the seams of your wall-to-wall carpet have begun to come apart, fix them as soon as you can. The longer you wait, the more likely your carpet is to fray and the more likely debris will start to accumulate under the carpet. The good news is that the repair requires only minimal skills and simple tools that you can rent at any carpet dealership. Read on . . . you can definitely solve the problem yourself.

CARPET SEAMS 101

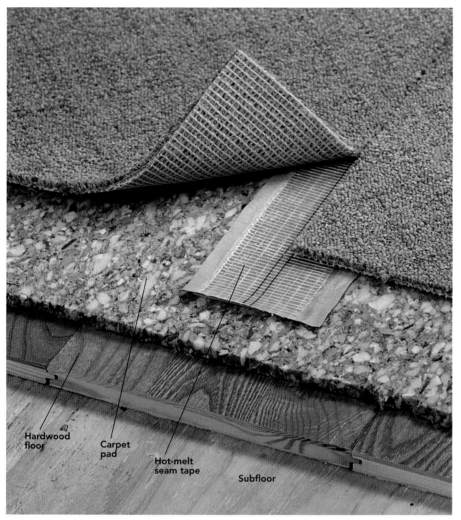

Hardwood floor
Carpet pad
Hot-melt seam tape
Subfloor

Carpet seams are held down with seam tape laid over the foam carpet pad. The tape sticks to the underside of the carpet. If the carpet is set onto the seam tape crookedly, it will leave a noticeable gap. In this case, the tape should be removed, and the seams should be reset.

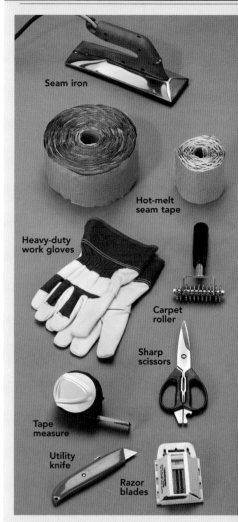

1 Separate the carpet fibers along the seam with your fingers, so you can clearly see the seam. Use a carpet or utility knife to cut through the seam tape stuck to the underside of the carpet. Open up the entire length of the seam and remove any remaining tape. Be careful not to cut the carpet pad. If you cut the pad, repair it with duct tape.

2 If there are any loose carpet fibers that could accidentally be pulled, snip them close to the base of the carpet.

3 Measure the length of the split seam and cut a new piece of hot-melt seam tape to size. Hold back one edge of carpet (not the carpet pad) while you slip the seam tape, adhesive side up, under the seam. Center the tape between the two pieces of carpet.

SAFETY FIRST

Be sure to regularly replace the blades in your utility knife. A dull utility knife requires you to use more pressure, which makes accurate cutting more difficult.

4 Place the seam iron on a board or old carpet remnant and pre-heat it to the appropriate temperature, as recommended by the seam-tape manufacturer (usually 250°).

5 Hold back one side of the carpet and place the hot iron directly on the tape at one end of the seam. Hold it there for about 30 seconds, so that it melts the tape glue. Let the carpet flop down over the iron and slowly draw the iron along the entire length of the seam. Go about a foot at a time. Check to make sure the carpet is not too hot and then press the carpet down into the heated adhesive with the other hand. As you go, make sure the backings are butted together. The glue will harden in just a couple of minutes.

6 Set the carpet to the seam tape by walking over the seam. Alternatively, roll over the seam with a handheld, spiked seam roller (available at most home-improvement stores).

HERE'S HOW

To ensure that the carpet will not fray at the seams, apply a continuous bead of seam glue along the seam edges.

Replacing Ceramic Tiles

7

Removing a damaged tile requires a little elbow grease. The first step is to weaken the tile with the appropriate tools (as will be explained in this project). From that point, the job is much easier if you have a large, sturdy chisel to remove chunks of the tile.

A CRACKED OR BROKEN CERAMIC TILE IS EASY ENOUGH TO REPLACE, PROVIDED you have a suitable replacement tile. Before starting this project, shop around a bit for the replacement tile. If you have to buy a new tile, make sure you only look at tile specifically for floors. Take the exact measurement of the broken tile with you. If possible, take a fragment of the tile along with you so the sales person can match the finish and composition. If you absolutely cannot find a replacement tile, consider turning the problem into a design challenge by replacing a few tiles in a pattern of your choice with a contrasting tile. If you need to replace multiple tiles for whatever reason, see page 276 for grouting and sealing large areas.

CERAMIC TILE MATERIALS 101

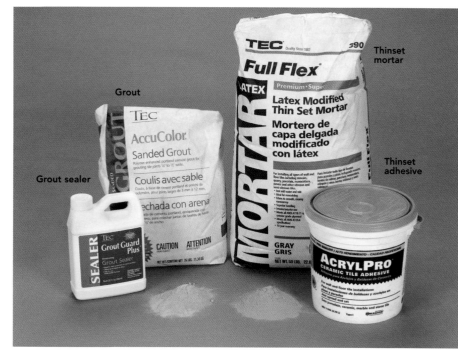

Grout sealer · Grout · Thinset mortar · Thinset adhesive

Replacing a tile requires a new tile, adhesive, grout, and a sealer. The joints between ceramic tiles are filled with a cement-based filler called "grout." This must be removed and replaced when a single tile is replaced. It is good to occasionally check the condition of the grout over the entire floor. (To regrout floors, see page 74). Grout is available in tinted colors to match your tile. You must also seal all grout lines with silicone sealer. Seal the joints every two years or so.

TERMS YOU NEED TO KNOW

SUBFLOOR—The base layer of wood or plywood that supports the underlayment and surface flooring.

UNDERLAYMENT—The intermediate layer between the surface flooring material and the subfloor. The underlayment for a ceramic tile floor can be plywood or cementboard.

THINSET MORTAR—A cement-based adhesive used to adhere ceramic tile to the underlayment.

TILE SPACERS—Small plastic spacers used to position tiles for uniform grout lines. Available in different sizes to create grout joints of different widths.

GROUT—A very fine cement mortar, sometimes tinted, used to fill the joints between ceramic tiles.

METAL LATHE—An open fabric of metal that holds poured mortar used as a base for ceramic tile. You are most likely to see this in older tile installations.

CARBIDE-TIPPED GROUT SAW—A scraping tool with a sharp carbide-coated blade to remove old, hardened grout.

TOOLS & SUPPLIES YOU NEED

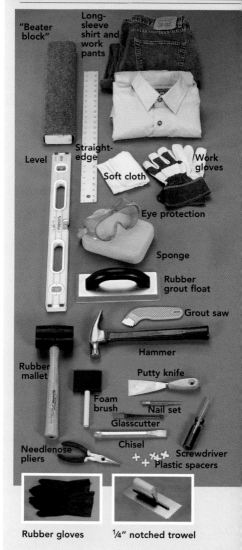

"Beater block" · Long-sleeve shirt and work pants · Level · Straight-edge · Soft cloth · Work gloves · Eye protection · Sponge · Rubber grout float · Grout saw · Hammer · Rubber mallet · Putty knife · Foam brush · Nail set · Glasscutter · Chisel · Screwdriver · Needlenose pliers · Plastic spacers

Rubber gloves · ¼" notched trowel

SKILLS YOU NEED

• Hammering and chiseling
• Trowel work
• Grouting and sealing

DIFFICULTY LEVEL

EASY · MODERATE

This project can be completed in a day or so, including drying time, depending on how many tiles need to be replaced.

HOW TO REPLACE A CERAMIC TILE

1 With a carbide-tipped grout saw, apply firm but gentle pressure across the grout until you expose the unglazed edges of the tile. Do not scratch the glazed tile surface. If the grout is stubborn, use a hammer and screwdriver to first tap the tile (Step 2).

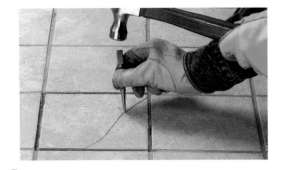

2 If the tile is not already cracked, use a hammer to puncture the tile by tapping a nail set or center punch into it. Alternatively, if the tile is significantly cracked, use a chisel to pry up the tile.

3 To remove the tile, insert a chisel into one of the cracks and gently tap the tile. Start at the center and chip outward so you don't damage the adjacent tiles. Be aware that cement board looks a lot like mortar when you're chiseling. Remove and discard the broken pieces.

4 Use a putty knife to scrape away old thinset adhesive; use a chisel for poured mortar installation. Note: If the underlayment is covered with metal lathe you won't be able to get the area smooth, just clean it out the best you can. Once the adhesive is scraped from the underlayment, smooth the rough areas with sandpaper. If there are gouges in the underlayment, fill them with epoxy-based thinset mortar (for cementboard) or a floor-leveling compound (for plywood). Allow the area to completely dry.

SAFETY FIRST

Chipping out a ceramic tile can create flying shards of very sharp ceramic fragments. When doing this work, use patient, gentle blows of your hammer on the chisel. Always wear eye protection when using a hammer and chisel.

TOOL TIP

Before puncturing the tile with a nail set, you may want to weaken the tile by scoring deep fracture lines into it with a glasscutter and straightedge.

5 Use a ¼" notched trowel to apply thinset adhesive to the back of the replacement tile. Set the tile down into the space, and use plastic spacers around the tile to make sure it is centered within the opening.

6 Set the tile in position and press down until it is even with the adjacent tiles. Twist it a bit to get it to sit down in the mortar. Use a mallet or hammer and a block of wood covered with cloth or a carpet scrap (a "beater block") to lightly tap on the tile, setting it into the adhesive. Use a level or other straight surface to make sure the tile is level with the surrounding tiles. If necessary, continue to tap the tile until it's flush with the rest of the surrounding tiles.

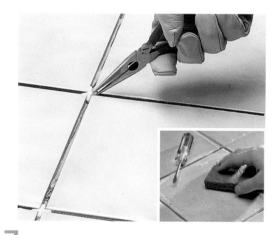

7 Remove the spacers with needlenose pliers. Get the mortar or thinset adhesive out of the grout joints with a small screwdriver and a cloth. Also, wipe away any adhesive from the surface of the tiles, using a wet sponge. Let the area dry for 24 hours (or according to the manufacturer's recommendations).

8 Use a putty knife to apply grout to the joints. Fill in low spots by applying and smoothing extra grout with your finger. Use the round edge of a toothbrush handle to create a concave grout line, if desired.

1 To grout and seal a large area, mix a batch of floor grout in a bucket, according to the directions on the label.

2 Pour the grout over the tile, then use a rubber grout float or rubber squeegee to spread it over the grout joints. Press down with a wiggling motion to force the grout deeply into the joints. Then tilt the face of the float 45° and diagonally drag the float across the joints to evenly apply the grout.

3 Let the grout set for 10 to 15 minutes, then use the grout float to remove excess grout from the surface of the tile. Hold the grout float on its edge and use a scraping motion.

HERE'S HOW

Before applying grout to porous tile, coat the tiles with a release agent (sold at tile shops) to keep the grout from discoloring the tile.

4 Use a barely damp sponge to wipe away excess grout from the surface of the tile. Be gentle with the joints themselves, though—you don't want to pull grout out of the joints you've just filled.

5 Let the grout dry for about 4 hours, then polish the tile with a soft cloth.

6 Use a foam brush to seal the grout after it cures. Do this every 1 to 2 years to protect against stains and to prevent it from crumbling.

HERE'S HOW

To determine if your grout needs to be resealed, test the existing sealer by putting a few drops of water on a grout line. If the water beads up, the sealer is still working. If the water absorbs into the grout, it needs to be resealed.

Replacing Laminate Floorboards

8

As indestructible as laminate floors may seem, minor scratches caused by normal day-to-day wear and tear are unavoidable. Whether the damaged plank is close to a wall or in the middle of the floor, this project will show you how to replace it.

IN THE EVENT THAT YOU NEED TO REPLACE A LAMINATE PLANK, YOU MUST first determine how to remove the damaged plank. If you have a glueless "floating" floor it is best to unsnap and remove each plank starting at the wall and moving in until you reach the damaged plank. However, if the damaged plank is far from the wall it is more time-efficient to cut out the damaged plank (see page 280). Fully-bonded laminate planks have adhesive all along the bottom of the plank and are secured directly to the underlayment. When you remove the damaged plank you run the risk of gouging the subfloor, so we recommend calling in a professional if you find that your laminate planks are completely glued to the subfloor.

LAMINATE FLOORBOARDS 101

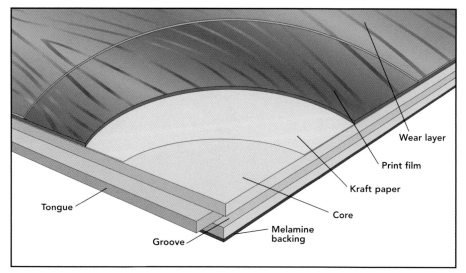

Wear layer

Print film

Kraft paper

Tongue

Core

Groove

Melamine backing

From bottom to top, laminate planks are engineered to resist moisture, scratches, and dents. A melamine base layer protects the inner core layer, which is most often HDF (high-density fiberboard). This is occasionally followed by kraft paper saturated in resins for added protection and durability. The print film is a photographic layer that replicates the look of wood or ceramic. The surface is a highly protective wear layer. The tongue-and-groove planks fit together tightly and may be (according to manufacturer's instructions) glued together for added stability.

TERMS YOU NEED TO KNOW

SUBFLOOR—The base layer of wood or plywood that supports the underlayment and surface flooring.

UNDERLAYMENT—The intermediate layer between the surface flooring material and subfloor. The rollout underlayment for laminate flooring combines a poly-water barrier and a foam cushion sound barrier.

FLOATING FLOORS—Flooring that does not fasten directly to the subfloor or underlayment, but rather "floats" on top. The flooring material is held together with a snap-together, interlocking system, either with or without adhesive at the joints. When replacing a cut out plank, you must use adhesive at the joints where the tongue-and-groove edges have been removed.

GLUELESS LAMINATE FLOORS—Flooring that does not require glue for installation, but instead relies upon a tight tongue-and-groove system.

FULLY-BONDED LAMINATE FLOORS—Laminate flooring that is attached to the subfloor with adhesive.

PLUNGE CUT—A technique used to cut out a rectangular area from the center of a piece of wood. Adjust the cut to the exact wood thickness. Turn on the saw and ease it down into the wood. Repeat along the entire cutline.

TOOLS & SUPPLIES YOU NEED

Laminate adhesive

Cardboard scraps

Circular saw

Replacement plank

Router

Wax paper

Protective eyewear

Drill

3/16" drill bit

Damp towel

Pry bar

Pliers

Hammer

Pencil

Marker

Wide painter's tape

Scrap of 2x4

Nail set

Suction cup

Plastic spatula

Chisel

Sandpaper

SKILLS YOU NEED

- Hammering using a nail set
- Drilling
- Using pry bar, chisel, and pliers
- Plunge cutting with a circular saw
- Using a router

DIFFICULTY LEVEL

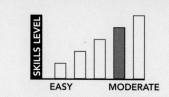

SKILLS LEVEL

EASY   MODERATE

This project can be completed in less than a day, not including 24 hours for adhesive drying time.

HOW TO REPLACE LAMINATE PLANKS

1 Draw a rectangle in the middle of the damaged board with a 1½" border between the rectangle and factory edges. At each rectangle corner and inside each corner of the plank, use a hammer and nail set to make indentations. At each of these indentations, drill ³⁄₁₆" holes into the plank. Only drill the depth of the plank.

2 To protect the floor from chipping, place painter's tape along the cutlines. Set the circular saw depth to the thickness of the replacement plank. Plunge cut the damaged plank and push the saw from the center of the line out to each end. Stop ¼" in from each corner. Pry up the middle section and remove.

3 Pry up the remaining outer edges of the damaged plank, using a scrap 2 x 4 wood block as leverage. Use a pliers to grab the 1½" border strip in front of the pry bar. Press downward until a gap appears at the joint, and then remove the border piece. Repeat for the other sides.

4 Place a scrap of cardboard in the opening to protect the underlayment foam while you remove all of the old glue from the factory edges with a chisel. Vacuum up the wood and glue flakes.

5 To remove the tongues on one long and one short end, lay the replacement plank face down onto a protective scrap of plywood (or 2 × 4). Clamp a straight cutting guide to the replacement plank so the distance from the guide causes the bit to align with the tongue and trim it off. Pressing the router against the cutting guide, slowly move along the entire edge of the replacement plank to remove the tongue. Clean the edges with sandpaper.

6 Dry-fit the grooves on the replacement board into the tongues of the surrounding boards and press into place. If the board fits snugly in between the surrounding boards, pry the plank up with a manufacturer suction cup. If the plank does not sit flush with the rest of the floor, check to make sure you routered the edges off evenly. Sand any rough edges that should have been completely removed and try to fit the plank again.

7 Set the replacement plank by applying laminate glue to the removed edges of the replacement plank and into the grooves of the existing planks. Firmly press the plank into place.

8 Clean up glue with a damp towel. Place a strip of wax paper over the new plank and evenly distribute some books on the wax paper. Allow the adhesive to dry for 12 to 24 hours.

Patching Carpet

9

Large spills often soak into carpet quickly and then start to spread. This can permanently damage a significant portion of your carpet. In such a case, a large carpet patch is in order.

IF A RELATIVELY LARGE AREA OF CARPET IS STAINED, BURNED, WORN, OR damaged, you can replace the damaged section with a matching carpet remnant. A large patch will likely be noticeable if the surrounding carpet is worn or faded, but a clean patch will prevent further damage—no matter how much you clean it, a large stain will attract oils and debris because the surface will be different from that of the surrounding carpet.

If you don't have a leftover remnant, you still have some options: If the carpet isn't too old, you may be able to find a matching remnant at a carpet dealer. If not, consider cutting a piece from the back of a closet or from under a couch that you don't intend to move. If these options are unsatisfactory, consider using a different type of carpet altogether and extending the patch to the nearest transition, such as a door threshold or wall. This will make your carpet design unique, and no one will track your inspiration to a damaged piece of carpet!

CARPET PATCHING 101

Before you start, be aware that even the best patching job may be noticeable if your carpet is faded or very worn. Any difference between the patch and the surrounding carpet will fade somewhat over time and become less noticeable. The difference is somewhat minimalized if you make sure the carpet nap of the patch matches the surrounding area (inset).

TERMS YOU NEED TO KNOW

WALL-TO-WALL CARPET—Two layers of woven backing are laid over separate padding. Installed by stretching onto tackless strips.

CUSHION-BACKED CARPET—One layer of woven backing is manufactured with a foam backing bonded to its underside and needs no additional padding. It is glued to the floor, rather than being installed under tension. Cushion-backed carpet was more common 15 years ago than it is now.

KNEE KICKER—A tool used for stretching carpet. The teeth at the front end of the tool grip the carpet; the back end is shaped so the user can apply forward pressure with the knee.

TOOLS & SUPPLIES YOU NEED

Carpet remnant

Heavy-duty work gloves

Carpet tape

Latex seam adhesive

Scrap of wood for cutting

Duct tape

Painter's tape

Utility knife

Hammer

Extra razorblades

Carpet tacks

Knee kicker

Awl

Phillips screwdriver

SKILLS YOU NEED

- Using simple knee kicker
- Cutting
- Hammering tacks
- Gluing

DIFFICULTY LEVEL

EASY   MODERATE

This project can be completed in a couple of hours, not including adhesive drying time.

HOW TO PATCH CARPET

1 Use a utility knife to cut four strips from a carpet remnant, each a little wider and longer than the cuts you plan to make around the damaged part of your carpet. Most wall-to-wall carpet is installed under tension; so to relieve that tension, set the knee kicker 6" to 1 ft. from the area to be cut out and nudge it forward (toward the patch area). If you create a hump in the carpet, you've pushed too hard and need to back off. Now place one of the strips upside down in front of the knee kicker and tack it to the floor at 2" to 4" intervals. Repeat the same process on the other three sides.

2 Use a marker to draw arrows on tape. Fan the carpet with your hand to see which direction the fibers are woven, and then use the pieces of tape to mark that direction on both the carpet surrounding the damaged area and the remnant you intend to use as a patch. Place a carpet remnant on plywood and cut out a carpet patch slightly larger than the damaged section, using a utility knife. As you cut, use a Phillips screwdriver to push carpet tufts or loops away from the cutting line. Trim loose pile, and then place the patch right side up over the damaged area.

TOOL TIP

Knee kickers have teeth that grab the carpet backing. These teeth should be set to grab the backing without grabbing the padding. There is an adjustable knob to do this. You can tell if the knee kicker is grabbing the padding by the increased pressure needed to move it forward. To release the tension just before a damaged area of carpet you intend to patch, place the feet on the floor and use your knee to press it toward the damaged area.

3 Tack one edge of the patch through the damaged carpet and into the floor, making sure the patch covers the entire damaged area. Use a utility knife to cut out the damaged carpet, following the border of the new patch as a template. If you cut into the carpet padding, use duct tape to mend it. Remove the patch and the damaged carpet square.

4 Cut four lengths of carpet seam tape, each about 1" longer than an edge of the cut out area, using a utility knife or scissors. Cover half of each strip with a thin layer of seam adhesive and then slip the coated edge of each strip, sticky side up, along the underside edges of the original carpet. Apply more adhesive to the exposed half of tape, and use enough adhesive to fill in the tape weave.

5 Line up your arrows and press the patch into place. Take care not to press too much, because glue that squeezes up onto the newly laid carpet creates a mess. Use an awl to free tufts or loops of pile crushed in the seam. Lightly brush the pile of the patch to make it blend with the surrounding carpet. Leave the patch undisturbed for 24 hours. Check the drying time on the adhesive used and wait at least this long before removing the carpet tacks.

WHAT IF . . . ?

If you have cushion-backed, fully-bonded carpet, you can follow the instructions above to make a large patch, except:

1. You won't need a knee kicker.

2. Use a putty knife to scrape away any dried cement from the hole you make.

3. Apply multi-purpose flooring adhesive to the floor with a $3/32$" trowel.

4. Instead of seam tape, just use a thin bead of cushion-back seam adhesive along the perimeter of the hole.

Removing Resilient Flooring

10

If adhesives are not properly removed before installing new resilient flooring, the oils may chemically react to the new material and produce a yellow discoloration, essentially destroying the vinyl floor. These spots cannot be removed with cleaning products. In these cases, the old resilient flooring should be removed entirely before you install new flooring.

REMOVING GLUED-DOWN RESILIENT FLOORING IS LABOR INTENSIVE, BUT IT'S necessary to do so if the surface is in very poor condition (or if you plan to replace the old resilient flooring with ceramic tile). Oils that cause yellow discoloration can eventually dry out and crack or seep through the vinyl, damaging new floor laid on top of it. Moreover, any unevenness or debris under the old vinyl will clearly show through new resilient flooring.

Note: It is true that resilient floor can serve as the foundation for most new floorings, including resilient flooring, hardwood, or carpet, but only if the existing surface is smooth and sound. Even if the existing flooring has loose seams, small tears, or air bubbles, then you must apply embossing leveler to the entire floor and let it dry before laying new resilient flooring. Alternatively, you can lay a new ¼" plywood underlayment over the old floor or you can remove the entire subfloor with the vinyl flooring and lay a new subfloor. These methods are worth consideration if you find that the subfloor is being heavily damaged as you begin to remove full-spread sheet vinyl, but they are also very time-consuming and require a considerable amount of precision.

SHEET FLOORING 101

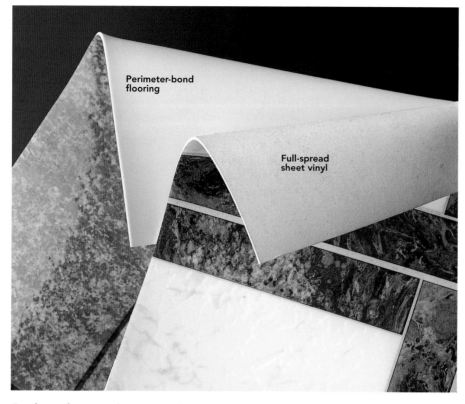

Perimeter-bond flooring

Full-spread sheet vinyl

Resilient sheet vinyl comes in full-spread and perimeter-bond styles. Full-spread sheet vinyl has felt-paper backing and is secured with adhesive that's spread over the entire floor before installation. Perimeter-bond flooring, identifiable by its smooth, white PVC backing, is laid directly on the underlayment and is secured by adhesive spread along the edges and seams.

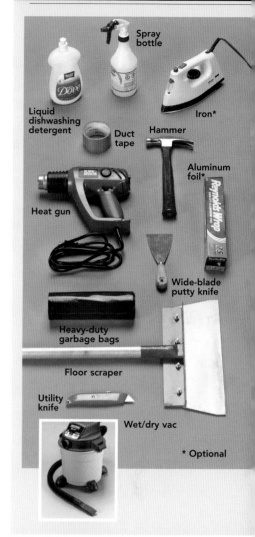

TERMS YOU NEED TO KNOW

SUBFLOOR—The base layer of wood or plywood that supports the underlayment and surface flooring.

UNDERLAYMENT—The intermediate layer between the surface flooring material and the subfloor.

PERIMETER-BOND SHEET VINYL—A synthetic resilient flooring that is installed in a single sheet, cut to fit the room it will be installed in, and glued to the underlayment at the room's edges.

FULL-SPREAD SHEET VINYL—A synthetic resilient flooring that is installed in a single sheet, cut to fit the room it will be installed in, and glued to the underlayment on a full-room bed of adhesive.

FLOOR SCRAPER—Designed like a shovel, a floor scraper removes resilient flooring products and scrapes off leftover adhesives or backings. The long handle provides leverage and force, and it allows you to work in a comfortable standing position.

SKILLS YOU NEED

• Cutting with a utility knife
• Scraping
• Using a heat gun

DIFFICULTY LEVEL

EASY   MODERATE

This project can be completed in a few hours.

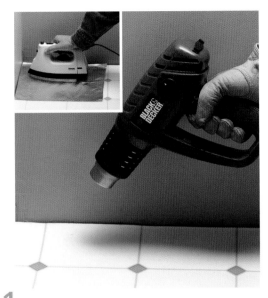

1 Remove baseboards. Beginning in a corner of the room, slowly move a heat gun back and forth 4 to 6" above the floor until you can pry up the corner. Alternatively, to use an iron, place aluminum foil on the floor to prevent melting or burning the floor, and keep the temperature at a low setting (inset).

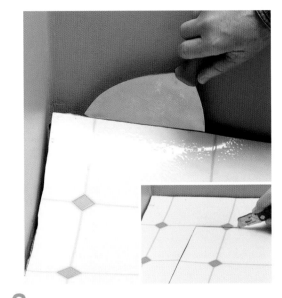

2 Once the adhesive is warm, insert a wide-blade putty knife under the loosened corner and pry back the flooring. If the glue is only around the perimeter of the room, measure from the wall to the approximate point where the glue stops and cut a strip that wide along the entire perimeter of the room (inset). Go on to Step 3, knowing you will remove the strip you just cut along the wall last.

3 With a utility knife, cut the flooring into strips about three feet wide (or smaller, if you find smaller strips are easier to handle and have the extra time needed for extra cutting and rolling). If you have perimeter-installed sheet flooring, start cutting the strips inside the perimeter cut you made in Step 2. Simply roll up the strips and bind them with duct tape (inset).

4 Start pulling up the strips by hand. Grip the material close to the floor to minimize tearing. Dispose of the waste in heavy-duty construction garbage bags.

5 Scrape the remaining sheet vinyl and backing, using a floor scraper. Use a hammer to tap a putty knife under loose edges to chip apart pieces.

6 For stubborn spots, peel up as much of the floor covering as possible, using a putty knife. Spray a solution of water and liquid dishwashing detergent under the surface layer to separate the backing. With the help of the detergent, continue to use the putty knife to scrape up the stubborn patches.

7 For very sticky and stubborn glue, hold a heat gun about 4 to 6" above the floor. Constantly move the heat gun as you scrape the gooey mess into a pile with a wide-blade putty knife. Occasionally pick up glue and dispose of it, and wipe the putty knife clean.

8 Now you just need to sweep up the debris and clean up with a wet/dry vacuum. To contain the dust, fill the wet vac with about 1" of water.

HERE'S HOW

Some old linoleum is secured to the floor with a tar-based adhesive. Tar-based adhesives are dark or tan colored and can be scrubbed away with steel wool and mineral spirits (or paint thinner).

Removing Carpet

11

When removing fully-bonded, cushion-backed carpet, be prepared to find carpet adhesive and foam padding on the floor underneath. It is a time-consuming process to remove the adhesive, but your new floor is well worth the effort needed to properly prepare a clean, level underlayment.

REMOVING CARPET IS NECESSARY IF IT HAS BEEN BADLY DAMAGED OR YOU ARE ready to install a different type of flooring. It is time-consuming work, but you can save money by removing carpet even if you intend to hire someone to install new flooring. Carpet is either installed with tack strips along the perimeter of a room, with adhesive spread along the perimeter of the room, or with adhesive spread along the entire floor.

CARPET BACKING 101

Perimeter tackless strips with an independent pad

Cushion-backed carpet

Wall-to-wall carpet is stretched and secured to tackless strips along the perimeter of the room. Once lifted from the strips, the carpet and pad can be rolled up. The tackless strips are often nailed down and must be removed. Cushion-backed carpet has a foam backing bonded to it. It is secured to the floor with general-purpose adhesive. When removing this carpet, pieces of the pad will stick to the floor. Removing all of the stubborn pieces requires time and a considerable amount of effort.

TERMS YOU NEED TO KNOW

SUBFLOOR—The base layer of wood or plywood that supports the underlayment and surface flooring.

WALL-TO-WALL CARPET—Carpet with two layers of woven backing. Usually, it's laid over separate padding. Installed by stretching onto tackless strips.

CUSHION-BACKED CARPET—One layer of woven backing is manufactured with a foam backing bonded to its underside and needs no additional padding. Usually, it's glued to the floor, rather than being installed under tension.

TACKLESS STRIPS ("TACK STRIPS")—Plywood strips with 2 to 3 rows of sharp nails angled away from the center of the room. The strips are installed along the perimeter to hold wall-to-wall carpet in place.

TOOLS & SUPPLIES YOU NEED

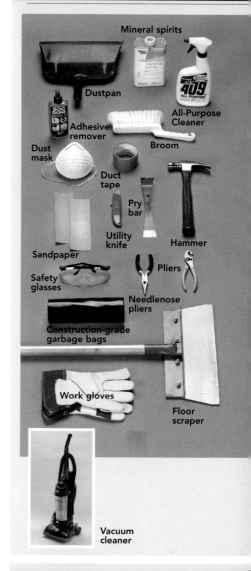

Mineral spirits

Dustpan

Adhesive remover

All-Purpose Cleaner

Dust mask

Broom

Duct tape

Pry bar

Sandpaper

Utility knife

Hammer

Safety glasses

Pliers

Needlenose pliers

Construction-grade garbage bags

Work gloves

Floor scraper

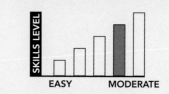

Vacuum cleaner

SKILLS YOU NEED

- Cutting
- Using a pry bar
- Pulling up staples

DIFFICULTY LEVEL

EASY   MODERATE

This project can be completed in a day.

HOW TO REMOVE CARPET

1 Because you're about to be handling your old carpet for a few hours, vacuum the entire floor thoroughly.

2 Use a utility knife to cut around metal threshold strips. Use a flat pry bar to lift up the strips until they release from the floor. Dispose the strips in construction-grade garbage bags. You may be able to pull the carpet up without removing the baseboards.

3 Use pliers to grab carpet fibers along the edge of the room; then lift the carpet to release it from the tack strips. Continue to release the carpet from tack strips along the room perimeter .

WHAT IF . . . ?

If you do not find tackless strips, your carpet is secured with adhesive—either around the perimeter or everywhere. If it's just around the perimeter, pull back the carpet in a corner of the room until it is no longer bonded to the floor with adhesive. From that point, measure out away from the wall about 1 ft. past the glue and cut around the perimeter of the room, using a utility knife. For now, leave one wall side uncut. This side will hold the carpet in place when you begin to cut strips.

4 Use your utility knife to cut the carpet into strips. Once part of the first strip of carpet is lifted, lay a scrap 2 × 4 under the carpet and use that as a cutting base—this step is necessary only if you want to protect the floor underneath (for example, if you have wood floors). After the first strip is cut, set the board on top of the carpet and fold the carpet back over the board, cutting from the underside. You may be able to cut the carpet pad and carpet at the same time; if not, you can cut the carpet pad separately later. Cut the strips into sizes that are manageable to you.

5 Roll up the strips of carpet and secure them with duct tape. You may have to pull up on the strips with some effort if the carpet pad is stapled down. If you were not able to cut through the carpet pad, you will have to cut that into strips and roll the strips up once the carpet is removed. If you have perimeter-bonded carpet you must now remove the remaining perimeter piece glued to the floor.

6 Sweep up pieces of carpet padding and put them into a construction-grade garbage bag. If the pad was held down with staples, don't clean away the bits of pad still attached to the staples—the padding makes it easier to find and remove the staples.

7 To remove tack strips, slowly and patiently lift the strips up with a pry bar. Place a thin piece of hard material (like a piece of ⅛" wood veneer) under the pry bar to protect the floor. Tack strips are attached to the floor with small nails spaced approximately 6 to 8" apart. The pry bar is most effective when placed directly under these points. If it is difficult to insert the pry bar under the tack strip in places, use a hammer to tap the short bent end of the pry bar underneath the tack strip where it is attached by a nail; then pry back.

Sealing Concrete Floors

12

Although concrete is most common in garages and basements, it is not limited to these parts of the house. Along with stainless steel appliances, warehouse and loft construction, and industrial design, concrete floors are part of today's design trends, making concrete maintenance and repair increasingly relevant to today's homeowner.

CONCRETE IS A VERSATILE BUILDING MATERIAL. MOST PEOPLE ARE ACCUSTOMED to thinking of concrete primarily as a utilitarian substance, but it can also mimic a variety of flooring types and be a colorful and beautiful addition to any room.

Whether your concrete floor is a practical surface for the garage or an artistic statement of personal style in your dining room, it should be sealed. Concrete is a hard and durable building material, but it is also porous. Consequently, concrete floors are susceptible to staining. Many stains can be removed with the proper cleaner, but sealing and painting prevents oil, grease, and other stains from penetrating the surface in the first place; thus, cleanup is a whole lot easier.

CONCRETE SEALING 101

Even after degreasing a concrete floor, residual grease or oils can create serious adhesion problems for coatings of sealant or paint. To check to see whether your floor has been adequately cleaned, pour a glass of water on the concrete floor. If it is ready for sealing, the water will soak into the surface quickly and evenly. If the water beads, you may have to clean it again. Detergent used in combination with a steam cleaner can remove stubborn stains better than a cleaner alone.

There are four important reasons to seal your concrete floor:

- To protect the floor from dirt, oil, grease, chemicals, and stains
- To dust-proof the surface
- To protect the floor from abrasion and sunlight exposure
- To repel water and protect the floor from freeze-thaw damage

TERMS YOU NEED TO KNOW

CONCRETE—A mixture of portland cement, water, and mineral aggregate (usually sand and gravel). Sometimes fly ash, pozzolans, or other additives are included in the mix.

ACID ETCHING—This is a technique in which acid is used to open the pores in concrete surfaces so a sealer can bond to it.

TOOLS & SUPPLIES YOU NEED

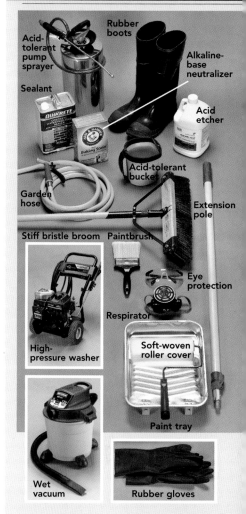

Rubber boots

Acid-tolerant pump sprayer

Alkaline-base neutralizer

Sealant

Acid etcher

Acid-tolerant bucket

Garden hose

Extension pole

Stiff bristle broom   Paintbrush

Eye protection

Respirator

High-pressure washer

Soft-woven roller cover

Paint tray

Wet vacuum

Rubber gloves

SKILLS YOU NEED

- Cleaning
- Sweeping
- Painting floors
- Vacuuming
- Working with strong acids

DIFFICULTY LEVEL

SKILLS LEVEL

EASY   MODERATE

This project can be completed in a weekend.

HOW TO SEAL CONCRETE

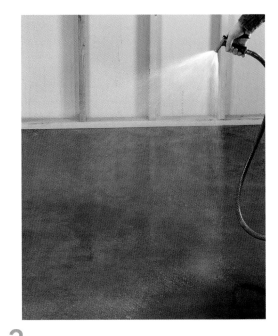

1 Clean and prepare the surface by first sweeping up all debris. Next, remove all surface muck: mud, wax, and grease. Finally, remove existing paints or coatings. See the chapter on cleaning concrete for tips on using cleaners specially designed for concrete floors.

2 Saturate the surface with clean water. The surface needs to be wet before acid etching. Use this opportunity to check for any areas where water beads up. If water beads on the surface, contaminants still need to be cleaned off with a suitable cleaner or chemical stripper.

HERE'S HOW

Prepare the concrete for sealer application by acid etching. Etching opens the pores in concrete surfaces, allowing sealers to bond with it. All smooth or dense concrete surfaces, such as garage floors, should be etched before applying stain. The surface should feel gritty, like 120-grit sandpaper, and allow water to penetrate it. If you're not sure whether your floor needs to be etched or not, it's better to etch. If you don't etch when it is needed, you have to remove the sealer residue before trying again. This easily becomes a time-consuming process that is best to avoid from the get-go.

THERE IS A VARIETY OF ACID ETCHING PRODUCTS AVAILABLE:

CITRIC ACID is a biodegradable acid that does not produce chlorine fumes. It is the safest etcher and the easiest to use, but it may not be strong enough for some very smooth concretes.

SULFAMIC ACID is less aggressive than phosphoric acid or muriatic acid, and it is perhaps the best compromise between strength of solution and safety.

PHOSPHORIC ACID is a stronger and more noxious acid than the previous two, but it is considerably less dangerous than muriatic acid. It is currently the most popular etching choice.

MURIATIC ACID (Hydrochloric Acid) is an extremely dangerous acid that quickly reacts and creates very strong fumes. This is an etching solution of last resort. It should only be used by professionals or by the most serious DIYers.

NOTE: **Never add water to acid—only add acid to water.**

3 Test your acid-tolerant pump sprayer with water to make sure it releases a wide, even mist. Once you have the spray nozzle set, check the manufacturer's instructions for the etching solution and fill the pump sprayer with the recommended amount of water.

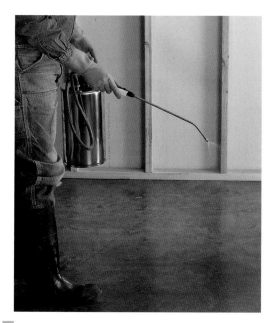

5 Apply the acid solution. Using the sprinkling can or acid-tolerant pump spray unit, evenly apply the diluted acid solution over the concrete floor. Do not allow acid solution to dry at any time during the etching and cleaning process. Etch small areas at a time, 10 × 10 ft. or smaller. If there is a slope, begin on the low side of the slope and work upward.

4 Add the acid etching contents to the water in the acid-tolerant pump sprayer (or sprinkling can). Follow the directions (and mixing proportions) specified by the manufacturer. Use caution.

SAFETY FIRST

All of these acids are dangerous. Use caution.

With any of these acid etches it is critical that there be adequate ventilation and that you wear protective clothing including:

- Safety goggles

- Respirator

- Rubber gloves

- Rubber boots

- Long pants and a long-sleeve shirt (to prevent acid contact with the skin)

6 Use a stiff bristle broom or scrubber to work the acid solution into the concrete. Let the acid sit for 5–10 minutes, or as indicated by the manufacturer's directions. A mild foaming action indicates that the product is working. If no bubbling or fizzing occurs, it means there is still grease, oil, or a concrete treatment on the surface that is interfering with the etching product.

7 Once the fizzing has stopped, the acid has finished reacting with the alkaline concrete surface and formed pH-neutral salts. Neutralize any remaining acid with an alkaline-base solution. Put a gallon of water in a 5-gallon bucket and then stir in an alkaline-base neutralizer. Using a stiff bristle broom, make sure the concrete surface is completely covered with the solution. Continue to sweep until the fizzing stops.

8 Use a garden hose with a pressure nozzle or, ideally, a pressure washer in conjunction with a stiff bristle broom to thoroughly rinse the concrete surface. Rinse the surface 2 to 3 times. Reapply the acid (repeat Steps 5, 6, 7, and 8).

WHAT IF . . . ?

If no fizzing occurs when the acid solution is put on the concrete, stop the process and clean the surface. Use a nylon bristle scrub brush to scrub the area with hot liquid dish soap and water, laundry soap and water, or a biodegradable degreasing cleaner. You can also try using a pressure washer. If degreasing doesn't solve the problem, the concrete may already be sealed with a concrete sealer. A surface sealer can only be removed mechanically by abrasive blasting; penetrant sealers may not be removable at all.

9 If you have any leftover acid you can make it safe for your septic system by mixing more alkaline solution in the 5-gallon bucket and carefully pouring the acid from the spray unit into the bucket until all of the fizzing stops.

10 Use a wet-vacuum to clean up the mess. Some sitting acids and cleaning solutions can harm local vegetation, damage your drainage system, and are just plain environmentally unfriendly. Check your local disposal regulations for proper disposal of the neutralized spent acid.

11 To check for residue, rub a dark cloth over a small area of concrete. If any white residue appears, continue the rinsing process. Check for residue again. You may be sick of the cleanup by now, but an inadequate acid rinse is even worse than not acid etching at all when it's time to add the sealant.

TOOL TIP

Mix one of these alkaline products with a gallon of water for a suitable acid-neutralizing solution:

- One cup of ammonia
  OR
- Four cups of gardener's lime
  OR
- A generous amount of baking soda
  OR
- 4 oz. of "Simple Green" cleaning solution

12 Let the concrete dry for at least 24 hours and sweep up dust, dirt, and particles leftover from the acid etching process. Your concrete should now have the consistency of 120-grit sandpaper and be able to accept concrete sealants.

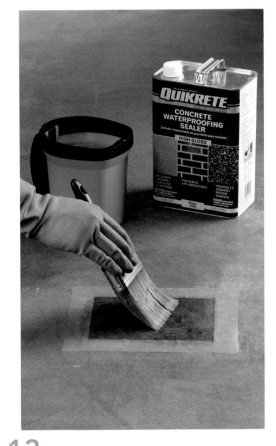

13 Once etched, clean, and dry, your concrete is ready for clear sealer or liquid repellent. Mix the sealer in a bucket with a stir stick. Lay painter's tape down for a testing patch. Apply sealer to this area and allow to dry to ensure desired appearance. Concrete sealers tend to make the surface slick when wet. Add an anti-skid additive to aid with traction, especially on stairs.

TOOL TIP

THERE ARE BASICALLY TWO CATEGORIES OF SEALERS:

FILM FORMERS create a barrier on the concrete's surface, blocking penetration of water and contaminants and providing a gloss or sheen. Film formers do not allow the concrete to breathe; they may trap moisture beneath the concrete surface. In cold areas this results in cracks due to the moisture freezing and expanding.

PENETRANTS increase water repellency and stain resistance by actually penetrating into the concrete surface to a depth of about 1 to 4 mils, providing an invisible protection without changing the surface appearance.

WHAT IF . . . ?

The most common sealing practice is to use clear sealant but there are also stained sealants and paints.

If you decide to paint instead of applying a clear or stained sealant, be sure to use paint designed for concrete floors. Also, once the paint has dried for a few days, apply two or three coats of water-based polyurethane.

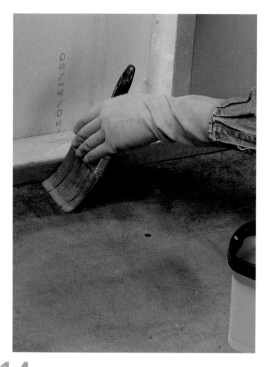

14 Use wide painter's tape to protect walls and then, using a good quality 4"-wide synthetic bristle paintbrush, coat the perimeter with sealer.

15 Use a long-handled paint roller with at least ½" nap to apply an even coat to the rest of the surface. Do small sections at a time (about 2' × 3'). Work in one orientation (e.g., north and south). Avoid lap marks by always maintaining a wet edge. Do not work the area once the coating has partially dried; this could cause it to lift from the surface. Allow surface to dry according to the manufacturer's instructions, usually 8 to 12 hours, minimum.

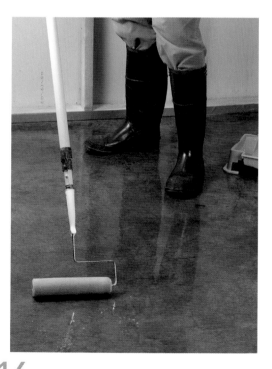

16 Apply a second coat in the opposite direction to the first coat, so if the first coat was north to south, the second coat should be east to west.

17 Clean tools, wet/dry vac and spray equipment with clean, warm water or mineral spirits.

Refinishing Hardwood Floors

13

Reviving your hardwood floors is definitely worth the hard work. By refinishing a tired-looking floor you suddenly realize why hardwood floors are so durable and long-lasting: They clean up beautifully.

MAKING WORN AND DULL HARDWOOD FLOORS LOOK NEW AGAIN DRAMATICALLY IMPROVES THE APPEARANCE OF A HOME. And the fact that very old hardwood floors can be completely restored to showroom condition is one of their real advantages over other types of flooring. Refinishing floors is time-consuming, messy, and disruptive to your household routine. Depending on the size of the room, be prepared to devote a weekend, minimally, to this project.

If you don't want to do the entire job yourself, you can still save money by doing some prep work yourself. Professionals often add on additional fees for removing and replacing shoe molding, nailing or gluing down loose boards, filling gouges and dents with wood putty, setting protruding nails, putting up plastic, cleaning the floor, and even moving furniture.

NOTE: If your floors are less than ½" thick, they are probably unsuitable for refinishing.

REFINISHING 101

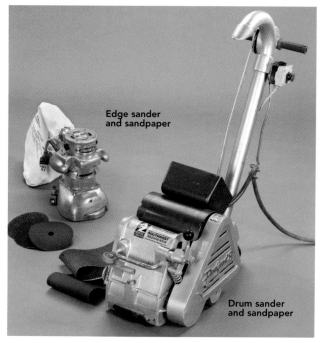

Edge sander and sandpaper

Drum sander and sandpaper

Refinishing a floor requires some heavy machinery, namely drum and edge sanders that may be rented from home stores or floor rental establishments. You can purchase sandpaper at the time of the rental.

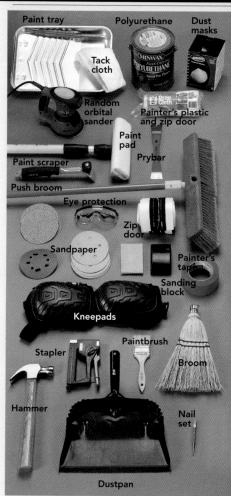
TYPES OF FINISHES

SURFACE FINISH—A floor finish applied to the wood surface, providing a harder and more durable coating than a sealer with a wax covering (for example, polyurethane (oil- or water-based) varnish, shellac, and lacquer).

PENETRANT FINISH—Penetrant floor finishes seep into the wood pores and become an integral part of the wood (for example, stains or sealers).

STAINS—Penetrants that alter the natural color of the wood. They can be used with a surface finish or protected with a sealer and wax.

SEALERS—Either clear or tinted penetrants that need to be protected with a wax or surface finish.

WAX—Wood floors not protected with a surface finish need to be covered with a coat of liquid, non-waterbased wax. Wax is not as durable as surface finish; periodically, it must be reapplied. The advantage is that patched areas easily blend in.

TERMS YOU NEED TO KNOW

REFINISHING FLOORS—Aggressively sanding floors to entirely remove previous finish and to level the floor before reapplying new floor finish.

FEATHER SAND—Sanding with lighter and lighter strokes as you move away from a more heavily sanded area. This creates a smooth transition between sanded and non-sanded areas.

ZIP DOOR—A plastic sheet with a long vertical zipper. It's taped over entryways for a convenient way to enter and exit rooms for the duration of a project.

HOW TO REFINISH HARDWOOD FLOORS

1 Staple plastic on all doorways. Place a zip door over the entryway you plan to use for the duration of the project.

2 Use painter's tape and plastic to cover heating and cooling registers, ceiling fans, and light fixtures.

3 Finally, place a fan in a nearby window to blow the circulating dust outside.

SAFETY FIRST

Even with proper ventilation, inhaling saw-dust is a health risk. We recommend getting a respirator. If you don't use one, you must at least wear a dust mask. Eye protection is also a must; and you'll thank yourself for buying a good pair of strong work gloves—they make the sander vibrations a little more bearable.

Important! Always unplug the sander whenever loading or unloading sandpaper.

SHOPPING TIP: SANDPAPER

Grits	Grade	Use
20, 30, 40, 60	Coarse	To level uneven boards.
100, 120	Medium	To minimize scratches from coarse grits.
150, 180	Fine	To eliminate scratches from medium grits.

Sandpaper becomes less effective over time; it may even rip. Buy 3–5 sheets of every grade for each room you want to refinish. You won't use them all, but most rentals allow you to return what you don't use. It's far better to have too many than to find yourself unable to continue until the next day because you ran out and the hardware store is closed.

Reminder: Before you leave the rental shop, have an employee explain to you how to load the paper. Every machine is a little different.

4 Wedge a pry bar between the shoe molding and baseboards. Move along the wall as nails loosen. Once removed, place a scrap 2 × 4 board against the wall and, with a pry bar, pry out baseboard at nails (inset). Maintain the gap with wood shims. Number the sections for easy replacement. Place wide masking tape along the baseboards. Drive protruding nails in floor ⅛" below the surface with a nail set.

5 Practice with the drum sander turned off. Move forward and backward. Tilt or raise it off the floor a couple of times. A drum sander is heavy, bulky, and awkward. Once it touches the floor, it walks forward; if you stop it, it gouges the floor.

6 For the initial pass with the drum sander, sand with the grain, using 40- or 60-grit paper; if there are large scratches, use 20 or 30. Start two-thirds down the room length on the right side; work your way to the left. Raise drum. Start motor. Slowly lower drum to floor. Lift the sander off the floor when you reach the wall. Move to the left 2 to 4" and then walk it backwards the same distance you just walked forward. Repeat.

7 When you get to the far left side of the room, turn the machine around and repeat the process. Overlap the sanded two-thirds to feather out the ridgeline.

Repeat the sanding process 3 or 4 more times using 120-grit sandpaper. Sand the entire floor. For the final passes, use finer sandpaper (150- to 180-grit) to remove scratches left by coarser papers.

Power edge sander

8 To sand hard-to-reach spots, first use a power edge sander along the walls, using the same grit that you last used with the drum sander. Make a succession of overlapping half-circles starting in the corner on one wall. Pull out in an arc and then swirl back to the wall. Continue around the room. Blend together any lines left by the drum and edge sanders by running a rotary buffer over the floor twice: first with an 80-grit screen and then with a 100-grit screen. Finally, use a 5" random orbital sander to smooth out the floor. The random motion naturally feathers out bumps.

9 Use a paint scraper to get to corners and hard-to-reach nooks and crannies. Pull the scraper toward you with a steady downward pressure. Pull with the grain. Next, sand with a sanding block.

HERE'S HOW

During the refinishing process it is very likely you will have to change the sandpaper and empty the contents of the dust bag. You should empty the contents of the dust bag when it is two-thirds full. When the machine is turned off, you can see how full the bag is. To check the wear of the sandpaper, turn off your machine every so often and tilt back the machine to check the paper on the underside. If it appears to be thinning, you want to change it.

Correctly replacing the sandpaper can be tricky. A rental professional should be able to walk you through the steps to change the paper and the dust bag, so be sure to consult with him or her before you leave the store.

10 Prepare the room for finish by sweeping and vacuuming. Remove plastic on the doors, windows, and fixtures. Sweep and vacuum again. Wipe up fine particles with a tack cloth.

11 Apply polyurethane finish. Mix equal parts water-based polyurethane and water. Use a natural bristle brush to apply the mixture along walls and around obstacles. To apply the mixture in the middle of the room, use a painting pad on a pole. Apply 2 coats diagonally across the grain and a final coat in the direction of the grain.

12 Allow the finish to dry after each coat. Lightly buff the floor with a fine to medium abrasive pad (or buffing pad). Clean the floor with a damp cloth and wipe the area dry with a towel.

13 Apply at least two coats of undiluted polyurethane finish to get a hard, durable finish. Allow the finish to dry; repeat Step 12 and then add a final coat. Do not overbrush.

14 After the final coat is dry, buff the surface with water and a fine abrasive pad. This removes surface imperfections and diminishes gloss. After finishing, wait at least 72 hours before replacing the shoe molding. Your newly refinished floor is now complete!

Painting Wood Floors

14

Just when it appears as though you've hit a wall in reviving your tired, wornout wood floor, try a coat of paint to bring back its brilliance. You'll be pleasantly surprised with the paint's ability to not only disguise flaws but its ability to add warmth and character to the room.

PAINT IS A QUICK, COST-EFFECTIVE WAY TO COVER UP WOOD FLOORS THAT may need work, but a floor doesn't have to be distressed or damaged to benefit from painting. Floors in perfect condition in both formal and informal spaces can be decorated with paint to add color and personality. For example, one could unify a space by extending a painted floor through a hallway to a staircase. And stencil designs or faux finishes can make an oversized room feel cozy and inviting. There are even techniques for disguising worn spots. One such disguising method also happens to create a fun, yet classical design: the checkerboard pattern allows homeowners to hide worn boards under a darker color while still maintaining a unique floor.

FLOOR PAINTING 101

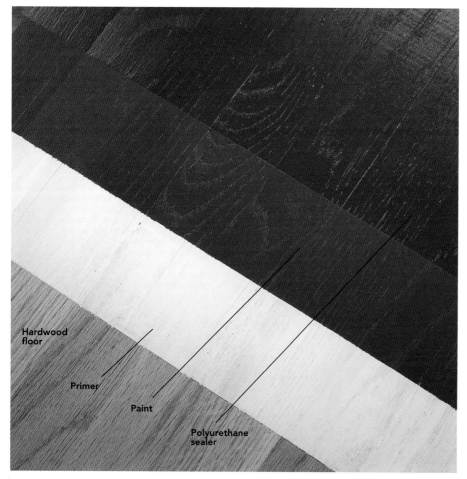

Hardwood floor

Primer

Paint

Polyurethane sealer

To paint a wood floor you must apply primer first; then you apply the paint and you follow that with a polyurethane sealer. Make sure the products you choose are specifically for floors.

TERMS YOU NEED TO KNOW

LACQUER THINNER—A strong, highly flammable solvent such as ethyl alcohol, ethyl acetate and toluene that is used to dilute, dissolve and clean up lacquer based paints, ink and adhesive residue.

PRIMER—A specially-formulated paint that is used to seal raw surfaces and to provide a base coat of paint that succeeding finish coats can better adhere to.

WATER-BASED POLYURETHANE—A clear finish used for coating natural or stained wood that provides a durable, glossy surface that is highly resistant to water, is just as durable as oil-based polyurethane, is easier to clean-up, and does not produce a yellowing discoloration.

SEALER—A finish coating, either clear or pigmented, that is applied on top of the paint.

TOOLS & SUPPLIES YOU'LL NEED

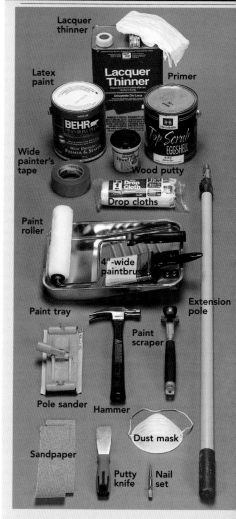

Lacquer thinner

Latex paint

Primer

Wide painter's tape

Wood putty

Drop cloths

Paint roller

4"-wide paintbrush

Extension pole

Paint tray

Paint scraper

Pole sander

Hammer

Dust mask

Sandpaper

Putty knife

Nail set

SKILLS YOU NEED

- Cleaning and sanding
- Using a hammer and nail set
- Using a paintbrush and roller

DIFFICULTY LEVEL

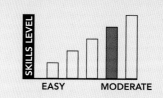

SKILLS LEVEL

EASY   MODERATE

This project can be completed in a day (not including drying time), depending upon how much prep work is needed and how large the room is.

HOW TO PAINT WOOD FLOORS

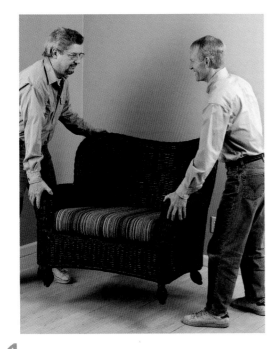

1 Prepare the painting area by first moving furniture. Lift pieces instead of dragging them to prevent gouges. Sweep or vacuum.

2 Use a paint scraper to smooth rough spots. Use a pole sander to sand with the grain of the wood. For coarse wood, use medium-grit sandpaper. Scuff glossy hardwoods with fine sandpaper (#120) for good adhesion.

3 When finished sanding, sweep or vacuum. Use a damp cloth to remove fine dust. Use a cloth dampened with lacquer thinner for a final cleaning. If you see any nails sticking up, tap them down with a hammer and nail set.

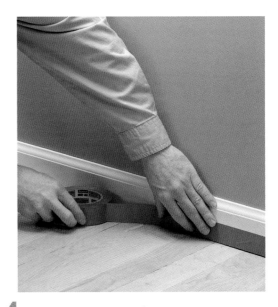

4 Protect the baseboards with wide painter's tape. Press the tape edges down so paint doesn't seep underneath.

5 Mix primer well. Use a 4"-wide brush to apply the primer around the perimeter of the room. Then paint the remaining floor with a roller on an extension pole. Allow the primer to dry.

6 To mix paint, pour half of the paint into another can, stirring the paint in both containers with a wooden stir stick before recombining them. As you stir, you want a smooth consistency.

7 Paint. Use a 4" brush to apply a semi-gloss paint around the border. To paint the rest of the floor, use a roller on an extension pole. Always roll from a dry area to a wet area to minimize lap lines. Allow paint to dry. Apply second coat of paint. Allow to dry.

8 Apply 2 or 3 coats of a matte-finish, water-based polyurethane sealer, using a painting pad on a pole. Allow the sealer to dry. Sand with a pole sander, using fine sandpaper. Clean up dust with a tack cloth.

Installing Laminate Flooring

15

The rich wood tones of beautiful laminate planks may cause you to imagine hours of long, hard installation work, but this is a DIY project that you can do in a single weekend. Buy the manufactured planks at a home-improvement or flooring store and install laminate flooring with the step-by-step instructions offered in the following pages.

LAMINATE FLOORING COMES IN A FLOATING SYSTEM THAT IS SIMPLE TO INSTALL, even if you have no experience with other home-improvement projects. You may install a floating laminate floor right on top of plywood, concrete slab, sheet vinyl, or hardwood flooring (follow the manufacturer's instructions). The pieces are available in planks or squares in a variety of different sizes, colors, and faux finishes—including wood and ceramic. Tongue-and-groove edges lock pieces together, and the entire floor floats on the underlayment. At the end of this project there are a few extra steps to take if your flooring manufacturer recommends using glue on the joints.

LAMINATE JOINTS 101

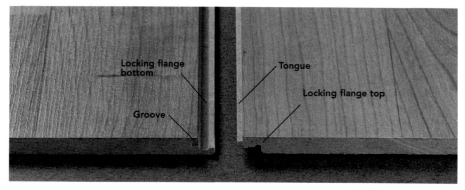

Locking flange bottom

Tongue

Locking flange top

Groove

The joint design for laminate planks and squares is intended to make installation and replacement a breeze, while also providing a barrier from moisture and debris. Today, tongue-and-groove joints are often supplemented with positively locking flanges to provide a tight fit on both the top and bottom of the board. The tongue on one side fits into the groove of the adjacent board; then the the plank is "clicked" into place by pressing down on the plank to join the flanges. Planks without the snap-together ("click") feature sometimes require glue for an extra snug fit (read the manufacturer's instructions carefully and follow all recommendations).

TERMS YOU NEED TO KNOW

SUBFLOOR—The base layer of wood or plywood that supports the underlayment and surface flooring.

UNDERLAYMENT—The intermediate layer between the surface floor and the subfloor.

FLOATING FLOORS—Floors that are not fastened to the subfloor or underlayment, but rather "float" on top. The flooring is held together with a snap-together, interlocking system.

GLUELESS LAMINATE FLOORING (also called "click-floors")—Laminate flooring that does not require glue for installation, but instead relies upon tight tongue-and-groove joints. No-glue flooring is far easier to install and repair than glued laminate flooring, but it may not be as resistant to moisture—so avoid installing it in bathrooms or basements.

GLUED LAMINATE FLOORING—Laminate flooring that requires glue at each plank joint in order to effectively seal together the tongue-and-groove planks.

DRAWBAR—A metal bar used to pull together the final two planks in a row. There are two hooks—one to attach to the end of a plank close to the wall (where a rubber mallet would not fit to tap the final plank into the adjacent plank), and one on the other end to pull the plank in tight with the adjacent board.

STRAP CLAMPS—A device used to hold several planks together tightly while adhesive in between joints dries.

TOOLS & SUPPLIES YOU NEED

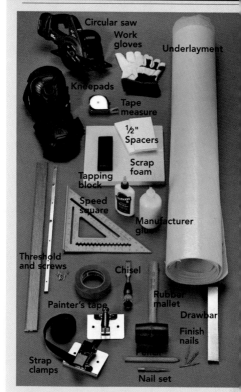

Circular saw
Work gloves
Underlayment
Kneepads
Tape measure
½" Spacers
Scrap foam
Tapping block
Speed square
Manufacturer glue
Threshold and screws
Chisel
Rubber mallet
Painter's tape
Drawbar
Finish nails
Strap clamps
Nail set

For shoe molding removal and replacement: pry bar, wood shims, chisel, hammer, nail set, finish nails.

For glued laminate flooring:
Wood block, rubber mallet, ½" spacers, strap clamps, damp cloth, plastic scraper.

SKILLS YOU NEED

- Measuring
- Using a drawbar
- Drilling
- Simple cuts with a circular saw
- Gluing
- Possibly ripcuts with a jigsaw

If removing base molding:
- Chiseling
- Hammering
- Countersinking nails

DIFFICULTY LEVEL

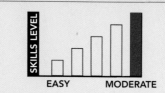

SKILLS LEVEL

EASY   MODERATE

This project can be completed in a weekend.

HOW TO INSTALL LAMINATE FLOORING

Laminate flooring, like hardwood, can shrink or expand when the temperature or humidity in a room changes. This movement can cause planks to buckle, so be sure to allow your new laminate flooring stock to acclimate to the conditions in your house. Simply keep the planks in the room where they will be used for a few days prior to installation.

1 Remove the shoe molding by wedging a pry bar between the shoe molding and baseboards and pry outward. Continue along the wall until the entire shoe is removed. Next, place a scrap board against the wall and use a pry bar to pull the baseboard away from the wall. Maintain the gap with wood shims. Number the sections for easy replacement. Drive protruding nails in floor ⅛" below the surface with a nail set.

2 To install the underlayment, start in one corner and unroll the underlayment to the opposite wall. Cut the underlayment to fit, using a utility knife or scissors. Overlap the second underlayment sheet according to the manufacturer's recommendations, and secure the pieces in place with adhesive tape.

3 Working from the left corner of the room to right, set wall spacers and dry lay planks (tongue side facing the wall) against the wall. The spacers allow for expansion. If you are flooring a room more than 26 ft. long or wide, you need to buy appropriate-sized expansion joints. Note: Some manufacturers suggest facing the groove side to the wall.

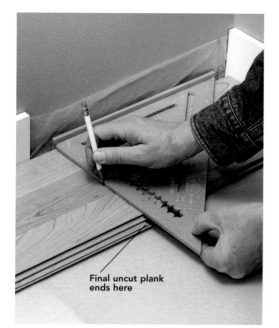

Final uncut plank ends here

4 Set a new plank right side up, on top of the previously laid plank, flush with the spacer against the wall at the end run. Line up a speed square with the bottom plank edge and trace a line. That's the cutline for the final plank in the row.

5 Press painter's tape along the cutline on the top of the plank to prevent chips when cutting. Score the line drawn in Step 4 with a utility knife. Turn the plank over and extend the pencil line to the backside.

6 Clamp the board (face down) and rigid foam insulation or plywood to a work table. The foam discourages chipping. Clamp a speed square on top of the plank, as though you are going to draw another line parallel to the cutline—use this to eye your straight cut. Place the circular saw's blade in front (waste side) of the actual cutline and cut.

7 To create a tight fit for the last plank in the first row, place a spacer against the wall and wedge one end of a drawbar between it and the last plank. Tap the other end of the drawbar with a rubber mallet or hammer. Protect the laminate surface with a thin cloth.

8 Continue to lay rows of flooring, making sure the joints are staggered. Staggering joints prevents the entire floor from relying on just a few joints, thus preventing the planks from lifting. Staggering also stengthens the floor, because the joints are shorter and evenly distributed.

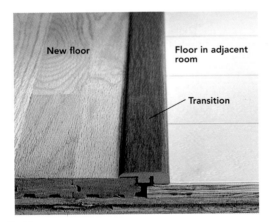

New floor   Floor in adjacent room

Transition

10 Install transition thresholds at room borders where the new floor joins another floor covering. These thresholds are used to tie together dissimilar floor coverings, such as laminate flooring and wood or carpet. They may also be necessary to span a distance in height between flooring in one room and the next.

9 To fit the final row, place two planks on top of the last course; slide the top plank up against the wall spacer. Use the top plank to draw a cut-line lengthwise on the middle plank. Cut the middle plank to size using the same method as in Step 4 (only now you are "ripcutting" a lengthwise cut—see page 319 for instructions on ripcuts). The very last board must be cut lengthwise and widthwise to fit.

HERE'S HOW

To stagger joints, first check the manufacturer's instructions to determine what the minimum distance should be between the staggered joints. The range is usually between 8" and 18" (minimum). The first plank in the second row can sometimes be the waste piece from the cut you made at the end of the last run. But if you don't have a long enough scrap, the first plank in each row should alternate between being ⅓ and ⅔ the length of a full plank. This creates a pattern that is not only pleasing to the eye, but it ensures a solid installation.

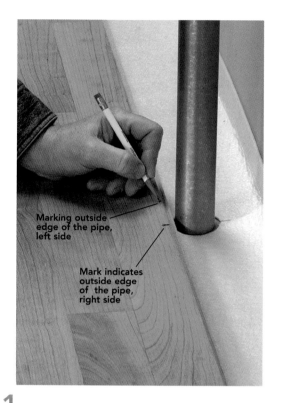

1 Position a plank end against the spacers on the wall next to the obstacle. Use a pencil to make two marks along the length of the plank, indicating the points where the obstacle begins and ends.

2 Once the plank is snapped into the previous row, position the plank end against the obstacle. Make two marks with a pencil, this time on the end of the plank to indicate where the obstacle falls along the width of the board.

3 Use a speed square to extend the four lines. The space at which they all intersect is the part of the plank that needs to be removed to make room for the obstacle to go through it. Use a drill with a Forstner bit, or a hole saw the same diameter as the space within the intersecting lines, and drill through the plank at the X. You'll be left with a hole; extend the cut to the edges with a jigsaw.

4 Install the plank by locking the tongue-and-groove joints with the preceding board. Fit the end piece in behind the pipe or obstacle. Apply manufacturer-recommended glue to the cut edges, and press the end piece tightly against the adjacent plank. Wipe away excess glue with a damp cloth.

HOW TO GLUE LAMINATE FLOORING

1 After dry-fitting each row, completely fill the groove of the plank with the manufacturer glue (or at least as instructed by the manufacturer).

2 Close the gaps between end joints and lengthwise joints, using a rubber mallet to gently tap a block (often supplied by the manufacturer) into the edge or end of the last plank. Use a drawbar for the last planks butted up to a wall. Wipe away excess glue in the joints with a damp cloth before it dries.

3 Rent 6 to 10 strap clamps to hold a few rows of planks together as adhesive dries (about an hour). Fit one end of the strap clamp over the plank nearest the wall, and the other end (the one with the ratchet lever) over the last plank. Use the ratchet to tighten straps until joints are snug.

If you need to cut a plank to fit snugly against another plank or a wall with an obstacle in the middle (such as a heat vent), measure in to the appropriate cutline to fit the board flush with the adjacent board or wall (on the other side of the obstacle). Draw a line across the plank in this location. Then measure the obstacle and transfer those measurements to the plank, using your pencil again. Mark a starter hole on the inside of the lines. Drill the hole just large enough to fit your jigsaw blade into it. Starting in the drilled hole, cut the plank along the drawn lines, using a jigsaw. Set the board in place by locking the tongue-and-groove joints with the preceding board.

1 Ripcut planks from the back side to avoid splintering the top surface. For accurate straight cuts, mark the cut with a chalk line. If you have drawn a pencil line that is not straight, double check your tracing—it may be that your wall is not perfectly straight, and in this case you'd cut along your hand-drawn pencil line.

2 Place another piece of flooring next to the piece marked for cutting to provide a stable surface for the foot of the saw. Also, clamp a cutting guide to the planks at the correct distance from the cutting line to ensure a straight cut.

FLOORING • Installing Laminate Flooring **319**

Installing Floor Tile

16

Tiles can be hand-picked to customize your floor. Picking out complementary colors within a single style is one way to make your floor unique.
Not only is it fun to design your floor with tiles, but the installation requires only a single weekend.

AS WITH ANY TILE INSTALLATION, RESILIENT TILE REQUIRES CAREFULLY POSITIONED LAYOUT lines. Before committing to any layout and applying tile, conduct a dry run to identify potential problems.

Keep in mind the difference between reference lines (see opposite page) and layout lines. Reference lines mark the center of the room and divide it into quadrants. If the tiles don't lay out symmetrically along these lines, you'll need to adjust them slightly, creating layout lines. Once layout lines are established, installing the tile is a fairly quick process. Be sure to keep joints between the tiles tight and lay the tiles square.

Tiles with an obvious grain pattern can be laid so the grain of each tile is oriented identically throughout the installation. You can also use the quarter-turn method, in which each tile has its pattern grain running perpendicular to that of adjacent tiles. Whichever method you choose, be sure to be consistent throughout the project.

REFERENCE LINES 101

1 Position a reference line (X) by measuring along opposite sides of the room and marking the center of each side. Snap a chalk line between these marks.

2 Measure and mark the center-point of the chalk line. From this point, use a framing square to establish a second reference line perpendicular to the first one. Snap the second line (Y) across the room.

3 Check the reference lines for squareness using the 3-4-5 triangle method. Measure along reference line X and make a mark 3 ft. from the centerpoint. Measure from the centerpoint along reference line Y and make a mark at 4 ft.

4 Measure the distance between the marks. If the reference lines are perpendicular, the distance will measure exactly 5 ft. If not, adjust the reference lines until they're exactly perpendicular to each other.

TOOLS & SUPPLIES YOU NEED

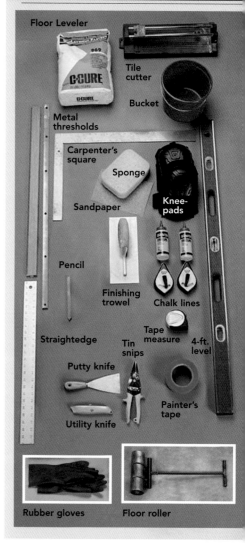

Floor Leveler

C-CURE

Tile cutter

Bucket

Metal thresholds

Carpenter's square

Sponge

Sandpaper

Knee-pads

Pencil

Finishing trowel

Chalk lines

Straightedge

Tin snips

Tape measure

4-ft. level

Putty knife

Painter's tape

Utility knife

Rubber gloves

Floor roller

SKILLS YOU NEED

- Measuring
- Cutting
- Pushing a 75- or 100-pound floor roller
- Using a trowel
- Hammering

TERMS YOU NEED TO KNOW

SUBFLOOR—The base layer of wood or plywood that supports the underlayment and surface flooring.

UNDERLAYMENT—The intermediate layer between the surface flooring material and the subfloor.

STICKY-BACK VINYL TILE—Resilient flooring available in 12" or 16" squares. Each vinyl tile has self-adhesive backing.

DIFFICULTY LEVEL

SKILLS LEVEL

EASY   MODERATE

This project can be completed in a weekend.

1 Snap perpendicular reference lines with a chalk line. Dry-fit tiles along layout line Y so a joint falls along reference line X. If necessary, shift the layout to make the layout symmetrical or to reduce the number of tiles that need to be cut.

2 If you shift the tile layout, create a new line that is parallel to reference line X and runs through a tile joint near line X. The new line, X1, is the line you'll use when installing the tile. Use a different colored chalk to distinguish between lines.

3 Dry-fit tiles along the new line, X1. If necessary, adjust the layout line as in steps 1 and 2.

4 If you adjusted the layout along X1, measure and make a new layout line, Y1, that's parallel to reference line Y and runs through a tile joint. Y1 will form the second layout line you'll use during installation.

5 Apply adhesive around the intersection of the layout lines using a trowel with ⅟₁₆" V-shaped notches. Hold the trowel at a 45° angle and spread adhesive evenly over the surface.

6 Spread adhesive over most of the installation area, covering three quadrants. Allow the adhesive to set according to the manufacturer's instructions, then begin to install the tile at the intersection of the layout lines. You can kneel on installed tiles to lay additional tiles.

7 When the first three quadrants are completely tiled, spread adhesive over the remaining quadrant, then finish setting the tile.

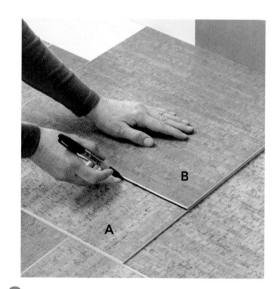

8 To cut tiles to fit along the walls, place the tile to be cut (A) face up on top of the last full tile you installed. Position a ⅛"-thick spacer against the wall, then set a marker tile (B) on top of the tile to be cut. Trace along the edge of the marker tile to draw a cutting line.

9 Cut tile to fit using a utility knife and straightedge. Hold the straightedge securely against the cutting line to ensure a straight cut. Option: You can use a ceramic-tile cutter to make straight cuts in thick vinyl tiles (see inset).

10 Install cut tiles next to the walls. If you're precutting all tiles before installing them, measure the distance between the wall and install tiles at various points in case the distance changes.

11 Continue installing tile in the remaining quadrants until the room is completely covered. Check the entire floor. If you find loose areas, press down on the tiles to bond them to the underlayment. Install metal threshold bars at room borders where the new floor joins another floor covering.

TOOL TIP

To mark tiles for cutting around outside corners, make a cardboard template to match the space, keeping a ⅛" gap along the walls. After cutting the template, check to make sure it fits. Place the template on a tile and trace its outline.

HOW TO INSTALL SELF-ADHESIVE RESILIENT TILE

1 Once your reference lines are established, peel off the paper backing and install the first tile in one of the corners formed by the intersecting layout lines. Lay three or more tiles along each layout line in the quadrant. Rub the entire surface of each tile to bond the adhesive to the floor underlayment.

2 Begin installing tiles in the interior area of the quadrant. Keep the joints tight between tiles. Use a floor roller to set tile and prevent bubbles.

3 Finish setting full tiles in the first quadrant, then set the full tiles in an adjacent quadrant. Set the tiles along the layout lines first, then fill in the interior tiles.

4 Continue installing the tile in the remaining quadrants until the room is completely covered. Check the entire floor. If you find loose areas, press down on the tiles to bond them to the underlayment. Install metal threshold bars at room border where the new floor joins another floor covering.

HOW TO INSTALL A GLASS MOSAIC FLOOR

1 Beginning at the intersection of the horizontal and vertical lines, apply the recommended adhesive in one quadrant. Spread it outward evenly with a notched trowel. Lay down only as much adhesive as you can cover in 10 to 15 minutes.

2 Stabilize a sheet of tile by randomly inserting plastic spacers into the open joints.

3 Pick up diagonally opposite corners of the square and move it to the intersection of the horizontal and vertical references lines. Align the sides with the reference lines and gently press one corner into place on the adhesive. Slowly lower the opposite corner, making sure the sides remain square with the reference lines. Massage the sheet into the adhesive, being careful not to press too hard or twist the sheet out of position. Continue setting tile, filling in one square area after another.

4 When two or three sheets are in place, lay a scrap of 2 × 4 wrapped in carpet across them and tap it with a rubber mallet to set the fabric mesh into the adhesive and force out any trapped air.

5 When you've tiled up close to the wall or another boundary, lay a full mosaic sheet into position and mark it for trimming. Use a glass cutter to score along the cut line.

6 After you've scored the tiles, cut them each individually with a pair of tile nippers.

7 Set tile in the remaining quadrants. Let the adhesive cure according to the manufacturer's instructions. Remove spacers with a needlenose pliers. Mix a batch of grout and fill the joints (see page 276). Allow the grout to dry, according to manufacturer's instructions.

8 Mosaic tile has a much higher ratio of grout to tile than larger tiles do, so it is especially important to seal the grout with a quality sealer after it has cured. Follow the manufacturer's instructions.

Painting & Decorating

YOU'VE SEEN THE HOME MAKEOVER SHOWS ON TV; YOU'VE ADMIRED YOUR FRIENDS' PROJECTS; YOU'VE READ ON-LINE ARTICLES ABOUT HOW EASY THIS ALL IS. AND YET, YOU'RE STILL JUST A LITTLE UNSURE ABOUT THIS IDEA OF TACKLING A DECORATING PROJECT.

Relax. You've come to exactly the right place. This book was written with you in mind—a new homeowner or, perhaps, someone who's just new to decorating. Even if you are seasoned with decorating experience, you will find valuable tips and professional procedures to incorporate into your next project. The information you need is all right here.

IN THIS CHAPTER:

- ❏ Before You Begin
    - Painting Tools
    - Decorating Tools
    - Prep Materials
    - Choosing Paint
- ❏ Hanging Pictures & Mirrors
- ❏ Replacing Towel Bars
- ❏ Hanging Curtains
- ❏ Installing Window Blinds & Shades
- ❏ Anchoring Bookcases
- ❏ Draping & Taping
- ❏ Painting Walls
- ❏ Preparing Unfinished Wood for Paint

- ❏ Painting Millwork & Trim
- ❏ Painting Wood Cabinets
- ❏ Painting Concrete Block Walls
- ❏ Stripping Wallcoverings
- ❏ Hanging Wallcoverings

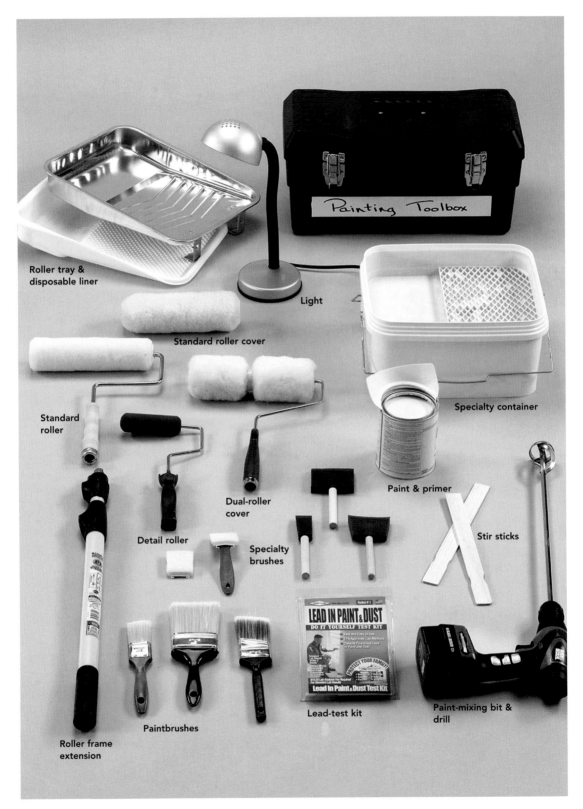

Roller tray &
disposable liner

Light

Standard roller cover

Specialty container

Standard
roller

Paint & primer

Detail roller

Dual-roller
cover

Stir sticks

Specialty
brushes

Roller frame
extension

Paintbrushes

Lead-test kit

Paint-mixing bit &
drill

These are the tools you'll need for your painting toolbox. All these tools are available at almost
every home improvement center, paint store, and hardware store.

WHEN IT COMES TO PAINTING TOOLS, SOME PEO-PLE PREFER DISPOSABLE TOOLS WHILE OTHERS value traditional versions. The differences between the two are cost and quality.

•PAINTBRUSHES: All-purpose brushes are made from a blend of polyester and nylon. Brushes blended with hog or ox bristles should only be used with oil-based paints. Your kit should include a 3" straightedged wall brush, 2" straightedged trim brush, and tapered sash brush. A good-quality brush has a shaped handle, non-corrosive metal ferrule, and several spacer plugs between bristles. Split ("flagged") and tapered ("chiseled") bristle ends make clean edges.

•ROLLER TRAYS: Sturdy trays are a must. Disposable pan liners minimize cleanup, but they are not substitutes for roller trays.

•STANDARD ROLLER FRAMES: Choose a well-balanced frame with nylon bearings and a comfortable handle. Extensions are available for painting ceilings.

•STANDARD ROLLER COVERS: Most jobs can be done with ⅜" synthetic rollers. Special corner roller covers allow you to paint corners without cutting in the edges. Good-quality roller covers create an attractive finish without leaving fibers in the paint.

•SPECIAL CONTAINERS: Large and small containers simplify large projects. For large projects, some paint manufacturers sell their paint in 5-gallon containers, so you can paint straight from the container. If the paint you choose doesn't come in a container like this, you may want to buy one. For cutting-in and touch-ups, small, easy-to-hold containers are a good idea.

•PAINT-MIXING BIT AND DRILL: Stirring paint is extremely important. The best way to stir large amounts of paint is with a drill and special paint-mixing bit. These bits are easy to use and clean up quickly.

•LEAD TEST KIT: If your home was built before 1978, it's critical that you test paint before cleaning, sanding, or repainting it. Easy-to-use lead test kits are available at home centers, hardware stores, and paint retailers everywhere. If the test indicates the presence of lead, consult a lead abatement specialist before starting any project.

Once you get to the chapters, you'll notice there may be a red toolbox in the Materials List. If you see that, it means you'll need your toolbox with all of the above tools in it for that particular project. There may be additional tools needed that are specific to the project at hand, but having this toolbox organized and at-hand will save a lot of time.

Before You Begin: Decorating Tools

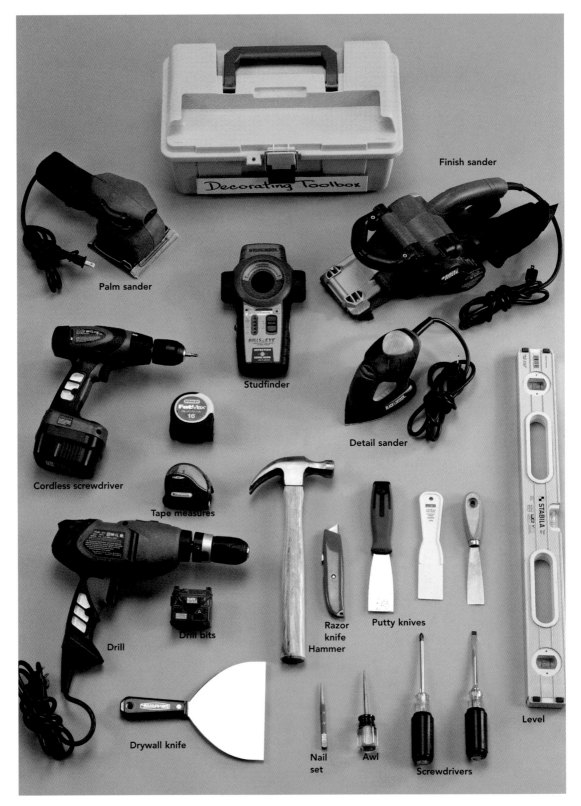

These are the tools you'll need for your decorating toolbox. All these tools are available at almost every home improvement center, paint store, and hardware store.

•CARPENTER'S OR LASER LEVEL: A carpenter's level contains two or more bubble gauges used to check the level of work surfaces. A laser level creates level, square lines on any surface.

•HAMMER: Designed for driving, setting, and pulling nails, hammers are essential. A 16-ounce, curved claw hammer with a high-carbon steel head and a handle made of hickory, fiberglass, or solid steel is a practical choice for typical home repairs.

•DRILL: Variable-speed reversing drills are handy for driving and removing screws, nuts, and bolts, as well as for drilling holes and stirring paint. For most decorating projects, a medium-voltage cordless drill is a good choice. Look for features such as a keyless chuck, adjustable clutch, and electronic level.

•CORDLESS SCREWDRIVER: For small projects, cordless power screwdrivers are a great alternative to standard screwdrivers. These tools come with a universal ¼" drive as well as a slotted bit and a #2 Phillips bit. Other bits, such as Torx and square drive, are also available.

•POWER SANDERS: Sanders smooth surfaces to be painted or decorated.

•SCREWDRIVERS: Standard screwdrivers—both slotted and Phillips—are essential. Choose quality screwdrivers with hardened-steel blades and easy-to-grip handles. Insulated handles protect you from electric shock, and oxide-coated tips provide a strong hold on screw heads.

•TAPE MEASURES: A high-quality, retractable steel tape measure will last for decades. Choose a tape that has a locking mechanism and a belt clip. Make sure the tape you choose has a standout of at least 7 ft.

•STUD FINDER: A stud finder has an indicator that lights up when it passes over a stud.

•AWL: An awl is a tool that has a metal shaft with a sharpened end. It is used to poke holes in drywall and other surfaces when drilling a pilot hole isn't necessary.

•NAIL SET: This is a metal shaft with a rounded end that is used to drive finish nails below a work surface.

•DRYWALL KNIVES ("PUTTY" KNIVES): These knives have thin, somewhat flexible blades attached to sturdy handles. They are used to spread spackle and drywall compound and can also be used to scrape away debris before cleaning walls or filling holes.

•RAZOR KNIFE: A razor knife is a sharp, retractable, disposable blade in a sturdy handle.

If you see a yellow toolbox in a materials list, it means that some or all of the above tools are needed to get that particular job done.

Before You Begin:
Prep Materials

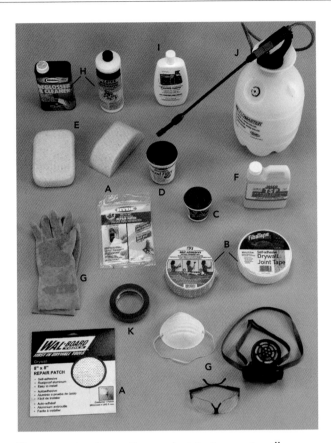

If you want a decorating project to turn out well, you simply have to do the necessary preparation work. With the help of the tools and materials available today, preparation stages go smoothly and easily.

A) HOLE-PATCHING KITS: Sturdy, self-adhesive mesh and backing materials used to repair large holes in walls.

B) SELF-ADHESIVE SEAM TAPE: Used to smooth drywall compound over joints and cracks.

C) SPACKLE: A quick-drying drywall compound. Some types of spackle are pink when wet and turn white as they dry, which makes it easy to tell when the patch is ready to be sanded.

D) WOOD FILLER: Compound used to fill holes in wood. It can be sanded and painted or stained.

E) SPONGES: Used to smooth damp joint compound, which reduces the amount of sanding needed later.

F) TRISODIUM PHOSPHATE: Cleaning agent used for washing walls before painting or hanging wallpaper.

G) SAFETY EQUIPMENT: Rubber gloves, safety glasses, and dust masks or respirators; these are necessary when using strong or caustic chemicals.

H) PREPARATION LIQUIDS: A latex-bonding agent makes plaster repairs more durable; liquid deglosser dulls glossy surfaces so paint can adhere properly.

I) WALLPAPER STRIPPER: A chemical agent that loosens wallpaper adhesive so it can be removed easily.

J) PRESSURE SPRAYER: Used to apply wallpaper stripper over large areas.

K) EASY-RELEASE PAINTER'S TAPE: Tape designed for easy and clean removal (does not leave an adhesive residue).

Before You Begin: Choosing Paint

Paint prices are often accurate reflections of quality. As a general rule, buy the best paint your budget allows. High-quality paint is easier to use and looks better than less expensive paint. Quality paints often last longer and require fewer coats, too.

LATEX PAINT: Water-based paint that's easy to use and cleans up with soap and water. Latex paint is suitable for nearly every application.

ALKYD PAINT: Oil-based paint that produces a durable finish; cleans up with paint thinner or mineral spirits. Some painters feel that alkyd paint produces a smoother finish, but local regulations restrict its use in some communities.

Paint comes in various sheens, ranging from flat to high-gloss enamel. Gloss enamels dry to a shiny finish and are best for surfaces that need to be washed often, such as bathroom or kitchen walls or woodwork in any room. Flat paints are used for walls and ceilings.

PRIMER: Primer bonds well to all surfaces and provides a durable base that helps keep the finish coat from cracking or peeling. Always use a good primer to prepare surfaces for painting.

TINTED PRIMER: When using deep colors, tinted primer reduces the number of coats of paint necessary to achieve good coverage.

Hanging Pictures & Mirrors

1

Hanging pictures and mirrors instantly personalizes a room, and it's easy to do when you approach it with the right tools and a good attitude. We'll show you how to position a piece properly and hang it securely—the first time.

IF YOU'VE EVER MADE SIX HOLES IN A WALL TO HANG ONE PICTURE, YOU KNOW HOW FRUSTRATING THE PROCESS CAN BE. Most of us have done it, and none of us want to repeat the experience. Great news! By following the steps outlined here and using the right hardware, you can hang a picture without making a single unnecessary hole.

Before getting out your tools, study the size and shape of the room. Designers and decorators often suggest placing the center of a picture or mirror at eye level—57 to 60 inches above the floor—but that's a guideline, not a hard and fast rule. If you're placing a mirror behind a sideboard or a picture over a mantle, let the style of the room and a sense of balance guide its placement.

HOW TO HANG PICTURES & MIRRORS

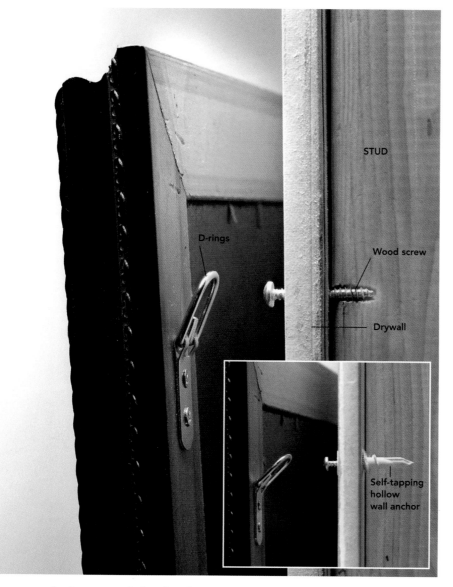

STUD

D-rings

Wood screw

Drywall

Self-tapping hollow wall anchor

Frames and mirrors remain level and secure when they're supported by wall studs and sturdy hardware. Before you can choose hardware, find out what the piece weighs. While shopping, check the labels on the hardware you're considering to make sure it will support the weight of the piece you're going to hang.

TERMS YOU NEED TO KNOW

STUD—The lumber used to frame a wall. Typically 2 × 4s spaced 16" apart.

STUD FINDER—A handheld device used to locate studs behind drywall and wall coverings.

TOOLS & SUPPLIES YOU NEED

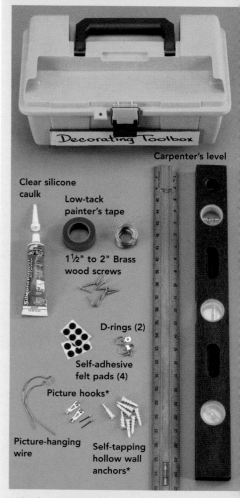

Decorating Toolbox

Carpenter's level

Clear silicone caulk

Low-tack painter's tape

1½" to 2" Brass wood screws

D-rings (2)

Self-adhesive felt pads (4)

Picture hooks*

Picture-hanging wire

Self-tapping hollow wall anchors*

* Match to weight of piece to be hung.

SKILLS YOU NEED

- Measuring accurately
- Light carpentry tool skills

DIFFICULTY LEVEL

This project takes less than 30 minutes.

HOW TO HANG A PICTURE

1 On each side of the frame, mark 8" down from the top. Purchase D-rings or picture hooks rated to support the approximate weight of the picture or mirror (package labels on the hardware give the suggested weight ranges).

2 Set the D-rings aside, and then use an awl to punch a hole at each mark on the frame. Reposition the first D-ring and drive a screw into the mark, securely attaching the D-ring to the frame. Repeat on the other side.

3 Attach a self-adhesive felt pad at each corner of the frame.

4 In the area where you want to hang the frame, place a piece of tape at the appropriate height, measured from the floor (usually 57 to 60", depending on the room's dimensions). Following manufacturer's directions, use a stud finder to locate the studs and mark the tape to indicate their positions.

5 Measure the width of the frame and divide that number by 2—this is the center of your frame. On the tape, mark the proposed center of the frame, and then mark the edge of the frame the calculated distance on each side. If possible, align the frame so that the three points are near your stud marks.

6 Measure down 8" from the frame side marks for the D-ring placement. If studs are not available, drive self-tapping hollow wall anchors into the holes (as shown), and then drill a screw into each anchor. If studs are available, drill wood screws directly into the studs.

7 Slip the D-rings or picture hooks over the screws on the wall. Your picture should now be straight and secure with nary an extra hole to repair.

QUICK FIX

Putting a felt pad at each corner of a frame helps it hang straight and keeps it from marking the walls. If you don't have any on hand, don't despair: Silicone caulk will do the trick quite nicely. Put a dot of caulk (about the diameter of a pencil eraser) on each corner. As soon as the caulk dries, you're good to go.

Replacing Towel Bars

2

New accessories update a bathroom in a flash, without much trouble or expense. The important thing is to make sure the hanging hardware is supported by studs or hollow wall anchors rated for the bar's weight.

EVEN WHEN IT COMES TO TOWEL BARS AND OTHER BATHROOM ACCESSORIES, STYLES CHANGE WITH THE TIMES. No matter how much we love them now, in a decade or so, today's hot styles will be hopelessly out of date. And so it goes.

If the towel bars in your bathroom are damaged, out of date, or just plain ugly, it's time to replace them. There are a few things to think about before you go shopping. First, take a look at the finish on the faucets in the room. Generally, it's best to choose accessories that match or coordinate with the faucets. Next, measure the mounting plates on the existing accessories. It's easier to produce professional-looking results if the plates on the new accessories are the same size or larger than the existing ones.

Although we're showing a towel bar in this project, most bathroom accessories are installed in a similar fashion. Once you understand the process, you'll be ready to add any accessory you want or need.

HOW TO REPLACE A TOWEL BAR

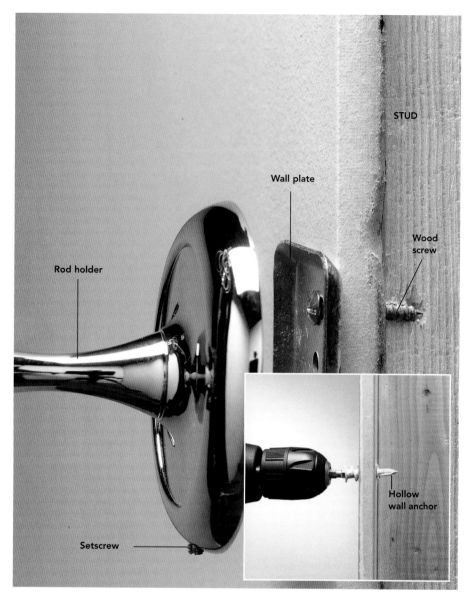

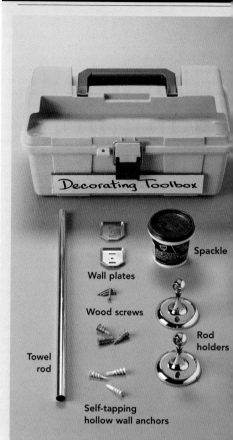

Decorating Toolbox

Spackle

Wall plates

Wood screws

Rod holders

Towel rod

Self-tapping hollow wall anchors

STUD

Wall plate

Wood screw

Rod holder

Hollow wall anchor

Setscrew

Towel bars and other bathroom accessories are supported by mounting plates attached to walls. The mounting plate must be securely supported by wall studs or hollow wall anchors.

SKILLS YOU NEED

- Measuring accurately
- Light carpentry tool skills

DIFFICULTY LEVEL

This project takes less than 30 minutes.

TERMS YOU NEED TO KNOW

SETSCREW—A small screw that holds a part in place. On towel bars, they're typically found on the bottom, out of sight as much as possible.

MOUNTING PLATE—The hardware that supports the weight of the towel bar or accessory.

SPACKLE—A filler for cracks and holes in walls. Available premixed in small containers for routine repairs.

HOW TO INSTALL A NEW TOWEL BAR

1 Position the towel bar and make a mark along the outside of the mounting trim on each side. (Try to avoid positioning the bar so the new holes will fall directly over the old ones.) Repeat for the other side.

2 Center the mounting plate between the marks made in step 1, and then make marks for the screw locations. Repeat this process on the other side. Check the marks with a level, and adjust if necessary. Use a stud finder to check if the marks are located over studs.

TOOL TIP

If the old plates are secure, leave them in place. To ensure the new towel bar fits your existing plates, measure the mounting plates remaining on the wall.

3 Drill pilot holes, and then hold the first mounting plate in place and drive screws to attach it to the wall. Repeat on the other side.

Option: If studs will not support the screws, use an awl to make a small hole at each mark, and then drive a self-tapping hollow wall anchor into the wall.

4 Settle the towel bar onto the mounting plates. Tighten the setscrews that hold the bar to the mounting plates. (Again, these setscrews typically are found on the bottom of the mounting trim.)

WHAT IF...?

What if I want to install a towel bar on a ceramic tile wall?

Follow the directions as given, but use a ceramic tile bit with a carbide tip to drill the pilot holes. Before beginning to drill, scratch a dimple into the tile with an awl or a sharp nail. (Starting beyond the tile's glaze helps keep the bit from dancing around on the tile.)

Hanging Curtains

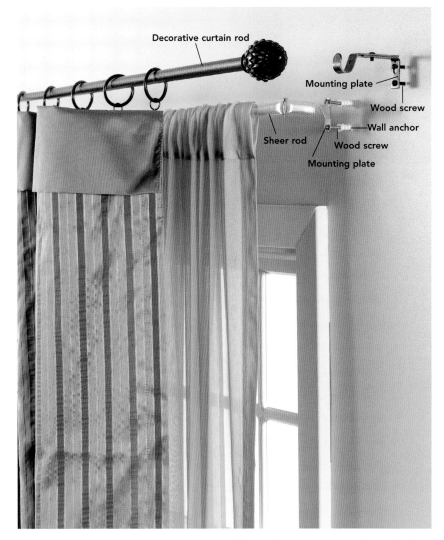

3

Decorative curtain rod

Mounting plate

Wood screw

Wall anchor

Wood screw

Sheer rod

Mounting plate

Curtains can dress a room in elegance, lighten the room's mood, or do little more than filter incoming light—it's completely up to you. Choosing them may take some time, but hanging them can be a breeze.

PUTTING UP CURTAINS IS ONE OF THOSE PROJECTS THAT MANY HOMEOWNERS DREAD: IT INVOLVES CREATING HOLES IN THE WALLS, AND MISTAKES OR MIS-CALCULATIONS SHOW IMMEDIATELY. Take a deep breath. There's no reason to let hanging curtains become an exercise in frustration. With the information we're about to give you and some advance planning, you'll be able to get it right the first time, every time. Honestly.

There are several decisions to be made long before the measuring and drilling starts, and each is important to the success of the project. First, how much of the window will the curtains cover? Do they need to open and close? And what kind of hanging hardware do you like?

HOW TO HANG CURTAINS

TOOLS & SUPPLIES YOU NEED

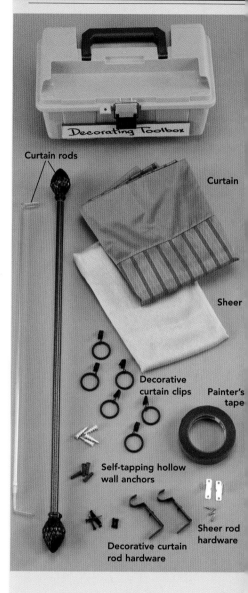

Curtain rods

Curtain

Sheer

Decorative curtain clips

Painter's tape

Self-tapping hollow wall anchors

Sheer rod hardware

Decorative curtain rod hardware

1 Measure the height and width of the window. Make a quick diagram of the window and note the measurements you took. Before purchasing curtains or hardware, decide where you want the curtains to start and stop, and indicate those measurements on your diagram. Attach the brackets for the sheer rod. Place the sheer rod and check for level. Adjust if necessary.

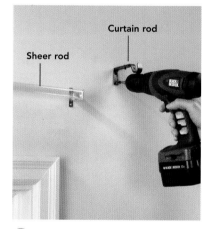

Sheer rod

Curtain rod

2 Attach the brackets for the decorative curtain rod a few inches outside and above the sheer brackets. Use wall anchors if the bracket is not located over a stud.

3 Place the curtain over the sheer rod, and then place the rod for the sheer into the mounting plate. Repeat for the decorative curtains and rod.

SKILLS YOU NEED

- Measuring accurately
- Light carpentry tool skills

DIFFICULTY LEVEL

This project takes 60 to 90 minutes.

Installing
Window Blinds & Shades

4

Horizontal blinds and shades improve energy efficiency and light control in an easy-to-install, reasonably priced package. Many retailers will cut them to fit while you wait—all you have to do is provide accurate measurements.

HORIZONTAL BLINDS AND SHADES CAN BE OPENED OR CLOSED COMPLETELY WITH A PUSH OF A BUTTON OR A TUG ON A CORD. Plus, just a twist of a rod tilts blinds to filter light or direct light as needed. And then there are hybrid products—sheer shades sandwiched around slats that can be louvered like blinds. With the many products available today, it's easy to find one that suits your needs as well as your room's needs.

With blinds and shades, as with most window treatments, the key to easy installation is careful measurement and good preparation. It's important to decide exactly what you want the blinds to accomplish before shopping—even before measuring. A quick evaluation of the room and window in question is the basis for all the decisions you'll have to make.

BLINDS & SHADES 101

Typical roll-up window shades are mounted to the inside edges of the jamb, as shown above. Many styles of blinds are mounted to the wall above the window (called "outside mount").

TERMS YOU NEED TO KNOW

WINDOW FRAME—The enclosure in which a window sash is mounted.

WINDOW JAMB—The vertical pieces that form the sides of a window.

HEAD RAIL—The top part of the blinds where the mechanisms are housed.

VALANCE—A decorative piece that covers the top of a window treatment. On blinds, the valance covers the head rail and brackets.

HOLD-DOWN CLIP—A small piece of hardware that holds the lower edge of a blind or shade in place. Keeps blinds from flapping against the frame when the window is open.

TOOLS & SUPPLIES YOU NEED

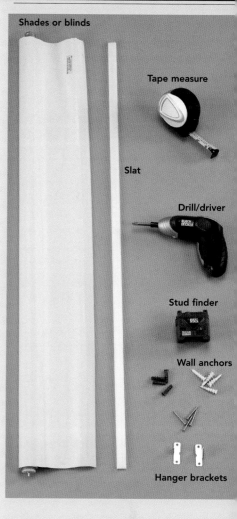

Shades or blinds

Tape measure

Slat

Drill/driver

Stud finder

Wall anchors

Hanger brackets

SKILLS YOU NEED

- Measuring accurately
- Light carpentry tool skills

DIFFICULTY LEVEL

This project takes 30 to 60 minutes.

HOW TO HANG ROLL-UP SHADES

1 At the top, bottom, and middle of the window frame, measure the opening between the side jambs. Make a quick diagram of the window and note the smallest of the three measurements.

2 Measure the height of the window frame (between the top and bottom), at each side, and in the middle. Add the largest of these measurements to your diagram. With your diagram in hand, purchase blinds or shades to fit the window. If possible, have the retailer cut the blinds or shades to your specifications. If that's not possible, buy the closest size (a bit smaller) to the window opening.

3 To cut standard roll-up shades to length, remove the slat from the bottom edge and cut through the hem with scissors. Carefully tear the material until you reach the roller tube. Follow the manufacturer's specific instructions.

4 Remove the excess cardboard, and then remove the roller end from the tube. Cut the tube to length with a hacksaw (metal) or finetooth wood saw (cardboard).

5 Roll the shade material back up, and then push the roller end inward and replace the end cap.

6 Cut the slat (that fits into hems) to length, according to manufacturer's instructions. For basic roller shades, you simply snap the slat apart at the desired location.

7 Position the first bracket flush with the upper front corner of the window frame, and mark its screw holes. Drill a pilot hole at each mark, hold the bracket in place, and then drive in the screws to secure it. Repeat for the other bracket, making sure the two brackets are level.

8 Slide the pin end of the head rail into the bracket on one end, and then slide the slatted end into the other bracket.

1 To mount blinds outside the window frame, measure the width from the outside edges of the window frame and the height from 2" to 3" above to 2" to 3" below the frame. If the window doesn't have a frame, measure the opening and add a few inches on each side. Make a diagram of the measurements and refer to it when purchasing blinds to fit.

2 Position the first bracket as indicated by the diagram you made in step 1, and mark its screw holes. Use a stud finder to locate nearby studs. If a stud is in the bracket area, drill pilot holes at the marks and attach the bracket to the wall. If no stud is available, use an awl to make a small hole at each mark, and then drive a self-tapping hollow wall anchor into each. Finally, drive a screw into each anchor.

3 Shoot a line with a laser level or use a standard level to draw a level line across the wall from the top edge of the bracket to the planned position for the second bracket. Position the second bracket and fasten it to the wall as described in step 2.

4 Lift the blinds into place and install them in the brackets on the wall. Follow the manufacturer's instructions to ensure a secure fit.

HORIZONTAL BLINDS are available in a variety of materials and slat sizes. Mini-blinds (½" to ⅝" slats) work well for small or shallow windows. Venetian blinds (approximately 2" slats) minimize the space the blinds take when closed.

CELLULAR SHADES are energy efficient, attractive, and blend well into most rooms. Their honey-comb construction and opaque materials provide excellent insulation and privacy.

WINDOW SHADINGS, a hybrid of blinds and cellular shades, consist of sheer shades sandwiched around opaque blinds that can be tilted to control light. They give you energy efficiency and privacy.

Metal, vinyl, and aluminum (shown) blinds offer unique colors and textures.

Wood blinds (shown), bamboo, and natural materials have a casual, green feel.

Honeycomb (cellular) shades come in a variety of colors and transparencies.

Mini-blinds have slats that range from ½" to ⅝".

Venetian blinds have larger slats, usually 2" or more.

There are several varieties of blinds/cellular shades. This combination allows for the perfect amount of light at any given time.

Anchoring Bookcases

5

Anchoring bookcases to a wall keeps them securely in place, no matter how they're loaded or used.

FREESTANDING BOOKCASES ARE TOP-HEAVY, ESPECIALLY WHEN FULLY LOADED WITH BOOKS AND OTHER OBJECTS. This can be dangerous, especially in homes with children. Anchoring bookcases eliminates the possibility of one falling over, which is especially valuable if you live in an earthquake-prone area.

Anchoring a bookcase is very easy to do, as long as you're comfortable using a circular saw. Don't worry! We'll walk you through the steps of using this tool as well.

FRENCH CLEAT 101

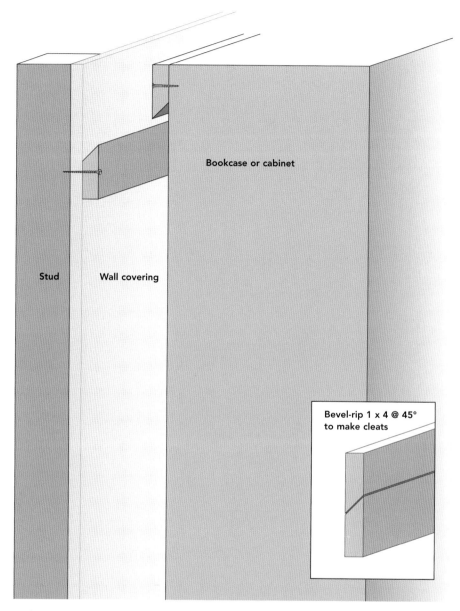

Stud   Wall covering

Bookcase or cabinet

Bevel-rip 1 x 4 @ 45°
to make cleats

A cleat is a simple device—really nothing more than a 1 × 4 or 1 × 6 rip-cut at a 45° bevel. One half of the cleat is attached to the bookcase with the angled edge down and the other is attached to the wall with the angled edge up. When the bookcase is in place, the cleat on the back of the bookcase is supported by the one attached to the wall. Studs or sturdy wall anchors must support the screws holding the cleat to the wall.

TERMS YOU NEED TO KNOW

FRENCH CLEAT—A piece of wood that's bevel-ripped and used to attach an item (such as a cabinet or bookcase) to a wall.

TOOLS & SUPPLIES YOU NEED

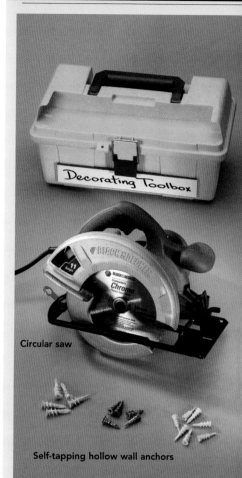

Circular saw

Self-tapping hollow wall anchors

SKILLS YOU NEED

- Measuring accurately
- Light carpentry tool skills

DIFFICULTY LEVEL

This project takes 60 minutes.

HOW TO ANCHOR A BOOKCASE

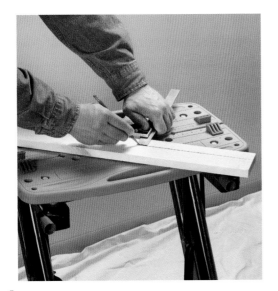

1 Cut a piece of 1 × 4 or 1 × 6 that is 8" less than the width of the bookcase. Mark a rip-cutting line that's offset about ½" from the middle.

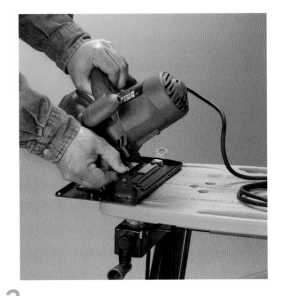

2 Set the bevel on a circular saw to 45° and cut along the marked line, rip-cut using a straitedge guide. Or, use a tablesaw if you have access to one.

TOOL TIP

The angle of the blade on a circular saw can be set for beveled cuts. Check the owner's manual for specific directions, but in general you push or unscrew a safety release, set the angle according to a marked gauge, then reset the safety.

3 Center one cleat so the square edge is flush with the top and bottom of the bookcase. Use wood screws to attach it to the bookcase, with the angled points facing down. Be sure to screw into the bookcase frame, not just the backing material.

4 Measure the height of the bookcase, and draw or shoot a level line onto the wall in the area where the bookcase will be anchored, flush with the top and as wide as the bookcase. Using a stud finder, locate and mark the studs above the line. If you are working near the ceiling, allow enough space for the top cleat to clear the bottom cleat.

5 Center the top of the wall cleat against the line marked on the wall, with the angled point facing up. Attach the cleat to the wall by driving 2½" drywall screws through it and into the studs as marked.

6 Lift the bookcase and settle the bookcase cleat onto the wall cleat. Adjust the bookcase until it's secure against the wall.

Draping & Taping

6

A little time spent applying tape and laying out plastic sheeting and drop cloths saves hours of cleanup at the end of a project.

NO MATTER HOW CAREFUL YOU ARE, PAINTING PROJECTS CAN GET MESSY. Dry paint—even latex paint—is virtually impossible to remove from most fabrics and not much fun to remove from any other surface. Careful draping and taping saves your precious belongings and reduces the amount of cleanup necessary when the project is complete.

DRAPING & TAPING 101

Painting projects go quickly and smoothly when the project area has been prepared and surfaces not to be painted have been draped and taped off to protect them from splatters and other mistakes. Tape off woodwork with easy-release painter's tape, cover floors with drop cloths, and cover walls that will not be painted with plastic sheeting.

TERMS YOU NEED TO KNOW

PLATE COVER—A decorative piece that covers the opening for a light fixture.

EASY-RELEASE PAINTER'S TAPE—A type of low-tack tape designed to be easy to remove without leaving adhesive residue.

Drop cloths

Plastic sheeting

Easy-release painter's tape

Screwdrivers

SKILLS YOU NEED

- Working on a ladder
- Taping with accuracy

DIFFICULTY LEVEL

This project takes 1 to 2 hours.

HOW TO DRAPE & TAPE
BEFORE PAINTING A CEILING

1 In rooms with hanging light fixtures, shut off the power to the circuit, lower the plate cover, and pull a trash bag up from the bottom of the fixture. Tie a knot at the top, neatly covering the entire piece. In bathrooms, place a lawn-sized trash bag over the toilet and tape it in place.

2 Remove as many objects as possible from the room, then cover everything else with plastic. Cover the remaining area of the floor with canvas drop cloths.

3 Press the top half of 2" masking tape along the joint between the ceiling and the wall. Leave the bottom half of the tape loose.

4 Slide sheet plastic under the masking tape, and press the tape down just enough to hold it in place. Make sure the plastic is long enough to protect the baseboards as well as the walls.

HOW TO TAPE
BEFORE PAINTING WALLS OR MILLWORK

1 Shut off the electricity to the circuits in the room. Remove the covers from receptacles and switches as well as heating and air-conditioning duct covers. Tape over gaps between the boxes and the switch or receptacle. Restore power.

2 Align painter's tape with the outside edge of the window molding; press in place. Run the tip of a putty knife along the edge of the tape to seal it so paint can't seep under the edges.

3 Align wide painter's tape with the top edge of the baseboard. Run the tip of a putty knife along the inside edge to seal it, but leave the tape parallel to the floor to shield the rest of the baseboard.

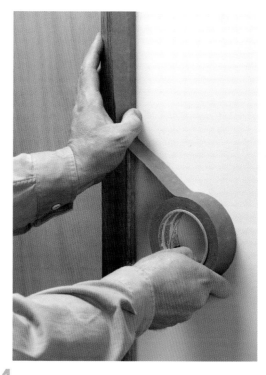

4 Before painting trim and millwork, tape off edges of the walls. Line up the tape with the edge of the millwork and press it into place.

Painting Walls

Painting a wall is a simple matter of distributing paint evenly. The simple techniques described here will help you do that with ease.

PREPARING TO PAINT CAN BE TEDIOUS. Actually painting is fun: It goes fairly quickly and progress is immediately obvious.

It's much easier to see missed areas in natural light, so try to complete the project in daylight. Use high-quality paint and tools, and work with full brushes and rollers to keep lap marks to a minimum.

When painting bare drywall or plaster, apply a coat of primer to the entire project area and let it dry before applying the paint. When applying dark or deep colors (especially reds), have the primer tinted to match the paint; tinted primer reduces the number of paint coats required for full coverage.

Roll one 2   4-ft. section at a time, cutting in the edges and corners before rolling the main area. Roll the area while the areas that have been cut in are still wet, and start the next section while the edges of the first are still wet. This technique, called "painting to a wet edge," keeps lap marks from showing on the finished wall.

WALL PAINTING 101

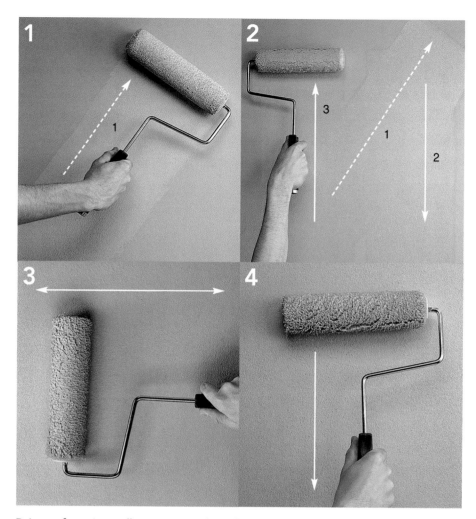

Primer

Paint

BEHR

Masking tape

Paint surfaces in small sections, working from dry surfaces back into wet paint to avoid roller marks. 1. With loaded roller, make a diagonal sweep (1) about 4' long on the surface. On walls, roll upward on the first stroke to avoid spilling paint. Use slow roller strokes to avoid splattering. 2. Draw the roller straight down (2) from the top of the diagonal sweep. Shift the roller to the beginning of the diagonal and roll up (3) to complete the unloading of the roller. 3. Distribute paint over the rest of the section with horizontal back-and-forth strokes. 4. Smooth the area by lightly drawing the roller vertically from the top to the bottom of the painted area. Lift the roller and return it to the top of the area after each stroke.

SKILLS YOU NEED

- Loading a roller
- Cutting in edges and corners
- Rolling paint smoothly

TERMS YOU NEED TO KNOW

CUT IN—To brush paint onto the edges of an area to be painted.

WET EDGE—Fresh paint. Rolling paint onto the main areas of the wall or ceiling while the paint is still wet in the areas that have been "cut in" prevents lines or shadows between those areas after the paint has dried.

DIFFICULTY LEVEL

This project takes 3 to 4 hours, depending on the size of the area being covered.

HOW TO PAINT A WALL

1 Stir the paint, using a variable-speed drill and paint-mixing bit. Set the drill on a low speed and keep the head of the bit in the paint until it completely stops turning. Paint separates quickly, so stir it thoroughly from time to time.

2 Cut in the edges of a 2 × 4-ft. section of the first wall, using the narrow edge of a paintbrush. Press down just enough to flex the bristles. Use long, slow strokes, and paint from dry areas back into wet paint.

3 Cut in any corners in the section, using the wide edge of the paintbrush or use a specialty corner roller.

HERE'S HOW

Here's how to avoid having the paint look different from one wall to the next. Paint—especially custom-mixed paint—can vary a tiny bit from one can to another. If your project is large, mix the cans together in a large pail and stir it thoroughly. This is known as boxing.

4 Load the roller with paint. With the loaded roller, make a diagonal sweep about 4 ft. long on the wall. Roll upward on the first stroke to avoid spilling paint. Roll slowly to avoid splattering.

5 Draw the roller straight down from the top of the diagonal sweep. Shift the roller to the beginning of the diagonal stroke and roll upward to complete the unloading of the roller.

6 Roll back and forth across the section to smooth the area. Lightly draw the roller down the section from top to bottom. Lift the roller and start again at the top after each stroke. Finally, slide the roller cover slightly off of the roller frame and roll the cut-in areas to minimize brush marks.

7 Cut in and roll the section directly under the first one. Continue with adjacent areas, cutting in and rolling the top sections before the bottom sections. Roll all finish strokes toward the floor.

Preparing Unfinished Wood for Paint

8

Raw wood needs to be carefully prepared before being painted.

PREPARING RAW WOOD FOR PAINT INVOLVES FILLING NAIL HOLES, SANDING THE SURFACE, AND APPLYING A COAT OF PRIMER. While none of this is difficult, it can be time consuming, so it's important to plan plenty of time for this project. A small putty knife works well for filling nail holes, but sometimes your index finger is the perfect tool.

RAW WOOD SANDING 101

Latex wood filler

Primer

Fine sanding sponges

Tack cloth

Paintbrush

New woodwork contains nail holes that must be filled with wood filler. The surface must then be sanded and the sanding dust removed. Finally, the woodwork must be sealed with a coat of primer.

SKILLS YOU NEED

- Sanding
- Light carpentry skills

DIFFICULTY LEVEL

This project takes 2 to 4 hours, depending on the amount of woodwork you need to finish.

TERMS YOU NEED TO KNOW

COUNTERSINK—To drive the head of a nail below the surface of the surrounding wood.

NAIL SET—A tool used to set nails below the surface.

HOW TO PREPARE WOOD FOR PAINT

1 Check the woodwork to identify any nail or screw heads that have not been countersunk below the wood surface.

2 Countersink nailheads by placing the end of a nail set on the head of the nail and striking the top of the nail set with a hammer. Continue until the head of the nail is $\frac{1}{16}$" below the wood's surface.

3 Apply wood filler to any nail holes, dents, or damaged areas. In detailed or carved areas, make sure the filler does not fill in the details or carvings. If necessary, remove filler with a small screwdriver or awl.

4 Sand the surface of the woodwork. Start with a fine-grit sponge and progress to an extra-fine grit sponge, sanding with the grain of the wood.

5 Tape off the woodwork (see page 370).

6 Apply a coat of primer, using a paintbrush (a 2½" sash brush works well). Let the primer dry, according to the manufacturer's directions.

SAFETY TIP

If your home was built before 1978 and you will be sanding painted wood, test the painted wood for lead before taking any further action. You can purchase a lead-testing kit for this job. If the test indicates the presence of lead, collect a sample and consult a lead-abatement specialist.

7 Lightly sand the primed woodwork and wipe the surface with a tack cloth.

Painting Millwork & Trim

9

Windows, doors, and trim are on the frontline of the daily bump and grind.
A new coat of paint makes them look more attractive and last longer.

WHEN PAINTING AN ENTIRE ROOM, PAINT THE TRIM FIRST, THEN THE WALLS.
When painting trim, start at the inside edges and work your way out toward the walls. On windows, that means working from the sashes toward the case molding. On doors, it means working from the main surface of the door out to the case molding. On baseboards, it's best to cut in the top edge and work down toward the floor.

MILLWORK PAINTING 101

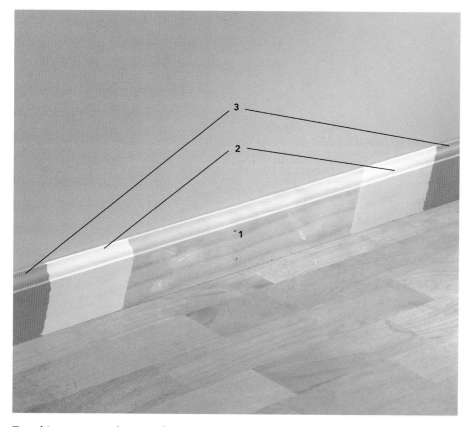

To achieve a smooth, even finish on millwork, nail holes and dents are filled with latex wood filler; the surface is sanded, primed, and sanded again. Finally, one or two coats of paint are applied.

TOOLS & SUPPLIES YOU NEED

Paint
Primer
Sanding sealer
Easy-release painter's tape
Hammer
Nails
1½" tapered sash brush
Tack cloth
Drill/driver
Corner masks
Extra-fine sanding sponge
Putty knife
Screw-driver
Stencil brush
Wide taping knife

TERMS YOU NEED TO KNOW

APRON—A vertical board at the bottom of a double-hung window.

BASEBOARDS—The wood that covers the joint between a wall and the floor.

CASEMENT WINDOW—A window with vertical sashes that open out from the frame on hinge-like mechanisms. Operated by means of a crank located on the lower sash.

CASE MOLDING—The trim that surrounds a window sash or door, covering the joint between the window sashes and the walls.

DOUBLE-HUNG WINDOW—A window that has two sashes that move up and down, one behind the other, along tracks in the opening.

MILLWORK—A generic term for door and window trim as well as baseboards and other trim.

RAILS—The horizontal framework of a door.

STILES—The vertical framework of a door.

WINDOWSILL—The horizontal board at the bottom of a window.

SKILLS YOU NEED

- Sanding
- Painting

DIFFICULTY LEVEL

This project takes approximately 2 hours, depending on the amount of millwork you are working on.

1 Prepare window to be painted. Remove hardware where possible and use painter's tape to mask the rest.

2 Apply tape or corner masks to glass and put tape around outside edges of case molding.

3 Remove double-hung window sashes from their frames when possible. To release a spring-mounted, double-hung window sash, press against the frame and pull the sash toward you.

4 To paint sashes that have been removed, drill holes and drive 3" nails into the legs of a wooden stepladder. Set the window on the nails as though on an easel. Windows can also be placed flat on a bench or sawhorses.

5 Using a tapered sash brush, begin by painting the wood next to the glass. Use the narrow edge of the brush, and overlap the paint onto the tape on the glass.

6 Paint the flat portions of the sash. Use slow brush strokes and smooth the paint carefully. Do not paint the sides or bottom of the window sash.

7 Paint the case moldings, sill, and apron. Again, paint slowly and evenly. Let the paint dry completely.

8 Sand lightly and apply a second coat of paint, using the same method as described above. When the second coat is dry, remove the tape and replace the sashes.

HOW TO PAINT A CASEMENT WINDOW

1 Apply tape and masks as described on page 370.

2 First paint the wood next to the glass, then the flat portions of the sash, followed by the case moldings and sills. Move the sash in and out to comfortably reach all areas. Do not paint sides, top, or bottom of the sash.

HOW TO PAINT BASEBOARDS AND TRIM

1 Prepare baseboards for painting. Starting at the top edge of the baseboard and working toward the floor, apply a light coat of paint. Hold a drywall knife or plastic shielding tool beneath the baseboard as you paint; wipe the tool each time it is moved.

2 Paint deeply patterned surfaces with a stiff-bristled brush, such as a stenciling brush. Use small circular strokes to penetrate recesses.

HOW TO A PAINT DOOR

1 Remove the door by driving out the lower hinge pin, using a screwdriver and hammer. Next, have a helper hold the door in place while you drive out the middle and then the upper hinge pins.

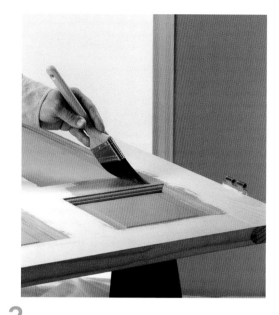

2 Place the door flat on a pair of sawhorses. On paneled doors, use a paintbrush to paint in the following order: 1) recessed panels, 2) horizontal rails, and 3) vertical stiles. Let the paint dry thoroughly. If a second coat is required, sand the door lightly and wipe it with a tack cloth before applying it.

3 Seal the unpainted edges of the door with clear wood sealer. Allow the sealer and paint to completely dry. Rehang the door in the same location, using the old screw locations as well.

TIP

If the screw holes in the wall no longer support the screws firmly, fill them with latex wood patch and drill pilot holes before hanging the door.

Painting Wood Cabinets

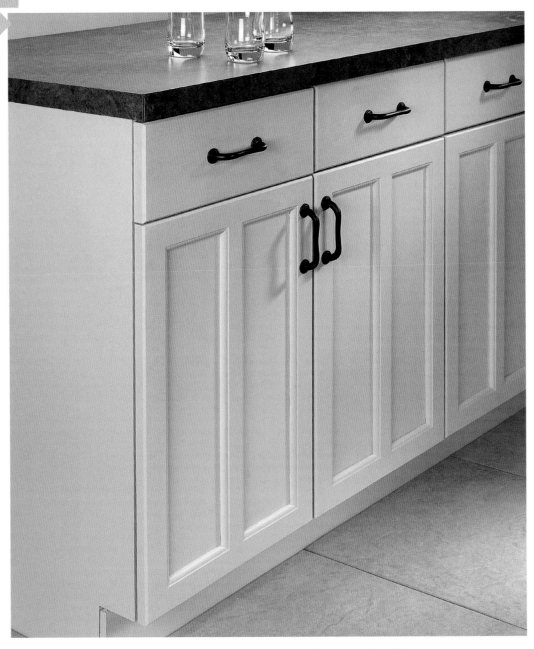

10

Painting wood cabinets is an inexpensive way to give a kitchen a face-lift.

PAINT IS A GOOD FINISH FOR CABINETS OF ALL SORTS: IT'S ATTRACTIVE, EASY TO CLEAN, AND (WHEN HEAVY-DUTY ENAMEL IS USED) DURABLE. Although painting cabinets is not difficult, it is time consuming: Most require two coats of paint, all surfaces have to be sanded lightly between coats, and both sides of the doors need to be painted.

HOW TO PAINT WOOD CABINETS

1 Empty the cabinets, and then remove the shelf pins and shelves. For stubborn shelf pins, use a pliers to pull them out. Unfasten the hinge screws and all hardware, then remove the cabinet doors from the frames.

2 Wash the cabinets with a mild detergent solution. Rinse with clean water and a sponge. Fill scratches, dents, or cracks with latex wood filler, using a putty knife. Let the wood filler dry completely. Sand all surfaces with an orbital sander and 150-grit sandpaper.

3 Brush paint onto the interior of the cabinet frames, starting with the back wall, then the top, sides, and bottom. Roll paint the outside surfaces, working from top to bottom.

4 Using a trim brush, paint the inside of each door. Once dry, paint the other side using a tapered sash brush. Let the drawers dry for several days, then replace the hardware and rehang the doors.

TOOLS & SUPPLIES YOU NEED

High-gloss enamel paint

Decorating Toolbox

Painting Toolbox

Paint remover

Detergent

Liquid deglosser

Latex wood filler

Paint tray and roller

Primer

Paintbrushes

Putty knife

150-grit sandpaper

Cheesecloth

Detail sander

Tack cloth

SKILLS YOU NEED

- Sanding
- Painting smoothly

DIFFICULTY LEVEL

This project takes about 2 hours per foot of cabinets

Painting Concrete Block Walls

11

Paint dresses up concrete block walls, and some products also help the blocks resist water infiltration.

UNPAINTED CONCRETE BLOCKS ARE DULL AND INSTITUTIONAL-LOOKING. They're also slightly porous, so in situations where hydrostatic pressure is present, water can seep through them. Paint provides a long-lasting, durable surface that improves the appearance of blocks as well as increases their water resistance.

Concrete blocks must be cured for at least 30 days before being painted. Before they can be patched and painted, they must also be free of mildew, dust and dirt, and efflorescence. The paint fills the pores of the blocks and helps them become more water resistant.

The products used to prepare concrete blocks for paint emit irritating fumes. Provide adequate ventilation or wear a respirator when working with them.

CONCRETE BLOCK PAINTING 101

Paint concrete walls in sections for a professional finish. First cut in corners and paint the perimeter with a paintbrush. Then paint the interior in 2-ft. sections, as shown above. Be sure to patch holes with hydraulic cement and allow to dry before painting.

TERMS YOU NEED TO KNOW

EFFLORESCENCE—A white, crystalline mineral deposit sometimes found on masonry surfaces.

ETCHER—A product used to "etch" or make tiny grooves in the surface of the concrete blocks.

TOOLS & SUPPLIES YOU NEED

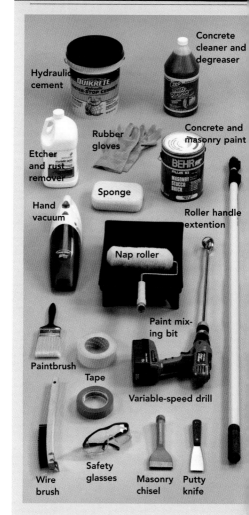

Concrete cleaner and degreaser

Hydraulic cement

Rubber gloves

Concrete and masonry paint

Etcher and rust remover

Sponge

Hand vacuum

Roller handle extention

Nap roller

Paint mixing bit

Paintbrush

Tape

Variable-speed drill

Wire brush

Safety glasses

Masonry chisel

Putty knife

SKILLS YOU NEED

- General cleaning skills
- Working with safety equipment
- Painting

DIFFICULTY LEVEL

This project takes 4 to 6 hours, not including curing times.

HOW TO PREPARE CONCRETE BLOCK FOR PAINT

1 Press a piece of masking tape onto the blocks in several places. Pull the tape away: If the tape doesn't pull concrete away from the surface, it can be painted. If loose concrete comes away with the tape, all loose bits need to be scraped away with a wire brush.

2 Apply hydraulic cement in layers no more than ½" thick, until the patch is slightly higher than the surrounding area. Feather the patch until the edges are even with the surface. Let the patch dry, according to manufacturer's directions.

3 Evaluate the blocks, looking for holes and cracks. If you find any, use a masonry chisel or a bottle opener and a wire brush to remove any debris or dirt. Clean all dust and debris from the surface with a hand vacuum.

4 Clean the concrete blocks with a cleaner and degreaser (or etcher). Thoroughly rinse the blocks with water and then let them dry. Be sure to wear safety glasses and heavy-duty rubber gloves. Check the ventilation in the area, and put on a respirator if necessary.

HOW TO PAINT A CONCRETE BLOCK WALL

1 Stir the paint, using a variable-speed drill and a paint-mixing bit. If the project requires more than one can of paint, mix the cans together in a large bucket before stirring. Use a paintbrush to cut in the edges of a 2 × 4-ft. section, starting at the top.

2 While the cut-in edges are still wet, roll paint onto the first section. Work the paint into the surface, making certain paint fills any pores or voids. Repeat with the section immediately beneath the first, and then continue to the next section (starting at the top once again). Let the paint dry according to manufacturer's instructions.

TIP

After painting the entire wall, apply a second coat of paint to cover the entire area and fill any voids left after the first coat. Let the paint dry and reevaluate the blocks. If water has been a problem in the past, check for leaks. If leaks are still present, apply more paint in these areas.

12

Stripping Wallcoverings

Stripping wallcoverings can be quite tedious, depending on the type of wallcovering it is and how it was applied.

NEWER VINYL WALLCOVERINGS ARE DESIGNED TO BE "STRIPPABLE," WHICH MEANS THEY CAN BE REMOVED BY HAND. All you have to do is find a loose edge and pull upward. Some other wallcoverings leave a layer of paper that can be scraped off easily when it's dampened with water. Still others can be removed only with a fair amount of time and effort.

If wallcovering is hung over unsealed drywall, it's virtually impossible to remove it without destroying the drywall. You may be able to paint or hang new wallcovering directly over the old, but you have to make sure the surface is smooth and prime it with an alkyd drywall primer.

The only way to find out what's lurking beneath your wallcovering is to grab an edge and pull!

WALLPAPER STRIPPING 101

Properly applied wallcovering—good-quality coverings that have been applied with good wallpaper adhesive over primed walls—can be stripped with a remover solution, drywall knife, and a little time and patience.

TERMS YOU NEED TO KNOW

ALKYD—An oil-based primer or paint.

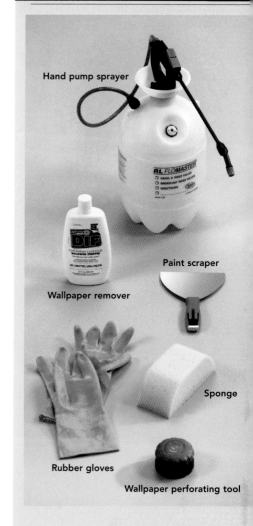

HOW TO STRIP WALLCOVERINGS

1 Find a loose corner and pull upward. If there are no loose corners, use a putty knife to pry one loose and pull. If the paper comes off easily, you're home free. Just keep pulling until it's all off the walls.

2 Dilute wallpaper remover in water, according to the manufacturer's directions. Wash the walls, working from the top toward the bottom of the walls. Rinse the walls with clear water and let them dry completely.

HOW TO REMOVE STUBBORN WALLCOVERINGS

1 If the wallcovering doesn't pull off easily, it's time to bring in the big guns. Cover the floor with drop cloths, and then dilute wallpaper remover in a bucket of water, following the manufacturer's directions.

2 Run a perforating tool over the surface of the wallcovering. (It creates holes that let the remover solution penetrate the surface to loosen the adhesive.)

3 Use a pressure sprayer to apply the remover solution. Let the solution soak into the covering, according to the manufacturer's directions.

4 Scrape away loosened wallcovering with a wide drywall knife. Be careful not to damage the wall behind the paper, and make sure you remove any backing paper or other layers.

5 Rinse adhesive residue from the wall with remover solution. Rinse with clear water and let the walls dry.

TIP

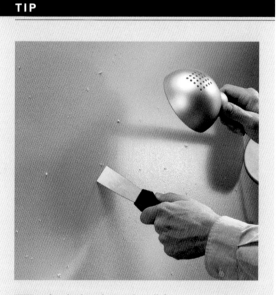

To check the cleaned wall for remaining adhesive, holes, or other flaws, illuminate the wall from the side, using a bright light. Inspect the walls carefully, making sure they are completely clean and repaired before painting or hanging new wallcoverings.

13

Hanging Wallcoverings

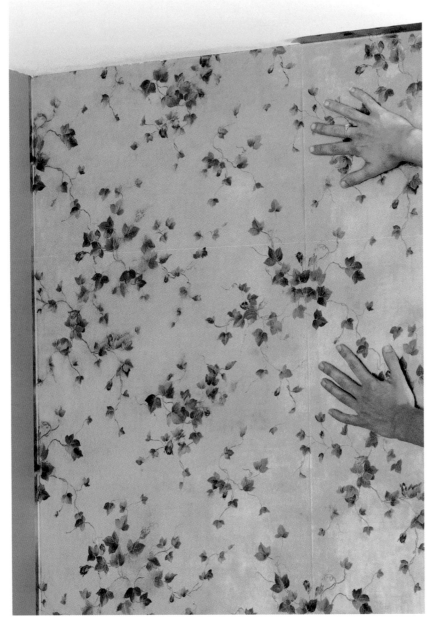

Hanging wallcoverings requires careful planning and attention to detail.
The work is not difficult, but it's a challenging project.

THE OLD ADAGE IN CARPENTRY, "MEASURE TWICE, CUT ONCE," IS JUST AS APPLICABLE TO WALLCOVERING PROJECTS. The materials are expensive and mistakes immediately obvious. The only way to avoid problems is to plan meticulously.

First, measure the room and sketch out a hanging plan. Next, prepare the room and recruit a helper or two. Plan to work during daylight hours whenever possible, as the light is better and the adhesive dries more evenly.

HANGING WALLCOVERING 101

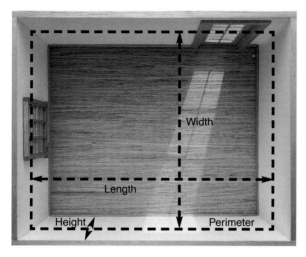

Clean, non-corrosive bucket

High-quality sponges

Bubblestick

Wallpaper paste

Smoothing brush

Razor knife

Smoothing tool

Wide drywall knife

Wallcovering scissors

Water tray

Seam roller

TERMS YOU NEED TO KNOW

BOOK—To lightly fold moistened wallcovering so that the pasted sides face one another. Allows adhesive to cure in preparation for hanging.

BUBBLESTICK—A plastic ruler with a level bubble in it. This tool is lightweight and easy to use when establishing plumb lines and when cutting.

MISMATCH—Point where a full strip meets a partial strip, typically placed behind a door or in an inconspicuous spot. Few rooms can be covered without one partial strip—the math just doesn't come out that way very often.

RAZOR KNIFE—A small, lightweight knife used for trimming wallcovering. Tip of blade can be snapped off to renew tip.

SMOOTHING BRUSHES—Tools used to press wallpaper onto wall. Short-nap brushes are best for vinyl wallcoverings. Brushes with a long, soft nap are used for fragile wallcoverings, such as grasscloth.

SMOOTHING TOOL—A lightweight piece of plastic used to smooth out bubbles in wallcovering.

SKILLS YOU NEED

- Measuring accurately
- Establishing plumb lines
- Cutting accurately

DIFFICULTY LEVEL

Allow at least one full day per room.

Successful wallcovering projects start with careful planning. The mismatch should be placed in an inconspicuous area, such as behind a door. The actual hanging starts at a focal point, such as a fireplace or large window. In rooms that don't have an obvious focal point, it starts at the corner farthest from the entry. The wallcovering should always overlap at the corners: at least ½" on inside corners and 1" on outside corners.

Each strip should start with a full pattern at the ceiling line and should overlap both the ceiling and baseboard by about 2" so it can be trimmed precisely during the hanging process.

Turn off the power to the circuit in the room and remove covers on receptacles and switches before starting a wallcovering project.

HOW TO CREATE A HANGING PLAN

1 Measure the room and create a sketch of the hanging plan. Center a plumb line on a focal point, such as a fireplace or window, and sketch out a plan in both directions from the center line.

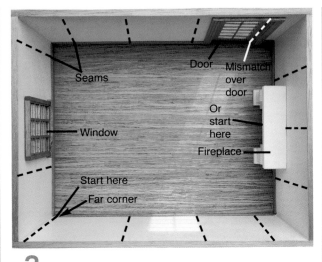

2 If the room doesn't have an obvious focal point, start at the corner farthest from the entry, measure a distance equal to the width of the wallcovering and mark a point. Work in both directions, marking the points where seams will fall.

3 Adjust the hanging plan for corners that fall exactly on seam lines. Make sure the wallcovering will overlap at least ½" on inside corners and 1" on outside corners.

4 Adjust for seams that fall in difficult locations, such as near the edges of windows or doors. Shift the starting point so the seams leave workable widths of wallcovering around obstacles.

HOW TO PREPARE WALLCOVERING STRIPS

1 Hold the wallcovering against the wall so there is a full pattern at the ceiling line and the strip overlaps both the ceiling and the baseboard by at least 2". Cut the strip to length, using scissors.

2 Fill a water tray half full of lukewarm water. Roll the cut strip loosely with the pattern side in. Soak the roll in the tray as directed by the manufacturer, usually about one minute, to activate the prepasted adhesive.

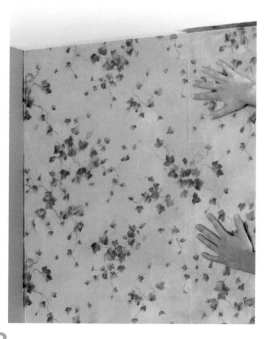

3 Hold up a second strip and find the pattern match with the previously hung strip. Measure and cut the new strip with about 2" of excess at each end.

TIP

If wallpaper can be "booked" (check manufacturer's directions), fold each end of the strip to the center, with the pasted side in. Do not crease the folds. Let the strip cure for about 10 minutes.

1 From the starting point shown in your hanging plan, measure a distance equal to the width of the wallcovering minus ½" and mark a point. Draw a vertical plumb line from the ceiling to the floor, using a bubblestick or level.

2 Cut and prepare the first strip (see page 387). Unfold the top portion of the booked strip and position it against the plumb line so the strip extends beyond the ceiling joint by about 2".

3 At the corner fold line, snip the top of the strip so the wallcovering wraps around the corner without wrinkling. Using your open palms, slide the strip into position with the edge butted against the plumb line. Smooth the strip with a smoothing brush.

4 Unfold the bottom of the strip. Use your open palms to position it against the plumb line. Smooth the strip with a smoothing brush, carefully pressing out any bubbles.

5 Trim the excess wallcovering at the ceiling and baseboard, using a drywall knife and a utility knife. With clean water and a sponge, rinse any adhesive from the surface of the wallcovering.

6 Hang additional strips, sliding strips into place so the pattern matches exactly. Let the strips stand for about half an hour, then roll the seams with a seam roller. (On embossed or fabric wallcoverings, set the seams with a smoothing brush.)

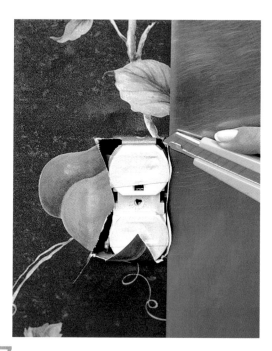

7 Where wallcovering covers receptacle or switch boxes, use a razor knife to make small diagonal cuts to expose the box. Finally, trim the paper to the edges of the box. Note: Turn off power to the circuit and remove switch and receptacle covers before starting the project.

TOOL TIP

Dull blades tear wallcovering rather than cutting it cleanly. To renew the blade on a disposable razor knife, break the tip away. For safety, grasp the blade with pliers and bend down until the old tip of the blade breaks away at the scored line.

HOW TO HANG WALLCOVERING AROUND AN INSIDE CORNER

1 Cut and prepare a full strip. While the strip cures, measure from the edge of the preceding strip to the corner at several points; add ½" to the longest of these measurements. Make sure the edges of the booked strip are aligned perfectly, then mark this distance near the top and bottom of the booked strip. Hold a straightedge against the marks and cut the strip.

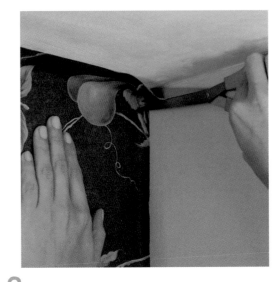

2 Position the strip. Make corner slits at the top and bottom of the strip to wrap the overlap around the corner without wrinkles. Smooth the strip with a smoothing brush, then trim the excess at the ceiling and baseboard.

3 Measure a distance equal to the remainder of the strip you cut in step 1, and mark a point equal to this measurement. At this mark, draw a plumb line from the ceiling to the floor on the next wall.

4 Position the strip on the wall with the cut edge in the corner and the uncut edge against the plumb line drawn in step 3. Smooth and trim the strip. If the wallcovering is vinyl, peel back the edge and apply a bead of vinyl-on-vinyl adhesive to the lapped area. Press the seam flat and let it cure before rolling the seams.

HOW TO HANG WALLCOVERING AROUND DOORS AND WINDOWS

1 Position the strip on the wall as usual, running the wallcovering over the window or door. Smooth the wallcovering, pressing the strip tightly against the case molding.

2 Use scissors to make diagonal cuts at the corners of the casings. Trim away excess wallcovering to about 1" around the inside of the frame.

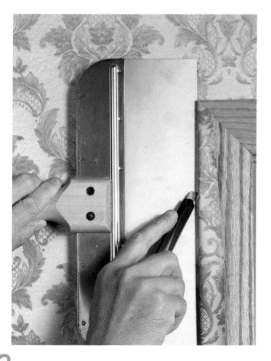

3 Hold a drywall knife and use a razor knife to trim the strip.

4 Cut short strips to hang above (and below, if this is a window) the opening. Check your scraps to see whether any will fill the space while maintaining the repeat of the pattern.

HOW TO HANG WALLCOVERING AROUND DOORS AND WINDOWS (CONTINUED)

5 At the other side of the opening, position a strip and smooth it into place. Snip the corner diagonally and trim away excess as described in step 2 above.

6 Match the pattern at the seam on the bottom half and slide the strip into place. Trim the excess as described in steps 2 and 3 above. Rinse the wall-covering and casings, using a damp sponge.

HOW TO HANG WALLCOVERING AROUND A WALL-MOUNTED SINK

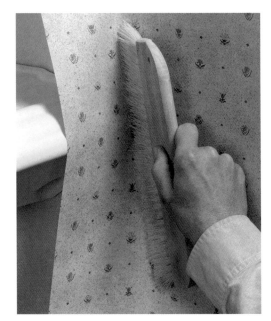

1 Cut and position the strip, brushing it up to the edge of the sink. Cut slits in the wallcovering, leaving a ¼" overlap around the edges of the sink.

2 Trim the wallcovering around the sink, leaving a slight overlap. Smooth the strip, tucking the overlap into a gap around the sink, if possible. Or, neatly trim the overlap.

1 Pull the escutcheon plate out from the wall. Hold the strip against the wall so the pattern matches the previous strip. From the closest edge of the strip, cut the slit to reach the pipe.

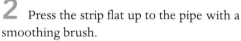
2 Press the strip flat up to the pipe with a smoothing brush.

3 Cut a hole at the end of the slit to fit around the pipe. Butt the edges of the slit together and brush them smooth.

HERE'S HOW

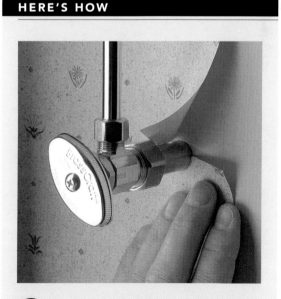

Cutting slits in your favorite wallpaper may feel intimidating at first. It gets easier with time, especially if you take the time to make the slits along a pattern line, which helps disguise them.

Outdoor Projects

THOUGH THEY'RE NOT ALWAYS THE FLASHIEST PROJECTS, REPAIRS TO THE EXTERIOR WALLS, ROOF, FOUNDATION, WINDOWS, SIDING, AND DOORS ARE AMONG THE MOST IMPORTANT YOU CAN DO. NEGLECT THEM, AND YOUR HOUSE BECOMES SUSCEPTIBLE TO DETERIORATION FROM THE OUTSIDE IN; DO THEM DILIGENTLY AND YOUR HOME WILL PROVIDE A SECURE AND COMFORTABLE LIVING PLACE FOR YOU AND YOUR FAMILY FOR YEARS TO COME (AND THE NEIGHBORS WILL APPRECIATE YOUR WORK, TOO).

In this section you'll learn how to repair and maintain your home to prevent and fix damage caused by the outside elements. Like all other sections in this book, the projects here can help you even if you know nothing at all about home repairs or improvements. All the information you'll need to get the job done is right here.

IN THIS CHAPTER:

- Before You Begin
   Outdoor Tool Kit
- Clearing Clogged Gutters
- Touching Up Exterior Paint
- Fixing Sliding Screen Doors
- Installing Storm Doors
- Tuning Up Double-Hung Windows
- Exterior Caulking
- Pestproofing
- Fixing Concrete Walkways
- Repairing Asphalt Driveways
- Fixing Broken Glass Panes
- Repairing Concrete Steps

- Repairing Siding
- Repairing Stucco
- Renewing Wood Decks
- Replacing Damaged Roof Shingles
- Installing Locksets & Deadbolts
- Tuning Up Garage Doors
- Installing House Gutters
- Installing Landscape Lighting
- Pressure Washing a House

Before You Begin:
Outdoor Tool Kit

The outdoor fix-it projects in this book really don't require much in the way of special tools and materials. Although a few of the projects may call for a specialty tool or two, most of them can be completed with a basic set of hand and power tools.

The group of tools shown here is a collection that will put you well on your way to doing the projects in this book, as well as most general carpentry repair projects around the house. But don't worrry if you don't yet own them. You can gradually assemble your tool kit as you take on project after project. Or, you can borrow them from a neighbor or friend as you need them.

Clearing Clogged Gutters

1

Gutter systems play a critical role in protecting both the exterior and interior of your house. By catching runoff water from the roof, gutters keep the siding dry. They also prevent water from pooling around the foundation— the most common cause of wet basements.

THE IDEA BEHIND GUTTERS IS SIMPLE: JUST COLLECT THE RAINWATER THAT FALLS ON A ROOF AND DIVERT IT FROM THE FOUNDATION OF THE HOUSE. Ironically the root cause of gutter dysfunction is rarely the water itself. Instead it's the leaves and twigs that get trapped in the gutters and clog the downspouts. When these exits are blocked, the water runs over the lip of the gutter and falls exactly where you don't want it to fall: next to the foundation. Clogged gutters lead to stained siding in the summer and ice dams in the winter. The solution is obvious: clean the gutters a couple of times a year.

Cleaning gutters means working from ladders. To do the job right, lean an extension ladder against the house (with rubber ladder end guards to protect the siding) or against the roof (using a ladder stabilizer). Climb up with a garden hose and bucket in hand. If there's just a little bit of debris, try washing it out with the garden hose. But heavy congestion has to be removed by hand. A putty knife is a good tool for this job. Just lift out the mess and put it in the bucket. To free clogged downspouts, push a garden hose down the pipe and run the water at full force until the clog breaks loose and the pipe is clear.

GUTTERS 101

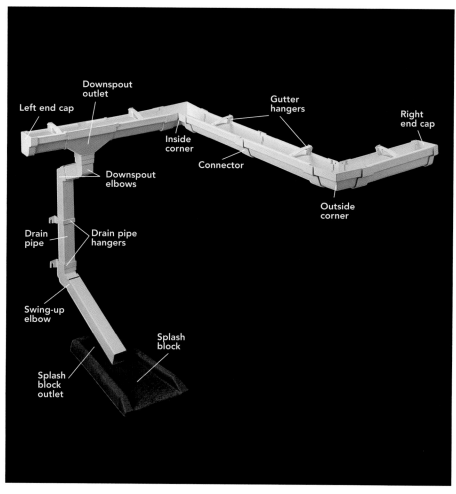

Clogs can occur anywhere in a gutter system, but the most likely trouble spots are at the downspout outlets and in the drain pipe.

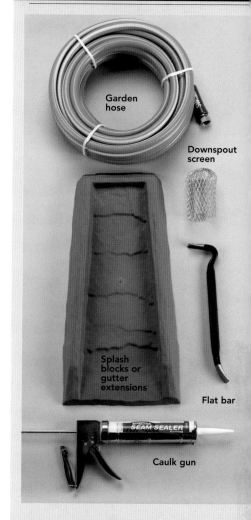

Garden hose

Downspout screen

Splash blocks or gutter extensions

Flat bar

Caulk gun

TERMS YOU NEED TO KNOW

END CAPS—Placed at the end of gutter runs.

INSIDE/OUTSIDE CORNERS—Used on corners with no water outlet to carry water around a corner.

DOWNSPOUT OUTLETS—Should be placed at least every 35 feet.

DRAIN PIPE HANGERS—Should use at least two per drain pipe.

DOWNSPOUT ELBOWS—Recommended three per downspout.

DIFFICULTY LEVEL

SKILLS LEVEL

EASY   MODERATE

This project can be completed in 4 to 6 hours.

1 Clean dense debris from gutters using a putty knife or a narrow drywall knife. Put the debris in a bucket instead of dropping it on the ground.

2 Stubborn clogs in downspouts can be loosened and flushed away with a garden hose. Just push the end of the hose down the pipe and turn on the water full blast.

3 If your gutter collects a lot of leaves and frequently clogs the downspouts, slide a ball-shaped screen into the top of each pipe or cover the entire gutter with a protective screen.

4 Leaky joints between sections of gutter or at downspout connections can be patched with gutter seal. Just clean out any debris, dry the seam, and fill it well with sealer. Smooth the bead with your fingertip or a putty knife.

5 To straighten a sagging gutter, remove hangers or spikes in the sagging area. Snap a chalkline at the correct height, raise the gutter to the line, and then reinstall the hangers.

6 To straighten gutters that are supported with hanging brackets, loosen the brackets, lift the gutter and reinstall the brackets.

7 Splash blocks are designed to direct water from the downspouts away from the house foundation. If you have these blocks, make sure they're positioned directly under the downspouts. If you don't have the blocks, buy and install them.

FYI

A folding extension is a gutter accessory that mounts on the bottom on a downspout and works like a splash block to send the water away from the house. Because it's hinged, the pipe can be folded up out of the way when mowing or working in planting beds next to the house.

2

Touching Up Exterior Paint

Few projects will go further than touching up painted siding when it comes to freshening up the appearance of your house.

IF YOU OWN A HOUSE WITH A PAINTED EXTERIOR, YOU ALREADY KNOW ABOUT PERPETUAL MAINTENANCE. It goes something like this. You painted your house the year your daughter graduated from eighth grade. It was a big deal because you had to get it done between her end-of-school party (in your backyard) and the family reunion in August (also in your backyard). Of course you spent your whole vacation doing it, except for the two days when nearly every in-law asked why you didn't hire a professional to do the job. Sometimes doing the right thing doesn't seem like the right thing to do.

But once the job was done, you enjoyed (for about three years) not thinking about paint. Then it started. At first it was just a little flaking along the bottom edge of the fascia. Then it spread to the window casing boards and the top edge of the water table, behind the bushes. Suddenly, it became clear that the whole house would need repainting just when your daughter would be graduating from high school. Talk about perpetual maintenance.

Unfortunately, there's no happy ending to this dark story. But there is a way to protect your flank while retreating: routine paint touch-ups. If you fix the little things when they go bad, you can easily postpone a major repainting for several years. And every summer without drop cloths and extension ladders is a blessing to be counted by all.

SANDING SIDING 101

Sanded to bare wood

Scraped and spot-sanded

Pressure-washed only

Garden hose

Primer
and paint

Car-
washing
brush

Palm
sander

Drill

Flap
sander

Paint brushes

Sanding block

Razor paint
scraper

Caulk
gun &
silicone
caulk

The amount of surface preparation you do will largely determine the final appearance of your paint job. Decide how much sanding and scraping you're willing to
do to obtain a finish you'll be happy with.

DIFFICULTY LEVEL

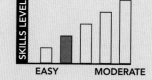

SKILLS LEVEL

EASY   MODERATE

This project can be completed in five
to seven days.

TERMS YOU NEED TO KNOW

CAR-WASHING BRUSH—A common automotive maintenance tool that consists of a
soft-bristle brush mounted on the end of a wand made of aluminum tubing. The
wand attaches to a garden hose.

FLAP SANDER—An accessory designed for electric drills made of narrow pieces of
abrasive paper attached to a steel arbor. The drill turns the arbor and paper in a
rotary motion.

1 Wash your siding with an inexpensive hose-mounted brush, such as a car-washing brush. Work from the top of the wall to the bottom. Use household detergent on tough spots and rinse all soapy areas thoroughly.

2 Scrape away peeling paint with a paint scraper. Don't gouge the wood, and be sure to change (or sharpen) the scraper blade frequently to make the work go faster.

3 Use 100-grit sandpaper over a sanding block to smooth the scraped areas. Feather the edges so they match the surrounding surface.

4 Use a flap sander mounted in an electric drill (or a cordless drill for very quick jobs) to remove peeling paint from curved surfaces. This tool works on both concave and convex boards.

5 On larger scraped areas, use an electric sander to smooth the surface. Use 100-grit sandpaper and be sure to brush the sanding dust off the siding or trim when you're done.

6 Fill any cracks between the siding and the door and window trim using a caulk gun and paintable, exterior caulk. Fill deep cracks in a couple of passes to keep the caulk from smearing on the siding.

7 Prime and then paint all sanded areas. And, try not to over-brush. Because paint tends to fade over time, your touch-ups will look brighter than the original paint covering. Keeping their size as small as possible will make them less noticeable.

8 Try to remove any paint splatters from window glass before they dry. Once the paint hardens it's much harder to remove.

Fixing Sliding Screen Doors

3

Screen doors are extremely vulnerable to damage from feet, pets and a host of other hazards. But fixing them is a breeze.

SLIDING GLASS DOORS ARE MOSTLY GOOD THINGS. They let in a lot of light and when the sliding panel is open, they let in a lot of air. And, because all these doors have sliding screens, the air they let in is reasonably bug free. The problem is, the large screen easily falls victim to pets and children and often needs repair.

To replace the screen, you need to remove the screen door panel. It is held in grooves by four spring-loaded wheels, one at each corner of the door. It is nearly impossible, and very frustrating, to try to replace a screen with the panel in place. The screen is held in place with a flexible plastic spline cord which you can easily pull out.

Take a short section of the old spline to a hardware store or home center and buy new spline material that matches the diameter of the old one. Also buy replacement screening and an installation tool that is designed for the size of spline you are installing. These tools come with a roller on both ends. One is convex shaped and is used to forced the screen into the door groove. The other roller has a concave edge to force the spline over the screen.

WINDOW SCREENING 101

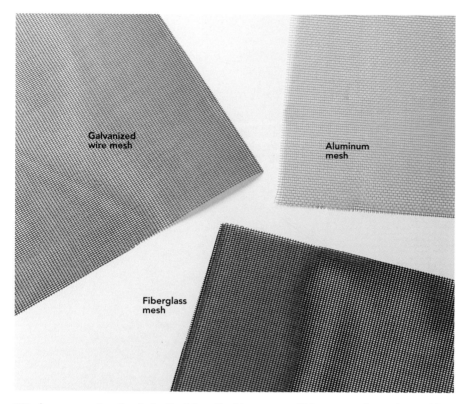

Galvanized wire mesh

Aluminum mesh

Fiberglass mesh

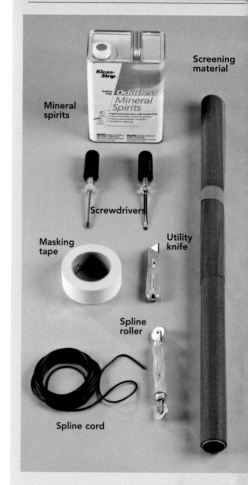

Screening material

Mineral spirits

Screwdrivers

Masking tape

Utility knife

Spline roller

Spline cord

Window screening (technically, it's called insect mesh) is woven from three different materials: galvanized wire, aluminum wire and black fiberglass strands. Each has its advantages and drawbacks: galvanized wire is inexpensive and easy to find, but can become misshapen or rusty; aluminum is less common, but it is strong and won't discolor as easily; fiberglass is easy to work with and won't rust or corrode, but it is prone to tearing. The best advice is simply to buy screening that matches the windows on the rest of your house.

TERMS YOU NEED TO KNOW

SPLINE—For sliding screen doors, a flexible plastic material (round in cross section) that holds screening tight in door grooves. Sold in long strings and sized to fit different width grooves.

SPLINE ROLLER—A specialty tool designed to force spline cords into the spline channel of the screen frame.

DIFFICULTY LEVEL

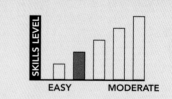

SKILLS LEVEL

EASY   MODERATE

This project can be completed in two to three hours.

1 You can't remove the screen door until you release the tension on the roller wheels. Back off the adjustment screws, then lift the door out of the channel that holds it captive.

2 Remove the door rollers using a screwdriver. Sometimes these rollers can just be pried out. Other times you'll have to remove a small screw.

3 Clean the rollers with mineral spirits and an old paint brush. Once all the dirt and grime is removed, dry the rollers and lubricate them with light oil.

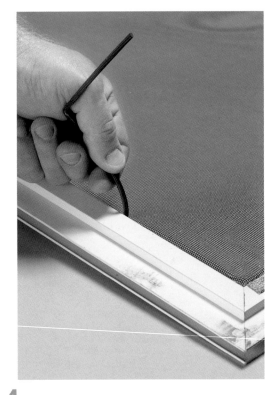

4 Pry up one corner of the old spline and then gently pull it out of the screen channel. If this plastic spline is still soft and flexible, it can be reused for the new screen.

5 Tape the new screen onto the door frame with masking tape. Then make a diagonal cut at each corner to remove the excess screen. This will keep the screen from bulging at the corner when it is pressed into its channel.

6 Force the screen into the door groove using the convex wheel on the spline roller installation tool. Don't force the screen in with a single pass. Rather, make several lighter passes until the screen reaches the bottom of the channel.

7 Once the screen is in the channel, install the spline material. Use the concave wheel and work slowly to make sure the spline is forced all the way into the channel. Several passes may be required.

8 Trim off any excess screening with a sharp utility knife. Do not cut the spline. Reinstall the wheels and replace the panel in the door.

4

A quality storm door helps seal out cold drafts, keeps rain and snow off your entry door, and lets a bug-free breeze into your home when you want one.

STORM DOORS PROTECT THE ENTRY DOOR FROM DRIVING RAIN OR SNOW. They create a dead air buffer between the two doors that acts like insulation. When the screen panels are in place, the door provides great ventilation on a hot day. And, they deliver added security, especially when outfitted with a lockset and a deadbolt lock.

If you want to install a brand new storm door or replace an old one that's seen better days, your first job is to go shopping. Storm doors come in many different styles to suit just about anyone's design needs. And they come in different materials, including aluminum, vinyl, and even fiberglass. (Wood storm doors are still available but not in preassembled form.) All these units feature a pre-hung door in a frame that is mounted on the entry door casing boards. Depending on the model you buy, installation instructions can vary. So be sure to check the directions that came with your door before starting the job.

STORM DOORS 101

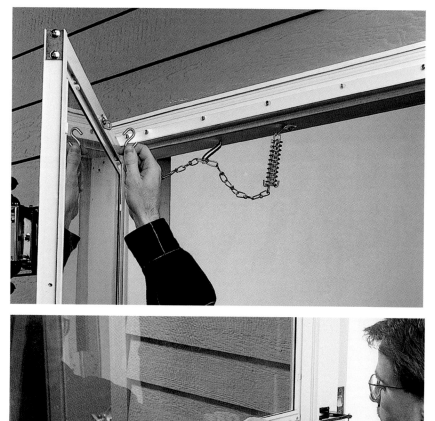

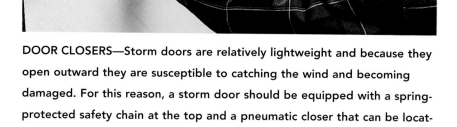

Drill and bits

Primer and paint

Level

Tape measure

Finish nails

Screwdrivers

Hammer

Paint brush

Masking tape

Hacksaw

DOOR CLOSERS—Storm doors are relatively lightweight and because they open outward they are susceptible to catching the wind and becoming damaged. For this reason, a storm door should be equipped with a spring-protected safety chain at the top and a pneumatic closer that can be located anywhere on the door (usually about handle level).

DIFFICULTY LEVEL

SKILLS LEVEL

EASY   MODERATE

This project can be completed in six to eight hours.

TERMS YOU NEED TO KNOW

DOOR JAMBS—The boards that line the rough opening of the doorway. The door swings between them and the hinges and strike plate are mounted on them.

DOOR CASING BOARDS—Boards that are nailed to the jambs and the wall surrounding any door opening. They lay flat against the wall covering inside, and flat against the wall sheathing on the outside.

HOW TO INSTALL A STORM DOOR

1 Test fit the door in the opening. If it is loose, add a shim to the hinge side of the door. Cut the piece with a circular saw and nail it to the side of the jamb, flush with the front of the casing.

2 Install the rain cap at the top of the door opening. The directions for the door you have will explain exactly how to do this. Sometimes it's the first step, like we show here; sometimes it's installed after the door is in place.

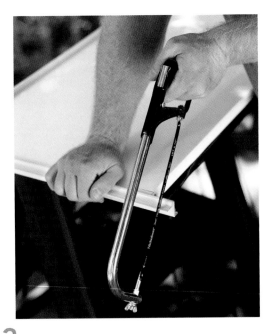

3 Measure the height of the opening and cut the hinge flange to match this measurement. Use a hacksaw and work slowly so the saw won't hop out of the cut and scratch a visible area of the hinge.

4 Lift the door and push it tightly into the opening. Partially drive one mounting screw near the bottom and another near the top. Check the door for plumb, and when satisfied, drive all the mounting screws tight to the flange.

5 Measure from the doorway sill to the rain cap to establish the length of the latch-side mounting flange.

6 Cut the latch-side flange with a hacksaw. Work carefully so you don't pull out the weather-stripping from the flange channel as you cut.

7 Install the latch-side flange with a couple of partially-driven screws. Then check that the opening width is the same at the top, middle and bottom. When you're satisfied that this flange is parallel to the hinge flange, install all the mounting screws securely.

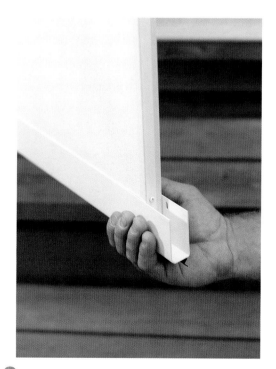

8 To install the door sweep, slide it over the bottom of the door and install its mounting screws loosely. Make sure the sweep forms a tight seal with the sill, then tighten the screws.

9 Install the lockset by pushing the outside half of the unit into the mounting holes from the outside of the door. Hold it in place with masking tape.

10 Mount the other half of the lockset on the inside of the door. Just line up the screws and push them into the threaded tubes on the outside half of the unit. Tighten the screws securely.

11 Install the deadbolt in the same way you installed the lockset. Slide the outside half in first and then add the inside half and tighten the mounting screws.

12 Install the strike plates for both the lockset (shown here) and the deadbolt locks. These plates are just screwed to the door jamb where the lock bolt and deadbolt fall (see pages 462 to 467).

13 Begin installing the door closer by screwing the jamb bracket in place. Most of these brackets have slotted screw holes so you can make minor adjustments without taking off the bracket.

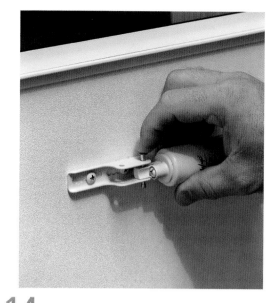

14 Install the door closer bracket on the inside of the door. Then mount the closer on the jamb bracket and the door bracket. Usually the closer is attached to these with some form of short locking pin.

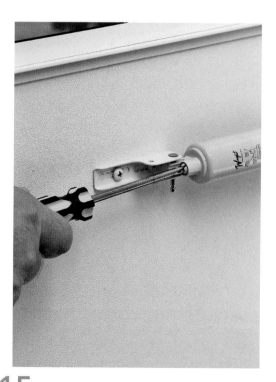

15 Adjust the automatic door closer so it closes the door completely without slamming it. The adjustment is usually made by turning a set screw in and out with a screwdriver.

16 Some doors feature a storage compartment for the glass sash and the screen sash between the bottom panels of the door. To change sashes, just unlock one and slide it down. Then pull up the other and lock it in place.

Tuning Up
Double-Hung Windows

5

Double-hung windows stick from time to time and often are painted shut.
A special serrated paint tool is made for breaking the paint lines, but a
plain putty knife can also do the job.

DOUBLE-HUNG WINDOWS ARE THE MOST COMMON WINDOW TYPES. It's not hard
to understand why. They don't open outward, which would expose them to more potential
weather damage than they already confront. And, they don't open inward, which would tangle curtains and drapes every time you wanted some air. They don't have elaborate hinge
mechanisms that wear over time and need service or replacement.

Newer models are much more energy efficient than older ones, and almost never need any
maintenance beyond cleaning. Unfortunately, they don't look as good as older versions,
unless you buy the top-drawer models. Many well-built windows still come with snap-in grills
to simulate the muntins found on old sashes.

If you are have old windows and you want to keep them, know this: there will be some window maintenance in your future to keep things running smoothly.

DOUBLE-HUNG WINDOWS 101

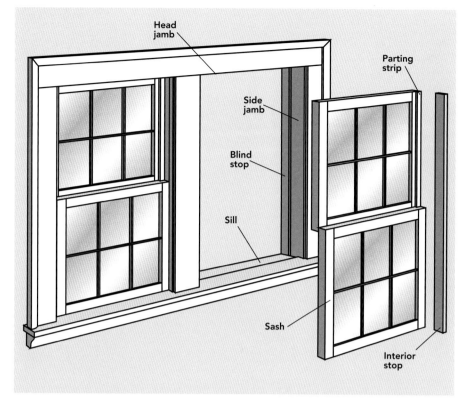

Head jamb

Parting strip

Side jamb

Blind stop

Sill

Sash

Interior stop

When they are working well, there's nothing like an old double-hung window. You can open and close a heavy sash with just one finger because the sashes are tied to counter weights that slide up and down in channels behind the side jambs. The balance between the weights and sash is so delicate that gentle finger pressure will start the weights moving down which will carry the sash up. Though the sash cords do break eventually, most poor performance is caused by binding sashes.

TERMS YOU NEED TO KNOW

MUNTINS—Secondary framing members that hold multiple glass panes within a single window sash.

SASH STOP—A small trim board that is nailed to both window jambs to hold the sash in place. Also called a window stop.

PARTING STRIP—A narrow strip that separates two sashes on a typical double-hung window.

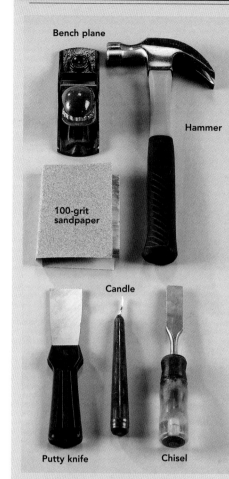
DIFFICULTY LEVEL

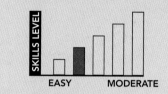

SKILLS LEVEL

EASY   MODERATE

This project can be completed in one to two hours per window.

1 Loosen a stuck window sash by forcing a putty knife between the sash and the window stop or parting strip. If hand pressure isn't enough to push in the blade, tap the handle with a hammer. Loosen both sides of the sash.

2 Once the sash is free, push it out of the way and clean out any debris from the sash channel using an old chisel or stiff, narrow putty knife.

3 Clean up the channel by sanding all three surfaces smooth. Use 100-grit paper wrapped around a scrap block of wood. Brush away the sanding dust or vacuum it up.

TIP:

Sashes that bind only slightly can often be freed by tapping the stop with a small block of wood. Don't strike the block too hard. This could split the stop. Firm taps should do the trick.

4 Paraffin is a good lubricant for sash channels. Just rub a candle vigorously against all three surfaces of both channels.

5 To remove a bottom sash, take off the stop trim on both jambs that hold the sash in place. Slide a chisel or putty knife between the two surfaces and pry gently to avoid splitting the stop.

6 Once the stops are removed the sash can swing free. Remove the weight cords from the sides and cut or plane the sash so it fits the channels better.

7 To free the upper sash, remove the parting strip on both jambs. Grip each strip at the bottom or top with pliers and pull. The parting strips are held only by friction, no fasteners are used. Protect the strip with small scrap blocks on both sides.

Exterior Caulking

6

Caulk guns are used to deliver a wide range of household products, not simply caulk. The guns are tricky to use at first, but with practice you'll get the hang of it.

WHEN YOU VISIT EVEN A MODEST HARDWARE STORE YOU WILL BE CONFRONT-ED WITH AT LEAST TEN DIFFERENT KINDS OF CAULK, ALL IN THE SAME-SIZE TUBES. It is possible, naturally, to read the labels and find out what the manufacturer says the caulk should do. But who wants to spend that kind of time and effort on cheap goop?

Well, maybe you should, if you want to save money on heating and air-conditioning costs, keep insects out, and prevent water from working its way behind your siding. Caulk can do all of this and more. You just have to buy a couple of tubes, spring for a caulk gun (about $4), and spend a little time filling house holes.

Any holes cut through the outside envelope of the house for services, like electricity, telephone, cable or satellite dishes, gas pipes, clothes dryer vents, outdoor receptacles and light fixtures, and garden hose sillcocks are candidates for caulking. Then hunt down the cracks that open up between the siding boards and the trim boards, like the window and door casings, the corner boards and baseboard trim along the bottom of the walls.

CAULK 101

Among the many products available for purchase in caulk-style cartridges are true caulks (usually made of silicone, acrylic, latex or a combination), but you'll also find specialty products that are formulated for specific materials, such as concrete. Some manufacturers list longevity ratings, which should really only be used for comparison purposes among similar brands.

TERMS YOU NEED TO KNOW

SILICONE ACRYLIC CAULK—A resilient gap-filling compound made with acrylic and silicone resins that's very flexible, durable, and has a low coefficient of thermal expansion. Cleans up with soap and water.

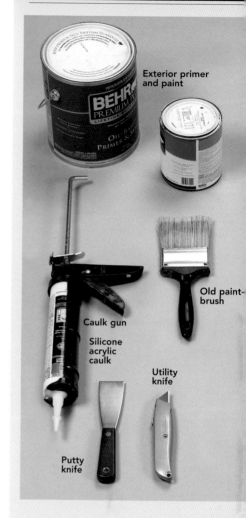
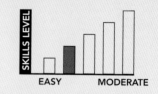

1 Exterior light fixtures rarely fit tightly to the siding. To block the air infiltration, apply a bead of caulk all the way around the base. Smooth the bead with a wet finger.

3 Dryer vent hoods occupy a lot of area and a loose one lets in a lot of air. If the hood rests on beveled siding, there may be large voids where the siding boards lap. Fill these holes with caulk and smooth the bead with your finger.

2 Exterior receptacles have a gasket between the cover plate and the box. However, nothing blocks the air movement around the box. Caulk around the box to fill these holes.

CAULK APPLICATIONS

Wading through the variety of caulks available is imposing but, fortunately, not impossible. For exterior use you want something flexible and durable, and the best choice is a silicone acrylic caulk. These products are more expensive than basic acrylic latex caulk but they perform better. They also clean up with water, which is a real plus. Sometimes this caulk is available in colors but usually you'll find it only in clear and white versions. If you need color, you'll have to paint over the caulk after it's dry—but make sure you buy paintable caulk.

Using caulk is messy, especially if you over-fill holes and then try to wipe off the excess. Cut the tip off the tube applicator to match the size of most of the holes you want to fill. Use a sharp utility knife and angle the cut to about 45 degrees to get the best bead. Poke the inside membrane of the tube by pushing a long nail down through the applicator. Then slide the tube into the gun, click the trigger a few times so the plunger bears against the bottom of the tube and squeeze the handle. As the caulk starts flowing, move the tip along the hole or crack until it's full.

4 Old caulk that is cracked or pulling away from the joint should be removed. Cut both sides of the old caulk using a carpet knife or utility knife and pull the debris from the joint. Remove dust with an old paintbrush.

5 Once the caulk is removed, prime the crack with exterior primer. Make sure to coat all the exposed wood.

6 After the primer dries, caulk the joint and smooth the bead with your finger or a putty knife.

7 Finish up the job by brushing on two coats of paint. Allow the caulk to dry, according to the manufacturer's instructions, before you paint.

Pestproofing
Your House

7

They might be cute as a button or perfectly gruesome, but uninvited pests
can do enormous damage to your home and need to be kept out.

IN THE END, IT MAY BE A SIMPLE QUESTION OF ETIQUETTE. If you invite pests into
your house, you can't feel put out when they decide to accept. And, what constitutes an invi-
tation? Well, lots of things, like holes that aren't caulked, chimneys without protective flue
covers, damaged vent screening and so on. Of course, taking such a hard line is a little bit like
blaming the victim. Is everybody really supposed to know where all the holes in the house
are and be familiar with the travel patterns of all the local squirrels? Probably not, at least
when it comes to the squirrels.

The most common entry points are small holes along the foundation and soffits, and sometimes next to windows and doors. These should all be filled with silicone acrylic caulk. Holes
much wider than ¼ in. should be stuffed with caulk backer before caulking. Also fill any gaps
around where phone, gas, cable, electric, water and other services enter the house. Once you
are done filling the obvious gaps, look for evidence of infestation like animal droppings or
nesting materials. Remove these and check the area for any entry points that you might have
missed. If the rodents persist, you can fight back with spring-loaded death traps or Havahart-
type traps that capture the animal so it can be released outside.

PESTPROOFING 101

The mudsill is the area formed by the foundation wall and the sill plates of your exterior walls. It is the most likely point of pest invasions and should be inspected (look for light coming in from outdoors) and caulked regularly.

GETTING THEM OUT WHEN THEY'RE IN

There are many hardware-store products designed to help you get rid of pests inside your house. For insects in the attic and basement, pesticide foggers are one option. These shouldn't be used around food prep areas or when anyone is in the house. The usual approach is to activate the fogger and then leave for a few hours. No matter which product you buy, follow the use instructions carefully.

Common roach and ant traps do capture a lot of pests, but will not solve the problem unless the source from outside is eliminated. The same is true of all sorts of mousetraps. If you've closed all the entry points that you can find, and you've trapped all the pests that should have been inside when you plugged the holes, then you need help. Call a reputable exterminator and let them handle the job.

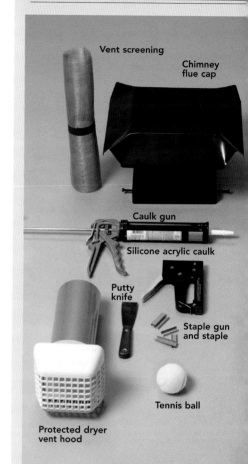

Vent screening

Chimney flue cap

Caulk gun

Silicone acrylic caulk

Putty knife

Staple gun and staple

Tennis ball

Protected dryer vent hood

DIFFICULTY LEVEL

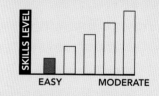

SKILLS LEVEL

EASY   MODERATE

This project can be completed in one to four hours.

1 If your chimney flue doesn't have a cap, you are inviting birds, bats, and squirrels into the flue, especially if you never use the fireplace. A chimney cap with screening or mesh on the sides will keep all these pests out.

2 Most roof vents come with screens installed to keep insects out of the house. If this screen is torn or missing, staple new screening (it's actually called insect mesh at the store) to the backside of the vent with ¼"-long staples.

3 Replace typical flap-type dryer vents (inset) with protected vent hoods. These keep out insects and small rodents, and are designed to be a universal replacement for standard vent hoods.

4 Sill plates are supposed to be installed over a sealer material that keeps out insects. But sometimes the sealer is left off. If you see evidence that insects are coming through the joint, fill it with caulk outside and inside (see page 425).

5 Insects can easily enter your house through a basement floor drain. The drain hole can be filled with a tennis ball that will float out of the way to allow water into the drain if the floor is flooded.

6 Check the foundation of your house for anthills, wasp's nests and termite tunnels. If you find any of these nests, remove them and close off the points of entry.

7 Be especially watchful in moist areas of the house where many insects prefer to be. Eliminate the access points and install a dehumidifier to make the area less attractive to pests.

8 If you ever find evidence of termite-eaten wood, call an exterminator immediately. These technicians can kill all the termites and check for other harmful species, like carpenter ants.

Fixing
Concrete Walkways

8

Once a concrete sidewalk or driveway starts to fail, you can bet that it's just the beginning of the problem. By fixing the crack or chip-out right away you can preserve the concrete.

CONCRETE CERTAINLY HAS AN ATTITUDE. It's hard, stubborn, and uncompromising; it won't bend even when a little give-and-take would make everything easier. Fortunately, it's more than just tough. It's also durable, long lasting, and faithful.

Everybody thinks concrete is so tough that they can do anything to it and it will be fine. Up to a point this is true. There isn't too much that puny humans can do, in the normal course of life, to cause any real damage. But the weather is something else, especially the kind of weather that gets below freezing in the winter. The freeze and thaw cycle creates little cracks that soon become bigger cracks as water seeps in, freezes and expands. If repairs aren't made when the problems are small, the problems will never be small again.

CONCRETE CRACKS 101

Hammer — Concrete patch — Edging tool

Wire brush — Pointing trowel

Crack filler — Paintbrush

Cold chisels

Masking tape

Whisk broom

Plastic sheeting

Scrap lumber for form board

Cracks in concrete typically must be made worse before they are made better. By chiseling the top of the crack so the walls slope down and away from the crack, you create a bell shape that will hold the repair material in place. You can fill cracks up to about ½" in. wide × ½" deep with a liquid polymer crack filler available at lumberyards and home centers. Fill the cracks just slightly below the surrounding surface for the best appearance. Then cover the cracks for two days so they aren't damaged by foot traffic. Deeper cracks should first be filled to within ½" of the top with foam backer rods. These should be compressed in the crack with a screwdriver or a putty knife and then covered with crack filler. If the crack is over ½" wide, fill the gap in a couple of applications so everything has time to cure properly. Breaks along the edge of the walk are the hardest to repair, but with a little effort, you can help that walk maintain its edge just a bit longer.

TERMS YOU NEED TO KNOW

FOAM BACKER RODS—Tube-shaped sections of foam for filling wide holes before caulking is applied. Commonly available in various lengths and in diameters from ¼" up to 2 in.

SPALLED CONCRETE—Concrete surface damage that appears as a flaking away of the top layer, usually less than 1/16" deep.

DIFFICULTY LEVEL

SKILLS LEVEL

EASY   MODERATE

This project can be completed in one to two hours per four foot square section of sidewalk.

HOW TO FIX A CONCRETE CHIP-OUT

1 Drive a form board next to the sidewalk and undercut the broken section with a cold chisel and hammer. This will create a modest keyway that will give the patch something extra to grip.

2 Just prior to applying the patch, brush some clean water onto the broken area to help the patch bond better.

CONCRETE REPAIR PRODUCTS

CONCRETE PATCHING materials contain additives and reinforcement to accomplish specific tasks. Shop carefully at your building center to make sure you buy the best product for your repair.

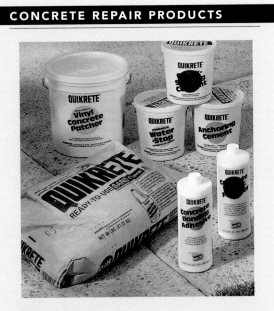

3 Use a small mortar trowel to apply the mortar patch. Be sure to force the patch to the bottom of the hole and feather the edges so the patch blends in well with the surrounding surfaces.

4 To reduce the chance of the edge breaking again, round it off using an edging tool. Gently move the tool over the patch and try to match the edge troweling on the rest of the walk.

5 Lightly brush the surface of the patch with a stiff broom. This creates better traction for bad weather conditions. When you're done, cover the patch with a plastic tarp for 6 or 7 days.

HOW TO FIX A CONCRETE CRACK

1 Remove any dust and debris from cracks with a wire brush, vacuum cleaner or a compressor with a hose-mounted spray nozzle.

2 Squeeze crack filler in the crack, stopping just below the surface of the walk. This protects the cracks without running the risk of smearing the filler across the surrounding surfaces.

Repairing Asphalt Driveways

9

Asphalt is a relatively forgiving paving material. When popouts or cracks occur, repairing them is basically a matter of dumping in fresh material and picking a way to compress it.

THE TWO MOST POPULAR HARD SURFACE DRIVEWAY MATERIALS ARE ASPHALT AND CONCRETE. Both are used, almost interchangeably, throughout the country in cold and hot climates. But there are some basic differences. Concrete generally costs more to install and asphalt generally costs more to maintain as the years go by. And, concrete doesn't always perform well in cold areas. It's susceptible to damage from the freeze-and-thaw cycle and it can be damaged by exposure to road salt. Asphalt, on the other hand, doesn't always perform well in hot climates. It absorbs a lot of heat from the sun and tends to stay soft during very hot periods. And, of course, when the surface is soft, it can wear more quickly.

It's a good thing that concrete doesn't need much routine maintenance because doing just about anything to concrete is difficult. Asphalt, however, is very easy to maintain and repair. And there are plenty of products in local home centers to help anyone do the work. In many ways, fixing an asphalt driveway is a lot like repainting a house that is in bad shape. Most of the work deals with surface preparation. Applying a new coat of driveway sealer is only the last of many steps.

DRIVEWAY SEALER 101

Some driveway sealers are made of coal tar, others are asphalt emulsions. Coal tar is compatible with asphalt paving and has some durability advantages over asphalt because it has ultra-violet stabilizers in the mix. These keep the black color of the sealer from fading quickly. Coal tar also resists damage from gas and oil spills better than asphalt. Both types are sold in 5 gal. buckets that sell for about $20 and cover between 300 and 400 sq. ft. of surface area.

The trick with applying sealers is to do it in warm weather (nothing below 50 degrees F.). Also, you should apply the sealer in thinner, rather than thicker, coats. If you build up too thick a coat, the sealer can peel. The container directions on the product you buy will indicate the proper coverage rate.

TERMS YOU NEED TO KNOW

ASPHALT—A combination of bitumens—that are by-products of coal tar distillation—and aggregates—that are a mixture of sand and gravel. Installed when hot.

ASPHALT SEALER—A bituminous coating, sometimes including sand as a fine aggregate, that is used to seal the surface of asphalt pavement.

ASPHALT—A paste-like combination of bitumens, very fine aggregate and additives to keep the mixture malleable.

ASPHALT CRACK FILLER—Comes in different formulations. One is a rubberized liquid emulsion that stays flexible permanently.

COLD-PATCH ASPHALT MIX—A combination of asphalt and synthetic polymers that keep the asphalt workable when it's cool.

TOOLS & SUPPLIES YOU NEED

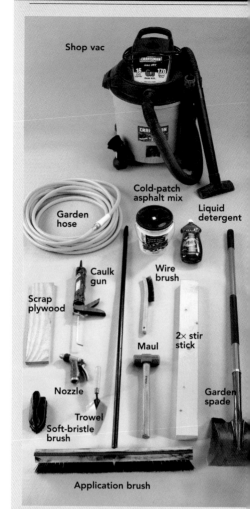

Shop vac

Cold-patch asphalt mix

Liquid detergent

Garden hose

Caulk gun

Wire brush

Scrap plywood

2× stir stick

Maul

Nozzle

Garden spade

Trowel

Soft-bristle brush

Application brush

DIFFICULTY LEVEL

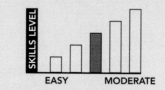

SKILLS LEVEL

EASY   MODERATE

This project can be completed in eight to twelve hours.

1 Begin the maintenance routine by removing any grass, weeds and other vegetation from the surface and sides of the driveway. Use a long-handle ice scraper or a square-tip shovel.

X-SECTION OF ASPHALT DRIVEWAY

Asphalt layer

Subbase

Soil

A typical asphalt driveway is formed by pouring and compressing a layer of hot asphalt over a subbase of compacted gravel.

2 Carefully inspect the asphalt surface for any oil and grease stains. Then remove them with driveway cleaner or household detergent. Scrub the cleaner into the surface with a soft brush and rinse the area clean with a garden hose. Repeat until the stain is gone. If using driveway cleaner, wear the recommended safety equipment.

3 Once the stains are removed, thoroughly rinse the entire driveway with a garden hose and nozzle. The goal is to wash away any debris and to remove the dust and dirt from the surface cracks.

4 Repair the small cracks first. Chip out any loose debris with a cold chisel and hammer. Then clean out all debris with a wire brush. Remove all the dust with a shop vacuum. A crevice tool on the end of the hose will do the best job.

6 Compact the patch material with a small piece of 2 × 4. Tamp the board up and down with your hand, or strike the board with a hammer. Keep working until you can't compress the patch any more.

5 Place asphalt patching compound in the holes with a small trowel. Overfill the hole so the patch material is about ½" higher than the surrounding asphalt surface.

7 Finish the patch by covering it with a piece of 2 × 6 and striking it with a hammer or mallet. Work back and forth across the board to smooth out the entire patch and make it flush to the surrounding surface.

8 On narrower patches, the compound can be smoothed with a small trowel. Just move the tool across the surrounding surface and then over the patch. This should flatten the patch. Finish up by compressing the compound by pushing it down with the trowel.

9 Prepare larger potholes by undercutting the edges with a cold chisel and a hammer. Then, remove all the debris and fill the hole with cold-patch asphalt mix. Working directly from the bag, fill the hole about 1 in. higher than the surrounding surface. Then compact it with a 2×4, as before.

10 One great way to compress cold-patch asphalt is to cover the patch with a piece of plywood. Then, drive your car onto the plywood and stop when one tire is centered on the panel. Wait a few minutes, then move the car back and forth a few times.

11 Once the hole patching is done, fill the routine cracks (less than ¼" wide) with asphalt crack filler. This material comes in a caulk tube, which makes it very easy to apply. Just clean the crack with a wire brush and a vacuum, then squeeze the filler into the crack.

12 After the crack filler has cured for about 10 or 15 minutes, smooth it out with a putty knife as you force the filler down into the crack. If this creates small depressions, fill these with a second application of filler.

13 Driveway sealer should always be mixed thoroughly before use. Take a 2× stir stick that's about 30 in. long and stir the sealer until it has a uniform consistency. Pour out enough to cover a strip across the driveway that's about 3-ft. or 4-ft. wide.

14 Spread the sealer with the squeegee side of the application brush. Try to keep this coat as uniform as possible. Work the sealer into the small cracks and pull it gently over the big patches.

15 Flip the squeegee over to the brush side and smooth out the lap marks and other irregularities that were left from the application coat. Work at right angles to the first pass.

Fixing Broken Glass Panes

10

Replacing a broken glass pane isn't nearly as common an occurrence today as it was a decade or two ago. But it's still a great skill to have for owners of older homes.

FOR PEOPLE WHO LIVE IN NEW, WELL-MADE HOUSES THE WINDOWS FROM THE GROUND TO THE RIDGE ARE BOUND TO BE DOUBLE-GLAZED UNITS THAT PER-FORM WITH COMMENDABLE ENERGY EFFICIENCY. This is a good thing, mostly. But these hi-tech units can break just like their older single-pane siblings, and you just can't fix double-glazed sashes yourself. People who live in older houses have it better. Their single pane sashes and storm windows are easy and inexpensive to repair. If you have just one pane to replace, most people can finish up the job in a couple of hours. Usually the hardest part of this chore is working off a ladder. You'll need one to remove the storm windows and to fix a regular sash because the repair needs to be made on the outside of the window.

GLASS PANES 101

Each glass pane in a typical wood sash is held in place on the inside by the wood that forms the sash and on the outside by glazing compound. This compound is a soft, caulk-like material when it's installed. But it hardens over time to form a durable seal that keeps the glass in the frame and the water out. If you wiggle the pieces of broken glass in-and-out, this will loosen the compound and you can pull the shards out. Measure the space, go to the hardware store for a $2 piece of glass, pop it in and glaze.

TERMS YOU NEED TO KNOW

WINDOW SASH—Any framework that holds window glazing, as in a double-hung window with two sashes (that is, two wood frames that each hold one or multiple pieces of glass).

GLAZIER'S POINTS—Small triangular pieces of steel with one side bent up at a 90-degree angle. Made for holding glass panes within wood frames, these points are pushed into place with a putty knife or flat blade screwdriver.

DIFFICULTY LEVEL

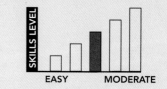

SKILLS LEVEL

EASY   MODERATE

This project can be completed in two to three hours.

HOW TO FIX A BROKEN WINDOW PANE

1 Wearing heavy leather gloves, remove the broken pieces of glass. Then, soften the old glazing compound using a heat gun or a hair dryer. Don't hold the heat gun too long in one place because it can be hot enough to scorch the wood.

2 Once a section of compound is soft, remove it using a putty knife. Work carefully to avoid gouging the wood frame. If a section is difficult to scrape clean, reheat it with the heat gun. Soft compound is always easy to remove.

3 Once the wood opening is scraped clean, seal the wood with a coat of linseed oil or primer. If the wood isn't sealed, the dry surface will draw too much moisture from the glazing compound and reduce its effectiveness.

4 Apply a thin bed of glazing compound to the wood frame opening and smooth it in place with your thumb.

5 Press the new pane into the opening, making sure to achieve a tight seal with the compound on all sides. Wiggle the pane from side-to-side and up-and-down until the pane is seated. There will be some squeeze-out, but do not press all the compound out.

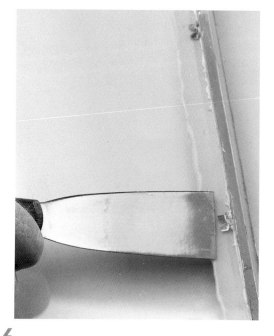

6 Drive glazier's points into the wood frame to hold the pane in place. Use the tip of a putty knife to slide the point against the surface of the glass. Install at least 2 points of each side of the pane.

7 Make a rope of compound (about ½" diameter) by rolling it between your hands. Then press it against the pane and the wood frame. Smooth it in place by drawing a putty knife, held at a 45-degree angle, across its surface. Scrape off excess.

8 Allow the glazing compound at least one week to dry completely. Then prime and paint it to match the rest of the sash. Be sure to spread the paint over the joint between the compound and the glass. This will seal the joint completely. When the paint is dry, scrape off the extra with a razor blade paint scraper.

Repairing Concrete Steps

11

A little concrete patching material and some know-how will keep your concrete steps looking brand new.

BUILDERS USE A LOT OF DIFFERENT MATERIALS FOR ENTRY STEPS. Many familiar varieties of stone and brick are common choices. Wood is also a favorite, especially for rustic buildings or those that are blessed with a large front porch. But when you look at all the houses and all the entry doors, including those at the back and side of the house, concrete has to be the top choice, by far. That's because it's cheap, durable, and long lasting.

The biggest problem involved in making a successful concrete step repair is binding the patch material to the existing material. Strong bonds can be created with the use of a bonding agent, usually part of the patching mix. The second bonding problem is that the repair surface must be free of all dust, dirt, grease and debris. Unless it is thoroughly cleaned, the patch won't hold for long.

CONCRETE CRACK REPAIR 101

Small cracks (about ¼ in. wide and deep) can be filled with concrete crack filler. Just brush out the crack and squeeze in the filler, stopping just a bit below the top of the crack. For wider cracks, one good approach is to fill the crack with mortar. Breaks along the edges and corners are repaired with a form board (or boards) nailed to the side of the steps. Then the edges of the break are undercut with a cold chisel and the void filled with a concrete patch mix. For big breaks, it's a good idea to drive masonry nails into the middle of the void to act as reinforcement for the patch. Make sure to drive these nails deep enough so their heads won't sit above the finished surface.

TERMS YOU NEED TO KNOW

CONCRETE CRACK FILLER—A liquid polymer substance that dries into a flexible, watertight seal.

BONDING AGENT—An adhesive chemical substance that's applied between a concrete substrate and a mortar patching mix.

MORTAR PATCHING MIX—A mixture of cement, sand, water and admixtures like bonding agents and plasticizers to make the material more workable.

TOOLS & SUPPLIES YOU NEED

Mortar patch mix

Bonding agent

Steel float

Edging tool

Circular saw with masonry blade

Pointing trowel

Paintbrush

Cold chisel

Wire brush

Plastic sheeting

Form boards

DIFFICULTY LEVEL

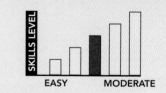

SKILLS LEVEL

EASY   MODERATE

This project can be completed in two to five hours.

OUTDOOR PROJECTS · Repairing Concrete Steps

1 Retrieve the broken corner, then clean it and the mating surface with a wire brush. Apply latex bonding agent to both surfaces. If you do not have the broken piece, you can rebuild the corner with patching compound.

2 Spread a heavy layer of fortified patching compound on the surfaces to be joined, then press the broken piece into position. Lean a heavy brick or block against the repair until the patching compound sets (about 30 minutes). Cover the repair with plastic and protect it from traffic for at least one week.

HOW TO REBUILD WITH PATCHING COMPOUND

1 Clean chipped concrete with a wire brush. Brush the patch area with latex bonding agent.

2 Mix patching compound with latex bonding agent, as directed by the manufacturer. Apply the mixture to the patch area, then smooth the surfaces and round the edges, as necessary, using a flexible knife or trowel.

3 Tape scrap lumber pieces around the patch as a form. Coat the insides with vegetable oil or commercial release agent so the patch won't adhere to the wood. Remove the wood when the patch is firm. Cover with plastic and protect from traffic for at least one week.

1 Make a cut in the stair tread just outside the damaged area, using a circular saw with a masonry-cutting blade. Make the cut so it angles toward the back of the step. Make a horizontal cut on the riser below the damaged area, then chisel out the area in between the two cuts.

2 Cut a form board the same height as the step riser. Coat one side of the board with vegetable oil or commercial release agent to prevent it from bonding with the repair, then press it against the riser of the damaged step, and brace it in position with heavy blocks. Make sure the top of the form is flush with the top of the step tread.

3 Apply latex bonding agent to the repair area with a clean paint brush, wait until the bonding agent is tacky (no more than 30 minutes), then press a stiff mixture of quick-setting cement into the damaged area with a trowel.

4 Smooth the concrete with a float, and let it set for a few minutes. Round over the front edge of the nose with an edger. Use a trowel to slice off the sides of the patch, so it is flush with the side of the steps. Cover the repair with plastic and wait a week before allowing traffic on the repaired section.

12

Repairing Siding

Siding is like the skin of your house and, like the skin on your body, sometimes it gets a scratch or bruise or cut. Here we'll show you how to bandage the damage.

EXPLAINING HOW TO MAKE BASIC SIDING REPAIRS IS HARDER THAN IT SOUNDS. That's because there are a lot of different siding types and a lot of variation in the way the same siding is installed. We show here the repair basics for the most common sidings: clapboard, tongue-and-groove, wood shingles, board-and-batten and vinyl or metal. The chance that your siding is installed exactly the way you see here is slight, but it's a good place to start.

Clapboard siding is bevel-lap siding boards made of redwood or cedar or pine. This siding can last for well over 100 years, if it's properly maintained.

Tongue-and-groove siding creates a very tight exterior seal and, if the paint and caulk are well maintained, it is virtually trouble free. But it is difficult and time-consuming to install.

Wood shingles are typically made of cedar or cyprus and may be either split or sawn. This type of siding may be painted or allowed to weather to a silvery gray.

Vinyl and aluminum siding are designed, installed and repaired in much the same way. Both products expand and contract a great deal with changes in temperature.

Board-and-batten, in this day and age, normally refers to wood panels (textured plywood) with thin strips of lumber installed to cover the seams between panels.

EXTERIOR WALLS 101

Wall sheathing

Wall stud

Interior vapor barrier

Siding (clapboard)

Insulation

Exterior moisture barrier (building paper or house-wrap)

Regardless of what type of siding you have, the inside of your exterior walls will look something like this. When you're working on siding, it's important that you identify the locations of wall studs and that you avoid penetrating or tearing the vapor barriers on either side of the wall.

Power miter saw

Trim saw

Caulk guns

Zip tool

Keyhole saw or wallboard saw

Hammer

Flat pry bar

Aviator snips

Fasteners

Mini hacksaw

Hacksaw blade

Siding material for patching

DIFFICULTY LEVEL

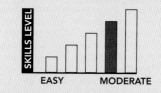

SKILLS LEVEL

EASY   MODERATE

This project can be completed in two to three hours, for simple repairs.

1 Locate and mark framing members inside the wall (use a stud finder) so you can draw cutting lines around the damage that fall over studs. Starting at the bottom, cut clapboards at the cutting lines with a keyhole saw or a wallboard saw. For access, slip wood shims under the clapboard above the one you're cutting. NOTE: The repair will look better if you stagger cutting lines so they don't fall on the same stud.

2 Cut replacement clapboards to fit, using a miter saw or power miter saw.

3 Nail the replacement clapboards in the patching area (you can use tape to hold them in place if you like). Follow the same nailing pattern used for the boards around it. Set nail heads with a nailset.

4 Caulk the gaps between clapboards and fill nailholes with exterior putty or caulk. Prime and paint the repaired section to match.

HOW TO REPAIR BOARD & BATTEN

1 With a flat pry bar, remove the battens on each side of the damaged area. To protect the painted surfaces, cut along the joints between the boards and battens with a utility knife before removing the battens.

2 Remove the damaged panel (or make vertical cuts with a circular saw underneath the batten locations if any of the battens are only decorative). Cut a replacement panel from matching material, sized to leave a ⅛" gap between the original panels and the new patch. Nail panel in place, caulk the repair seams and reinstall the battens. Prime and paint to match.

HOW TO REPAIR TONGUE & GROOVE

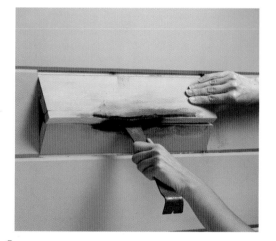

1 To repair tongue-and-groove siding, first mark both ends of the damage and rip-cut the board down the middle, from end to end, with a circular saw or trim saw. Then use the trim saw to cut along the vertical lines. Finish all cuts with a keyhole saw. Split the damaged board with a pry bar or a wide chisel. Then pull the pieces apart and out of the hole. If the building paper below the damaged section was cut or torn, repair it.

Back of groove area on patch is removed

2 Cut the replacement board to fit, then cut off the backside of the groove so the board can clear the tongue on the course below. Prime the board, let it dry, then nail it into place. Paint to match.

Small stucco problems rarely turn into major problems—if you catch them when they are still small. A caulk product designed for masonry will fix small stucco woes. The patched area can then be covered with touch-up paint so that it blends in.

STUCCO IS ONE OF THE MOST DURABLE SIDING MATERIALS USED ON HOMES. But damp climates can be especially hard on these surfaces, and if left unattended, small cracks can lead to some pretty big problems. A few years of water damage can cause large sections of stucco to loosen and even fall away from your house.

Fortunately, these problems aren't all that hard to repair, even for beginners. And keeping stucco in good condition is one of the easiest maintenance tasks of all. All you really need to do is inspect your stucco once each year and fill any small cracks you find—which won't happen that often. But let's say you forgot, and your stucco has a more major problem. Don't panic; just keep reading.

STUCCO 101

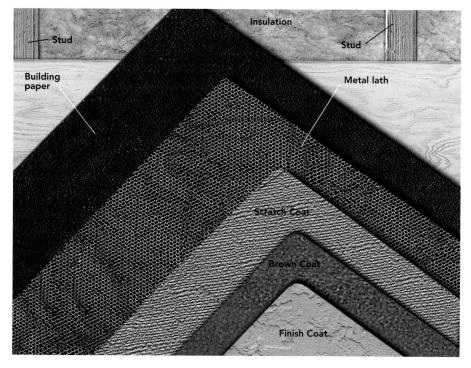

Stud — Insulation — Stud

Building paper — Metal lath

Scratch Coat

Brown Coat

Finish Coat

Your original stucco walls were made from three layers of cement-based stucco laid over a metal fabric, called lathe, which is nailed over the building paper and plywood or plank sheathing covering the skeleton of the walls. Today, though, you can just use a single premixed stucco product, sold in plastic buckets, to make repairs to stucco.

TERMS YOU NEED TO KNOW

BROWN COAT—The second of three stucco layers, the brown coat uses the same formulation as the scratch coat, but is applied in a smooth layer.

SCRATCH COAT—The first of three layers of stucco, it earns its name because it is scored with grooves while still wet so that the following coats will adhere to it.

FINISH COAT—The top layer of stucco, which is often tinted and textured to provide a decorative finish.

METAL LATH—This porous steel fabric is nailed to wall sheathing to provide the base for the first, or scratch coat of stucco.

SQUARE-END TROWEL—a straight, smooth metal tool used to apply stucco and other masonry substances.

TOOLS & SUPPLIES YOU NEED

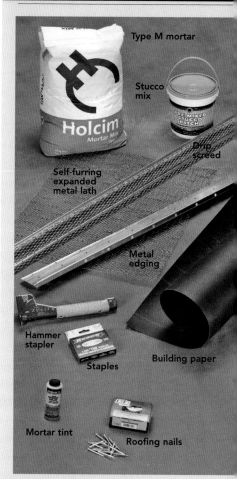

Type M mortar

Stucco mix

Drip screed

Self-furring expanded metal lath

Metal edging

Hammer stapler

Staples

Building paper

Mortar tint

Roofing nails

DIFFICULTY LEVEL

SKILLS LEVEL

EASY   MODERATE

This project can be completed in two to four days.

HOW TO PATCH STUCCO

1 Remove loose material from the repair area, using a wire brush. If the underlying metal lath has any rust, brush this away, too.

2 Use a broad putty knife or small trowel to apply premixed stucco repair compound to the repair area, with enough depth to slightly overfill the depression.

3 Smooth out the repair area with your knife or trowel, taking care to make the borders of the repair blend smoothly into the surrounding wall surface. Use a whisk broom or trowel to duplicate the texture of the wall.

4 If you have any bigger patch areas, chip away the loose stucco, cut away the loose metal lath, then cut and attach new lath to the wall sheathing.

5 If your large patch area includes a corner, cut and install a piece of metal edging along the corner of the wall. Sheet metal is sharp, so make sure you wear gloves and eye protection when cutting it.

6 Apply a base, or scratch coat of premixed stucco compound over the lath, with a thickness of about ⅜". Score closely spaced horizontal lines in the wet surface, using a scratching tool or a nail. Let the stucco dry for a couple of days.

7 Apply the second coat of stucco patch compound, to withing ¼" of the original surface. Let the patch dry for a day or two.

8 Apply the final coat of stucco, then texture it to match the surrounding wall, using a whisk broom or trowel. After the stucco dries, you can either paint the patch area to match the surrounding wall, or paint the entire wall for nearly invisible blend.

Renewing Wood Decks

14

Weathered wood has true romantic appeal, but when the wood is the only thing between your feet and the ground it ought to be in pristine shape. Refinishing a wood deck is vital to that cause (and you'll need to learn how, since you'll be doing it practically every year).

WOOD DECKS CAN BE GREAT THINGS. They give you a place to relax and entertain outside, while maintaining one of the big advantages of staying in: a flat stable floor. In the last 30 years, decks have overtaken the old fashioned patio. One reason for this is that decks are made of wood, not masonry, so the design possibilities are almost limitless. Masonry products, whether concrete, brick, or natural stone, are much harder to work with and are more expensive. Wood decks do wear out and must be maintained to last a long time and look good while doing it.

If you have a small deck (anything under 200 sq. ft.), refinishing is a pretty easy job. But on larger decks, refinishing can develop into quite a chore. The thing to remember, when you've been scrubbing off the old finish for hours, is that replacing a deck can eat up $10,000 nearly as fast as a college bursar. So it pays to take care of things before the deck damage gets out of control.

DECK FINISHING 101

Refinishing a deck involves three separate steps. The first is to remove the old finish. The second is to wash away all the dirt, mildew, and other residues. And the third is to reseal the surface with a new finish. There are lots of products on the market for cleaning decks. The trick is to get the product that's right for your situation. Anything that just says "deck cleaner" is not what's needed. These help lift off dirt and grime but won't do much to remove an old finish. If your deck is covered with just a transparent sealer or a light stain, then a product called a "stain/sealer remover" is what you need. If you have a heavy, solid-color stain, you'll want something stronger. These are sometimes called simply "deck finish strippers," and are made to lift off everything from the surface.

TERMS YOU NEED TO KNOW

DRILL/DRIVER—A cordless drill outfitted with an adjustable clutch that lets the user preset the amount of force used to drive any fastener. Once the drill reaches the preset torque limit, the clutch prevents the chuck from rotating and thus the bit from turning.

LAG SCREWS—A steel screw with a hexagonal head and a thin body with a coarse thread. Used for drawing heavy boards together without using a standard bolt, nut and washers.

CUPPED BOARD—A board that has a convex deviation (a bump) across its width, not its length or thickness.

TOOLS & SUPPLIES YOU NEED

Pressure washer

Deck cleaner

Deck cleaner

Drill

Deck finish

Garden hose

Pressure washer roller

Paint brush

Fasteners

Long-nap roller

Nail set

Plastic tarps

Rubber gloves

Hammer

Spray nozzle

Scrub brush

DIFFICULTY LEVEL

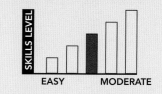

SKILLS LEVEL

EASY   MODERATE

This project can be completed in one to two days depending on size of deck.

1 Apply a heavy coat of deck stripper to the deck boards. Usually a garden sprayer works for this job. But you can also use a paint roller with a long nap roller to spread the stripper.

2 Let the stripper set for as long as the container directions recommend (usually around 15 minutes). Then brush it vigorously with a stiff bristle deck brush. Try to avoid splattering the stripper on nearby plants, the siding, trim or windows and doors.

3 Rinse off the stripper using a garden hose with a spray attachment or use a pressure washer. Be sure to rinse any adjacent surfaces that might have been splattered with stripper.

4 Next comes the deck cleaner, which is often sold in a concentrated form. Mix it thoroughly in a large bucket, according to the container's directions.

5 Using a stiff deck brush, spread the deck cleaner over the boards and scrub until the wood brightens. Usually, this happens almost immediately. Keep scrubbing until the surface looks new.

TIP

Keep in mind, when working with the brush, that it tends to hold less sealer than a paint roller. So, to ensure even coverage, load up the brush with extra sealer and apply it in a heavier coat.

6 Protect surrounding surfaces with masking tape and paper, then start brushing on the sealer. Use the brush just for hard to reach areas. Use a roller on everything else.

7 Apply sealer to the open areas with a roller that has a ¾"-nap roller cover. As you move, press the roller down forcefully so the sealer squeezes between the boards and covers their edges.

Replacing Damaged Roof Shingles

15

A little bit of localized damage doesn't mean it's time to reroof your whole house. Replacing an old shingle or two can buy you many more years of coverage, but only if the roof doesn't show widespread wear.

THE WORLD OF RESIDENTIAL ROOFING IS PRETTY VARIED. Asphalt, fiberglass-reinforced asphalt, rolled asphalt, wood shingles, wood shakes, slate, concrete, terra cotta tiles, steel, and rubber are just some of the current roofing choices. Why is it with all this choice what you see practically everywhere is asphalt shingles, row after row, all clean-cut, well behaved and just a little bit dull? Well, cost is one thing. Standard three-tab asphalt shingles are priced at about $80 per square (100 square feet of coverage), which is a lot cheaper than other options. Asphalt is also reliable and durable. Twenty-year lifespans are not uncommon.

If you have asphalt shingles on your roof and a small section is damaged, you're in luck. The repair is easy and quick, if only a couple of shingles are involved, so you can do it yourself. There are only two significant obstacles to the job. The first is working from a ladder. If this makes you uncomfortable, hire the job done. The second is that the repair involves a small amount of plastic roof cement. No matter how much you use, this material will get all over you and every tool you touch.

ROOF SAFETY 101

Caulk gun with roof cement

Flat pry bar or nail puller

Roofing nails

Hammer

Shingles that match the existing roof color

If your roof pitch is 6:12 (6 in. of vertical rise for every 12 in. of horizontal run) or less, then you should be able to work on the roof comfortably and safely. But if your roof is steeper than 6:12, consider getting a contractor. A fall, from even a one-story roof, is a serious matter. To measure a slope, hold a carpenter's square against the roofline, with the top arm horizontal (check it with a level). Position the square so it intersects the roof at the 12" mark. On the vertical arm, measure down from the top to the point of intersection to find the rise.

DIFFICULTY LEVEL

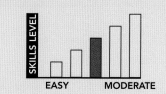

SKILLS LEVEL

EASY   MODERATE

This project can be completed in three to five hours.

PROBLEMS YOU'LL NEED TO SOLVE

You can't repair a roof if you don't have some replacement shingles. Fortunately many builders save the shingles that were left over from the original installation. These will be a bit brighter than the ones on the roof that have been faded by the sun. But they'll be close enough. If you don't have any original shingles and can't buy a good match at your local lumberyard, your best strategy is to harvest repair shingles from a less noticeable section of the roof. This means you'll have to repair two roof sections instead of one, but you'll end up with a better looking job.

HOW TO REPLACE DAMAGED ROOF SHINGLES

1 To flatten a buckled shingle, squeeze some plastic roof cement under the buckle then weigh down the shingle with a brick or two for a couple of hours.

2 To remove a damaged shingle, grip its bottom edge (with gloves on) and wiggle it back and forth as you pull down. This will pull it free from the roofing nails that hold it in place.

3 Remove any exposed nails with a flat pry bar or a nail puller. If the roofing felt (the layer below the shingles) is damaged, repair the patch with some plastic roof cement.

4 Nail the new shingles in place, starting at the lowest course and working up. The new shingle will not be as faded as the old ones surrounding it. But over time the difference between the two will be less noticeable.

5 Before installing the last shingle, turn it over and apply a bead of plastic roof cement to the back top edge. Keep this bead about 1 in. below the top edge.

7 If the damaged shingle falls in a roof valley, take it out and clean any old cement from the valley flashing. Then apply two beads of plastic roof cement along the edge of the valley.

6 Carefully slide the last shingle into place. The plastic roof cement will smear across the underside of the shingle, which will improve the bond with the shingle below. Press the repair shingle flat, then lift up the shingle above and drive nails in the typical way.

8 Cut the repair shingle to size and slide it into position. Press it firmly into the valley cement to achieve the best bond.

Installing
Locksets & Deadbolts

16

You never know when you'll need to replace a door lockset or deadbolt, but there are many situations when you'll be glad you know how to do it.

HOME SECURITY IS NOT SO MUCH A MATTER OF TENACIOUS CRIME PREVENTION AS IT IS A QUESTION OF PEACE OF MIND. If you have been burglarized, you're bound to feel vulnerable. So we all have an interest in keeping what's outside, outside. There are many different approaches to accomplishing this. Some cost a lot of money, and some don't cost much at all. The first (and most expensive) is having a whole-house security system installed that notifies the police if there's any trouble. But not everyone needs or wants something so involved. A more passive approach serves their needs. This generally means a combination of motion-activated floodlights and quality door locks. When someone carefully approaches a back door at night, there are few things as alarming as having a bright light suddenly flash in their eyes. And there's nothing quite as discouraging as trying to break through a door with a deadbolt lock when you want to go unnoticed. If you only care to do one of these security building jobs, pick installing better locks. They're on the job every day, all day and all night, whether the power is on or off.

LOCKSETS & DEADBOLTS 101

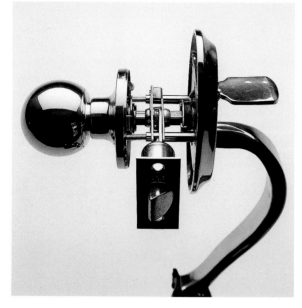

LOCKSETS—A good door deserves a good lockset. Inexpensive locksets are available for $10 to $15 and high quality ones cost around $40. Locksets for interior doors are called passage locks and are not suitable for exterior doors.

DEADBOLTS—A good deadbolt should cost around $25. There are several styles to choose from that differ in ways other than finish. Some are keyed on the outside and have a thumblatch on the interior side. If you have a glass sidelight or door panel, think about buying a model that's keyed on both the exterior and interior so an intruder can't break your glass and reach in to unlock the deadbolt.

TERMS YOU NEED TO KNOW

DOOR JAMB—Boards that define a door opening. The door hinges are hung on one jamb board and the strike plates for any locks are installed on the opposite jamb.

TEMPLATE—A pattern that establishes the proper layout for a procedure. In this case, a piece of paper taped to a door to indicate where clearance holes should be drilled.

LOCKSET—A complete locking system including knobs, locking mechanism, locking bolt, and decorative roses. Used on entry doors and interior doors where locking is desired.

DEADBOLT—A heavy-duty locking bolt that goes deep into the door jamb to prevent tampering.

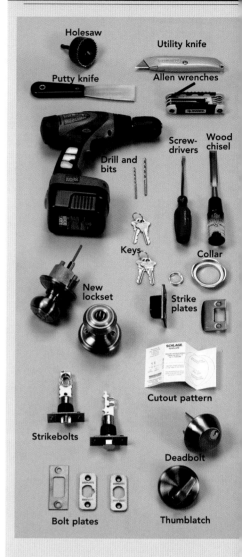
DIFFICULTY LEVEL

SKILLS LEVEL

EASY   MODERATE

This project can be completed in two to three hours.

HOW TO INSTALL A LOCKSET

1 Remove the old lockset. The knob on the inside of the door is usually held in place with a small clip. This is located on the side of the sleeve that extends from the knob to the flange on the door surface. To release this clip, just push it into the flange with a screwdriver or an awl. Then pull off the knob.

2 Remove the flange next. These are usually snapped in place over the lock mechanism underneath. To remove one, just pry it off with a screwdriver pushed into a slot designed for it. Other flanges are held by small spring clips. By pushing down on the clip with a screwdriver, the flange can easily be pulled off with your fingers.

3 Once the flange is off, the lock mechanism will be accessible. The two sides of the lock are joined together by two screws. Remove these screws and take the lock components out of the lockset hole in the door.

4 With both sides of the lock removed, the lock bolt can be taken out. Remove the screws that hold the bolt plate to the edge of the door. Then pull out the bolt mechanism.

Bolt plate

5 Install the new bolt assembly and make sure that the screws in the bolt plate are driven tightly into the door. Separate the lock halves and slide them together with the door and bolt assembly sandwiched between.

6 While holding one side of the lock against the door, maneuver the other side of the lock so the screws fall in the slots made for them. Once the screw heads have cleared the slots, tighten the screws so both halves of the lock are tight against the door. Install the new knobs and new strike plate.

HOW TO INSTALL A DEADBOLT

TEMPLATE TIP

Many doors sold today come with holes for the lockset predrilled. Some also are predrilled for a deadbolt, but very often you'll need to drill holes for the actual deadbolt you purchase. To assist in this, manufacturers provide a template that you tape to the door for reference. Following the manufacturer's instructions, tape the hole template to the door (make sure you've oriented the template to correspond to the actual thickness of your door) and mark the center point of each hole, including the bolt hole in the edge of the door. The deadbolt is usually located 7" or 8" above the lockset.

1 Determine the size of holesaw you need by checking the installation instructions that came with the lock. Then chuck this tool into a drill and bore the hole. Stop boring when the tip of the drill bit, at the center of the holesaw, breaks through the other side.

2 Go to the other side of the door and slide the pilot bit of the hole saw into the hole and cut out the rest of the waste material. If you try to cut through the door in a single pass, you risk tearing the steel covering (on steel-clad doors) as the hole-saw teeth break through the surface.

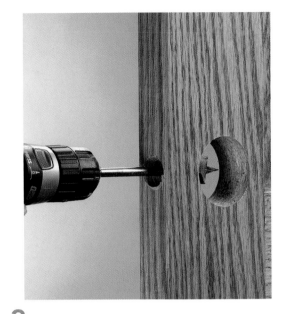

3 Drill the bolt hole through the edge of the door, using a spade bit or forstner bit. Make sure to keep the bit level so the bolt hole will enter the lock hole at the proper point.

4 Push the bolt assembly into the bolt hole so the bolt plate is flat on the edge of the door. Trace around the plate with a utility knife. Remove the mechanism and cut a ⅛"-deep mortise in the edge of the door with a sharp chisel (see next page).

5 Once you're satisfied with the fit, press the bolt plate into its mortise and attach it by driving in the two plate screws. Slide both sides of the lock into the bolt mechanism (inset) and attach them by driving the screws that hold the two parts together. Make sure these screws are tight.

MORTISING TECHNIQUE

Installing hardware plates requires using a wood chisel to create a mortise for the hardware.

1 Deepen the outline for the mortise to ⅛" with a wood chisel (try to find a chisel the same width as the mortise). With the beveled face of the chisel blade facing into the mortise, rap the handle with a mallet.

2 Chisel a series of ⅛"-deep parallel cuts about ¼" apart.

3 Position the chisel bevel-side down at about a 45-degree angle. Strike with a mallet to chisel out the waste. Smooth the mortise bottom.

6 Extend the lock bolt and color its end with lipstick, a grease pencil, or a crayon. Then retract the bolt, close the door and extend the bolt so its end hits the jamb. This will yield the precise location of the bolt hole that's needed on the jamb. Drill a hole (usually 1½" deep) for the bolt with a spade bit (see installation instructions for actual hole size requirements).

7 Close the door and test the deadbolt to make sure the bolt fits into the bolt hole in the jamb. If not, enlarge the hole slightly. Once the bolt fits, center the strike plate over the bolt hole and trace it with a utility knife. Cut a mortise for the strike plate using a sharp chisel.

8 Finish up by installing the strike plate on the jamb. Some of these plates are oversized like the one above. But most look more like standard lockset strike plates. Both types, however, feature long screws that are driven through the jamb and deep into the wall studs behind.

Tuning Up
Garage Doors

17

A garage door that's well maintained and a working garage door opener are modern conveniences that are easy to take for granted.

IS THIS A GREAT COUNTRY OR WHAT? YOU'RE DRIVING HOME LATE AT NIGHT, IT'S POURING OUTSIDE, AND YOU'RE FREEZING BECAUSE YOU'VE GOT THE FLU. Then, you turn into your driveway, punch a little button, and your garage door opens, a light comes on, you pull in, and you're HOME. You didn't have to get drenched, or lift a door that felt like heavy metal, or scream at the heavens for making you so miserable. You danced away from all of this, and that is a good thing.

Unfortunately, over time, many good things become bad things, especially if they aren't well-maintained. And an overhead garage door is no exception. To keep everything running smoothly requires effort on three fronts: the door, the opener, and the electronic safety sensors that prevent the door from closing on cars, pets or people.

GARAGE DOORS 101

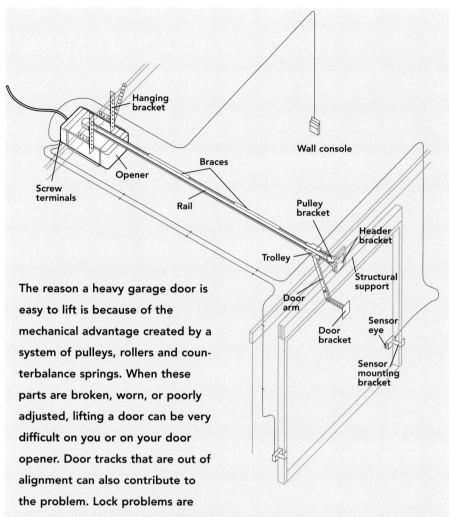

The reason a heavy garage door is easy to lift is because of the mechanical advantage created by a system of pulleys, rollers and counterbalance springs. When these parts are broken, worn, or poorly adjusted, lifting a door can be very difficult on you or on your door opener. Door tracks that are out of alignment can also contribute to the problem. Lock problems are common in garage doors: either the cylinder is hard to operate or the lock bar doesn't fit in its track opening.

Most door openers have a chain drive that may require tightening or lubrication. And sensors located on both sides of the door can be easily knocked out of alignment.

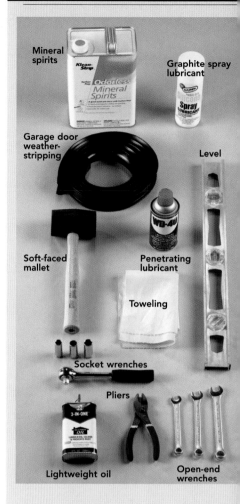

Mineral spirits

Graphite spray lubricant

Garage door weather-stripping

Level

Soft-faced mallet

Penetrating lubricant

Toweling

WD-40

Socket wrenches

Pliers

Lightweight oil

3-IN-ONE OIL

Open-end wrenches

DIFFICULTY LEVEL

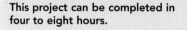

SKILLS LEVEL

EASY   MODERATE

This project can be completed in four to eight hours.

TERMS YOU NEED TO KNOW

CHAIN-DRIVE OPENER—An electric opener that lifts and lowers a garage door with a chain that's driven by a motor mounted sprocket.

SCREW-DRIVE OPENER—An electric opener that lifts and lowers a garage door with a continuous screw that's driven by a gear in the motor.

CLOSING FORCE SENSITIVITY—This is a measurement of how quickly a garage door opener will stop and reverse the door's travel when an obstruction is sensed or hit.

HOW TO TUNE-UP A GARAGE DOOR

1 Begin the tune-up by lubricating the door tracks, pulleys and rollers. Use a lightweight oil, not grease, for this job. The grease catches too much dust and dirt.

2 Remove clogged or damaged rollers from the door by backing off the nuts that hold the roller brackets. The roller will come with the bracket when the bracket is pulled free.

3 Mineral spirits and kerosene are good solvents for cleaning roller bearings. Let the bearing sit for a half-hour in the solvent. Then brush away the grime build-up with an old paint brush or toothbrush.

4 If the rollers are making a lot of noise as they move over the tracks, the tracks are probably out of alignment. To fix this, check the tracks for plumb. If they are out of plumb the track mounting brackets must be adjusted.

5 To adjust out-of-plumb tracks, loosen all the track mounting brackets (usually 3 or 4 per track) and push the brackets into alignment.

6 It's often easier to adjust the brackets by partially loosening the bolts and tapping the track with a soft-faced mallet. Once the track is plumb, tighten all the bolts.

7 Sometimes the door lock bar opens sluggishly because the return spring has lost its tension. The only way to fix this is to replace the spring. One end is attached to the body of the lock; the other end hooks onto the lock bar.

8 If a latch needs lubrication, use graphite in powder or liquid form. Don't use oil because it attracts dust that will clog the lock even more.

9 Sometimes the lock bar won't lock the door because it won't slide into its opening on the door track. To fix this, loosen the guide bracket that holds the lock bar and move it up or down until the bar hits the opening.

10 Worn or broken weatherstripping on the bottom edge of the door can let in a lot of cold air and stiff breezes. Check to see if this strip is cracked, broken, or has holes along its edges. If so, remove the old strip and pull any nails left behind.

11 Measure the width of your garage door, then buy a piece of weatherstripping to match. These strips are standard lumber yard and home center items. Sometimes they are sold in kit form, with fasteners included. If not, just nail the stripping in place with galvanized roofing nails.

12 If the chain on your garage door opener is sagging more than ½" below the bottom rail, it can make a lot of noise and cause drive sprocket wear. Tighten the chain according to the directions in the owner's manual.

13 On openers with a drive screw instead of a chain, lubricate the entire length of the screw with lightweight oil. Do not use grease.

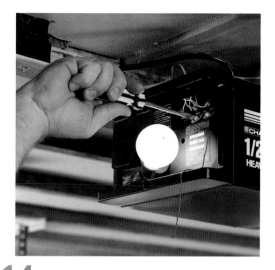

14 Test the door's closing force sensitivity and make adjustments at the opener's motor case if needed. Because both the sensitivity and the adjustment mechanism vary greatly between opener models, you'll have to rely on your owner's manual for guidance. If you don't have the owner's manual, you can usually download one from the manufacturer's website.

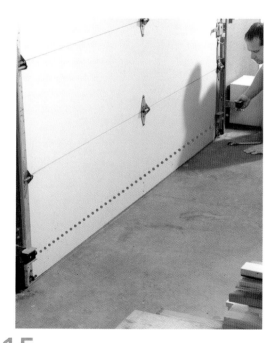

15 Check for proper alignment on the safety sensors near the floor. They should be pointing directly at one another and their lenses should be clean of any dirt and grease.

16 Make sure that the sensors are talking to the opener properly. Start to close the door, then put your hand down between the two sensors. If the door stops immediately and reverses direction, it's working properly. If it's not, make the adjustment recommended in the owner's manual. If that doesn't do the trick, call a professional door installer and don't use the door until it passes this test.

Installing
House Gutters

18

Installing a snap-together vinyl gutter system is a manageable task for most do-it-yourselfers. Before you purchase new gutters, create a detailed plan and cost estimate. Include all the necessary parts, not just the gutter and drain pipe sections; they make up only part of the total system. Test-fit all the pieces on the ground before you begin the actual installation.

GUTTERS PREVENT RUNOFF FROM YOUR ROOF THAT CAN DAMAGE FOUNDATION PLANTINGS. THEY HELP KEEP WATER OUT OF YOUR BASEMENT, AND THEY REDIRECT WATER AWAY FROM ENTRYWAYS. In short, there are plenty of good reasons to install gutters on a house that doesn't have a gutter system, or to replace a failing gutter system. However, be aware that installing new gutters in cold climates can be a real problem. (As the old saying goes: You can't live with them and you can't live without them.) They have a bad rep because they cause so many ice dams. Without gutters, this water would just run off the edge of the roof. So consider all the pluses and minuses carefully before investing in a gutter system. If you decide to go for it, here's one tip: When calculating the costs, don't be fooled by the relatively low per-foot cost for a run of gutter or downspouts, since it's the fittings and connectors that make up most of the cost of DIY gutter installations.

GUTTERS 101

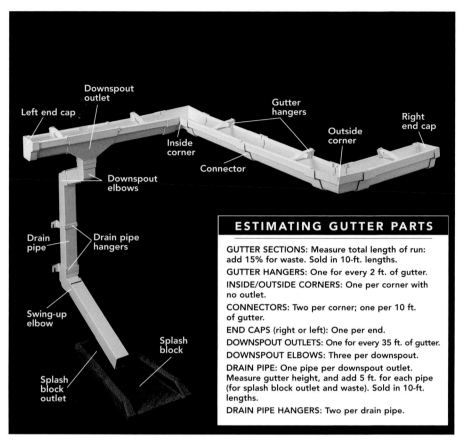

Left end cap
Downspout outlet
Gutter hangers
Right end cap
Inside corner
Outside corner
Connector
Downspout elbows
Drain pipe
Drain pipe hangers
Swing-up elbow
Splash block
Splash block outlet

ESTIMATING GUTTER PARTS

GUTTER SECTIONS: Measure total length of run: add 15% for waste. Sold in 10-ft. lengths.

GUTTER HANGERS: One for every 2 ft. of gutter.

INSIDE/OUTSIDE CORNERS: One per corner with no outlet.

CONNECTORS: Two per corner; one per 10 ft. of gutter.

END CAPS (right or left): One per end.

DOWNSPOUT OUTLETS: One for every 35 ft. of gutter.

DOWNSPOUT ELBOWS: Three per downspout.

DRAIN PIPE: One pipe per downspout outlet. Measure gutter height, and add 5 ft. for each pipe (for splash block outlet and waste). Sold in 10-ft. lengths.

DRAIN PIPE HANGERS: Two per drain pipe.

Steel, aluminum and vinyl gutter materials are available at a number of different outlets, including lumber yards, home centers and some hardware stores. To make a shopping list, first measure the length of gutter you need. Then calculate the amount of downspout required (generally sold in 10-ft. lengths.) A good rule of thumb for 5-in. gutters says that any gutter run less than 40 ft. only needs one downspout. For longer ones, a downspout should be installed at both ends of the run. After you total up the gutters and downspouts, list the fittings. Each downspout requires an outlet fitting, and both ends of the completed gutter need an end cap. Any joints need a splice fitting, and any inside or outside corners need inside or outside corner fittings. Two elbows are required to make the transition between the outlet fitting and its downspout. And two fastener brackets are needed for each section of downspout. You'll also need hanging brackets for the gutters. Buy enough to install one every 2 ft.

TERMS YOU NEED TO KNOW

GUTTER PITCH—This is the amount that a gutter slopes from its high to low points, usually expressed as difference in height per 10 ft. of run.

GUTTER RUN—The gutter sections and fittings that fall between gutter end caps.

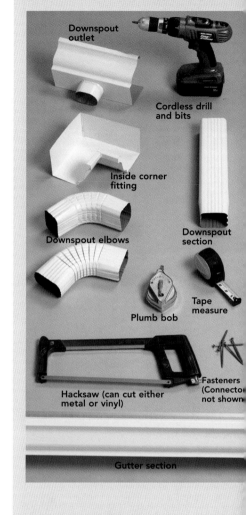

1 Mark a point at the high end of each gutter run, 1" from the top of the fascia. Snap chalk lines that slope toward downspouts. For runs longer than 35 ft., mark a slope from a high point in the center toward downspouts at each end.

2 Install downspout outlets near the ends of gutter runs (at least one outlet for every 35 ft. of run). The tops of the outlets should be flush with the slope line, and they should align with end caps on the corners of the house, where drain pipes will be attached.

3 Following the slope line, attach hangers or support clips for hangers for a complete run. Attach them to the fascia at 24" intervals, using deck screws.

4 Following the slope line, attach outside and inside corners at all corner locations that don't have end caps.

5 Use a hacksaw to cut gutter sections to fit between outlets and corners. Attach the end caps and connect the gutter sections to the outlets. Cut and test-fit gutter sections to fit between outlets, allowing for expansion gaps.

6 Join the gutter sections together, using connectors. Attach gutter hangers to the gutter (for models with support clips mounted on the fascia). Hang the gutters, connecting them to the outlets.

7 Cut a section of drain pipe to fit between two downspout elbows. One elbow should fit over the tail of the downspout outlet and the other should fit against the wall. Assemble the parts, slip the top elbow onto the outlet, and secure the other to the siding with a drain pipe hanger.

8 Cut a piece of drain pipe to fit between the elbow at the top of the wall and the end of the drain pipe run, staying at least 12" above the ground. Attach an elbow, and secure the pipe to the wall with a drain pipe hanger. Add accessories, such as splash blocks, to help channel water away from the house (inset).

19

Installing Landscape Lighting

Low-voltage lights are safe to install and use to beautify your outdoor spaces. Unlike solar landscape lights, they are powered by good old reliable electricity, so they really can stay on all night if you wish them to.

SOME LANDSCAPE LIGHTING MANUFACTURERS PITCH THEIR SYSTEMS AS SECURITY PRODUCTS. If you keep the outside of your house well lit, the reasoning goes, the thieves will turn elsewhere to find easier pickings. It's possible that the companies are right about this. But probably the stronger arguments are for improved safety and appearance.

It can't be surprising that adding some light to the dark makes going places safer. This idea has been around for a long time—a very long time. But the notion that you can improve the look of your house, by adding some nightlights, is more recent. In fact, decorating with exterior lights became widespread only in the last 25 years, when low-voltage landscape lighting showed up. The beauty of low-voltage lighting is that it can be installed by anyone without the risk of being shocked.

Low-voltage lights are powered by a transformer that steps 120-volt current down to a safe 12 volts. Choosing the location for the transformer is an important part of planning. You have two options: inside the house and outside the house. The outside installation is a little easier, but the inside one is a little better, especially from a security standpoint. Also take some time to review your light placement. Once you are happy with the plan, drive a small stake where you want each light to go.

LOW-VOLTAGE LIGHT KITS 101

Landscape lighting can be ordered in kit form or as individual pieces. Kits include a few light heads, some wire and a transformer that changes standard house current into low-voltage power. If you want half a dozen lights along the front walk, for example, then the kit is a good idea. It's cheaper, very easy to install and will last a long time unless the lights get run over by a lawnmower. Predictably, the individual parts approach offers a much wider range of light heads, a selection of transformers that can handle bigger jobs, and all the wire and other accessories anyone could need. Of course, this choice costs more money. A typical starter kit retails for about $150, while a collection of 20 expensive light heads, a big transformer and lots of wire can gobble up $1000 or more.

TERMS YOU NEED TO KNOW

LOW-VOLTAGE—Usually about 12 volts of current, instead of the standard 120 volts, used to power devices like outdoor landscape lights.

TRANSFORMER—A smaller version of the gray pods that are mounted at the top of electrical power poles. Changes current of one voltage to another. In this case, from the standard (and dangerous) 120-volt electrical service to a much safer 12-volt service.

TOOLS & SUPPLIES YOU NEED

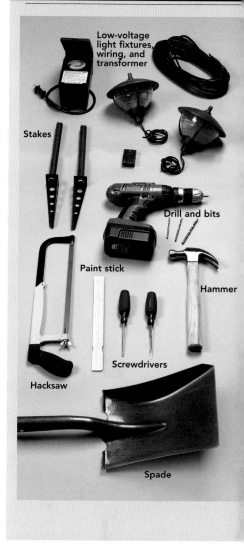

DIFFICULTY LEVEL

EASY   MODERATE

This project can be completed in eight to twelve hours.

1 Install your transformer or transformers. If you are installing one in a garage, mount it on a wall within 24" of the GFCI receptacle and at least 12" off the floor. If you are using an outdoor receptacle on a wall or a post, mount the transformer on the same post or an adjacent post at least 12" off the ground and not more than 24" inches from the receptacle. Do not use an extension cord.

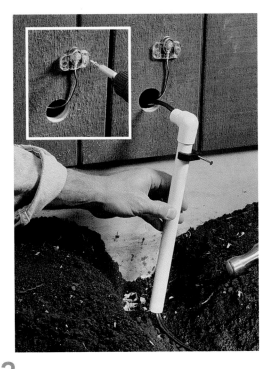

2 Drill a hole through the wall or rim joist for the low-voltage cable and any sensors to pass through (inset). If a circuit begins in a high-traffic area, it's a good idea to protect the cable by running it through a short piece of PVC pipe or conduit and then into the shallow trench.

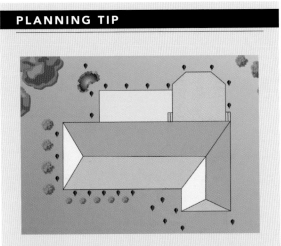

PLANNING TIP

Make a diagram of your yard and mark the location of new fixtures. Note the wattages of the fixtures and use the diagram to select a transformer and plan the circuits.

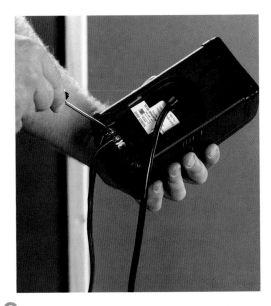

3 Attach the end of the low-voltage wire to the terminals on the transformer. Make sure that both strands of wire are held tightly by their terminal screws.

4 Transformers usually have a simple mechanism that allows you to set times for the lights to come ON and go OFF automatically. Set these times before hanging the transformer.

5 Many low-voltage light fixtures are modular, consisting of a spiked base, a riser tube and a lamp. On these units, feed the wires and the wire connector from the light section down through the riser tube and into the base.

6 Take apart the connector box and insert the ends of the fixture wire and the low voltage landscape cable into it. Puncture the wire ends with the connector box leads. Reassemble the connector box.

7 Feed the wire connector back into the light base and attach it according to directions that came with the lamp. In this model, all that was required was pushing the connector into a locking slot in the base.

8 After the bulb is installed, assemble the fixture parts that cover it, including the lens cap and reflector.

9 Lay out the lights, with the wires attached, in the pattern you have chosen. Then cut the sod between fixtures with a spade. Push the blade about 5 in. deep and pry open a seam by rocking the blade back and forth.

10 Gently force the cable into the slot formed by the spade; don't tear the wire insulation. A paint stick (or a cedar shingle) is a good tool for this job. Push the wire to the bottom of the slot.

11 Firmly push the light into the slot in the sod. It the lamp doesn't seat properly, pull it out and cut another slot at a right angle to the first and try again.

12 Once the lamp is stabilized, tuck any extra wire into the slot using the paint stick. If you have a lot of extra wire, you can fold it and push the excess to the bottom of the slot. No part of the wire should be exposed when you are done with the job.

FIXTURE TIPS:

Specialty lights can cost a lot more than the standard plastic spike-base lamps. Because of this, many people modify the cheaper units to serve other purposes. To do this, first cut off the spike-base with a hacksaw.

To install a modified light on a deck, bore a wire-clearance hole through a deck board. Then feed the low-voltage wire through this hole and attach the base to the deck with screws. The same technique can be used to install modified units on planters or railings.

Many different specialty lights are available for use on a wood deck. This model mounts directly on the surface and the wires feed through an access hole under the light. Other lights that are thinner, but mount the same way, are designed for the underside of stair treads. These light up the stairs and reduce the chance of people stumbling in the dark.

20

Pressure Washing
a House

Pressure washers can be rented or you can buy your own light-duty model for around $100. Washing your siding is just one of the many useful chores a pressure washer can perform.

SELF-SERVICE CAR WASHES ARE A GREAT IDEA. THEY LET YOU WASH YOUR CAR THE WAY YOU WANT TO WASH IT, AND THEY LEAVE YOU ALONE. If you could fit your house into a self-serve car wash, you might never need a pressure washer of your own. That is, until you think a little. What about washing the car at home, getting off the caked-on grass from the bottom of the mower, blowing away the stains on the garage floor, banishing the dirt from your backyard deck, and prevailing over the mildew on all that plastic outdoor furniture? A pressure washer makes all these jobs easier and quicker than other approaches. And, it does a wonderful job of washing your house.

PRESSURE WASHERS 101

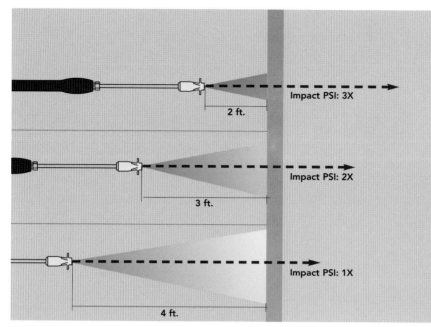

Impact PSI: 3X
2 ft.

Impact PSI: 2X
3 ft.

Impact PSI: 1X
4 ft.

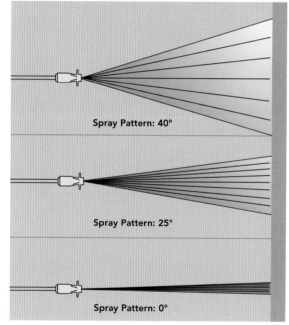

Spray Pattern: 40°

Spray Pattern: 25°

Spray Pattern: 0°

There are two ways to adjust cleaning power using the pressure washer. You can adjust the distance (above) that you hold the nozzle from the surface you are cleaning. The second way is to change the spray pattern (left). Some pressure washers also allow you to adust the pressure regulator knob on the engine or water pump. This enables you to fine-tune the water pressure without altering the distance or spray pattern.

TOOLS & SUPPLIES YOU NEED

Pressure washer with detergent siphon tube

Degreaser solution

Liquid detergent

Bleach

Rotating scrub brush

Plastic sheeting

Rubber gloves

Detergent siphon tube

Scrub brush

DIFFICULTY LEVEL

SKILLS LEVEL

EASY   MODERATE

This project can be completed in one to three days.

BUYING A PRESSURE WASHER

You can find a very good pressure washer for as little as $100, but it won't be a 3000 psi machine that you could use to spruce up the Sears Tower. Instead, it will be an electric model that delivers about 1500 psi and about 2 gallons per minute (gpm) of flow. Multiplying the pressure (psi) and water flow (gpm) ratings yields a rating a figure called the cleaning power (CP) for each model. A machine with a CP rating of 3000 will do everything you want around the house without the risk of injury from puncture wounds that are possible with the higher pressure machines.

HOW TO PRESSURE WASH A HOUSE

1 If using detergents, cover the plants around your house with tarps or plastic sheeting. Leave the cover on only when you are working. If it stays on for long periods during hot weather, the plants can die from exposure to too much heat.

2 You have the option to add cleaning detergent to the machine's water flow by installing a standard siphon tube between the machine and a container of detergent.

TIP FOR REMOVING STAINS

Stubborn mildew and rust stains usually need hand scrubbing with a weak bleach solution. Use a sponge or brush to clean the area and rinse the area thoroughly. Be sure to wear protective gloves.

3 If the siding is very dirty, you may have to use a rotating scrub brush accessory to clean the surface. The brush can use either clean water or dispense a soapy solution. This is a bit like pre-cleaning stains on clothing before laundering.

4 To prevent streaks on house siding, start pressure washing on the bottom and work up. Use the same approach whether you're using plain water or soapy water.

5 To rinse the side, start at the top and work down. The clean water will flush away any dirt and soap residue and leave behind a clean surface.

CLEANING OTHER OUTDOOR SURFACES

A pressure washer also works on surfaces like wood decks. Sometimes a quick spraying with plain water will do the trick. But more typically, the deck has to be cleaned chemically and then rinsed with plain water.

Concrete steps, walks and driveways respond very well to pressure washing. Because the spray tip can be held so close to the surface without causing any damage, usually water alone will do the trick. But oil stains on a garage floor will require a detergent wash and possibly a prewash with a degreaser solution.

RESOURCES

American Standard
American Standard and Porcher brand lavatories, toilets, shower systems, bathtubs, kitchen sinks, faucets
800-442-1902
www.americanstandard-us.com

Armstrong World Industries
717-397-0611
www.armstrong.com

Clopay Garage Doors
800-225-6729
www.clopaydoor.com

Crane Plumbing
Crane, Fiat, Sanymetal, Showerite and Universal Rundle toilets and plumbing products
www.craneplumbing.com

Delta Faucet Co.
Kitchen and bathroom faucets
800-345-3358
www.deltafaucet.com

Electric Eel
Power augers for sale or rent
(937) 323-4644
www.electriceel.com

Eljer, Inc.
Eljer, Titan and Endurocast toilets, tubs, lavatories, faucets
800-423-5537
(972) 560-2000
www.eljer.com

Elkay Cos.
Sinks and faucets
(630) 572-3192 (U.S.)
800-661-1795 (Canada)
www.elkayusa.com

Fluidmaster
Fill valves, flush valves, toilet repair parts
www.fluidmaster.com

Grohe
Kitchen and bathroom faucets
(630) 582-7711 (U.S.)
(905) 271-2929 (Canada)
www.groheamerica.com

Hunter Douglas
800-265-1363
www.hunterdouglas.com

In-Sink-Erator
Garbage disposers and hot water dispensers
800-558-5700
www.insinkerator.com

International Association of Plumbing and Mechanical Officials
20001 E. Walnut Drive South
Walnut, CA 91789-2825
www.iapmo.org

International Conference of Building Officials
5360 Workman Mill Rd.
Whittier, CA 90601-2298
800-284-4406

Kohler Plumbing
Kohler brand kitchen and bathroom fixtures
800-456-4537
www.kohler.com

LASCO Bathware
Tub and shower products
800-945-2726
www.lascobathware.com

Moen
Sinks, faucets and related accessories for kitchen and bath
800-289-6636
www.moen.com

National Kitchen & Bath Association
800-843-6522
www.nkba.com

Plumbing and Drainage Institute
45 Bristol Drive
South Easton, MA 02375
www.pdionline.org

Plumbing Heating Cooling Information Bureau
222 Merchandise Mart Plaza
Chicago, IL 60654

Price Pfister
Kitchen and bathroom faucets
800-732-8238 (U.S.)
800-340-7608 (Canada)
www.pricepfister.com

Sterling Plumbing
Sterling brand tub and shower surrounds, shower doors, toilets, kitchen sinks and related kitchen and bathroom fixtures
888-783-7546
www.sterlingplumbing.com

The Institute of Plumbing and Heating Engineering
64 Station Lane, Hornchurch
Essex, RM12 6NB, England
www.worldplumbing.org

Toto USA Inc.
Toilets, faucets, lavatories and other bathroom fixtures
888-295-8134
www.totousa.com

PHOTO CREDITS

p. 242 (lower left)
© Inside/Beateworks.com,
(lower right) photo courtesy of Armstrong Flooring

p. 320 photo courtesy of Armstrong Flooring

p. 336 © George Mayer / www.istock.com

p. 351 photos courtesy of Hunter Douglas

P. 424 photo Rebecca Grabill / www.istock.com

P. 468 photo courtesy of Clopay

Metric Equivalents

Inches (in.)	1/64	1/32	1/25	1/16	1/8	1/4	3/8	2/5	1/2	5/8	3/4	7/8	1	2	3	4	5	6	7	8	9	10	11	12	36	39.4
Feet (ft.)																								1	3	3½
Yards (yd.)																									1	1½
Millimeters (mm)	0.40	0.79	1	1.59	3.18	6.35	9.53	10	12.7	15.9	19.1	22.2	25.4	50.8	76.2	101.6	127	152	178	203	229	254	279	305	914	1,000
Centimeters (cm)							0.95	1	1.27	1.59	1.91	2.22	2.54	5.08	7.62	10.16	12.7	15.2	17.8	20.3	22.9	25.4	27.9	30.5	91.4	100
Meters (m)																								.30	.91	1.00

Converting Measurements

TO CONVERT:	TO:	MULTIPLY BY:
Inches	Millimeters	25.4
Inches	Centimeters	2.54
Feet	Meters	0.305
Yards	Meters	0.914
Miles	Kilometers	1.609
Square inches	Square centimeters	6.45
Square feet	Square meters	0.093
Square yards	Square meters	0.836
Cubic inches	Cubic centimeters	16.4
Cubic feet	Cubic meters	0.0283
Cubic yards	Cubic meters	0.765
Pints (U.S.)	Liters	0.473 (Imp. 0.568)
Quarts (U.S.)	Liters	0.946 (Imp. 1.136)
Gallons (U.S.)	Liters	3.785 (Imp. 4.546)
Ounces	Grams	28.4
Pounds	Kilograms	0.454
Tons	Metric tons	0.907

TO CONVERT:	TO:	MULTIPLY BY:
Millimeters	Inches	0.039
Centimeters	Inches	0.394
Meters	Feet	3.28
Meters	Yards	1.09
Kilometers	Miles	0.621
Square centimeters	Square inches	0.155
Square meters	Square feet	10.8
Square meters	Square yards	1.2
Cubic centimeters	Cubic inches	0.061
Cubic meters	Cubic feet	35.3
Cubic meters	Cubic yards	1.31
Liters	Pints (U.S.)	2.114 (Imp. 1.76)
Liters	Quarts (U.S.)	1.057 (Imp. 0.88)
Liters	Gallons (U.S.)	0.264 (Imp. 0.22)
Grams	Ounces	0.035
Kilograms	Pounds	2.2
Metric tons	Tons	1.1

Converting Temperatures

Convert degrees Fahrenheit (F) to degrees Celsius (C) by following this simple formula: Subtract 32 from the Fahrenheit temperature reading. Then, mulitply that number by 5/9. For example, 77°F - 32 = 45. 45 × 5/9 = 25°C.

To convert degrees Celsius to degrees Fahrenheit, multiply the Celsius temperature reading by 9/5. Then, add 32. For example, 25°C × 9/5 = 45. 45 + 32 = 77°F.

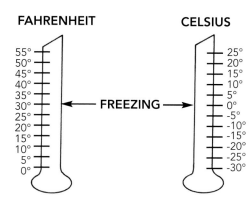

Adhesive — Bonding agent used to adhere the floor covering to the underlayment. Adhesives are also available for installing a floor covering on nonporous surfaces, such as sheet vinyl.

American National Standards Institute (ANSI) — A standards-making organization that rates tile for water permeability.

Baseboard — Strip of wood molding, available in various designs and thicknesses, applied at the bottom of the wall to cover the gap between the floor covering and the wall.

Baseboard shoe — A narrow piece of molding, often quarter round, attached to the bottom of baseboard to hide gaps between the floor covering and baseboard and to add a decorative edge.

Baseboard tile — Baseboard-shaped tile used instead of wood baseboards. Used in conjunction with tile floors.

Base-shoe molding — A strip of molding nailed to baseboard at the floor to conceal gaps and add a decorative edge.

Berber carpet — Looped pile running in parallel lines. Berber carpet has the same color throughout the fibers.

Bevel cut — An angled cut through the width or thickness of a board or other piece of stock.

Blindnail — Driving nails at an angle through the tongues of hardwood flooring so the next piece of flooring will cover the nail.

Box nail — A nail similar in appearance to a common nail, but with a thinner shaft. Used for lighter construction and on materials that split easily.

Brick molding — Used between the exterior surface of a house and a window or doorframe.

Building code — A set of building regulations and ordinances regulating the way a house can be built or remodeled. Most building codes are controlled by a local municipality.

Building permit — Permit obtained from the local building department allowing you to remodel your home.

Casing — Any trim around a window, door, or other opening.

Casing nail — Similar to a finishing nail, but with a slightly larger dimpled head for better holding power.

Cat's paw — A type of prying tool used primarily in demolition; the tool is good for extracting nails.

Cementboard — Underlayment used for ceramic tile and some hardwood installations. Cementboard is the best underlayment in areas likely to get wet.

Chalk line — The line left by chalk, usually blue or red, after the chalk string is pulled tight between two points and snapped against the floor.

Coefficient of friction — A measurement of a tile's slip resistance. Tiles with high numbers are more slip resistant.

Common nail — A heavy-shaft nail used primarily for framing work, available from 2d to 60d.

Coping saw — A handsaw with a flexible blade and fine teeth for cutting intricate curves and bends in wood.

Cripple stud — A short stud that is normally located above or below window and door openings.

Crosscut — Cutting a piece of wood perpendicular to the wood grain.

Cut-pile carpet — Individual carpet fibers woven tightly together. The fibers are colored on the outside, but not on the inside.

Door casing — Wood molding and trim placed around a door opening to give it a finished look.

Drip edge — A piece of molding placed over any exterior opening so that water runs or drips away from the opening.

Dry-fit — Installing tile without mortar to test the layout.

Dry mix — Packaged mix (usually sold in bags) that can be combined with water to form mortar.

Embossing leveler — A mortarlike substance used to prepare resilient flooring or ceramic tile for use as an underlayment.

Endnailing — Joining two boards at a right angle by driving nails through the face of one board into the end of another.

Engineered flooring — Flooring that's manufactured to look like solid hardwood, but is easier to install, less expensive, and more resistant to wear. Engineered flooring is available in strips or planks.

Expansion joint — A joint in a tile layout filled with a flexible material, such as caulk, instead of grout. The expansion joint allows the tile to shift without cracking.

Facenailing — Joining two parallel boards by driving nails through the faces of both boards.

Fiber/cementboard underlayment — A thin, high-density underlayment used under ceramic tile and resilient flooring where floor height is a concern.

Field tile — Tile that's not part of a design or border.

Finish nail — A nail with a small, dimpled head, used for fastening wood trim and other detailed work.

Flagstone — Quarried stone cut into slabs usually less than 3" thick, used for outdoor floors.

Floating floor — Wood or laminate floor covering that rests on a thin foam padding and is not fastened or bonded to the subfloor or underlayment.

Floor board — A strip or plank in a wood floor.

Floor tile — Any type of tile designated for use on floors.

Floor-warming systems — A system of heating elements installed directly under the floor covering. Floor-warming systems provide supplemental radiant heat to warm up a floor.

Framing member — A common term for a single structural element of a construction framework, such as a stud, joist, truss, or beam.

Full-, half-, quarter-sheet — Referring to the size of a sheet good relative to a 4 × 8-ft. sheet. A half-sheet is 4 × 4-ft., a quarter-sheet is 2 × 4-ft.

Full-spread vinyl — Sheet vinyl with a felt-paper backing that is secured to the underlayment with adhesive.

GFCI receptacle — A receptacle outfitted with a ground-fault circuit-interrupter. Also used on some extension cords to reduce the possibility of electric shock when operating an appliance or power tool.

Glue laminate — A type of engineered lumber specifically created for headers or support beams, in which layers of wood are bonded to form a solid unit.

Grout — A dry powder, usually cement-based, that is mixed with water and pressed into the joints between tiles. Grout also comes with latex or acrylic additive for greater adhesion and impermeability.

Header — A piece of lumber used as a support beam over a doorway or window opening.

Isolation membrane — A flexible material installed in sheets or troweled onto an unstable or damaged base floor or subfloor before installing tile. Isolation membrane prevents shifts in the base from damaging the tile above.

Jack stud — A wall-framing member used to support a header in a doorway or window opening.

Jamb — The top and side pieces that make up the finished frame of a door opening.

Joists — The framing members that support the floor.

King studs — The first studs on either side of a framed opening to span from the sole plate to the top plate.

Latex patching compound — Compound used to fill cracks and chips in old underlayment and to cover screw or nail heads and seams in new underlayment.

Load-bearing wall — Any wall (interior or exterior) that bears some of the structural weight of a house. All exterior walls are load-bearing.

Locknailing — Strengthening a miter joint in window or door casings by driving nails through the middle of the joint from the outer edge of the casing. This technique also works well with picture frames.

Miter cut — An angle cut in the end of a piece of flooring or molding.

Molding — Decorative strips of wood installed along walls and floors.

O.C. (on center) — The distance from the center of one framing member to the center of the next.

Partition wall — An interior, non-loadbearing wall.

Pennyweight — A measure used to indicate nail size and length, commonly shown as a lower case "d."

Perimeter-bond vinyl — Sheet vinyl with a PVC backing that is placed directly on underlayment and secured by adhesives along the edges and seams.

Planks — Wood or laminate flooring that is 4" or more wide.

Platform framing — A type of framing construction in which the studs only span a single story, and each floor acts as a platform to build and support the next higher level. Most common framing method in modern home construction.

Plumb bob — A device consisting of a pointed weight on the end of a string, used to determine whether a surface is exactly vertical or to transfer marks along a vertical plane.

Plunge cut — A cut that begins in the field of a board or piece of plywood by slowly pivoting the blade into the wood.

Plywood — A common underlayment for resilient and ceramic tile installations.

Portland cement — A combination of silica, lime, iron, and alumina that has been heated, cooled, and pulverized to form a fine powder from which mortar products are made.

PVC — Acronym for polyvinyl chloride. PVC is a rigid plastic material that is highly resistant to heat and chemicals.

Reciprocating saw — A type of power saw that cuts with a back and forth action through wood, metal, and plastic.

Reference lines — Lines marked on the subfloor to guide the placement of the floor covering.

Rip — Cutting a piece of wood parallel to the grain.

Rise — The height of a step in a stairway.

Rough opening — The opening of the rough framing for a window or door.

Run — The length of a step in a stairway.

Sealants — Product used to protect non- and semi-vitreous tile from stains and water damage. Sealants are also used to protect grout.

Sheet vinyl — Flooring material made from vinyl and other plastics in the form of sheets that are 6 ft. or 12 ft. wide and approximately ⅛" thick.

Shim — A thin wedge of wood used to make slight adjustments in doors or windows during installation.

Sister joist — Dimensional lumber attached alongside an existing joist to provide additional strength.

Soffits & chases — Boxes made with dimensional lumber and plywood or wallboard to cover up existing mechanicals or other obstructions.

Spacers — Plastic lugs inserted between tiles to help maintain uniform installation during installation.

Stain — Water-based or oil-based agent used to penetrate and change the color of a wood floor.

Strip flooring — Wood flooring that has multiple strips, usually three, fastened together to form a single plank.

Strips — Wood or laminate flooring that is less than 4" wide.

STC (sound transmission class) — A rating system referring to how well sound is contained within a room due to the construction. Normal wall construction has a rating of 32 STC.

Stud — A vertical framing member used in the framework of a house or building.

Subfloor — The surface, usually made of plywood, attached to the floor joists.

Tack cloth — Lint free cloth, usually cheese cloth, used to clean floors and wipe away dust. Tack cloth is treated with a resin to make it sticky.

Tackless strips — Strips of wood nailed around the perimeter of a room. The teeth of the strips hold carpet in place.

Threshold — The area in a doorway where two floor coverings meet.

Toenailing — Joining two boards at a right angle by driving nails at a 45° angle through the side of one board into the face of another.

Tongue-and-groove flooring — Wood or laminate floor coverings that have a tongue and a groove in each individual piece. The flooring is assembled by placing the tongue and groove joints together.

Top plate — A piece of dimensional lumber that rests on top of the studs in a wall and supports the ends of rafters.

Treated wood — Lumber that has been impregnated with chemicals to make it resistant to pests and rot.

Underlayment — Material placed on top of the subfloor, such as plywood, fiber/cementboard, cementboard, and isolation membrane.

Vapor barrier — Plastic sheeting used as a barrier to keep water from a concrete floor from penetrating the floor covering installed over it.

Wallboard — Also known as drywall; flat panels available in various sizes made of gypsum covered with durable paper; Used for most interior wall and ceiling surfaces.

FLOORING INDEX

DECORATING INDEX

OUTDOOR INDEX